T0134422

Adaptive Autonomous Secure Cyber Systems

Sushil Jajodia • George Cybenko
V.S. Subrahmanian • Vipin Swarup
Cliff Wang • Michael Wellman
Editors

Adaptive Autonomous Secure Cyber Systems

 Springer

Editors
Sushil Jajodia
Center for Secure Information Systems
George Mason University
Fairfax, VA, USA

V.S. Subrahmanian
Department of Computer Science
Dartmouth College
Hanover, NH, USA

Cliff Wang
Computing and Information Science
Division
Army Research Office
Durham, NC, USA

George Cybenko
Thayer School of Engineering
Dartmouth College
Hanover, NH, USA

Vipin Swarup
MS T310
MITRE Corporation
McLean, VA, USA

Michael Wellman
Computer Science & Engineering
University of Michigan
Ann Arbor, MI, USA

ISBN 978-3-030-33434-5   ISBN 978-3-030-33432-1   (eBook)
https://doi.org/10.1007/978-3-030-33432-1

© Springer Nature Switzerland AG 2020
This work is subject to copyright. All rights are reserved by the Publisher, whether the whole or part of the material is concerned, specifically the rights of translation, reprinting, reuse of illustrations, recitation, broadcasting, reproduction on microfilms or in any other physical way, and transmission or information storage and retrieval, electronic adaptation, computer software, or by similar or dissimilar methodology now known or hereafter developed.
The use of general descriptive names, registered names, trademarks, service marks, etc. in this publication does not imply, even in the absence of a specific statement, that such names are exempt from the relevant protective laws and regulations and therefore free for general use.
The publisher, the authors, and the editors are safe to assume that the advice and information in this book are believed to be true and accurate at the date of publication. Neither the publisher nor the authors or the editors give a warranty, expressed or implied, with respect to the material contained herein or for any errors or omissions that may have been made. The publisher remains neutral with regard to jurisdictional claims in published maps and institutional affiliations.

This Springer imprint is published by the registered company Springer Nature Switzerland AG.
The registered company address is: Gewerbestrasse 11, 6330 Cham, Switzerland

Preface

Autonomy in physical and cyber systems promises to revolutionize cyber operations. The ability of autonomous systems to execute at scales, scopes, and tempos exceeding those of humans and human-controlled systems will introduce entirely new types of cyber defense strategies and tactics, especially in highly contested physical and cyber environments. The development and automation of cyber strategies that are responsive to autonomous adversaries pose basic new technical challenges for cyber security.

The recent advances in adaptive cyber defense (ACD) have developed a range of new ACD techniques and methodologies for reasoning in an adaptive environment. Building on that work, this book explores fundamental scientific problems essential for autonomous cyber defense. Specific areas include:

- The extent to which autonomous cyber systems can be designed and operated in a framework that is significantly different from the human-based systems we now operate
- Game and control theory-based moving target defenses (MTDs) and ACDs for fully autonomous cyber operations
- Online learning algorithms, including deep recurrent networks and reinforcement learning, for the kinds of situation awareness and decisions that autonomous cyber systems will require
- Use machine leaning (ML) and cyber deception methods and to reason about the situation and appropriate responses
- Defending against attacks on ML-based autonomous cyber defensive agents

It is our sincere hope that this volume inspires researchers to build upon the knowledge we present to further establish scientific foundations for autonomous adaptive cyber systems and ultimately bring about a more secure and reliable Internet.

Fairfax, VA, USA   Sushil Jajodia
Hanover, NH, USA   George Cybenko
Hanover, NH, USA   V.S. Subrahmanian
McLean, VA, USA   Vipin Swarup
Durham, NC, USA   Cliff Wang
Ann Arbor, MI, USA   Michael Wellman

Acknowledgments

We are extremely grateful to the numerous contributors to this volume. In particular, it is a pleasure to acknowledge the authors for their contributions. Special thanks go to Susan Lagerstrom-Fife, senior publishing editor at Springer, for her support of this project. We also wish to thank the Army Research Office for their financial support under the grant numbers W911NF-17-1-0486 and W911NF-13-1-0421.

Contents

Reference Architecture of an Autonomous Agent for Cyber Defense of Complex Military Systems

Paul Theron, Alexander Kott, Martin Drašar, Krzysztof Rzadca, Benoît LeBlanc, Mauno Pihelgas, Luigi Mancini, and Fabio de Gaspari

1 Future Military Systems and the Rationale for Autonomous Intelligent Cyber Defense Agents

Modern defense systems incorporate new technologies like cloud computing, artificial intelligence, lasers, optronics, electronics and submicronic processors, on-board power-generation systems, automation systems, sensors, software defined radios

This chapter reuses portions of an earlier paper: Theron, P., et al, "Towards an Active, Autonomous and Intelligent Cyber Defense of Military Systems: the NATO AICA Reference Architecture", Proceedings of the International Conference on Military Communications and Information Systems Warsaw, Poland, 22nd - 23rd May 2018; © 2018 IEEE.

P. Theron
Aerospace Cyber Resilience Chair, Paris, France
e-mail: paul.theron@thalesgroup.com

A. Kott (✉)
U.S. Army Research Laboratory, Adelphi, MD, USA
e-mail: alexander.kott1.civ@mail.mil

M. Drašar
Masaryk University, Brno, Czech Republic
e-mail: drasar@ics.muni.cz

K. Rzadca
University of Warsaw, Warsaw, Poland
e-mail: krzadca@mimuw.edu.pl

B. LeBlanc
Ecole Nationale Supérieure de Cognitique, Bordeaux, France
e-mail: benoit.leblanc@ensc.fr

© Springer Nature Switzerland AG 2020
S. Jajodia et al. (eds.), *Adaptive Autonomous Secure Cyber Systems*,
https://doi.org/10.1007/978-3-030-33432-1_1

1

and networks, etc. They are more and more relying on software, and will also embed new hardware technologies, including high performance computers and quantum technologies, nanoparticles, metamaterials, self-reconfigurable hardware, etc.

While defense infrastructures and systems engaged on the battle ground may not fail, the multitude of high-tech features and interconnections that they embed make cyber-attacks a good way to affect their functionality and the missions in which they are involved.

Today, five broad classes of systems coexist in Land, Sea and Air operations:

- Office and information management systems: these include web services, email-ing systems, and information management applications ranging from human resource management to logistics through maintenance and project management;
- C4ISR systems for the command of war operations: they include associated Battlefield Management Systems that extend the C4ISR down to single vehicles and platoons;
- Communication systems: they include SATCOM, L16, line of sight networks, software defined radios, and the Internet of Battle Things (IoBT) can be seen as a major operational innovation and extension of communication capabilities;
- Platform and life automation systems: they are similar to industrial systems and provide sea vessels or armored vehicles, for instance, with capabilities such as air conditioning, refrigeration, lifts, video surveillance, etc.;
- Weapon systems: these include sensors and effectors of all kinds, operating in all kinds of situations and contested battle grounds.

On the battlefield, these platforms and technologies will operate together in complex large scale networks of massively interconnected systems.

Autonomy can be defined as the capacity of systems to decide by themselves on their course of action in uncertain and challenging environments without the help of human operators. It should not be confused with automation, the aptitude of systems to perform set tasks according to set rules in environments where uncertainty is low and characterized [11].

Despite the fact that "Full autonomy might not necessarily be the objective" and the existence of a variety of definitions [5], the number of autonomous military systems will grow [10]. They will be able to mitigate operational challenges such as needs for rapid decision-making, high heterogeneity and/or volumes of data, intermittent communications, the high complexity of coordinated actions, or the danger of missions, while they will require persistence and endurance [11, p. 12].

M. Pihelgas
NATO Cooperative Cyber Defence Centre of Excellence, Tallinn, Estonia
e-mail; mauno.pihelgas@ccdcoe.org

L. Mancini · F. de Gaspari
Sapienza University, Rome, Italy
e-mail: mancini@di.uniroma1.it; degaspari@di.uniroma1.it

Examples of autonomous capabilities and systems [11] include:

- Unmanned Air Systems, Unmanned Surface Vehicles and Unmanned Underwater Vehicles, will be able to carry out reconnaissance or attack missions stealthily, some of them with a large endurance. For instance, the Haiyan UUV [24] is a mini-submarine built on a civilian platform that China's People's Liberation Army Navy (PLAN) sponsors to create an autonomous UUV capable of carrying out dangerous missions like minesweeping and submarine detection operations without any human intervention. Weighing only 70 kg, energy efficient and fitted with advanced computing capacities, it has an endurance of up to 30 days.
- Today's Intelligence, Surveillance & Recognition (ISR) missions request more and more high-definition (HD) images and videos being captured and transmitted back to ground stations for analysis. As HD means large volumes of raw data (possibly encrypted, which adds to volumes), communication means cannot provide the ad hoc transmission throughput (and continuity in contested environments). Autonomous sensors equipped with artificial intelligence will be capable of generating on the ground aggregated, high-level information that can be more easily transmitted to command posts as they require much less bandwidth than raw data, also lowering the human workload needed to process high volumes of complex multi-source raw data.
- Autonomous Unmanned Ground Vehicles can be employed in dealing with chemical, biological, radiological and nuclear (CBRN) threats as well as with Improvised Explosive Devices (IED), as was the case in Iraq and Afghanistan conflicts.
- The US MK-18 Mod 2 program has demonstrated significant progress in utilizing Remote Environmental Monitoring UnitS (REMUS) Unmanned Underwater Vehicles for mine countermeasure missions, thus allowing pulling military personnel away from dangerous mine fields and reducing tactical reaction times.
- Unmanned Aircrafts (UA) could be used in anti-access and area denial (A2/AD) missions to perform functions that today require the intervention of personnel such as aerial refueling, airborne early warning, ISR, anti-ship warfare, command, offensive strike facilitation (electronic warfare, communications jamming, decoys) and actions supporting defense by creating confusion, deception or attrition through decoys, sensors and emitters, target emulators. Similar functions could be used in underwater combat.
- Agile ground forces could get local tactical support from Unmanned Aircraft Systems (UAS) embarking sensors, ISR capacities, communication means, electronic warfare functions and weapon systems. These UAS would reach greater levels of efficiency and could better deal with large numbers of ground, air and possibly sea sensors and actuators if they could themselves work in swarms or cohorts and collectively adapt their action dynamically on the basis of mission and environment-related data collected in real time.
- Logistics could be another area of utilization of autonomous land, sea and air vehicles and functions. Autonomous capabilities could be used in contested changeable environments either in support and defense of friendly logistic deployment and operation, or to disturb or strike enemy logistics.

Another two fundamental issues need to be taken into account.

The first of these issues is the fact that the level of interconnectedness, and therefore of interdependence and cross-vulnerability, of military systems will increase to unseen heights [42].

The Internet of Things is increasing rapidly in both numbers and types of smart objects, and this is a durable trend with regards to Defense [11] despite the massive scale of their deployment, their meager configurability and the new (cyber) risks they create. In effect, with the shift to the IPv6 addressing standard, the number of devices that can be networked is up to 340 undecillion unique devices (340 with 36 zeroes after it) and this immense network of interconnected devices could become a global platform for massively proliferated, distributed cyber-attacks [11].

This multitude of devices will work together in clusters, likely hard to map out, likely subject to unstable changing configurations of their dependencies. These changes will occur beyond our control because of the degrees of autonomy conferred to objects in shifting operative conditions.

Massively interconnected military systems will become more and more difficult to engineer, test, maintain, operate, protect and monitor [42], which leads the authors to recommend "reducing the number of interconnections by reversing the default culture of connecting systems whenever possible" to improve cybersecurity. This recommendation, however intelligent it seems, is very likely never to be listened to . . .

Thus, cyber defending such complex systems will become arduous. For instance, they will not anymore allow for the sort of cybersecurity monitoring we currently deploy across IT and OT systems as they will prevent the implementation of classic, centralized, and even big data/machine learning-based security operations centers (SOCs).

They will also overwhelm human SOC operators' cognitive capacities as it will become impossible for the latter to get instantly a clear and adequate picture of the systems they defend, of their condition, of the adverse events taking place and of the remedies to apply and of their possible impacts.

To defend them against cyber-attacks, only locally implemented distributed and resilient swarms of cyber defense agents adapting to these frequent reconfigurations and emerging circumstances will be able to monitor and defend this vast fuzzy network, learning superior abilities from cumulated experience.

In this particular context, different from the previously exposed context of the cyber defense of a few well-identified and carefully managed autonomous mission systems, cyber defense agents will evolve themselves into more and more unknown, less and less controllable and maintainable states.

Given this last parameter, they may either show decreasing levels of efficiency or generate uncontrollable adverse effects.

The second issue stems from the fundamental military need to proceed successfully with defense missions while operational personnel of Air, Land and Sea forces are not primarily specialists of cybersecurity and cyber defense. This is not to mention that on the battlefield there will always be a scarcity of cyber competencies [22].

Cyber-attacks may cause human operators sometimes to be fooled, for instance when radar or GPS data are spoofed, or stressed, for instance when anomalies multiply while their cause appears unclear and their consequences detrimental. Studies in a variety of domains such as air, sea and ground transportation have drawn attention to this phenomenon. Attacks may trigger human errors of varying consequences. For instance, NAP [29] points out that "Inaccurate information sent to system operators, either to disguise unauthorized changes, or to cause the operators to initiate inappropriate actions, [] could have various negative effects".

The burden of cyber defending systems must therefore be relieved from unqualified operators' shoulders, while the lack of specialists of cybersecurity on the ground prohibits calling upon rapid response teams in case of trouble.

In this context, handling cyber-attacks occurring in the course of operations requires an embedded, undisturbing, seamless autonomous intelligent cyber defense technology [45]. Autonomous intelligent cyber defense agents should resolve (at - least most of) cyber-attacks without technology users being aware of issues at hand.

Only when they would reach their limits, i.e. when being unable to understand situations, to reconciliate disparate pieces of information, or to elaborate cyber defense counter-measures, such multiple agents should collaborate with human operators. NAP [28] provides inspiring examples of machine-human collaboration in a variety of contexts. Such a need for collaboration might also exist in the context of massively interconnected systems of systems evoked earlier.

2 NATO's AICA Reference Architecture: A Concept for Addressing the Need for an Autonomous Intelligent Cyber Defense of Military Systems

Inspired by the above rationale, NATO's IST-152 Research and Technology Group (RTG) is an activity that was initiated by the NATO Science and Technology Organization and was kicked-off in September 2016. The group has developed is developing a comprehensive, use case focused technical analysis methodology in order to produce a first-ever reference architecture and technical roadmap for active autonomous intelligent cyber defense agents. In addition, the RTG worked to identify and evaluate selected elements that may be eligible contributors to such capabilities and that begin to appear in academic and industrial research.

Scientists and engineers from several NATO Nations have brought unique expertise to this project. Only by combining multiple areas of distinct knowledge along with a realistic and comprehensive approach can such a complex software agent be provided.

The output of the RTG may become a tangible starting point for acquisition activities by NATO Nations. If based on a common reference architecture, software agents developed or purchased by different Nations will be far more likely to be interoperable.

Related research includes Mayhem (from DARPA Cyber Challenge, but also Xandra, etc.), agents from the Pechoucek's group, Professor Mancini's work on the AHEAD architecture [9] and the Aerospace Cyber Resilience research chair's research program [45], Anti-Virus tools (Kaspersky, Bitdefender, Avast, Norton, etc.), HBSS, OSSEC, Various host-based IDS/IPS systems, Application Performance Monitoring Agents, Anti-DDOS systems and Hypervisors. Also, a number of related research directions include topics such as deep learning (especially if it can be computationally inexpensive), Botnet technology (seen as a network of agents), network defense games, flip-it games, the Blockchain, and fragmentation and replication. The introduction of Artificial Intelligence into military systems, such as C4ISR, has been studied, for instance by Rasch et al. [35, 36]. Multi Agent Systems form an important part of AI.

Since the emergence of the concept of Multi Agent Systems, e.g., [46], MAS have been deployed in a number of contexts such as power engineering [25] and their decentralized automated surveillance [7], industrial systems [33], networked and intelligent embedded systems [16], collective robotics [19], wireless communication [21], traffic simulation and logistics planning [8], home automation [20], etc.

However, if the use of intelligent agents for the cyber defense of network-centric environments has already long been envisaged [43], effective research in this area is still new.

In the context of the cyber defense of friendly systems, an "agent" has been defined [45] as a piece of software or hardware, a processing unit capable of deciding on its own about its course of action in uncertain, possibly adverse, environments:

- With an individual mission and the corresponding competencies, i.e. in analyzing the milieu in which the agent is inserted, detecting attacks, planning the required countermeasures, or steering and adapting tactically the execution of the latter, or providing support to other agents like for instance inter-agent communication;
- With proactivity, i.e. the capacity to engage into actions and campaigns without the need to be triggered by another program or by a human operator;
- With autonomy, i.e. a decision making capacity of its own, the capacity to function or to monitor, control and repair itself on its own, without the need to be controlled by another program or by a human operator, and the capacity to evaluate the quality of its own work and to adjust its algorithms in case of deviance from its norm or when its rewards (satisfaction of its goals) get poor;
- Driven by goals, decision making and other rules, knowledge and functions fit for its purpose and operating circumstances;
- Learning from experience to increase the accuracy of its decisions and the power of its reactions;
- With memories (input, process, output, storage);
- With perception, sensing and action, and actuating interfaces;
- Built around the adequate architecture and appropriate technologies;
- Positioned around or within a friendly system to defend, or patrolling across a network;

- Sociable, i.e. with the capacity to establish contact and to collaborate with other agents, or to enter into a cyber cognitive cooperation when the agent requires human help or to cooperate with a central Cyber C2;
- Trustworthy, i.e. that will not deceive other agents nor human operators;
- Reliable; i.e. that do what they are meant to do, during the time specified and under the conditions and circumstances of their concept of operation;
- Resilient, i.e. both robust to threats (including cyber-threats aimed at disabling or destroying the agent itself; the agent being able to repel or withstand everyday adverse events and to avoid degrading), and resistant to incidents and attacks that may hit and affect the agent when its robustness is insufficient (i.e. the agent is capable of recovering from such incidents or attacks);
- Safe, i.e., conceived to avoid harming the friendly systems the agent defends, for instance by calling upon a human supervisor or central cyber C2 to avoid making wrong decisions or to adjust their operating mode to challenging circumstances, or by relocating when the agent is the target of an attack and if relocation is feasible and allows protecting it, or by activating a fail-safe mode, or by way of self-destruction when no other possibility is available.

In the same context (ibid), a multi agent system is a set of agents:

- Distributed across the parts of the friendly system to defend;
- Organized in a swarm (horizontal coordination) or cohort (vertical coordination);
- In which agents may have homogeneous or heterogeneous roles and features;
- Interoperable and interacting asynchronously in various ways such as indifference, cooperation, competition;
- Pursuing a collective non-trivial cyber defense mission, i.e. allowing to piece together local elements of situation awareness or propositions of decision, or to split a counter-attack plan into local actions to be driven by individual agents;
- Capable of self-organization, i.e. as required by changes in circumstances, whether external (the attack's progress or changes in the friendly system's health or configuration) or internal (changes in the agents' health or status);
- That may display emergent behaviors [26], i.e. performances that are not explicitly expressed in individual agents' goals, missions and rules; in the context of cyber defense, "emergence" is likely to be an interesting feature as, consisting in the "way to obtain dynamic results, from cooperation, that cannot easily be predicted in a deterministic way" [26]; it can be disturbing to enemy software in future malware-goodware "tactical" combats within defense and other complex systems;
- Extensible or not, i.e. open or closed to admitting new agents in the swarm or cohort;
- Safe, trustworthy, reliable and resilient as a whole, which is a necessity in the context of cyber defense whereas in other, less challenging contexts may be unnecessary. Resilience, here, may require maintaining a system of virtual roles as described in a human context by Weick [47].

AICA will not be simple agents. Their missions, competencies, functions and technology will be a challenging construction in many ways.

Among many such challenges, we can mention [45] working in resource-constrained environments, the design of agents' architecture and the attribution of roles and possible specialization to each of them, agents' decision making process [3], the capacity to generate and execute autonomously plans of counter-measures in case of an attack, agents' autonomy, including versus trustworthiness, MAICA's safety to defense systems, cyber cognitive cooperation [23], agents' resilience in the face of attacks directed at them by enemy software, agents' learning capacities and the development of their functional autonomy, the specification and emergence of collective rules for the detection and resolution of cyber-attacks, AICA agents' deployment concepts and rationale, their integration into host hardware as [33] showed in industrial system contexts, etc.

To start the research with an initial assumption about agents' architecture, the IST-152-RTG designed the AICA Reference Architecture [22] on the basis of classical perspective reflected in [37].

At the present moment, it is assumed to include the following functional components (Fig. 1).

The AICA Reference Architecture delivers five main high-level functions (Fig. 2):

- Sensing and world state identification.
- Planning and action selection.
- Collaboration and negotiation.
- Action execution.
- Learning and knowledge improvement.

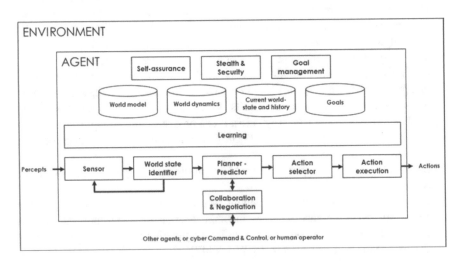

Fig. 1 Assumed functional architecture of the AICA

Fig. 2 The AICA's main five high-level functions

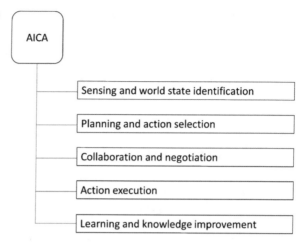

2.1 Sensing and World State Identification

Definition: Sensing and World state identification is the AICA's high-level function that allows a cyber-defense agent to acquire data from the environment and systems in which it operates as well as from itself in order to reach an understanding of the current state of the world and, should it detect risks in it, to trigger the Planning and Action selection high-level function. This high-level function relies upon the "World model", "Current world state and history", "Sensors" and "World State Identifier" components of the assumed functional architecture.

The Sensing and World state identification high-level function includes two functions: (1) Sensing; (2) Word state identification.

2.1.1 Sensing

Description: Sensing operates from two types of data sources: (1) External (system and device-related) current world state descriptors; (2) Internal (agent-related) current state descriptors.

Current world state descriptors, both external and internal, are captured on the fly by the agent's Sensing function. They may be double-checked, formatted or normalized for later use by the World state identification function (to create processed current world state descriptors).

2.1.2 World State Identification

Description: The World state identification function operates from two sources of data: (1) Processed current world state descriptors; (2) Learnt world state patterns.

Learnt world state patterns are stored in the agent's world knowledge repository. Processed current world state descriptors and Learnt world state patterns are compared to identify problematic current world state patterns (i.e. presenting an anomaly or a risk). When identifying a problematic current world state pattern, the World state identification function triggers the Planning and Action selection high-level function.

2.2 Planning and Action Selection

Definition: Planning and action selection is the AICA's high-level function that allows a cyber-defense agent to elaborate one to several action proposals and to propose them to the Action selector function that decides the action or set of actions to execute in order to resolve the problematic world state pattern previously identified by the World state identifier function. This high-level function relies upon the "World dynamics" that should include knowledge about "Actions and effects", "Goals", "Planner - Predictor" and "Action selector" components of the assumed functional architecture.

The Planning and action selector high-level function includes two functions: (1) Planning; (2) Action selector.

2.2.1 Planning

Description: The Planning function operates on the basis of two data sources: (1) Problematic current world state pattern; (2) Repertoire of actions (Response repertoire).

The Problematic current world state pattern and Repertoire of actions (Response repertoire) are concurrently explored in order to determine the action or set of actions (Proposed response plan) that can resolve the submitted problematic current world state pattern. The action or set of actions so determined are presented to the Action selector. It may be possible that the Planning function requires some form of cooperation with human operators (cyber cognitive cooperation, C3).

It may alternatively require cooperation with other agents or with a central cyber C2 (command and control) in order to come up with an optimal set of actions forming a global response strategy. Such cooperation could be either to request from other agents or from the cyber C2 complementary action proposals, or to delegate to the cyber C2 the responsibility of coordinating a global set of actions forming the wider response strategy.

It may be possible that the Planning function requires some form of cooperation with human operators (cyber cognitive cooperation, C3). It may alternatively require cooperation with other agents or with a central cyber C2 (command and control) in order to come up with an optimal set of actions forming a global response strategy. Such cooperation could be either to request from other agents or from the cyber C2 complementary action proposals, or to delegate to the cyber C2 the responsibility of coordinating a global set of actions forming the wider response strategy.

These aspects have been the object of an initial study in [3] where options such as offline machine learning, pattern recognition, online machine learning, escalation to a human operator, game theoretic option search, and failsafe have been envisaged, and in [23] for cyber cognitive cooperation processes.

2.2.2 Action Selector

Description: The Action selector function operates on the basis of three data sources: (1) Proposed response plans; (2) Agent's goals; (3) Execution constraints and requirements, e.g., the environment's technical configuration, etc.

The proposed response plan is analyzed by the Action selector function in the light of the agent's current goals and of the execution constraints and requirements that may either be part of the world state descriptors gained through the Sensing and World state identifier high-level function or be stored in the agent's data repository and originated in the Learning and Knowledge improvement high-level function. The proposed response plan is then trimmed from whatever element does not fit the situation at hand, and augmented of prerequisite, preparatory or precautionary or post-execution recommended complementary actions. The Action selector thus produces an Executable Response Plan, and then submitted to the Action execution high-level function.

Like with the Planning function, it is possible that the Action selector function requires to liaise with human operators, other agents or a central cyber C2 (command and control) in order to come up with an optimal Executable Response Plan forming part of and being in line with a global response strategy. Such cooperation could be to exchange and consolidate information in order to come to a collective agreement on the assignment of the various parts of the global Executable Response Plan and the execution responsibilities to specific agents. It could alternatively be to delegate to the cyber C2 the responsibility of elaborating a consolidated Executable Response Plan and then to assign to specific agents the responsibility of executing part(s) of this overall plan within their dedicated perimeter. This aspect is not yet studied in the present release of the AICA Reference Architecture.

2.3 Collaboration and Negotiation

Definition: Collaboration and negotiation is the AICA's high-level function that allows a cyber-defense agent (1) to exchange information (elaborated data) with other agents or with a central cyber C2, for instance when one of the agent's functions is not capable on its own to reach satisfactory conclusions or usable results, and (2) to negotiate with its partners the elaboration of a consolidated conclusion or result. This high-level function relies upon the "Collaboration & Negotiation" component of the assumed functional architecture.

The Collaboration and negotiation high-level function includes, at the present stage, one function: Collaboration and negotiation.

Description: The Collaboration and negotiation function operates on the basis of three data sources: (1) Internal, outgoing data sets (i.e. sent to other agents or to a central C2); (2) External, incoming data sets (i.e. received from other gents or from a central cyber C2); (3) Agents' own knowledge (i.e. consolidated through the Learning and knowledge improvement high-level function).

When an agent's Planning and action selector function or other function needs it, the agent's Collaboration and negotiation function is activated. Ad hoc data are sent to (selected) agents or to a central C2. The receiver(s) may be able, or not, to elaborate further on the basis of the data received through their own Collaboration and negotiation function. At this stage, when each agent (including possibly a central cyber C2) has elaborated further conclusions, it should share them with other (selected) agents, including (or possibly not) the one that placed the original request for collaboration. Once this (these multiple) response(s) received, the network of involved agents would start negotiating a consistent, satisfactory set of conclusions. Once an agreement reached, the concerned agent(s) could spark the next function within their own decision making process.

When the agent's own security is threatened the agent's Collaboration and negotiation function should help warning other agents (or a central cyber C2) of this state.

Besides, the agent's Collaboration and negotiation function may be used to receive warnings from other agents that may trigger the agent's higher state of alarm.

Finally, the agent's Collaboration and negotiation function should help agents discover other agents and establish links with them.

2.4 Action Execution

Definition: The Action execution is the AICA's high-level function that allows a cyber-defense agent to effect the Action selector function's decision about an Executable Response Plan (or the part of a global Executable Response Plan assigned to the agent), to monitor its execution and its effects, and to provide the agents with the means to adjust the execution of the plan (or possibly to dynamically adjust the plan) when and as needed. This high-level function relies upon the "Goals" and "Action execution" components of the assumed functional architecture.

The Action execution high-level function includes four functions:

- Action effector;
- Execution monitoring;
- Effects monitoring;
- Execution adjustment.

2.4.1   Action Effector

Description: The Action effector function operates on the basis of two data sources:

- Executable Response Plan;
- Environment's Technical Configuration.

Taking into account the Environment's Technical Configuration, the Action effector function executes each planned action in the scheduled order.

2.4.2   Execution Monitoring

Description: The Execution monitoring operates on the basis of two data sources:

- Executable Response Plan;
- Plan execution feedback.

The Execution monitoring function should be able to monitor (possibly through the Sensing function) each action's execution status (for instance: done, not done, and wrongly done). Any status apart from "done" should trigger the Execution adjustment function.

2.4.3   Effects Monitoring

Description: The Effects monitoring function operates on the basis of two data sources: (1) Executable Response Plan; (2) Environment's change feedback.

It should be able to capture (possibly through the Sensing function) any modification occurring in the plan execution's environment. The associated dataset should be analyzed or explored. The result of such data exploration might provide a positive (satisfactory) or negative (unsatisfactory) environment change status. Should this status be negative, this should trigger the Execution adjustment function.

2.4.4   Execution Adjustment

Description: The Execution adjustment function operates on the basis of three data sources: (1) Executable Response Plan; (2) Plan execution feedback and status; (3) Environment's change feedback and status.

The Execution adjustment function should explore the correspondence between the three data sets to find alarming associations between the implementation of the Executable Response Plan and its effects. Should warning signs be identified, the Execution adjustment function should either adapt the actions' implementation to circumstances or modify the plan.

2.5   Learning and Knowledge Improvement

Definition: Learning and knowledge improvement is the AICA's high-level function that allows a cyber-defense agent to use the agent's experience to improve progressively its efficiency with regards to all other functions. This high-level function relies upon the Learning and Goals modification components of the assumed functional architecture.

The Learning and knowledge improvement high-level function includes two functions: (1) Learning; (2) Knowledge improvement.

2.5.1   Learning

Description: The Learning function operates on the basis of two data sources: (1) Feedback data from the agent's functioning; (2) Feedback data from the agent's actions.

The Learning function collects both data sets and analyzes the reward function of the agent (distance between goals and achievements) and their impact on the agent's knowledge database. Results feed the Knowledge improvement function.

2.5.2   Knowledge Improvement

Description: The Knowledge improvement function operates on the basis of two data sources: (1) Results (propositions) from the Learning function; (2) Current elements of the agent's knowledge.

The Knowledge improvement function merges Results (propositions) from the Learning function and the Current elements of the agent's knowledge.

3   Use Cases

The use-case of military UAVs that operate in teams illustrates a possible deployment of the AICA Reference Architecture. It is based on the AgentFly project developed within the Agent Technology Center [44].

The AgentFly project facilitates the simulation of multi agent Unmanned Aerial Vehicles (UAV). Its features include flight path planning, decentralized collision avoidance and models of UAVs, physical capabilities and environmental conditions [41]. In addition to simulation, AgentFly was implemented on a real fixed-wing Procerus UAV [32].

The basis of this use-case is the set of missions selected for the AgentFly project. It is here extended to include an adversarial cyber-attack activity against the AgentFly UAV to disrupt its mission. The use case is that a swarm of AgentFly

UAVs perform a routine tactical aerial surveillance mission in an urban area. Collaboration between AgentFly UAVs aims at collision avoidance, trajectory planning, automatic distributed load-balancing and mission assurance.

The AgentFly UAVs use case is built around the following assumptions:

- AgentFly UAVs self-assess and share information with neighboring UAVs.
- When setting up a communication channel, AgentFly UAVs have to determine whether they trust their correspondent.
- Network-wide collaboration and negotiation is affected by timing, range, and reachability issues.
- The AgentFly UAV lacks modern cyber defense capabilities and is thus vulnerable to potential cyberattacks.
- Due to environmental conditions, AgentFly UAVs might be offline for some time and later re-join the swarm when connectivity allows.
- A single AICA agent is implemented within each AgentFly UAV.
- The AICA connects with the modules of the UAV and can supervise the activity and signals in and between various UAV modules (e.g., sensors, navigation, and actuators).
- The AICA can function in isolation from other AgentFly UAVs' AICA agents present in the AgentFly UAV swarm.

Attackers have acquired a technology similar to that used in AgentFly UAVs' COMMS module. They have discovered a zero-day vulnerability that can be exploited remotely over the radio link from the ground and they plan to use the vulnerability in order to gain control over the swarm of UAVs and cut them off from the theatre's Command & Control (C2) system. The UAVs are using the COMMS module to collaborate among themselves and report to the C2 when needed.

The vulnerability lies in the functionality responsible for dynamically registering new UAV agents in the swarm upon due request. The COMMS module is interconnected with other intrinsic modules of the AgentFly UAV via a central control unit.

The adversary has set up a ground station in the area of the surveillance mission. When AgentFly UAVs enter the area, the cyberattack is launched.

The AICA detects a connection to the COMMS module and allows the incoming connection for the dynamic registration of a new UAV agent into the swarm. Due to the nature of zero-day attacks, an Intrusion Detection System (IDS) would not have any corresponding signatures to detect a compromised payload.

The AICA's Sensor monitors the entire set of modules of the AgentFly UAV.

The AICA's World-state identifier module flags the connection from a newly connected UAV agent as anomalous since it does not follow the baseline pattern that has been established out of previous connections with legitimate UAVs. It also detects a change in the UAV's system configuration and deems it anomalous because no new configurations have been received from the C2. The AICA launches, through its Sensor module, a system integrity check. A compromise within the UAV's COMMS module is detected.

The AICA decides (Planner-Selector and Action selection modules) to isolate (Action execution module) the COMMS module from other UAV modules in order to prevent further propagation. Alerting the C2 is not possible because of the compromised COMMS module.

In order to reduce the attack surface, the AICA requests (Action execution module) that the UAV's central control unit resets the COMMS module, raises the security level and disables auxiliary functions (among others, the dynamic inclusion of new UAVs into the swarm).

The AICA performs another integrity check to verify that no other compromise exists. It keeps its Sensor and World-state identifier modules on a high-level of vigilance in relation to integrity monitoring. The AICA adds the signature of the payload that caused the anomaly into its knowledge base. And it sends out an alert along with malware signature updates to other agents as well as to the C2.

This basic, single AICA agent, use case should be expanded to Multi AICA agents deployed across the AgentFly UAV's architecture and modules. Future research will benchmark Multi AICA agents versus Single AICA agent deployments in order to assess the superiority and context of Multi AICA agent solutions.

4 Discussion and Future Research Directions

The AICA Reference Architecture (AICARA) [22] was elaborated on the basis of [37, 38].

Since the end of 70's and the early works on Artificial Intelligence (AI), the concept of agent was used by different authors to represent different ideas. This polymorphic concept was synthesized by authors such as [30, 48]. Since 1995, Russell and Norvig [38] proposed an architecture and functional decomposition of agents widely regarded as reference work in the ever-growing field of AI.

Their agent architecture can be seen as an extension of the developments in object-oriented methods for software development that culminated in the Unified Modeling Language [4] and design patterns [17]. Both concepts form the basis of modern software development.

The concept of cooperating cognitive agents [38] perfectly matches requirements for AICA agents.

First, AICA agents need to prove trustworthy, and therefore the AICA Reference Architecture is conceived as a white-box. The agent's architecture involves a set of clearly defined modules and specifies the links connecting information perception to action actuation or else the agent to external agents or a central cyber defense C2.

Second, the AICA agents must go beyond merely reactive agents because in situations of autonomy they will need to make decisions by themselves. Reactive agents are today widely used in cybersecurity and are based on rule sets in the form of "if X suspicious, then trigger Y".

Third, Russell and Norvig [38] has attributes highly required by AICA agents: autonomous decision making, learning and cooperation. This is important because these agents may operate for prolonged periods of time if deployed in autonomous weapon systems. The latter may face multiple and unknown cyber-attacks and AICA agents, by learning and cooperating with one another, will sustain their capacity to equip the weapon system with an autonomous intelligent cyber defense.

Applied to the field of the autonomous cyber defense of military systems [38], well-known concepts must be reassessed, prototypes must be built and tested, and the superiority of the concept must now be benchmarked.

Developing the concepts described here also presents many other challenges that require research in the coming years.

Agents' integrity, agent communications' security, the inclusion of cyber defense techniques such as deception, or else identifying and selecting the right actions, are only a few of them.

4.1   Agents' Integrity

A compromise of agents can potentially threaten the entire military platform they are supposed to defend. It is paramount to harden the agents' architecture in order to minimize the chance of such compromise. Methods that assess the integrity of the agent during runtime are required.

Virtualization techniques have been successfully employed to improve systems' resiliency [2, 18]. For instance, systems such as [18] allow providing security guarantees to applications running on untrusted operating systems. It is possible to build upon such techniques in order to harden AICA agents and to maintain their functionality even under attack or in case of partial compromise. Furthermore, periodical assessment of agents' integrity can be performed through attestation techniques [15], based on a trusted hardware core (Trusted Platform Module, TPM). Such techniques allow ensuring that the software of the agent has not been altered at any time, even during the operations of the platform, and can easily scale up to millions of devices [1]. Finally, while the topic of protecting machine learning systems from adversarial examples is still relatively new, techniques such as distillation [31] could be leveraged to increase robustness.

4.2   Agent Communications' Security

Sensors are the fundamental building blocks providing the agents with a consistent world view. As such, they are a part of the AICA architecture most exposed to adversarial tampering. The AICA architecture needs to provide secure communications to ensure that the agent's world view is not corrupted.

To this end, cryptographic protocols such as random key pre-distribution [12, 13], can be employed to provide secure agent-sensor communication even when one or more sensor channels are compromised.

4.3   The Inclusion of Cyber Defense Techniques
Such as Deception

Deception is a key component of active defense systems and, consequently, could be part of the AICA architecture. Active defense deception tools can be used to thwart an ongoing attack. To provide this functionality, the AICA architecture can employ deception techniques such as honeyfiles [6, 49], mock sensors [14] and fake services [34]. Moreover, implementing dynamic tools deployment and reconfiguration is required for actuating functions. To this end container technologies can be employed, such as in [9] to provide isolation and configuration flexibility.

4.4   Identifying and Selecting the Right Actions

Identifying the appropriate actions to take in response to external stimuli is one of the key requirements for the AICA architecture. The AICA agent should include autonomous decision making that can adapt to the current world state. Machine learning-based techniques can be employed [39] to this end, to devise complex plans of action [40] to mitigate an attack, and to learn from previous experiences. However, Blakely and Theron [3] have shown that a variety of techniques may be called upon by AICA agents to elaborate their decisions.

5   In Conclusion

AICA agents are required by foreseeable evolutions of military systems, and it is likely that civil systems, such as the wide-scale deployment of the Internet of Things, will generate similar demands.

The AICA Reference Architecture (AICARA) [22] is a seminal proposition to answer the needs and challenges of the situation.

NATO's IST-152 Research and Technology Group (RTG) has initiated this piece of work and in a recent meeting held in Warsaw, Poland, has evaluated that future research is likely to span over the next decade before efficient solutions be operated.

The AICARA opens discussions among the scientific community, from computer science to cognitive science, Law and moral philosophy.

Autonomous intelligent cyber defense agents may change the face of the fight against malware. This is our assumption.

References

1. Ambrosin, M. et al., 2016. *SANA: Secure and Scalable Aggregate Network Attestation.* New York, NY, USA, ACM, pp. 731–742.
2. Baumann, A., Peinado, M. & Hunt, G., 2015. Shielding Applications from an Untrusted Cloud with Haven. *ACM Trans. Comput. Syst.,* 8, Volume 33, pp. 8:1–8:26.
3. Blakely, B. & Theron, P., 2018. *Decision flow-based Agent Action Planning.* Prague, 18–20 October 2017: https://export.arxiv.org/pdf/1804.07646.
4. Booch, G., 1991. *Object-Oriented Analysis and Design with Applications.* The Benjamin Cummings Publishing Company ed. San Francisco, CA: Pearson Education.
5. Boulanin, V. & Verbruggen, M., 2017. *Mapping the development of autonomy in weapon systems,* Solna, Sweden, available at https://www.sipri.org/publications/2017/other-publications/mapping-development-autonomy-weapon-systems: SIPRI.
6. Bowen, B. M., Hershkop, S., Keromytis, A. D. & Stolfo, S. J., 2009. *Baiting Inside Attackers Using Decoy Documents.* s.l., Springer, Berlin, Heidelberg, pp. 51–70.
7. Carrasco, A. et al., 2010. Multi-agent and embedded system technologies applied to improve the management of power systems. *JDCTA,* 4(1), pp. 79–85.
8. Chen, B. & Cheng, H. H., 2010. A review of the applications of agent technology in traffic and transportation systems. *Trans. Intell. Transport. Sys.,* 11(2), pp. 485–497.
9. De Gaspari, F., Jajodia, S., Mancini, L. V. & Panico, A., 2016. *AHEAD: A New Architecture for Active Defense,* Vienna, Austria: SafeConfig'16, October 24 2016.
10. Defense Science Board, 2012. *Task Force Report: The Role of Autonomy in DoD Systems,* Washington, D.C.: Office of the Under Secretary of Defense for Acquisition, Technology and Logistics.
11. Defense Science Board, 2016. *Summer Study on Autonomy,* Washington, D.C.: Office of the Under Secretary of Defense for Acquisition, Technology and Logistics.
12. Di Pietro, R., Mancini, L. V. & Mei, A., 2003. *Random Key-assignment for Secure Wireless Sensor Networks.* New York, NY, USA, ACM, pp. 62–71.
13. Di Pietro, R., Mancini, L. V. & Mei, A., 2006. Energy Efficient Node-to-node Authentication and Communication Confidentiality in Wireless Sensor Networks. *Wireless Networks,* 11, Volume 12, pp. 709–721.
14. Disso, J. P., Jones, K. & Bailey, S., 2013. *A Plausible Solution to SCADA Security Honeypot Systems.* IEEE, Eighth International Conference on Broadband, Wireless Computing, Communication and Applications, pp. 443–448.
15. Eldefrawy, K., Francillon, A., Perito, D. & Tsudik, G., 2012. *SMART: Secure and Minimal Architecture for (Establishing a Dynamic) Root of Trust.* 19th Annual Network and Distributed System Security Symposium, February 5–8 ed. San Diego, CA: NDSS 2012.
16. Elmenreich, W., 2003. Intelligent methods for embedded systems. In: J. 2. Vienna University of Technology 2003, ed. *Proceedings of the First Workshop on Intelligent Solutions in Embedded Systems.* Austria: Vienna: Vienna University of Technology, pp. 3–11.
17. Gamma, E., Helm, R., Johnson, R. & Vlissides, J., 1994. *Design patterns: elements of reusable object-oriented software.* Reading, Massachusetts: Addison-Wesley.
18. Hofmann, O. S. et al., 2013. *InkTag: Secure Applications on an Untrusted Operating System.* New York, NY, USA, ACM, pp. 265–278.
19. Huang, H.-P., Liang, C.-C. & Lin, C.-W., 2001. Construction and soccer dynamics analysis for an integrated multi-agent soccer robot system. *Natl. Sci. Counc. ROC(A),* Volume 25, pp. 84–93.
20. Jamont, J.-P. & Occello, M., 2011. A framework to simulate and support the design of distributed automation and decentralized control systems: Application to control of indoor building comfort. In: *IEEE Symposium on Computational Intelligence in Control and Automation.* Paris, France: IEEE, pp. 80–87.
21. Jamont, J.-P., Occello, M. & Lagrèze, A., 2010. A multiagent approach to manage communication in wireless instrumentation systems. *Measurement,* 43(4), pp. 489–503.

22. Kott, A. et al., 2019. *Autonomous Intelligent Cyber-defense Agent (AICA) Reference Architecture, Release 2.0*, Adelphi, MD: US Army Research Laboratory, ARL SR-0421, September 2019, available from https://arxiv.org/abs/1803.10664.

23. LeBlanc, B., Losiewicz, P. & Hourlier, S., 2017. *A Program for effective and secure operations by Autonomous Agents and Human Operators in communications constrained tactical environments*. Prague: NATO IST-152 workshop.

24. Lin, J. & Singer, P. W., 2014. *University Tests Long-Range Unmanned Mini Sub*. [Online] Available at: https://www.popsci.com/blog-network/eastern-arsenal/not-shark-robot-chinese-university-tests-long-range-unmanned-mini-sub [Accessed 11 May 2018].

25. McArthur, S. D. et al., 2007. Multi-Agent Systems for Power Engineering Applications - Part I: Concepts, Approaches, and Technical Challenges. *IEEE TRANSACTIONS ON POWER SYSTEMS*, 22(4), pp. 1743–1752.

26. Muller, J.-P., 2004. Emergence of collective behaviour and problem solving. In: A. Omicini, P. Petta & J. Pitt, eds. *Engineering Societies in the Agents World IV*. volume 3071: Lecture Notes in Computer Science, pp. 1–20.

27. NAP, 2012. *Intelligent Human-Machine Collaboration: Summary of a Workshop*, available at http://nap.edu/13479: National Academies Press.

28. NAP, 2014. *Autonomy Research for Civil Aviation: Toward a New Era of Flight*, available at http://nap.edu/18815: National Academies Press.

29. NAP, 2016. *Protection of Transportation Infrastructure from Cyber Attacks: A Primer*, Available at http://nap.edu/23516: National Academies Press.

30. Nwana, H. S., 1996. Software agents: An overview. *The knowledge engineering review, 11(3)*, pp. 205–244.

31. Papernot, N. et al., 2016. *Distillation as a Defense to Adversarial Perturbations Against Deep Neural Networks*. IEEE, 37th IEEE Symposium on Security & Privacy, pp. 582–597.

32. Pěchouček, M., Jakob, M. & Novák, P., 2010. Towards Simulation-Aided Design of Multi-Agent Systems. In: R. Collier, J. Dix & P. Novák, eds. *Programming Multi-Agent Systems*. Toronto, ON, Canada: Springer, 8th InternationalWorkshop, ProMAS 2010, 11 May 2010, Revised Selected Papers, pp. 3–21.

33. Pechoucek, M. & Mařík, V., 2008. Industrial deployment of multi-agent technologies: review and selected case studies. *Autonomous Agents and Multi-Agent Systems,* Volume 17, p. 397–431.

34. Provos, N., 2004. *A Virtual Honeypot Framework*. Berkeley, USENIX Association, pp. 1–1.

35. Rasch, R., Kott, A. & Forbus, K. D., 2002. AI on the battlefield: An experimental exploration. *AAAI/IAAI*.

36. Rasch, R., Kott, A. & Forbus, K. D., 2003. Incorporating AI into military decision making: an experiment. *IEEE Intelligent Systems,* 18(4), pp. 18–26.

37. Russell, S. J. & Norvig, P., 2003. *Artificial Intelligence: A Modern Approach*. 2nd ed. Upper Saddle River, New Jersey: Prentice Hall.

38. Russell, S. J. & Norvig, P., 2010. *Artificial Intelligence: a Modern Approach*. 3rd ed. Upper Saddle River, NJ: Pearson Education.

39. Seufert, S. & O'Brien, D., 2007. *Machine Learning for Automatic Defence Against Distributed Denial of Service Attacks*. IEEE, ICC 2007 proceedings, pp. 1217–1222.

40. Silver, D. et al., 2017. Mastering the game of Go without human knowledge. *Nature,* 10, Volume 550, p. 354.

41. Sislak, D., Volf, P., Kopriva, S. & Pěchouček, M., 2012. AgentFly: Scalable, High-Fidelity Framework for Simulation, Planning and Collision Avoidance of Multiple UAVs. In: P. Angelov, ed. *Sense and Avoid in UAS: Research and Applications*. Wiley Online Library: Wiley: John Wiley&Sons, Inc., https://onlinelibrary.wiley.com/doi/pdf/10.1002/9781119964049.ch9, pp. 235-264.

42. Snyder, D. et al., 2015. *Improving the Cybersecurity of U.S. Air Force Military Systems Throughout Their Life Cycles*, Santa Monica, CA: RAND Corporation.

43. Stytz, M. R., Lichtblau, D. E. & Banks, S. B., 2005. *Toward using intelligent agents to detect, assess, and counter cyberattacks in a network-centric environment,* Alexandria, VA: Institute For Defense Analyses.
44. Tactical AGENTFLY, 2018. *Agent Technology Center.* [Online] Available at: http:// agents.felk.cvut.cz/projects/agentfly/tactical [Accessed 6 June 2018].
45. Théron, P., 2017. *La cyber résilience, un projet cohérent transversal à nos trois thèmes, et la problématique particulière des Systèmes Multi Agent de Cyber Défense.* Leçon inaugurale, 5 décembre 2017, ed. Salon de Provence, France: Chaire Cyber Résilience Aérospatiale (Cyb'Air).
46. Von Neumann, J., 1951. The General and Logical Theory of Automata. In: L. A. Jeffress, ed. *Cerebral Mechanisms in Behavior: The Hixon Symposium, September 1948, Pasadena.* New York: John Wiley & Sons, Inc, pp. 1–31.
47. Weick, K., 1993. The Collapse of Sensemaking in Organizations: The Mann Gulch Disaster. *Administrative Science Quarterly,* 38(4), pp. 628–652.
48. Wooldridge, M. & Jennings, N. R., 1995. Intelligent agents: Theory and practice. *The knowledge engineering review, 10(2),* pp. 115–152.
49. Yuill, J., Zappe, M., Denning, D. & Feer, F., 2004. *Honeyfiles: deceptive files for intrusion detection.* IEEE Xplore, Information Assurance Workshop, 2004. Proceedings from the Fifth Annual IEEE SMC, 10–11 June 2004, pp. 116–122.

Defending Against Machine Learning Based Inference Attacks via Adversarial Examples: Opportunities and Challenges

Jinyuan Jia and Neil Zhenqiang Gong

1 Introduction

As ML provides more and more powerful tools for data analytics, attackers increasingly use ML to perform automated inference attacks in various domains. Roughly speaking, an ML-equipped inference attack aims to infer private data of an individual, a software, or a system via leveraging ML classifiers to automatically analyze their certain public data. Inference attacks pose pervasive privacy and security threats to individuals and systems. Example inference attacks include, but are not limited to, *attribute inference attacks* in online social networks [1–10], *author identification attacks* [11–16], *website fingerprinting attacks* in anonymous communications [17–21], *side-channel attacks* to steal a system's cryptographic keys [22, 23], *membership inference attacks* [24–26], *sensor-based location inference attacks* [27, 28], *feature inference attacks* [29, 30], *CAPTCHA breaking attacks* [31–33], etc. For instance, in attribute inference attacks, an attacker uses ML classifiers to infer online social network users' private attributes (i.e., private data)—such as location, gender, sexual orientation, and political view—from their publicly available data such as page likes, rating scores, and social friends. The Facebook data privacy scandal in 2018 is a real-world example of attribute inference attack, where Cambridge Analytica leveraged an ML classifier to infer a large amount of Facebook users' private attributes via their public page likes [34].

Existing defenses against inference attacks can be roughly grouped into two categories, i.e., *game-theoretic methods* [35–39] and *(local) differential privacy* [40–46]. These methods are not practical: they either are computationally intractable or incur large utility loss of the public data. Specifically, in game-theoretic methods,

J. Jia · N. Z. Gong (✉)
Duke University, Durham, NC, USA
e-mail: jinyuan.jia@duke.edu; neil.gong@duke.edu

© Springer Nature Switzerland AG 2020
S. Jajodia et al. (eds.), *Adaptive Autonomous Secure Cyber Systems*,
https://doi.org/10.1007/978-3-030-33432-1_2

an attacker performs the optimal inference attack based on the knowledge of the defense, while the defender defends against the optimal inference attack. These methods are computationally intractable. In particular, the computation cost to find the noise that should be added to the public data is *exponential* to the dimensionality of the public data [39], which is often large in practice. Salamatian et al. [47] proposed to quantize the public data to approximately solve the game-theoretic optimization problem [38]. However, quantization incurs a large utility loss of the public data [39]. Differential privacy (DP) [40] or its variant called local differential privacy (LDP) [41–46] can also be applied to defend against inference attacks. DP/LDP provides a strong privacy guarantee. However, DP/LDP aims to achieve a privacy goal that is different from the one in inference attacks. For instance, LDP's privacy goal is to add random noise to a true public data record such that two arbitrary true public data records have close probabilities (their difference is bounded by a privacy budget) to generate the same noisy public data record. However, in defending against inference attacks, the privacy goal is to add noise to a public data record such that the private data cannot be accurately inferred by the attacker's classifier. As a result, DP/LDP achieves a suboptimal privacy-utility tradeoff at defending against inference attacks [39].

In this chapter, we discuss the opportunities and challenges of defending against inference attacks via adversarial examples. Our key intuition is that attackers use ML classifiers in inference attacks. ML classifiers were shown to be vulnerable to adversarial examples [48–50], which add carefully crafted noise to normal examples such that an ML classifier makes predictions for the examples as we desire. Based on this observation, we can add carefully crafted noise to a public data record to turn it into an adversarial example such that attacker's classifiers incorrectly predict the private data. However, existing methods to construct adversarial examples are insufficient because they did not consider the unique challenges of defending against inference attacks. Specifically, the first challenge is that the defender does not know the the attacker's classifier, since there are many possible choices for the classifier. Second, in certain application domains, the true private data value is not available when turning the public data into an adversarial example, i.e., the "true label" is not known when constructing the adversarial example. Third, the noise added to the public data should satisfy certain utility-loss constraints, which may be different for inference attacks in different application domains. We take AttriGuard [39],[1] the first adversarial example based practical defense against inference attacks (in particular, attribute inference attacks in online social networks), as an example to illustrate how to address the challenges.

AttriGuard works in two phases. Phase I addresses the first two challenges, while Phase II addresses the third challenge. Specifically, in Phase I, the defender itself learns an ML classifier to perform attribute inference. The defender constructs

---

[1]Code and dataset of AttriGuard are publicly available: https://github.com/jjy1994/AttriGuard.

adversarial examples based on its own classifier and the adversarial examples are also likely to be effective for the attacker's classifier because of *transferability* [50–53]. For each possible attribute value, the defender finds a carefully crafted noise vector to turn a user's public data into an adversarial sample, for which the defender's classifier predicts the attribute value. Existing adversarial example methods (e.g., [50, 52–55]) are insufficient because they did not consider users' privacy preference. In particular, different users may have different preferences on what types of noise can be added to their public data. For instance, a user may prefer modifying its existing rating scores, or adding new rating scores, or combination of them. To address the challenge, AttriGuard optimizes the method developed by Papernot et al. [54] to incorporate such constraints.

In Phase II, the defender randomly picks a noise vector found in Phase I according to a probability distribution $\mathbf{q}$ over the noise vectors. AttriGuard finds the probability distribution $\mathbf{q}$ via minimizing its distance to a *target probability distribution* $\mathbf{p}$ subject to a bounded utility loss of the public data. The target probability distribution is selected by the defender. For instance, the target probability distribution could be a uniform distribution over the possible attribute values, with which the defender aims to make the attacker's inference close to random guessing. Formally, AttriGuard formulates finding the probability distribution $\mathbf{q}$ as solving a constrained convex optimization problem. Moreover, according to the *Karush–Kuhn–Tucker (KKT) conditions* [56], the solution of the probability distribution $\mathbf{q}$ is intuitive and interpretable.

Jia and Gong [39] compared AttriGuard with existing defenses using a real-world dataset [7, 57]. In the dataset, a user's public data are the rating scores the user gave to mobile apps on Google Play, while the attribute is the city a user lives/lived in. First, the results demonstrated that the adapted adversarial example method in Phase I outperforms existing ones. Second, AttriGuard is effective at defending against attribute inference attacks. For instance, by modifying at most 4 rating scores on average, the attacker's inference accuracy is reduced by 75% for several defense-unaware attribute inference attacks and attacks that adapt to the defense. Third, AttriGuard adds significantly smaller noise to users' public data than existing defenses when reducing the attacker's inference accuracy by the same amount.

In the rest of this chapter, we will review inference attacks and their defenses, how to formulate the problem of defending against inference attacks, and describe AttriGuard to solve the formulated problem. Finally, we will discuss further opportunities, challenges, and future work for leveraging adversarial machine learning to defend against inference attacks.

2   Related Work

2.1   *Inference Attacks*

Attribute Inference Attacks A number of studies [1–10] have demonstrated that
users in online social networks are vulnerable to *attribute inference attacks*. In these
attacks, an attacker has access to a set of data (e.g., rating scores, page likes, social
friends) about a target user, which we call *public data*; and the attacker aims to
infer *private attributes* (e.g., location, political view, or sexual orientation) of the
target user. Specifically, the attacker could be a social network provider, advertiser,
or data broker (e.g., Cambridge Analytica). The attacker first collects a dataset from
users who disclose both their public data and attributes, and then the attacker uses
them as a training dataset to learn a ML classifier, which takes a user's public data
as input and predicts the user's private attribute value. Finally, the attacker applies
the classifier to predict the target user's private attribute value via its public data.
Attribute inference attacks can accurately infer users' various private attributes via
their publicly available rating scores, page likes, and social friends. For instance,
Cambridge Analytica inferred Facebook users' various private attributes including,
but not limited to, age, gender, political view, religious view, and relationship status,
using their public page likes [34].

Other Inference Attacks Other than attribute inference attacks in online social
networks, inference attacks are also pervasive in other domains. Table 1 shows
some inference attacks and the corresponding public data and private data. In
author identification attacks [11–16], an attacker can identify the author(s) of an
anonymous text document or program via leveraging ML to analyze the writing
style. In website fingerprinting attacks [17–21], an attacker can infer the website a
user visits via leveraging ML to analyze the network traffic, even if the traffic is

Table 1 Some inference attacks

Attack	Public data	Private data
Attribute inference attacks [1–10]	Rating scores, page likes, social friends, etc.	Age, gender, political view, etc.
Author identification attacks [11–16]	Text document, program	Author identity
Website fingerprinting attacks [17–21]	Network traffic	Website
Side-channel attacks [22, 23]	Power consumption, processing time, access pattern	Cryptographic keys
Membership inference attacks [24–26]	Confidence scores, gradients	Member/non-member
Location inference attacks [27, 28]	Sensor data on smartphone	Location
Feature inference attacks [29, 30]	Partial features, model prediction	Missing features
CAPTCHA breaking attacks [31–33]	CAPTCHA	Text, audio, etc.

encrypted and anonymized. In side-channel attacks [22, 23], an attacker can infer a system's cryptographic keys via leveraging ML to analyze the power consumption, processing time, and access patterns. In membership inference attacks [24–26], an attacker can infer whether a data record is in a classifier's training dataset via leveraging ML to analyze the confidence scores of the data record predicted by the classifier or the gradient of the classifier with respect to the data record. In sensor-based location inference attacks [27, 28], an attacker can infer a user's locations via leveraging ML to analyze the user's smartphone's aggregate power consumption as well as the gyroscope, accelerometer, and magnetometer data available from the user's smartphone. In feature inference attacks [29, 30],[2] an attacker can infer a data point's missing features (e.g., an individual's genotype) via analyzing an ML model's prediction for the data point. In CAPTCHA breaking attacks [31–33], an attacker can solve a CAPTCHA via ML.

2.2 Defenses

Game-Theoretic Methods and Differential Privacy Shokri et al. [35], Calmon et al. [38], and Jia and Gong [39] proposed game-theoretic methods to defend against inference attacks. These methods rely on optimization problems that are computationally intractable when the public data is high dimensional. Salamatian et al. [47] proposed *Quantization Probabilistic Mapping (QPM)* to approximately solve the game-theoretic optimization problem formulated by Calmon et al. [38]. Specifically, they cluster public data and use the cluster centroids to represent them. Then, they approximately solve the optimization problem using the cluster centroids. Huang et al. [58] proposed to use generative adversarial networks to approximately solve the game-theoretic optimization problems. However, these approximate solutions do not have formal guarantees on utility loss of the public data. Differential privacy or local differential privacy [40–46] can also be applied to add noise to the public data to defend against inference attacks. However, as we discussed in Introduction, they achieve suboptimal privacy-utility tradeoffs because they aim to provide privacy guarantees that are stronger than needed to defend against inference attacks.

Other Methods Other methods [2, 59] leveraged heuristic correlations between the entries of the public data and attribute values to defend against attribute inference attacks in online social networks. Specifically, they modify the k entries that have large correlations with the attribute values that do not belong to the target user. k is a parameter to control privacy-utility tradeoffs. For instance, Weinsberg et al. [2] proposed BlurMe, which calculates the correlations based on the coefficients of a logistic regression classifier that models the relationship between public data entries

---

[2]These attacks are also called attribute inference attacks [30]. To distinguish with attribute inference attacks in online social networks, we call them feature inference attacks.

and attribute values. Chen et al. [59] proposed ChiSquare, which computes the correlations between public data entries and attribute values based on chi-square statistics. These methods suffer from two limitations: (1) they require the defender to have direct access to users' private attribute values, which makes the defender become a single point of failure, i.e., when the defender is compromised, the private attribute values of all users are compromised; and (2) they incur large utility loss of the public data.

3 Problem Formulation

We take attribute inference attacks in online social networks as an example to illustrate how to formulate the problem of defending against inference attacks. However, our problem formulation can also be generalized to other inference attacks. We have three parties: *user*, *attacker*, and *defender*. Next, we discuss each party one by one.

3.1 User

We focus on protecting the private attribute of one user. We can protect different users separately. A user aims to publish some data while preventing inference of its private attribute from the public data. We denote the user's public data and private attribute as $\mathbf{x}$ (a column vector) and s, respectively. For instance, an entry of the public data vector $\mathbf{x}$ could be the rating score the user gave to an item or 0 if the user did not rate the item; an entry of the public data vector could also be 1 if the user liked the corresponding page or 0 otherwise. For simplicity, we assume each entry of $\mathbf{x}$ is normalized to be in the range $[0, 1]$. The attribute s has m possible values, which we denote as $\{1, 2, \cdots, m\}$; $s = i$ means that the user's private attribute value is i. For instance, when the private attribute is political view, the attribute could have two possible values, i.e., democratic and republican. We note that the attribute s could be a combination of multiple attributes. For instance, the attribute could be $s = $ (politicalview, gender), which has four possible values, i.e., (democratic, male), (republican, male), (democratic, female), and (republican, female).

Policy to Add Noise Different users may have different preferences over what kind of noise can be added to their public data. For instance, a user may prefer modifying its existing rating scores, while another user may prefer adding new rating scores. We call a policy specifying what kind of noise can be added a *noise-type-policy*. In particular, we consider the following three types of noise-type-policy.

- **Policy A: Modify_Exist.** In this policy, the defender can only modify the non-zero entries of $\mathbf{x}$. When the public data are rating scores, this policy means that the defender can only modify a user's existing rating scores. When the public data

correspond to page likes, this policy means that the defender can only remove a user's existing page likes.
- **Policy B: Add_New.** In this policy, the defender can only change the zero entries of **x**. When the public data are rating scores, this policy means that the defender can only add new rating scores for a user. When the public data represent page likes, this policy means that the defender can only add new page likes for a user. We call this policy *Add_New*.
- **Policy C: Modify_Add.** This policy is a combination of Modify_Exist and Add_New. In particular, the defender could modify any entry of **x**.

3.2 Attacker

The attacker has access to the noisy public data and aims to infer the user's private attribute value. We consider an attacker has an ML classifier that takes a user's (noisy) public data as input and infers the user's private attribute value. Different users might treat different attributes as private. In particular, some users do not treat the attribute s as private, so they publicly disclose it. Via collecting data from such users, the attacker can learn the ML classifier.

We denote the attacker's classifier as C_a, and $C_a(\mathbf{x}) \in \{1, 2, \cdots, m\}$ is the predicted attribute value for the user whose public data is **x**. The attacker could use a standard ML classifier, e.g., logistic regression, random forest, and neural network. Moreover, an attacker can also adapt its attack based on the defense. For instance, the attacker could first try detecting the noise and then perform attribute inference attacks. We assume the attacker's classifier is unknown to the defender, since there are many possible choices for the attacker's classifier.

3.3 Defender

The defender adds noise to a user's true public data according to a noise-type-policy. The defender can be a software on the user's client side, e.g., a browser extension. The defender has access to the user's true public data **x**. The defender adds a noise vector **r** to **x** and the attacker has access to the noisy public data vector $\mathbf{x} + \mathbf{r}$. The defender aims to achieve two goals:

- **Goal I.** The attacker's classifier is inaccurate at inferring the user's private attribute value.
- **Goal II.** The utility loss of the public data vector is bounded.

However, achieving the two goals faces several challenges.

Achieving Goal I The first challenge to achieve Goal I is that the defender does not know the attacker's classifier. To address the challenge, the defender itself trains a classifier C to perform attribute inference using the data from the users who share both public data and attribute values. Then, the defender adds a noise vector to a user's public data vector such that its own classifier is inaccurate at inferring the user's private attribute value. We consider the defender's classifier C is implemented in the popular *one-vs-all* paradigm. Specifically, the classifier has m decision functions denoted as $C_1, C_2, \cdots, C_m$, where $C_i(\mathbf{x})$ is the confidence that the user has an attribute value i. The classifier's inferred attribute value is $C(\mathbf{x}) = \text{argmax}_i\, C_i(\mathbf{x})$. Note that, when the attribute only has two possible values (i.e., $m = 2$), we have $C_2(\mathbf{x}) = -C_1(\mathbf{x})$ for classifiers like logistic regression and SVM.

The second challenge is that the defender does not know the user's true private attribute value. Therefore, for a given noise vector, the defender does not know whether its own classifier makes incorrect prediction on the user's private attribute value or not. One method to address the challenge is to add noise vectors to users' public data vectors such that the defender's classifier always predicts a certain attribute value for the users. However, for some users, such method may need noise that violates the utility-loss constraints of the public data. Therefore, the defender adopts a *randomized noise addition mechanism* denoted as $\mathcal{M}$. Specifically, given a user's true public data vector $\mathbf{x}$, the defender samples a noise vector $\mathbf{r}$ from the space of possible noise vectors with a probability $\mathcal{M}(\mathbf{r}|\mathbf{x})$ and adds it to the true public data vector.

Since the defender adds random noise, the defender's classifier's prediction is also random. We denote by $\mathbf{q}$ the probability distribution of the attribute values predicted by the defender's classifier for the particular user when the defender adds random noise to the user's public data vector according to a randomized noise addition mechanism $\mathcal{M}$. Moreover, the defender aims to find a mechanism $\mathcal{M}$ such that the output probability distribution $\mathbf{q}$ is the closest to a *target probability distribution* $\mathbf{p}$ subject to a utility-loss budget, where $\mathbf{p}$ is selected by the defender. For instance, without knowing anything about the attributes, the target probability distribution could be the uniform distribution over the m attribute values, with which the defender aims to make the attacker's inference close to random guessing. The target probability distribution could also be estimated from the users who publicly disclose the attribute, e.g., the probability p_i is the fraction of such users who have attribute value i. Such target probability distribution naturally represents a baseline attribute inference attack. The defender aims to reduce an attack to the baseline attack with such target probability distribution.

The next challenge is how to quantify the distance between $\mathbf{p}$ and $\mathbf{q}$. While any distance metric could be applied, AttriGuard measures the distance between $\mathbf{p}$ and $\mathbf{q}$ using their Kullback–Leibler (KL) divergence, i.e., $KL(\mathbf{p}||\mathbf{q}) = \sum_i p_i \log \frac{p_i}{q_i}$. AttriGuard chooses KL divergence because it makes the formulated optimization problem convex, which has efficient, accurate, and interpretable solutions.

Achieving Goal II The key challenge to achieve Goal II is how to quantify the utility loss of the public data vector. A user's (noisy) public data are often leveraged by a service provider to provide services. For instance, when the public data are rating scores, they are often used to recommend items to users that match their personalized preferences. Therefore, utility loss of the public data can essentially be measured by the service quality loss. Specifically, in a recommender system, the decreased accuracy of the recommendations introduced by the added noise can be used as utility loss. However, using such service-dependent utility loss makes the formulated optimization problem computationally intractable.

Therefore, we resort to utility-loss metrics that make the formulated optimization problems tractable but can still well approximate the utility loss for different services. In particular, we can use a distance metric $d(\mathbf{x}, \mathbf{x} + \mathbf{r})$ to measure utility loss. Since $\mathbf{r}$ is a random value generated according to the mechanism $\mathcal{M}$, we can measure the utility loss using the expected distance $E(d(\mathbf{x}, \mathbf{x} + \mathbf{r}))$. For instance, the distance metric can be L_0 norm of the noise, i.e., $d(\mathbf{x}, \mathbf{x} + \mathbf{r}) = ||\mathbf{r}||_0$. L_0 norm is the number of entries of $\mathbf{x}$ that are modified by the noise, which has semantic interpretations in a number of real-world application domains. For instance, when the public data are rating scores, L_0 norm means the number of items whose rating scores are modified. Likewise, when the public data are page likes, an entry of $\mathbf{x}$ is 1 if the user liked the corresponding page, otherwise the entry is 0. Then, L_0 norm means the number of page likes that are removed or added by the defender. The distance metric can also be L_2 norm of the noise, which considers the magnitude of the modified rating scores when the public data are rating scores.

Attribute-Inference-Attack Defense Problem With quantifiable defender's goals, we can formally define the problem of defending against attribute inference attacks. Specifically, the user specifies a noise-type-policy and an utility-loss budget β. The defender specifies a target probability distribution $\mathbf{p}$, learns a classifier C, and finds a mechanism $\mathcal{M}^*$, which adds noise to the user's public data such that the user's utility loss is within the budget while the output probability distribution $\mathbf{q}$ of the classifier C is closest to the target probability distribution $\mathbf{p}$. Formally, we have:

Definition 1 Given a noise-type-policy $\mathcal{P}$, an utility-loss budget β, a target probability distribution $\mathbf{p}$, and a classifier C, the defender aims to find a mechanism $\mathcal{M}^*$ via solving the following optimization problem:

$$\mathcal{M}^* = \mathrm{argmin}_{\mathcal{M}} \, KL(\mathbf{p}||\mathbf{q})$$
$$\text{subject to } E(d(\mathbf{x}, \mathbf{x} + \mathbf{r})) \le \beta, \tag{1}$$

where $\mathbf{q}$ depends on the classifier C and the mechanism $\mathcal{M}$. AttriGuard uses the L_0 norm of the noise as the metric $d(\mathbf{x}, \mathbf{x} + \mathbf{r})$ because of its semantic interpretation.

4   Design of AttriGuard

4.1   Overview

The major challenge to solve the optimization problem in Eq. (1) is that the number of parameters of the mechanism M, which maps a given vector to another vector probabilistically, is exponential to the dimensionality of the public data vector. To address the challenge, Jia and Gong [39] proposed AttriGuard, a *two-phase framework* to solve the optimization problem approximately. The intuition is that, although the noise space is large, we can categorize them into m groups depending on the defender's classifier's output. Specifically, we denote by G_i the group of noise vectors such that if we add any of them to the user's public data, then the defender's classifier will infer the attribute value i for the user. Essentially, the probability q_i that the defender's classifier infers attribute value i for the user is the probability that M will sample a noise vector in the group G_i, i.e., $q_i = \sum_{\mathbf{r} \in G_i} M(\mathbf{r}|\mathbf{x})$. AttriGuard finds one representative noise vector in each group and assumes M is a probability distribution concentrated on the representative noise vectors.

Specifically, in Phase I, for each group G_i, AttriGuard finds a minimum noise $\mathbf{r}_i$ such that if we add $\mathbf{r}_i$ to the user's public data, then the defender's classifier predicts the attribute value i for the user. AttriGuard finds a minimum noise in order to minimize utility loss. In *adversarial machine learning*, this is known as *adversarial example*. However, existing adversarial example methods [50, 52–55] are insufficient to find the noise vector $\mathbf{r}_i$, because they do not consider the noise-type-policy. AttriGuard optimizes the adversarial example method developed by Papernot et al. [54] to incorporate noise-type-policy. The noise $\mathbf{r}_i$ optimized to evade the defender's classifier is also likely to make the attacker's classifier predict the attribute value i for the user, which is known as *transferability* [50–53] in adversarial machine learning.

In Phase II, AttriGuard simplifies the mechanism M^* to be a probability distribution over the m representative noise vectors $\{\mathbf{r}_1, \mathbf{r}_2, \cdots, \mathbf{r}_m\}$. In other words, the defender randomly samples a noise vector $\mathbf{r}_i$ according to the probability distribution M^* and adds the noise vector to the user's public data. Under such simplification, M^* only has at most m non-zero parameters, the output probability distribution $\mathbf{q}$ of the defender's classifier essentially becomes M^*, and we can transform the optimization problem in Eq. (1) to be a convex problem, which can be solved efficiently and accurately. Moreover, Jia and Gong derived the analytical forms of the solution using the *Karush–Kuhn–Tucker (KKT) conditions* [56], which shows that the solution is intuitive and interpretable.

4.2 Phase I: Finding $\mathbf{r}_i$

Phase I aims to find a minimum noise $\mathbf{r}_i$ according to the noise-type-policy $\mathcal{P}$, such that the classifier C infers the attribute value i for the user after adding $\mathbf{r}_i$ to its public data $\mathbf{x}$. Formally, AttriGuard finds such $\mathbf{r}_i$ via solving the following optimization problem:

$$\mathbf{r}_i = \text{argmin}_{\mathbf{r}} \, ||\mathbf{r}||_0$$
$$\text{subject to} \quad C(\mathbf{x} + \mathbf{r}) = i. \tag{2}$$

The formulation of finding $\mathbf{r}_i$ can be viewed as finding an adversarial example [48–50] to the classifier C. However, existing adversarial example methods (e.g., [50, 52–55]) are insufficient to solve $\mathbf{r}_i$. The key reason is that they do not consider the noise-type-policy, which specifies the types of noise that can be added. Papernot et al. [54] proposed a *Jacobian-based Saliency Map Attack* (JSMA) to deep neural networks. They demonstrated that JSMA can find small noise (measured by L_0 norm) to evade a deep neural network. Their algorithm iteratively adds noise to an example ($\mathbf{x}$ in our case) until the classifier C predicts i as its label or the maximum number of iterations is reached. In each iteration, the algorithm picks one or two entries of $\mathbf{x}$ based on saliency map, and then increase or decrease the entries by a constant value.

Jia and Gong also designed their algorithm, which is called *Policy-Aware Noise Finding Algorithm (PANDA)*, based on saliency map. However, PANDA is different from JSMA in two aspects. First, PANDA incorporates the noise-type-policy, while JSMA does not. The major reason is that JSMA is not developed for preserving privacy, so JSMA does not have noise-type-policy as an input. Second, in JSMA, all the modified entries of $\mathbf{x}$ are either increased or decreased. In PANDA, some entries can be increased while other entries can be decreased. Jia and Gong demonstrated that PANDA can find smaller noise than JSMA.

4.3 Phase II: Finding $\mathcal{M}^*$

After the defender solves $\{\mathbf{r}_1, \mathbf{r}_2, \cdots, \mathbf{r}_m\}$, the defender randomly samples one of them with a certain probability and adds it to the user's public data $\mathbf{x}$. Therefore, the randomized noise addition mechanism $\mathcal{M}$ is a probability distribution over $\{\mathbf{r}_1, \mathbf{r}_2, \cdots, \mathbf{r}_m\}$, where $\mathcal{M}_i$ is the probability that the defender adds $\mathbf{r}_i$ to $\mathbf{x}$. Since $q_i = \text{Pr}(C(\mathbf{x} + \mathbf{r}) = i)$ and $C(\mathbf{x} + \mathbf{r}_i) = i$, we have $q_i = \mathcal{M}_i$, where $i \in \{1, 2, \cdots, m\}$. Therefore, the optimization problem in Eq. (1) can be transformed to the following optimization problem:

$$\mathcal{M}^* = \text{argmin}_{\mathcal{M}} \, KL(\mathbf{p}||\mathcal{M})$$
$$\text{subject to} \quad \sum_{i=1}^{m} \mathcal{M}_i ||\mathbf{r}_i||_0 \leq \beta$$

$$\mathcal{M}_i > 0, \forall i \in \{1, 2, \cdots, m\}$$

$$\sum_{i=1}^{m} \mathcal{M}_i = 1, \tag{3}$$

where AttriGuard uses the L_0 norm of the noise as the utility-loss metric $d(\mathbf{x}, \mathbf{x}+\mathbf{r})$ in Eq. (1). The above optimization problem is convex because its objective function and constraints are convex, which implies that $\mathcal{M}^*$ is a global minimum. Moreover, many methods can be applied to solve the optimization problem exactly and efficiently. For instance, Jia and Gong [39] described an KKT conditions based method to solve the optimization problem. We can also use the cvxpy package [60] to solve the problem.

Interpreting the Mechanism $\mathcal{M}^*$ According to the standard KKT conditions, the solved mechanism satisfies the following equations:

$$\nabla_{\mathcal{M}}(KL(\mathbf{p}||\mathcal{M}^*) + \mu_0(\sum_{i=1}^{m} \mathcal{M}_i^*||\mathbf{r}_i||_0 - \beta) - \sum_{i=1}^{m} \mu_i \mathcal{M}_i^*$$

$$+\lambda(\sum_{i=1}^{m} \mathcal{M}_i^* - 1)) = 0 \tag{4}$$

$$\mu_i \mathcal{M}_i^* = 0, \forall i \in \{1, 2, \cdots, m\} \tag{5}$$

$$\mu_0(\sum_{i=1}^{m} \mathcal{M}_i^*||\mathbf{r}_i||_0 - \beta) = 0, \tag{6}$$

where ∇ indicates gradient, while μ_i and λ are KKT multipliers. According to Eq. (5) and $\mathcal{M}_i^* > 0$, we have $\mu_i = 0, \forall i \in \{1, 2, \cdots, m\}$. Therefore, according to Eq. (4), Jia and Gong derived the following analytical form of the solved mechanism:

$$\mathcal{M}_i^* = \frac{p_i}{\mu_0||\mathbf{r}_i||_0 + \lambda} \tag{7}$$

If we do not have the utility-loss constraint $\sum_{i=1}^{m} \mathcal{M}_i||\mathbf{r}_i||_0 \leq \beta$ in the optimization problem in Eq. (3), then the mechanism $\mathcal{M}^* = \mathbf{p}$ reaches the minimum KL divergence $KL(\mathbf{p}||\mathcal{M})$, where $\mathbf{p}$ is the target probability distribution selected by the defender. In other words, if we do not consider utility loss, the defender samples the noise $\mathbf{r}_i$ with the target probability p_i and adds it to the user's public data. However, when we consider the utility-loss budget, the relationship between the mechanism $\mathcal{M}^*$ and the target probability distribution $\mathbf{p}$ is represented in Eq. (7). In other words, the defender samples the noise $\mathbf{r}_i$ with a probability that is the target probability p_i normalized by the magnitude of the noise $\mathbf{r}_i$. The solved mechanism is intuitive and interpretable.

5   Discussion, Limitations, and Future Work

Generalizing AttriGuard to Defend Against Other Inference Attacks We believe that there are many opportunities for both the adversarial machine learning community and the security and privacy community to leverage adversarial machine learning to defend against inference attacks in various domains. For the adversarial machine learning community, there are opportunities to develop new adversarial machine learning methods that consider the unique privacy and utility-loss challenges. For the privacy community, adversarial machine learning brings new opportunities to achieve better privacy-utility tradeoffs. For the security community, adversarial machine learning brings new opportunities to enhance system security such as designing more secure and usable CAPTCHAs as well as mitigating side-channel attacks. Specifically, we envision that AttriGuard's two-phase framework can be applied to defend against other inference attacks, e.g., the ones we discussed in Sect. 2.1. However, Phase I of AttriGuard should be adapted to different inference attacks, as different inference attacks may have their own unique privacy, security, and utility requirements on the representative noise vectors. Phase II can be used to satisfy the utility-loss constraints via randomly sampling a representative noise vector according to a certain probability distribution. We note that some recent studies [61, 62] have tried to leverage adversarial examples to defend against website fingerprinting attacks and side-channel attacks. However, they did not consider the utility-loss constraints, which can be satisfied by extending their methods using Phase II of AttriGuard. Moreover, recent studies [63, 64] have explored adversarial example based defenses against author identification attacks for programs.

Data Poisoning Attacks Based Defenses Other than adversarial examples, we could also leverage data poisoning attacks [65–72] to defend against inference attacks. Specifically, an attacker needs to train an ML classifier in inference attacks. For instance, in attribute inference attacks on social networks, an attacker may train a classifier via collecting a training dataset from users who disclose both public data and attribute values. In such scenarios, the defender could inject fake users with carefully crafted public data and attribute values to poison the attacker's training dataset such that the attacker's learnt classifier is inaccurate. In other words, the defender can perform data poisoning attacks to the attacker's classifier. For instance, an online social networking service provider could inject such fake users to defend against inference attacks performed by third-party attackers.

Adaptive Inference Attacks We envision that there will be an arms race between attackers and defenders. Specifically, an attacker could adapt its attacks when knowing the defense, while a defender can further adapt its defense based on the adapted attacks. For instance, an attacker could first detect the noise added to the public data or detect the fake users, and then the attacker performs inference attacks. Jia and Gong tried a low-rank approximation based method to detect the noise added by AttriGuard and AttriGuard is still effective against the method. However, this does not mean an attacker cannot perform better attacks via detecting the noise. An attacker could also leverage fake-user detection (also known as Sybil detection) methods (e.g., [73–82]) to detect and remove the fake users when the defender uses data poisoning attacks as defenses. We believe it is an interesting future work to systematically study the possibility of detecting noise and fake users both theoretically and empirically. We note that detecting noise is different from *detecting adversarial examples* [83–86], because detecting adversarial examples is to detect whether a given example has attacker-added noise or not. However, detecting adversarial examples may be able to help perform better inference attacks. Specifically, if an attacker detects that a public data vector is an adversarial example, the attacker can use a defense-aware inference attack for the public data vector, otherwise the attacker can use a defense-unaware attack.

Moreover, an attacker could also use classifiers, which are more robust to adversarial examples, to perform inference attacks. Jia and Gong evaluated three robust classifiers: adversarial training [50], defensive distillation [87], and region-based classification [88]. They showed that AttriGuard is still effective for attacks using such robust classifiers. As the adversarial machine learning community develops more robust classifiers (e.g., [89–91]), an attacker could leverage them for inference attacks. However, we speculate that robust classifiers are always vulnerable to adversarial examples that have large enough noise. In other words, we could still leverage adversarial examples to defend against inference attacks, but we may need larger noise (thus larger utility loss) for the public data when the attacker uses a classifier that is more robust to adversarial examples.

Transferability Transferability of adversarial examples is key to the success of adversarial example based defenses against inference attacks. Therefore, it is important to generate transferable adversarial examples. To enhance transferability, the defender can add larger noise to the adversarial examples (thus larger utility loss) or generate adversarial examples based on an ensemble of classifiers [52].

6   Conclusion

ML-equipped inference attacks pose growing privacy and security threats to users and systems in various domains. Attackers rely on the success of ML, but they also share the limitations of ML. In particular, ML classifiers are vulnerable to adversarial examples. In this chapter, we discuss the opportunities and challenges of turning the weaknesses of ML into weapons to defend against inference attacks. For instance, we can add carefully crafted noise to the public data to turn them into adversarial examples such that attackers' classifiers make incorrect predictions for the private data. There are many opportunities and challenges for both the adversarial machine learning community and the privacy and security community to study adversarial machine learning based defenses against inference attacks.

Acknowledgement This work was supported by NSF grant No. 1801584.

References

1. Jahna Otterbacher. Inferring gender of movie reviewers: exploiting writing style, content and metadata. In *CIKM*, 2010.
2. Udi Weinsberg, Smriti Bhagat, Stratis Ioannidis, and Nina Taft. Blurme: Inferring and obfuscating user gender based on ratings. In *RecSys*, 2012.
3. E. Zheleva and L. Getoor. To join or not to join: The illusion of privacy in social networks with mixed public and private user profiles. In *WWW*, 2009.
4. Abdelberi Chaabane, Gergely Acs, and Mohamed Ali Kaafar. You are what you like! information leakage through users' interests. In *NDSS*, 2012.
5. Michal Kosinski, David Stillwell, and Thore Graepel. Private traits and attributes are predictable from digital records of human behavior. *PNAS*, 2013.
6. Neil Zhenqiang Gong, Ameet Talwalkar, Lester Mackey, Ling Huang, Eui Chul Richard Shin, Emil Stefanov, Elaine(Runting) Shi, and Dawn Song. Joint link prediction and attribute inference using a social-attribute network. *ACM TIST*, 5(2), 2014.
7. Neil Zhenqiang Gong and Bin Liu. You are who you know and how you behave: Attribute inference attacks via users' social friends and behaviors. In *USENIX Security Symposium*, 2016.
8. Jinyuan Jia, Binghui Wang, Le Zhang, and Neil Zhenqiang Gong. AttriInfer: Inferring user attributes in online social networks using markov random fields. In *WWW*, 2017.
9. Neil Zhenqiang Gong and Bin Liu. Attribute inference attacks in online social networks. *ACM TOPS*, 21(1), 2018.
10. Yang Zhang, Mathias Humbert, Tahleen Rahman, Cheng-Te Li, Jun Pang, and Michael Backes. Tagvisor: A privacy advisor for sharing hashtags. In *WWW*, 2018.
11. Arvind Narayanan, Hristo Paskov, Neil Zhenqiang Gong, John Bethencourt, Emil Stefanov, Eui Chul Richard Shin, and Dawn Song. On the feasibility of internet-scale author identification. In *IEEE S&P*, 2012.
12. Mathias Payer, Ling Huang, Neil Zhenqiang Gong, Kevin Borgolte, and Mario Frank. What you submit is who you are: A multi-modal approach for deanonymizing scientific publications. *IEEE Transactions on Information Forensics and Security*, 10(1), 2015.
13. Aylin Caliskan-Islam, Richard Harang, Andrew Liu, Arvind Narayanan, Clare Voss, Fabian Yamaguchi, and Rachel Greenstadt. De-anonymizing programmers via code stylometry. In *USENIX Security Symposium*, 2015.
14. Aylin Caliskan, Fabian Yamaguchi, Edwin Tauber, Richard Harang, Konrad Rieck, Rachel Greenstadt, and Arvind Narayanan. When coding style survives compilation: De-anonymizing programmers from executable binaries. In *NDSS*, 2018.
15. Rakshith Shetty, Bernt Schiele, and Mario Fritz. A4nt: Author attribute anonymity by adversarial training of neural machine translation. In *USENIX Security Symposium*, 2018.
16. Mohammed Abuhamad, Tamer AbuHmed, Aziz Mohaisen, and DaeHun Nyang. Large-scale and language-oblivious code authorship identification. In *CCS*, 2018.
17. Dominik Herrmann, Rolf Wendolsky, and Hannes Federrath. Website fingerprinting: attacking popular privacy enhancing technologies with the multinomial naïve-bayes classifier. In *ACM Workshop on Cloud Computing Security*, 2009.
18. Andriy Panchenko, Lukas Niessen, Andreas Zinnen, and Thomas Engel. Website fingerprinting in onion routing based anonymization networks. In *ACM workshop on Privacy in the Electronic Society*, 2011.
19. Xiang Cai, Xin Cheng Zhang, Brijesh Joshi, and Rob Johnson. Touching from a distance: Website fingerprinting attacks and defenses. In *CCS*, 2012.
20. Marc Juarez, Sadia Afroz, Gunes Acar, Claudia Diaz, and Rachel Greenstadt. A critical evaluation of website fingerprinting attacks. In *CCS*, 2014.
21. Tao Wang, Xiang Cai, Rishab Nithyanand, Rob Johnson, and Ian Goldberg. Effective attacks and provable defenses for website fingerprinting. In *USENIX Security Symposium*, 2014.

22. Liran Lerman, Gianluca Bontempi, and Olivier Markowitch. Side channel attack: an approach based on machine learning. In *COSADE*, 2011.
23. Yinqian Zhang, Ari Juels, Michael K. Reiter, and Thomas Ristenpart. Cross-vm side channels and their use to extract private keys. In *CCS*, 2012.
24. Reza Shokri, Marco Stronati, Congzheng Song, and Vitaly Shmatikov. Membership Inference Attacks Against Machine Learning Models. In *IEEE S&P*, 2017.
25. Milad Nasr, Reza Shokri, and Amir Houmansadr. Machine Learning with Membership Privacy using Adversarial Regularization. In *CCS*, 2018.
26. Ahmed Salem, Yang Zhang, Mathias Humbert, Pascal Berrang, Mario Fritz, and Michael Backes. ML-Leaks: Model and Data Independent Membership Inference Attacks and Defenses on Machine Learning Models. In *NDSS*, 2019.
27. Y. Michalevsky, G. Nakibly, A. Schulman, and D. Boneh. Powerspy: Location tracking using mobile device power analysis. In *USENIX Security Symposium*, 2015.
28. Sashank Narain, Triet D. Vo-Huu, Kenneth Block, and Guevara Noubir. Inferring user routes and locations using zero-permission mobile sensors. In *IEEE S & P*, 2016.
29. Matthew Fredrikson, Eric Lantz, Somesh Jha, Simon Lin, David Page, and Thomas Ristenpart. Privacy in pharmacogenetics: An end-to-end case study of personalized warfarin dosing. In *USENIX Security Symposium*, 2014.
30. S. Yeom, I. Giacomelli, M. Fredrikson, and S. Jha. Privacy risk in machine learning: Analyzing the connection to overfitting. In *CSF*, 2018.
31. Guixin Ye, Zhanyong Tang, Dingyi Fang, Zhanxing Zhu, Yansong Feng, Pengfei Xu, Xiaojiang Chen, and Zheng Wang. Yet another text captcha solver: A generative adversarial network based approach. In *CCS*, 2018.
32. Elie Bursztein, Romain Beauxis, Hristo Paskov, Daniele Perito, Celine Fabry, and John Mitchell. The failure of noise-based non-continuous audio captchas. In *IEEE S & P*, 2011.
33. Elie Bursztein, Matthieu Martin, and John C. Mitchell. Text-based captcha strengths and weaknesses. In *CCS*, 2011.
34. Cambridge Analytica. https://goo.gl/PqRjjX, May 2018.
35. Reza Shokri, George Theodorakopoulos, and Carmela Troncoso. Protecting location privacy: Optimal strategy against localization attacks. In *CCS*, 2012.
36. Reza Shokri. Privacy games: Optimal user-centric data obfuscation. In *PETS*, 2015.
37. Reza Shokri, George Theodorakopoulos, and Carmela Troncoso. Privacy games along location traces: A game-theoretic framework for optimizing location privacy. *ACM TOPS*, 19(4), 2016.
38. Nadia Fawaz Flávio du Pin Calmon. Privacy against statistical inference. In *Allerton*, 2012.
39. Jinyuan Jia and Neil Zhenqiang Gong. Attriguard: A practical defense against attribute inference attacks via adversarial machine learning. In *USENIX Security Symposium*, 2018.
40. Cynthia Dwork, Frank McSherry, Kobbi Nissim, and Adam Smith. Calibrating noise to sensitivity in private data analysis. In *TCC*, 2006.
41. S. Warner. Randomized response: a survey technique for eliminating evasive answer bias. *Journal of the American Statistical Association*, 60(309), 1965.
42. J. C. Duchi, M. I. Jordan, and M. J. Wainwright. Local privacy and statistical minimax rates. In *FOCS*, 2013.
43. Aleksandra Korolova Úlfar Erlingsson, Vasyl Pihur. Rappor: Randomized aggregatable privacy-preserving ordinal response. In *CCS*, 2014.
44. R. Bassily and A. D. Smith. Local, private, efficient protocols for succinct histograms. In *STOC*, 2015.
45. Tianhao Wang, Jeremiah Blocki, Ninghui Li, and Somesh Jha. Locally differentially private protocols for frequency estimation. In *USENIX Security Symposium*, 2017.
46. Jinyuan Jia and Neil Zhenqiang Gong. Calibrate: Frequency estimation and heavy hitter identification with local differential privacy via incorporating prior knowledge. In *INFOCOM*, 2019.
47. Salman Salamatian, Amy Zhang, Flavio du Pin Calmon, Sandilya Bhamidipati, Nadia Fawaz, Branislav Kveton, Pedro Oliveira, and Nina Taft. Managing your private and public data: Bringing down inference attacks against your privacy. In *IEEE Journal of Selected Topics in Signal Processing*, 2015.

48. Marco Barreno, Blaine Nelson, Russell Sears, Anthony D Joseph, and J Doug Tygar. Can machine learning be secure? In *ACM ASIACCS*, 2006.

49. Battista Biggio, Igino Corona, Davide Maiorca, Blaine Nelson, Nedim ŚrndićPavel Laskov, Giorgio Giacinto, and Fabio Roli. Evasion attacks against machine learning at test time. In *ECML-PKDD*, 2013.

50. Jonathon Shlens Ian J. Goodfellow and Christian Szegedy. Explaining and harnessing adversarial examples. In *ICLR*, 2014.

51. Nicolas Papernot, Patrick McDaniel, Ian Goodfellow, Somesh Jha, Z Berkay Celik, and Ananthram Swami. Practical black-box attacks against machine learning. In *AsiaCCS*, 2017.

52. Yanpei Liu, Xinyun Chen, Chang Liu, and Dawn Song. Delving into transferable adversarial examples and black-box attacks. In *ICLR*, 2017.

53. Nicholas Carlini and David Wagner. Towards evaluating the robustness of neural networks. In *IEEE S & P*, 2017.

54. Nicolas Papernot, Patrick McDaniel, Somesh Jha, Matt Fredrikson, Z. Berkay Celik, and Ananthram Swami. The limitations of deep learning in adversarial settings. In *EuroS&P*, 2016.

55. Mahmood Sharif, Sruti Bhagavatula, Lujo Bauer, and K Michael Reiter. Accessorize to a crime: Real and stealthy attacks on state-of-the-art face recognition. In *CCS*, 2016.

56. *Convex Optimization*. Cambridge University Press, 2004.

57. Neil Zhenqiang Gong, Wenchang Xu, Ling Huang, Prateek Mittal, Emil Stefanov, Vyas Sekar, and Dawn Song. Evolution of social-attribute networks: Measurements, modeling, and implications using google+. In *IMC*, 2012.

58. Chong Huang, Peter Kairouz, Xiao Chen, Lalitha Sankar, and Ram Rajagopal. Generative adversarial privacy. In *Privacy in Machine Learning and Artificial Intelligence Workshop*, 2018.

59. Terence Chen, Roksana Boreli, Mohamed-Ali Kaafar, and Arik Friedman. On the effectiveness of obfuscation techniques in online social networks. In *PETS*, 2014.

60. cvxpy. https://www.cvxpy.org/, June 2019.

61. Mehmet Sinan Inci, Thomas Eisenbarth, and Berk Sunar. Deepcloak: Adversarial crafting as a defensive measure to cloak processes. In *arxiv*, 2018.

62. Mohsen Imani, Mohammad Saidur Rahman, Nate Mathews, and Matthew Wright. Mockingbird: Defending against deep-learning-based website fingerprinting attacks with adversarial traces. In *arxiv*, 2019.

63. Xiaozhu Meng, Barton P Miller, and Somesh Jha. Adversarial binaries for authorship identification. In *arxiv*, 2018.

64. Erwin Quiring, Alwin Maier, and Konrad Rieck. Misleading authorship attribution of source code using adversarial learning. In *USENIX Security Symposium*, 2019.

65. Battista Biggio, Blaine Nelson, and Pavel Laskov. Poisoning attacks against support vector machines. In *ICML*, 2012.

66. Matthew Jagielski, Alina Oprea, Battista Biggio, Chang Liu, Cristina Nita-Rotaru, and Bo Li. Manipulating machine learning: Poisoning attacks and countermeasures for regression learning. In *IEEE S & P*, 2018.

67. Bo Li, Yining Wang, Aarti Singh, and Yevgeniy Vorobeychik. Data poisoning attacks on factorization-based collaborative filtering. In *NIPS*, 2016.

68. Guolei Yang, Neil Zhenqiang Gong, and Ying Cai. Fake co-visitation injection attacks to recommender systems. In *NDSS*, 2017.

69. Luis Muñoz-González, Battista Biggio, Ambra Demontis, Andrea Paudice, Vasin Wongrassamee, Emil C Lupu, and Fabio Roli. Towards poisoning of deep learning algorithms with back-gradient optimization. In *AISec*, 2017.

70. Ali Shafahi, W Ronny Huang, Mahyar Najibi, Octavian Suciu, Christoph Studer, Tudor Dumitras, and Tom Goldstein. Poison frogs! targeted clean-label poisoning attacks on neural networks. In *NeurIPS*, 2018.

71. Octavian Suciu, Radu Marginean, Yigitcan Kaya, Hal Daume III, and Tudor Dumitras. When does machine learning fail? generalized transferability for evasion and poisoning attacks. In *Usenix Security Symposium*, 2018.

72. Minghong Fang, Guolei Yang, Neil Zhenqiang Gong, and Jia Liu. Poisoning attacks to graph-based recommender systems. In *ACSAC*, 2018.
73. H. Yu, M. Kaminsky, P. B. Gibbons, and A. Flaxman. SybilGuard: Defending against Sybil attacks via social networks. In *SIGCOMM*, 2006.
74. Qiang Cao, Michael Sirivianos, Xiaowei Yang, and Tiago Pregueiro. Aiding the detection of fake accounts in large scale social online services. In *NSDI*, 2012.
75. Gang Wang, Tristan Konolige, Christo Wilson, and Xiao Wang. You are how you click: Clickstream analysis for sybil detection. In *Usenix Security Symposium*, 2013.
76. Neil Zhenqiang Gong, Mario Frank, and Prateek Mittal. Sybilbelief: A semi-supervised learning approach for structure-based sybil detection. *IEEE Transactions on Information Forensics and Security*, 9(6):976–987, 2014.
77. Binghui Wang, Le Zhang, and Neil Zhenqiang Gong. Sybilscar: Sybil detection in online social networks via local rule based propagation. In *INFOCOM*, 2017.
78. Binghui Wang, Neil Zhenqiang Gong, and Hao Fu. Gang: Detecting fraudulent users in online social networks via guilt-by-association on directed graphs. In *ICDM*, 2017.
79. Peng Gao, Binghui Wang, Neil Zhenqiang Gong, Sanjeev R. Kulkarni, Kurt Thomas, and Prateek Mittal. Sybilfuse: Combining local attributes with global structure to perform robust sybil detection. In *CNS*, 2018.
80. Binghui Wang, Le Zhang, and Neil Zhenqiang Gong. Sybilblind: Detecting fake users in online social networks without manual labels. In *RAID*, 2018.
81. Binghui Wang, Jinyuan Jia, and Neil Zhenqiang Gong. Graph-based security and privacy analytics via collective classification with joint weight learning and propagation. In *NDSS*, 2019.
82. Zenghua Xia, Chang Liu, Neil Zhenqiang Gong, Qi Li, Yong Cui, and Dawn Song. Characterizing and detecting malicious accounts in privacy-centric mobile social networks: A case study. In *KDD*, 2019.
83. Jan Hendrik Metzen, Tim Genewein, Volker Fischer, and Bastian Bischof. On detecting adversarial perturbations. In *ICLR*, 2017.
84. Weilin Xu, David Evans, and Yanjun Qi. Feature squeezing: Detecting adversarial examples in deep neural networks. In *NDSS*, 2018.
85. Dongyu Meng and Hao Chen. Magnet: a two-pronged defense against adversarial examples. In *CCS*, 2017.
86. Warren He, Bo Li, and Dawn Song. Decision boundary analysis of adversarial examples. In *ICLR*, 2018.
87. Nicolas Papernot, Patrick McDaniel, Xi Wu, Somesh Jha, and Ananthram Swami. Distillation as a defense to adversarial perturbations against deep neural networks. In *IEEE S & P*, 2016.
88. Xiaoyu Cao and Neil Zhenqiang Gong. Mitigating evasion attacks to deep neural networks via region-based classification. In *ACSAC*, 2017.
89. Mathias Lecuyer, Vaggelis Atlidakis, Roxana Geambasu, Daniel Hsu, and Suman Jana. Certified robustness to adversarial examples with differential privacy. In *IEEE S & P*, 2019.
90. Jeremy M Cohen, Elan Rosenfeld, and J. Zico Kolter. Certified adversarial robustness via randomized smoothing. In *ICML*, 2019.
91. Shiqi Wang, Yizheng Chen, Ahmed Abdou, and Suman Jana. Mixtrain: Scalable training of verifiably robust neural networks. In *arxiv*, 2018.

Exploring Adversarial Artificial Intelligence for Autonomous Adaptive Cyber Defense

Erik Hemberg, Linda Zhang, and Una-May O'Reilly

1 Introduction

Even a well prepared cyber defender can never rest. The defender knows that the only certainty is that an intelligent adversary will repeatedly try to adapt to gain advantage. Whenever a defender is reacting to events it can mean that it is too late. So, how can a defender create autonomous adaptive cyber defenses to maintain the edge when the advantages seems to be heaped to the attacker's advantage and the defender seems doomed to always be vulnerable?

One approach, *adversarial Artificial Intelligence*, is to deploy defensive configurations, that consider multiple possible *anticipated* adversarial behaviors and take into account their expected impact, goal, strategies or tactics. For example, impact can be a combination of financial cost, disruption level or outcome risk. Or, a defender could prioritize a worst case, average case or an equilibrium.

Defensive configurations can be found by using stochastic search methods that explore the simulated competitive behavior of adversaries and generate ranked configurations according to a variety of objectives so a decision maker can choose among them [31]. The research field of coevolutionary algorithms [34] provides search heuristics for competitive engagements. The engagements are between members of adversarial populations with opposing objectives that each are selected on the basis of performance and are varied to adapt. Figure 1 shows an engagement environment where pairs of adversaries engage with a set of actions and measures the outcome for each adversary. These measures can be used by the coevolutionary algorithm to determine an adversary's fitness(quality).

E. Hemberg (✉) · L. Zhang · U.-M. O'Reilly
MIT CSAIL, Cambridge, MA, USA
e-mail: hembergerik@csail.mit.edu; lolzhang@alumn.mit.edu; unamay@csail.mit.edu

© Springer Nature Switzerland AG 2020   41
S. Jajodia et al. (eds.), *Adaptive Autonomous Secure Cyber Systems*,
https://doi.org/10.1007/978-3-030-33432-1_3

Fig. 1 Overview of coevolutionary adversarial AI framework concept. The coevolutionary component performs search over the actions of adversary controllers. The engagement component evaluates the strategies of the adversaries and returns the measurements of the engagement

Coevolutionary search methods results in population-wide adversarial dynamics. Such dynamics can expose adversarial behaviors for a defense to anticipate.

We present an extension of a framework called RIVALS that we previously have used to generate robust defensive configurations [31]. It is composed of different coevolutionary algorithms to help it generate diverse behavior. The algorithms, for further diversity, use different "solution concepts", i.e. measures of adversarial success and quality measures.

One way to evaluate solutions in a multi-player setting is to consider Nash equilibria. These are points which satisfy every player's optimizing condition given the other players' choices. That is, a player does not have incentive to deviate from its strategy given the other players' strategies. This concept has been used to understand the strategic actions of multiple players in a deterministic gaming environment [28]. We can model different threat scenarios in RIVALS and Nash equilibria may offer insight into possible outcomes in the attacker-defender coevolution.

The RIVALS framework supports a number of threat scenario use-cases using simulation and emulation of varying model granularity. These include:

(a) Defending a peer-2-peer network against Denial of Service (DOS) attacks [13, 40]
(b) Defenses against spreading device compromise in a segmented enterprise network [15], and
(c) Deceptive defense against the internal reconnaissance of an adversary within a software defined network [16]

The RIVALS framework is linked to a decision support module named ESTABLO [35, 40]. The engagements of every run of any of the coevolutionary algorithms are cached and, later, ESTABLO collects adversaries from the cache for its *compendium*. It then evaluates all the adversaries of each side against those of the other side inn the environment and ranks them according to multiple criteria. It can also provide comparisons of adversarial behaviors. This information can be incorporated in the decision process of a defensive manager.

The RIVALS adversarial AI framework we present contributes the following:

- The use of coevolutionary algorithms to adaptively generate adversarial dynamics supporting preemptive investigation of possible adversarial arms races.
- A suite of different coevolutionary algorithms that diversify the behavior of the adversaries, including ones focusing on finding Nash equilibria.
- Use cases that model a variety of adversarial threat and defensive models.
- A decision support module that supports selection of anticipatory defensive configuration. Herein, we highlight quality measurement that use Nash Averaging [6].

The paper proceeds as follows. In Sect. 2 we provide context on modeling and simulation and coevolutionary search algorithm. Section 3 describes our coevolutionary method, engagement component and decision support module. Section 4 provides examples applying to cyber security and network attacks. Finally, Sect. 5 summarizes and addresses future work.

2   Background

We provide background regarding coevolutionary search algorithms. In particular, modeling and simulation and the use of coevolutionary algorithms to find Nash equilibria.

A possible analogy to the strategy of testing the security of a system by trying to successfully attack it is software fuzzing [26]. Fuzzing tests software adaptively to search for bugs while adaptive attacks test defenses. In contrast to software where a bugs are fixed by humans, our approach automatically adapts a defense. Fuzzing can be driven by genetic algorithms (GA) [5] whereas, to drive cyber arms races in which both adversaries adapt, our approach uses a setup of coupled GAs called competitive coevolutionary algorithms.

2.1   Coevolutionary Search Algorithms

Figure 2 shows an outline of a basic coevolutionary algorithm that evolves two coupled populations, each with selection and variation (crossover and mutation). One population is comprised of *tests* and the other of *solutions* [34]. Tests and solutions may also be referred to as players. In each generation, different competitions are formed by pairing a test and a solution from their respective populations. This couples the two populations as they share a fitness evaluation component. A basic coevolutionary algorithm evolves two populations with selection and for variation uses crossover and mutation. One population comprises tests(attacks) and the other solutions(defenses). In each generation, competitions are formed by pairing attackers and defenders. The populations are evolved in alternating steps: first the

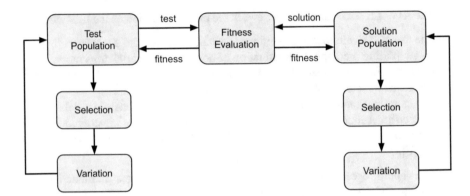

Fig. 2 A simple coevolutionary algorithm with coupled populations of tests(attackers) and solutions(defenders). Individuals in each population are evaluated against each other. For each population the most fit individuals are selected and varied to create a new population for the next generation

attacker population is selected, varied, updated and evaluated against the defenders, and then the defender population is selected, varied, updated and evaluated against the defenders. Each attacker–defender pair is dispatched to the engagement environment component to compete and the result is used as a component of fitness for each of them. Fitness is calculated over all the engagements.

Coevolutionary algorithms explore domains in which the quality of a candidate *solution* is determined by its ability to successfully pass some set of *tests*. Reciprocally, a *test*'s quality is determined by its ability to force errors from some set of *solutions*. In competitive coevolution, similar to game theory, the search can lead to an arms race between *test* and *solution*, both evolving while pursuing opposite objectives [34]. The dynamic of the coevolutionary algorithm, driven by conflicting objectives and guided by performance-based selection and random variation can gradually produce better and more robust solutions (i.e defenses) [36, 41]. Competitive coevolutionary algorithms are often applied in domains in which there are no exogenous objective measures of performance, but wherein performance relative to others is a good measure. These have been called *interactive* domains [18, 34] and include games, e.g., hybrid coevolutionary programming for Nash equilibrium search in games with local optima [42].

A fitness score is derived from some function of both players' performance outcomes in their competitions. Methods have been defined depending on the specific problem domain, e.g., [2, 8, 12, 20, 50]. A more formal approach, using the *test* and *solution* perspective, describes fitness assignments as *solution concepts* [34]. Solution concepts include: maximization of expected utility (MEU), best worst case (MinMax), Nash equilibrium, and Pareto optimality. One of the key challenges with coevolution is how to train and rate the performance of solutions [4, 6], both objectively and relative to others, because not every solution competes against every test during the evolutionary search.

The representation of *tests* (and *solutions*) is customizable in any coevolutionary algorithm [37] under the design constraint that it be amenable to stochastic variation, e.g. "genetic crossover" or mutation. It may directly express the test or it may do so indirectly, e.g. with a grammar. In the latter case, an intermediate interpreter works with a rule-based grammar to map from a "genome" that undergoes variation to a "phenome" that expresses an executable behavior. Grammars (and GA representations, in general) offer design flexibility: changing out a grammar and the environment of behavioral execution does not require any changes to the rest of the algorithm.

Coevolutionary algorithms can encounter problematic dynamics where *tests* are unable to improve *solutions*, or drive toward a solution that is the *a priori* intended goal. There are *remedies* to specific coevolutionary pathologies [7, 11, 34]. They generally include maintaining population diversity so that a search gradient is always present and using more explicit memory, e.g. a *Hall of Fame* or an archive, to prevent regress [25]. The pathologies of coevolutionary algorithms are similar to those encountered by generative adversarial networks (GANs) [3, 14]

2.2 Nash Equilibrium

In this contribution we introduce the search for Nash Equilibira in RIVALS, motivated by interest in the dynamics it drives. A strategy is a Nash equilibrium if no player can improve by unilaterally changing their strategy [30]. Let (S, f) be a game with n players, where S_i is the strategy set for player i, $S = \{S_1 \times S_2 \times \cdots \times S_n\}$ is the set of all possible strategies, and $f(x) = (f_1(x), \ldots, f_n(x))$ is the payoff function for strategy $x \in S$. Let x_i be a strategy of player i and x_{-i} be a strategy of all players except player i. When each player $i \in \{1, \ldots, n\}$ chooses strategy x_i, giving the strategies $x = (x_1, \ldots, x_n)$, then player i obtains payoff $f_i(x)$. The chosen strategies $x^* \in S$ are a Nash equilibrium (NE) if no unilateral deviation in strategy by any single player is profitable for that player, that is,

$$\forall i, x_i \in S_i : f_i(x_i^*, x_{-i}^*) \geq f_l(x_i, x_{-l}^*).$$

When the inequality above holds strictly, then the equilibrium is called a "strict Nash equilibrium." If there is a player with an exact equality between x_i^* and another strategy in the set S, then the equilibrium is called a "weak Nash equilibrium."

Nash equilibria can be difficult to find with populations of strategies, as with coevolutionary algorithms used in RIVALS. In the context of populations, it is the evolutionary stable strategies that are of interest. An evolutionarily stable strategy occurs when the whole population uses this strategy, and any small group of invaders using a different strategy will eventually die off over multiple generations [45]. That is, a strategy is evolutionarily stable if whenever the population is disturbed and a small subpopulation switches to a different state, its average payoff in the perturbed state will be less than the average payoff of the remaining population. If a strategy is evolutionarily stable then it is a Nash equilibrium, but the reverse is not necessarily true.

2.2.1 Nash Averaging

In this paper we introduce Nash averaging to the ESTABLO (compendium) component in RIVALS, motivated by Nash averaging being an evaluation method for comparing agents vs tasks or agents vs agents that is proposed as invariant, continuous, and interpretable. That is, adding redundant copies of an agent or tasks to the data should make no difference, the evaluation method should be robust to small changes in data, and the procedure should agree with intuition in basic cases [6].

Nash averaging relies on the creation of an antisymmetric matrix **A**, where the entries are processed from one of the following scenarios: agents vs. tasks, or agents vs. agents. For agents vs. tasks, algorithms are evaluated on suites of datasets or environments, while for agents vs. agents, algorithms compete directly against each other. From **A**, we can find a maximum entropy Nash equilibrium, and thus the Nash average, which we can use to rank the performance of different algorithms. For example the Gambit strategic game solver [24] can be used to calculate the max entropy(maxent) Nash equilibria.

2.3 Modeling and Simulation with Coevolutionary Algorithms

A coevolutionary algorithm includes an environment that supports executing the tests(attackers) and solutions(defenders) to compete against each other in each engagement. We use modeling and simulation(mod-sim) with a varying range of complexity, level of abstraction and resolution. Modeling and simulation comprise a powerful approach, for investigating general security scenarios [44], computer security [19, 47, 49] and network dynamics in particular, e.g., in CANDLES—the Coevolutionary, Agent-based, Network Defense Lightweight Event System of [38], attacker and defender strategies are coevolved in the context of a single, custom, abstract computer network defense simulation.

3   Method

Figure 3 shows the RIVALS Adversarial AI framework. In this section we describe the different components in it: the AI search heuristics, engagement environment, adversary representation and decision support.

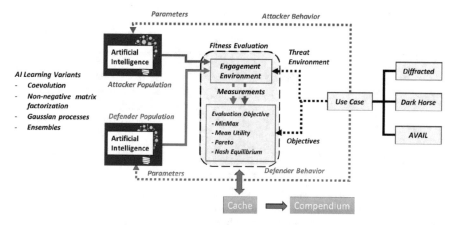

Fig. 3 Adversarial AI with the RIVALS framework. The different use-cases are shown to the right. Each use-case has different parameters, actions, objectives and therat environment. These are input for the engagement environments and the AI search heuristics. The fitness evaluations are stored in a cache and processed in a compendium for decision support. We have investigated different AI search heuristics in RIVALS, which are listed to the left

3.1 Coevolutionary Algorithms—AI Search Heuristic

The RIVALS framework supports diverse behavior by executing algorithms that vary in synchronization of the two populations and solution concepts [32, 35]. Working within a fixed time or fitness evaluation budget, the framework can also:

1. Cache engagements to avoid repeating them;
2. Use Gaussian process estimation to identify and evaluate the most uncertain engagement [32];
3. Use a recommender technique to approximate some adversary's fitnesses [32];
4. Use a *spatial grid* to reduce complete pairwise engagements to a Moore neighborhood quantity [27, 48];
5. Evolve solutions based on ensembles of search heuristics [35]

3.2 Engagement Environment

The engagement component is flexible and can support a problem-specific network testbed, simulator or model (as illustrated in Sect. 4). The abstraction level of the use case determines the choice of a simple to more detailed modeling and simulation or even the actual engagement environment. For example, mod-sim is appropriate when testbeds incur long experimental cycle times or has too many irrelevant details. Section 4 describes some engagement environments.

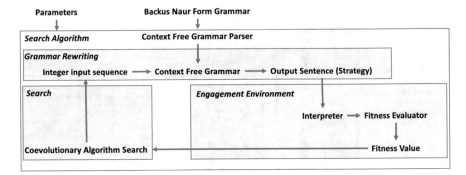

Fig. 4 A BNF grammar and search parameters are used as input. The grammar rewrites the integer input to a sentence. The fitness is calculated by interpreting the sentence and then evaluating it. The search component, here a coevolutionary algorithm, modifies the solutions using two central mechanisms: fitness based selection and random variation

3.3 Adversary Representation

The RIVALS framework uses grammars to express open ended behavioral action sequences for attack and defense strategies, see Fig. 4 and [29] for more details. A grammar is introduced in Backus Naur Form (BNF) and describes a language in the problem domain. The BNF description is parsed to a context free grammar representation. Its rewrite rules express how a sentence can be composed by rewriting a start symbol. The adversaries are represented as fixed length integer vectors that are used to control the rewriting. To interpret them, in sequence each of the vector's integers is translated. This resulting sentence is the strategy that is executed.

For solving different problems, only the BNF grammar, engagement environment and fitness function of the adversaries need to be changed. This modularity, and reusability of the parser and rewriter allows efficient software engineering. The grammar additionally helps communicate the framework's functionality to stake-holders by enabling conversations and validation at the domain level. This contributes to stake-holder confidence in solutions and the framework.

3.4 Decision Support

Competitive coevolution has the following challenges [35, 40]: 1. Solutions and tests are not on comparable to each other on a "level playing field" because fitness is subjective, i.e. based solely on the context of engagements. 2. Blind spots, unvisited by the algorithms may exist. 3. From multiple runs, with one or more algorithms, it is not always obvious how to automatically select a "best" solution.

The RIVALS framework's decision support module, ESTABLO addresses these challenges. ESTABLO: (a) runs competitive coevolutionary search algorithms with different solution concepts; (b) combines the best solutions and tests at the end of each run into a compendium; (c) competes each solution against different test sets, including the compendium and a set of unseen tests, to measure its performance according to different solution concepts; (d) selects the "best" solutions from the compendium using a ranking and filtering process; and (e) visualizes the best solutions to support a transparent and auditable decision.

During each coevolutionary run, we calculate the fitness of strategies at every generation. However, the fitness of a strategy is relative to the fitness of the adversary population at that generation during the run. Additionally, different algorithms may have different ways of computing fitness these fitness scores within the same game or problem. Thus, the fitness scores calculated during the experiments are not absolute, and algorithm performance cannot be objectively compared in this way.

In order to objectively compare the performances of different algorithms and solutions, we create a randomly generated "hold-out set" for each population. This is a set of unseen strategies with a distribution that favors both strategies that are similar to ones that have already been observed and strategies that are very different [40]. Then, we can compare fitness against this hold-out set as a constant standard for performance in addition to our relative comparisons against the adversary population.

The next section presents an overview of RIVALS use cases, and a deep-dive and discussion regarding methods of how to measure the quality of the solutions.

4 Experiments

In this section we demonstrate the utility of the RIVALS adversarial AI framework by presenting some use cases. Broadly the goal is to identify defensive configurations that are effective against a range of potential adversaries. We provide and overview of Dark Horse [16], AVAIL [15] and a deep dive into Diffracted. We will focus on comparing algorithm performance with different measures in the compendium.

4.1 Internal Reconnaissance in Software Defined Networks—Dark Horse

To gain strategic insight into defending against the network reconnaissance stage of advanced persistent threats, we recreate the escalating competition between scans and deceptive views on a Software Defined Network (SDN). Once an adversary has compromised a network endpoint, they can perform network reconnaissance [43].

After reconnaissance provides a view of the network and an understanding of where vulnerable nodes are located, they are able to continue their attack. One way to protect against reconnaissance is by obfuscating the network to delay the attacker. This approach is suited to software defined networks (SDN) such as those being used in many cloud server settings because it requires programmability that they support [17]. The SDN controller knows which machines are actually on the network and can alter, without function loss, the network view of each node, as well as place decoys (honeypots) on the network to mislead, trap and slow down the reconnaissance of the adversary.

One such multi-component deceptive defense system [1] foils scanning by generating "deceptive" versions of the actual network and providing them to hosts when they renew their DHCP leases. We use this deception system in conjunction with mininet [46] within the RIVALS framework as an engagement environment. This enables us to explore the dynamics between attacker and defender on a network where deception and reconnaissance strategies are adapted in response to each other [32]. A deception strategy is executed through a modified POX SDN controller. A reconnaissance strategy is executed by a NMAP scan[23]. The attacker strategy includes choices of: which IP addresses to scan, how many IP addresses to scan, which subnets to scan, the percent of the subnets to scan, the scanning speed, and the type of scan. The defender strategy includes choices of: the number of subnets to setup, the number of honeypots, the distribution of the real hosts throughout the subnets, and the number of real hosts that exist on the network. Fitness has four components: how fast the defender detects that there is a scan taking place, the total time it takes to run the scan, the number of times that the defender detects the scanner, and the number of real hosts that the scanner discovers. The experiments and analysis show that it is possible to discover certain configurations that the defender can use to significantly increase its ability to detect scans. Furthermore, there are specific reconnaissance configurations that have a better chance of being undetected.

4.2   Availability Attacks on Segmented Networks—AVAIL

Attackers often introduce malware into networks. Once an attacker has compromised a device on a network, they contaminate connected devices. This use case considers *network segmentation*, a widely recommended defensive strategy, deployed against the threat of network security attacks that delay the mission of the network's operator [15] in the context of malware spread.

Network segmentation divides the network topologically into isolated *enclaves* to deter inter-enclave contagion. How much network segmentation is helpful is a tradeoff. One complication is that the isolation of a more segmented network provides less mission efficiency because of increased overhead in inter-enclave communication. The other complication is that smaller enclaves contain compromise by limiting the spread rate, and their cleansing incurs fewer mission delays.

In addition, given a segmentation, a network operator can use threat monitoring and network cleansing policies to detect and dislodge attackers, however they come with a tradeoff of cost versus efficacy as well.

The RIVALS AVAIL use case assumes a network supports an enterprise in carrying out its business or *mission*, and that an adversary employs *availability attacks* against the network to disrupt this mission. In particular, the attacker starts by exploiting a vulnerable device on the network. This compromise inflicts a mission delay when a mission critical device is infected. Then, the attacker moves laterally to compromise more devices to delay the mission as much as possible. The network and its segmentation of enclaves are pre-defined but the placement of mission critical devices within an enclave and the deployment of defensive threat monitoring devices(taps) are possible to optimize.

The AVAIL use case employs a simulation model as its engagement environment. The contagion spread rate is pre-specified. The defender selects placement of mission devices and tap sensitivities in the different enclaves. The attacker selects the strength, duration and number of attacks in an attack plan targeting all enclaves. For a network with a set of four different enclave topologies, the framework is able to generate strong availability attack patterns that were not *a priori* identified. It also identifies effective configurations that minimize mission delay when facing these attacks.

4.3   DOS Attacks on Peer-to-Peer Networks—Diffracted

This section presents a deep dive in the results of a RIVALS experiment. We describe the problem, called Mobile Asset Problem (MAP), and experimental settings before presenting results from it. One of the challenges is to determine the quality of solutions when the fitness is subjectively based on the adversaries that it has been evalauted against. In addition, there are multiple search heuristics to choose from. The objective here is to compare the performance of algorithms based on different solution concepts. The comparisons highlight the difficulty in identifying Nash equilibria and evaluating results.

4.3.1   Mobile Asset Placement Problem

The Mobile Asset Placement (MAP) problem is based on the cyber security-related problem described in RIVALS [13] and will make up the core of our experiments. MAP illustrates the worst-case scenario in a network. The following mission is simulated on a network running the Chord protocol: an attacker tries to take out a set of nodes for the entirety of the mission, while a defender attempts to complete a set of tasks. A task consists of a start node and an end node, and it succeeds as long as both nodes in the task are not taken out by the attacker. The mission succeeds if all tasks succeed. Note that MAP models DoS threats and looks at where to allocate resources, so the problem determines quality of service, not detection. Additionally, MAP is a static problem, so we can quickly evaluate strategies while considering a worst-case vulnerability. A sample grammar for a MAP topology [13] is given below:

```
<attacker> ::= [<attacks>]
<attacks> ::= <node>, <attacks> | <node>
<node> ::= 0 | 1 | 2 | 3 | 4 | 5 | 6 | ... | 23

<defender> ::=
    [task(<node>,<node>), task(<node>,<node>),
        task(<node>,<node>), task(<node>,<node>)]
<node> ::= 0 | 1 | 2 | 3 | 4 | 5 | 6 | ... | 23
```

We ran experiments on a MAP topologies, with 23 Nodes and 4 tasks. The topology is a medium-sized networks with very different edge connections that are more reflective of security problems. Illustrations of these topologies are shown in Fig. 5.

The attacker fitness is calculated by

$$f_a = \frac{n_{failed}}{n_{tasks}} - \frac{n_{attacks}}{c \cdot n_{tasks}}$$

where n_{tasks} is the total number of tasks, n_{failed} is the number of tasks the attacker was able to disrupt, $n_{attacks}$ is the number of attacks the attacker used, and c is some constant used to express importance of effort relative to success. This formula helps incentivize attackers to disrupt tasks using as few attacks as possible.

The defender fitness is calculated by

$$f_d = \frac{n_{successful}}{n_{tasks}} - n_{same\_nodes} - n_{duplicate\_tasks}$$

where $n_{successful}$ is the number of successful tasks, n_{same_nodes} is the number of tasks with the same starting and ending node, and $n_{duplicate\_tasks}$ is the number of

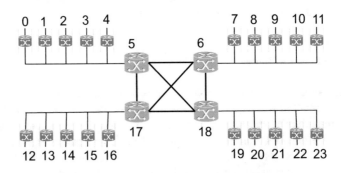

Fig. 5 Mobile Asset Placement topology, previously tested in RIVALS [13]

duplicated tasks. This function helps incentivize defenders to succeed at as many tasks as possible while penalizing approaches that use trivial tasks (same start and end node) or resort to redundant(duplicate) tasks. While the latter convey resiliiency they are costly in a resource sense.

4.3.2 Settings

It was necessary in this use case of RIVALS to find a balance of producing high-fitness strategies while still being cost efficient in terms of time and computation. The most computationally costly element of a coevolutionary algorithm is the fitness evaluation, and the number of fitness evaluations is proportional to population size and number of generations. Thus, we ran experiments varying these parameters with ratios multiplying to a constant number of 100 to determine performance differences between heuristics. We ran 30 trials for each of the following (population_size p, generations g) pairs: $(p = 2, g = 50), (p = 5, g = 20), (p = 10, g = 10), (p = 20, g = 5)$.

Settings used for all heuristics, as well as experiment-specific settings for the algorithms evaluated, are shown in Table 1.

4.3.3 Results for MAP

We first show results from one MAP topology with one set of RIVALS hyperparameter settings. We are interested in the comparative performance of the differenct algorithms. We believe that this data is a good representation of the general performance of these algorithms with average population sizes and generations on larger topologies. We picked the settings of $(p = 10, g = 10)$ to analyze here. The measurements we are concerned with at average fitness of each heuristic, comparisons using the ESTABLO compendium and Nash Averaging measure.

We calculate average fitness using maximum expected utility (MEU). For each trial, the best individuals per generation are saved, and their fitness scores (both against the hold-out set and relative to the adversary population) are recorded. We define two different average fitness measurements. The *final fitness score* for a population is calculated by taking the best *final* generation fitness value and averaging across all trials. The *average fitness score* for a population is calculated by taking the average of the best fitness values across *all* generations and averaging across all trials.

We first looked at the average and final best fitness scores averaged across all runs. Table 2 displays results for the attacker and defender populations for various algorithms. When looking at MAP attacker strategies ranked by average fitness against the hold-out set, we found that HybridCoev (measured by best strategy score) performed very well, while the NashSolve variants produced mediocre strategies. For the MAP defender population, IPCACoev, rIPCACoev,

Table 1 Competitive coevolutionary algorithm-specific settings

Algorithm	Settings

ALL	`tournament_size=2,`
	`crossover_probability=.8,`
	`mutation_probability=.1`

DiscoCoev [21]	`n_clusters=3`
DofCoev [22]	`dof_impute_strategy=mean,` `dof_alpha=.8, dof_num_components=2`
GaupRecCoev [33]	`gauprec_alpha=.25`
GridCoev [33]	`host_population=defender,` `host_solution_concept=meu`

HybridCoev [42]	`num_strategies=3,`
	`rival_matching_rate=.9,`
	`max_hill_climber_iter=5`

IPCACoev [10]	`win_threshold=.1,` `parent_archive_probability=.9`
MaxSolveCoev [9]	`archive_size=20`

MEULockstepCoev [33]	`locked_population=defender,`
	`locked_population_generations=2,`
	`locked_population_elite_size=1,`
	`locked_population_parents_size=2`

MinMaxCoev [13]	`N/A`

MinMaxLockstepCoev [33]	`locked_population=defender,`
	`locked_population_generations=2,`
	`locked_population_elite_size=1,`
	`locked_population_parents_size=2`

MuleGE [13]	`mule_ge_elite_size=1,` `one_way_population=attacker`
NashSolve [39]	`lower_threshold=-2,` `max_archive_size=3`
RIPCACoev [13]	`win_threshold=.1,` `parent_archive_probability=.9`
SimpleCoev [13]	`N/A`

Each algorithm uses a specific solution concept

and `MinmaxLockstepCoev` tended to produce the strongest solutions, while `HybridCoev` and `NashSolve` did not perform particularly well. These results were observed for all (`population_size`, `generations`) pairs, including the example shown in Table 2.

We expected `IPCACoev` and `rIPCACoev` to perform well for the defender population based on previous empirical data; however, these algorithms have long running time and require more evaluation steps. Additionally, note that some `NashSolve` and `HybridCoev` final scores are less then the average scores. This implies that the final best strategies did not necessarily perform better than previous generation strategies.

Table 2 Average and final fitness scores against hold-out sets on MAP topology 2 with (`population_size=10, generations=10`), averaged over 30 runs

Algorithm	Attacker		Defender	
	Avg fitness	Final fitness	Avg fitness	Final fitness
DiscoCoev	0.822 ± 0.005	0.830 ± 0.035	0.284 ± 0.071	0.400 ± 0.195
DofCoev	0.809 ± 0.005	0.807 ± 0.037	0.218 ± 0.043	0.177 ± 0.282
GaupRecCoev	0.807 ± 0.003	*0.806 ± 0.046*	-0.040 ± 0.062	-0.011 ± 0.328
GridCoev	0.802 ± 0.007	*0.806 ± 0.032*	*0.267 ± 0.053*	0.327 ± 0.191
HybridCoevAvg	0.796 ± 0.018	0.777 ± 0.189	0.011 ± 0.057	-0.061 ± 0.199
HybridCoevBest	**0.945 ± 0.018**	**0.911 ± 0.191**	0.283 ± 0.018	*0.289 ± 0.187*
HybridCoevWorst	<u>0.652 ± 0.033</u>	0.633 ± 0.277	-0.272 ± 0.104	<u>-0.433 ± 0.405</u>
IPCACoev	0.815 ± 0.003	0.818 ± 0.040	0.413 ± 0.076	**0.494 ± 0.227**
MaxSolveCoev	0.822 ± 0.013	0.830 ± 0.047	0.337 ± 0.087	0.387 ± 0.215
MEULockstepCoev	0.805 ± 0.008	0.803 ± 0.045	0.324 ± 0.054	0.320 ± 0.205
MinMaxCoev	0.790 ± 0.006	0.783 ± 0.030	0.148 ± 0.039	0.093 ± 0.153
MinMaxLockstepCoev	0.801 ± 0.005	0.801 ± 0.043	**0.423 ± 0.106**	0.479 ± 0.265
NashAvgSolve	0.793 ± 0.004	0.800 ± 0.030	0.162 ± 0.021	0.157 ± 0.188
NashBestSolve	0.792 ± 0.006	0.792 ± 0.027	0.148 ± 0.028	0.173 ± 0.204
NashSolve	0.787 ± 0.004	0.787 ± 0.028	<u>0.125 ± 0.025</u>	0.106 ± 0.163
RIPCACoev	*0.803 ± 0.002*	*0.806 ± 0.036*	0.337 ± 0.069	0.422 ± 0.220
SimpleCoev	0.811 ± 0.005	*0.806 ± 0.030*	0.286 ± 0.069	0.363 ± 0.185

The **best**, *median*, and <u>worst</u> scores are marked

4.3.4 Compendium

The heuristics are also compared against each other by creating a compendium. Table 3 displays the combined score, as well as the score for each different solution concept, for the highest combined ranking individual solution produced by each algorithm.

When looking at this compendium, we noticed that the algorithms rank similarly to the average fitness evaluation, particularly for defender solutions. Interestingly, for some attacker strategies, the corresponding algorithms that achieve these high combined scores did not perform well in the previous Table 2 comparison. The Nash equilibrium algorithm NashBestSolve and RIPCACoev are prime examples of this. However, the Table 3 compendium results do not necessarily contradict the results from Table 2 fitness averages. The compendium considers the highest combined score for an individual strategy rather than averaging over all runs, so algorithms that perform well in Table 3 but do not perform well in Table 2 may be good at finding strong individual strategies but not strong strategies on average.

We apply the concept of Nash averaging to our evaluations in the compendium. Note that MAP is not a symmetric game, so adversarial populations have different tasks and different fitness functions, and we cannot determine Elo ratings from a competition. Thus, strategies from a single population cannot be placed on the rows

Table 3 Compendium rankings on MAP topology 2 with (population_size=10, generations=10)

Algorithm	Attacker				Defender			
	Coev MEU	Coev MinMax	Inv Pareto front	Total score	Coev MEU	Coev MinMax	Inv Pareto front	Total score
DiscoCoev	0.897	0.330	21	1.338	**0.867**	0.333	130	2.200
DofCoev	**0.932**	0.665	19	1.668	0.467	0	**422**	1.467
GaupRecCoev	0.930	0.663	11	1.693	0.500	0	212	1.500
GridCoev	0.898	0.322	7	1.282	0.600	0.333	126	1.933
HybridCoev	0.898	0.332	1	1.238	0.567	0.333	211	1.900
IPCACoev	0.930	0.663	14	1.718	**0.867**	0.333	12	2.200
MaxSolveCoev	0.928	0.662	3	1.652	0.467	0	56	0.967
MEULockstepCoev	0.930	0.663	7	1.638	0.883	0.333	128	2.167
MinMaxCoev	**0.932**	0.665	22	1.688	0.883	0.333	221	1.967
MinMaxLockstepCoev	0.930	0.663	13	1.664	0.883	**0.667**	61	**2.500**
NashAvgSolve	0.899	0.332	5	1.281	0.533	0	238	1.533
NashBestSolve	**0.932**	**0.666**	22	**1.798**	0.533	0	222	1.533
NashSolve	0.897	0.331	3	1.259	0.600	0.333	216	1.933
RIPCACoev	0.930	0.663	12	1.793	0.600	0.333	7	1.933
SimpleCoev	0.930	0.664	16	1.685	0.500	0.333	40	1.083

The **best**, *median*, and worst scores are marked

and columns of matrix **A** in the same way as described in [6], because strategies from the same population cannot play themselves.

For an agents vs. agents approach we designed **A** such that the rows and columns of the matrix are composed of strategies from the same population. Because MAP is asymmetric and we cannot play same-population strategies against each other, we developed an alternative to the original Elo ratings and predictions used in [6]. For each best-performing final generation strategy i from each algorithm, we calculated the fitness f_i against the hold-out set. We then constructed intermediary matrix **S** such that $\mathbf{S}_{ij} = \frac{1}{1+e^{-(f_i-f_j)}}$. Finally, we assigned $\mathbf{A} = logit(\mathbf{S}) = log(\frac{\mathbf{S}_{ij}}{1-\mathbf{S}_{ij}})$. Table 4 shows Nash averaging results for some selected sizes of **A**.

Note that while we were able to produce and interpret results from the this agents vs. agents approach, these results are limited in scope. Due to the computational costs of running GAMBIT, we could only analyze relatively small **A**. Additionally, because the Nash average evaluation method involves comparing individual

Table 4 Nash averaging results for various sizes of **A** on MAP topology 2 with (population_size=10, generations=10)

Size of **A**	Maxent Nash equilibrium value	Maxent Nash equilibrium algorithms
Attacker		
15 × 15	0.167	DofCoev, IPCACoev, GridCoev, MEULockstepCoev, MinMaxCoev, RIPCACoev
30 × 30	0.100	DofCoev, GaupRecCoev, IPCACoev, GridCoev, MEULockstepCoev, MinMaxCoev, MinMaxLockstepCoev, NashSolve, RIPCACoev, SimpleCoev
45 × 45	0.056	DiscoCoev, DofCoev, GaupRecCoev, GridCoev, IPCACoev, IPCACoev, GridCoev, MEULockstepCoev, MEULockstepCoev, MinMaxCoev, MinMaxCoev, MinMaxLockstepCoev, MinMaxLockstepCoev, NashBestSolve, NashSolve, RIPCACoev, RIPCACoev, SimpleCoev, SimpleCoev
Defender		
15 × 15	0.25	GaupRecCoev, MinMaxCoev, NashBestSolve, NashSolve
30 × 30	0.111	GaupRecCoev, GaupRecCoev, GridCoev, MinMaxCoev, MinMaxCoev, NashBestSolve, NashBestSolve, NashSolve
45 × 45	0.083	DofCoev, GaupRecCoev, GaupRecCoev, GridCoev, MinMaxCoev, MinMaxCoev, MinMaxCoev, NashBestSolve, NashBestSolve, NashSolve, NashSolve

strategies, we were left with a further issue of how to filter through all the strategies generated by an algorithm to a select just a few to use in **A**. We chose to filter in the following way: for each algorithm, randomly choose 1 or 2 trials out of the original 30. Then, from those trials, choose the best-performing final generation strategy to be used as an agent in **A**.

From this evaluation method, we observed that the Nash equilibrium-finding algorithms are able to produce individual high-performing strategies, see Table 4. Additionally, it looks like these high-performing strategies could have the same fitness value because the same algorithms appear in the maxent Nash equilibria set as **A** grows.

Discussion of Nash Averaging

We performed further experiments with using Nash Averaging in RIVALS for the MAP problem, here we summarize and discuss the outcomes of this investigation. We tried the agents vs. tasks approach, in which the agent rows are the best performing final generation strategies from each of the 15 algorithms, and the task columns are the strategies from the hold-out set of size 10. This creates a 25×25 matrix **A** in which the top-right block is agent performance on tasks, the bottom-left is task difficulty for agents, the top-left block compares agents by their average skill on tasks, and the bottom-right compares tasks by their average difficulty for agents. However, when calculating maxent Nash equilibria, we found it difficult to analyze the results because the blocks in **A** had different interpretations. For example, we found maxent Nash equilibria that averaged over multiple blocks, which suggests a combined ranking of tasks (hold-out set strategies) and agents (coevolutionary algorithm strategies) at the same time.

We also tried an agents vs. agents approach. We construct a 30×30 matrix **A** by concatenating the best performing final generation strategies from each algorithm for both populations and then using that concatenated list for both rows and columns. In this construction, the top left and bottom right blocks are populated with zeros because those are entries in which the row and column strategies are from the same population.

We also attempted two ways of populating the nonzero blocks to form an antisymmetric **A**, both of which required choosing a single population for fitness score calculations. For the first method, we considered the top right block of **A** and assigned $\mathbf{A}_{ij}$ to be the fitness score of row strategy i against column strategy j. To make **A** antisymmetric, we then set $\mathbf{A}_{ji}$ to be the negative of that score. For the second method, we created a intermediary matrix **S**, and for the top right block we assigned $\mathbf{S}_{ij}$ to be the proportion of tasks that row strategy i completed against column strategy j. We then assigned $\mathbf{S}_{ji}$ to be $1 - \mathbf{S}_{ij}$. To construct antisymmetric matrix **A**, we assigned $\mathbf{A}_{ij} = logit(\mathbf{S}_{ij}) = log(\frac{\mathbf{S}_{ij}}{1-\mathbf{S}_{ij}})$ for all nonzero entries of **S**. However, calculating maxent Nash equilibria using both of these constructions also yielded results that we found difficult to interpret. Again, we found maxent Nash equilibria that averaged over multiple blocks and thus over both populations, even though we chose only one population's fitness function for constructing **A**.

5 Summary and Future Work

We have described an adversarial AI framework, called RIVALS, that recreates, in an abstract way, the adversarial, competitive coevolutionary process that occurs in security scenarios. The objective was to create a system that can be used for pro-active cyber defense against autonomous adaptive adversaries. We presented its current use cases and how we harvest defensive solutions from it.

Future work includes extending it to support more cyber security applications and developing more efficient or true to reality algorithms. In addition, we would like to further explore Nash averaging as an evaluation technique. Because GAMBIT was computationally intensive, we were only able to observe results for a very limited number of strategies per algorithm. Investigating other methods of calculating the maxent Nash equilibrium could allow us to look at larger datasets. Finally, we want to apply other Nash equilibrium-finding algorithms, to other cyber security problems that have known Nash equilibria and analyze performance there.

Acknowledgements This material is based upon work supported by DARPA. The views and conclusions contained herein are those of the authors and should not be interpreted as necessarily representing the official policies or endorsements. Either expressed or implied of Applied Communication Services, or the US Government.

References

1. Stefan Achleitner, Thomas Laporta, and Patrick McDaniel. Cyber deception: Virtual networks to defend insider reconnaissance. *In Proceedings of the 2016 International Workshop on Managing Insider Security Threats*, pages 57–68, 2016.
2. Peter J. Angeline and Jordan B. Pollack. Competitive environments evolve better solutions for complex tasks. In *Proceedings of the Fifth International Conference (GA93), Genetic Algorithms*, pages 264–270, 1993.
3. Sanjeev Arora, Rong Ge, Yingyu Liang, Tengyu Ma, and Yi Zhang. Generalization and Equilibrium in Generative Adversarial Nets (GANs). *arXiv preprint arXiv:1703.00573*, 2017.
4. Kai Arulkumaran, Antoine Cully, and Julian Togelius. Alphastar: An evolutionary computation perspective. *arXiv preprint arXiv:1902.01724*, 2019.
5. Thomas Bäck. *Evolutionary Algorithms in Theory and Practice: Evolution Strategies, Evolutionary Programming, Genetic Algorithms*. Oxford University Press, 1996.
6. David Balduzzi, Karl Tuyls, Julien Perolat, and Thore Graepel. Re-evaluating evaluation. In *Advances in Neural Information Processing Systems*, pages 3272–3283, 2018.
7. Josh C Bongard and Hod Lipson. Nonlinear system identification using coevolution of models and tests. *IEEE Transactions on Evolutionary Computation*, 9(4):361–384, 2005.

8. A. B. Cardona, J. Togelius, and M. J. Nelson. Competitive coevolution in ms. pac-man. In *2013 IEEE Congress on Evolutionary Computation*, pages 1403–1410, June 2013.
9. Edwin De Jong. The maxsolve algorithm for coevolution. In *Proceedings of the 7th annual conference on Genetic and evolutionary computation*, pages 483–489. ACM, 2005.
10. Edwin D. De Jong. A monotonic archive for pareto-coevolution. *Evol. Comput.*, 15(1):61–93, March 2007.
11. Sevan Gregory Ficici. *Solution concepts in coevolutionary algorithms*. PhD thesis, Citeseer, 2004.
12. D Fogel. Blondie24: Playing at the edge of artificial intelligence, 2001.
13. Dennis Garcia, Anthony Erb Lugo, Erik Hemberg, and Una-May O'Reilly. Investigating coevolutionary archive based genetic algorithms on cyber defense networks. In *Proceedings of the Genetic and Evolutionary Computation Conference Companion*, GECCO '17, pages 1455–1462, New York, NY, USA, 2017. ACM.
14. Ian Goodfellow, Jean Pouget-Abadie, Mehdi Mirza, Bing Xu, David Warde-Farley, Sherjil Ozair, Aaron Courville, and Yoshua Bengio. Generative adversarial nets. In *Advances in Neural Information Processing Systems*, pages 2672–2680, 2014.
15. Erik Hemberg, Joseph R Zipkin, Richard W Skowyra, Neal Wagner, and Una-May O'Reilly. Adversarial co-evolution of attack and defense in a segmented computer network environment. In *Proceedings of the Genetic and Evolutionary Computation Conference Companion*, pages 1648–1655. ACM, 2018.
16. Jonathan Kelly, Michael DeLaus, Erik Hemberg, and Una-May O'Reilly. Adversarially adapting deceptive views and reconnaissance scans on a software defined network. In *2019 IFIP/IEEE Symposium on Integrated Network and Service Management (IM)*, pages 49–54. IEEE, 2019.
17. Keith Kirkpatrick. Software-defined networking. *Communications of the ACM*, 56(9), 2013.
18. Krzysztof Krawiec and Malcolm Heywood. Solving complex problems with coevolutionary algorithms. In *Proceedings of the Genetic and Evolutionary Computation Conference Companion*, pages 880–906. ACM, 2018.
19. Mona Lange, Alexander Kott, Noam Ben-Asher, Wim Mees, Nazife Baykal, Cristian-Mihai Vidu, Matteo Merialdo, Marek Malowidzki, and Bhopinder Madahar. Recommendations for model-driven paradigms for integrated approaches to cyber defense. *arXiv preprint arXiv:1703.03306*, 2017.
20. Chong-U Lim, Robin Baumgarten, and Simon Colton. Evolving behaviour trees for the commercial game DEFCON. In *European Conference on the Applications of Evolutionary Computation*, pages 100–110. Springer, 2010.
21. Pawel Liskowski and Krzysztof Krawiec. Discovery of implicit objectives by compression of interaction matrix in test-based problems. In *International Conference on Parallel Problem Solving from Nature*, pages 611–620. Springer, 2014.
22. Paweł Liskowski and Krzysztof Krawiec. Non-negative matrix factorization for unsupervised derivation of search objectives in genetic programming. In *Proceedings of the 2016 on Genetic and Evolutionary Computation Conference*, pages 749–756. ACM, 2016.
23. Gordon Lyon. Nmap network scanner. https://nmap.org/, 2018. [Online; accessed 6-July-2018].
24. McLennan Andrew M. McKelvey, Richard D. and Theodore L. Turocy. Gambit: Software tools for game theory, 2016.
25. Thomas Miconi. Why coevolution doesn't "work": superiority and progress in coevolution. In *European Conference on Genetic Programming*, pages 49–60. Springer Berlin Heidelberg, 2009.
26. Barton P Miller, Louis Fredriksen, and Bryan So. An empirical study of the reliability of unix utilities. *Communications of the ACM*, 33(12):32–44, 1990.
27. Melanie Mitchell. Coevolutionary learning with spatially distributed populations. *Computational intelligence: principles and practice*, 2006.
28. Roger B Myerson. *Game theory*. Harvard university press, 2013.

29. Michael O'Neill and Conor Ryan. *Grammatical evolution: evolutionary automatic programming in an arbitrary language*, volume 4. Springer, 2003.
30. Martin J. Osborne and Ariel Rubinstein. *A course in game theory*. The MIT Press, Cambridge, USA, 1994. electronic edition.
31. Una-May O'Reilly and Erik Hemberg. An artificial coevolutionary framework for adversarial ai. In *AAAI Fall Symposia*, 2018.
32. Marcos Pertierra. Investigating coevolutionary algorithms for expensive fitness evaluations in cybersecurity. Master's thesis, Massachusetts Institute of Technology, 2018.
33. Marcos Pertierra Arrojo. Investigating coevolutionary algorithms for expensive fitness evaluations in cybersecurity, 2018.
34. Elena Popovici, Anthony Bucci, R Paul Wiegand, and Edwin D De Jong. Coevolutionary principles. In *Handbook of natural computing*, pages 987–1033. Springer, 2012.
35. Daniel Prado Sanchez. Visualizing adversaries - transparent pooling approaches for decision support in cybersecurity. Master's thesis, Massachusetts Institute of Technology, 2018.
36. Christopher D Rosin and Richard K Belew. New methods for competitive coevolution. *Evolutionary Computation*, 5(1):1–29, 1997.
37. Franz Rothlauf. *Design of modern heuristics: principles and application*. Springer Science & Business Media, 2011.
38. George Rush, Daniel R Tauritz, and Alexander D Kent. Coevolutionary agent-based network defense lightweight event system (candles). In *Proceedings of the Companion Publication of the 2015 on Genetic and Evolutionary Computation Conference*, pages 859–866. ACM, 2015.
39. Spyridon Samothrakis, Simon Lucas, ThomasPhilip Runarsson, and David Robles. Coevolving game-playing agents: Measuring performance and intransitivities. *IEEE Transactions on Evolutionary Computation*, 17(2):213–226, 2013.
40. Daniel Prado Sanchez, Marcos A Pertierra, Erik Hemberg, and Una-May O'Reilly. Competitive coevolutionary algorithm decision support. In *Proceedings of the Genetic and Evolutionary Computation Conference Companion*, pages 300–301. ACM, 2018.
41. Karl Sims. Evolving 3d morphology and behavior by competition. *Artificial life*, 1(4):353–372, 1994.
42. You Seok Son and Ross Baldick. Hybrid coevolutionary programming for nash equilibrium search in games with local optima. *IEEE Transactions on Evolutionary Computation*, 8(4):305–315, 2004.
43. Aditya Sood and Richard Enbody. Targeted cyberattacks: a superset of advanced persistent threats. *IEEE security & privacy*, 11(1):54–61, 2013.
44. Milind Tambe, editor. *Security and Game Theory: Algorithms, Deployed Systems, Lessons Learned*. Cambridge University Press, 2012.
45. Peter D. Taylor and Leo B. Jonker. Evolutionary stable strategies and game dynamics. *Mathematical Biosciences*, 40(1):145–156, 1978.
46. Mininet Team. Mininet - realistic virtual sdn network emulator. http://mininet.org/, 2018. [Online; accessed 6-July-2018].
47. Brian Thompson, James Morris-King, and Hasan Cam. Controlling risk of data exfiltration in cyber networks due to stealthy propagating malware. In *Military Communications Conference, MILCOM 2016-2016 IEEE*, pages 479–484. IEEE, 2016.
48. Nathan Williams and Melanie Mitchell. Investigating the success of spatial coevolution. In *Proceedings of the 7th annual conference on Genetic and evolutionary computation*, pages 523–530. ACM, 2005.
49. Michael L Winterrose and Kevin M Carter. Strategic evolution of adversaries against temporal platform diversity active cyber defenses. In *Proceedings of the 2014 Symposium on Agent Directed Simulation*, page 9. Society for Computer Simulation International, 2014.
50. Forhad Zaman, Saber M Elsayed, Tapabrata Ray, and Ruhul A Sarkerr. Evolutionary algorithms for finding nash equilibria in electricity markets. *IEEE Transactions on Evolutionary Computation*, 22(4):536–549, 2018.

Can Cyber Operations Be Made Autonomous? An Answer from the Situational Awareness Viewpoint

Chen Zhong, John Yen, and Peng Liu

1 Introduction

Inspired by the recent significant advances in deep learning systems, such as AlphaGo [1], and autonomous vehicles, such as Tesla autopilot,[1] the notion of "autonomous cyber-defense" has been drawing an increasing amount of attention in the field of cybersecurity. Although many building blocks of today's cyber-defense solutions, including but are not limited to non-executable stack or heap, ASLR (address space layout randomization), signature-based intrusion detection and prevention systems, alert correlation, worm signature generation, vulnerability scanners, and secure data communication over a computer network, are already fully automatic, there is still a debate on whether next generation cyber-defense solutions should be *wholly* autonomous.

In this paper, we contribute to the debate in the context of Cybersecurity Operations Centers (CSOCs). Below, we firstly give a brief overview of real-world CSOCs. Then we comment on how likely CSOCs could be made wholly autonomous in the foreseeable future.

---

[1]https://www.tesla.com/autopilot.

C. Zhong
Indiana University Kokomo, Kokomo, IN, USA

J. Yen · P. Liu (✉)
College of Information Sciences and Technology, Pennsylvania State University, State College, PA, USA
e-mail: pliu@ist.psu.edu

© Springer Nature Switzerland AG 2020
S. Jajodia et al. (eds.), *Adaptive Autonomous Secure Cyber Systems*,
https://doi.org/10.1007/978-3-030-33432-1_4

1.1   Overview of Today's CSOCs

Cybersecurity Operations Centers (CSOCs) have been widely established in prominent companies, government organizations and military departments to achieve cyber situational awareness. Specifically, the goal of CSOCs includes learning what attacks are happening/have happened within an organizational network, recovering how these attacks happened and suggesting what actions are needed to prevent/mitigate an attack. A CSOC typically employs various automated cyber defense measures and cybersecurity professionals to conduct 24*7 monitoring and intrusion detection. The common automated measures include traffic monitors, firewalls, vulnerability scanners, and Intrusion Detection/Prevention System (IDS/IPS).

Cybersecurity analysts play a significant role in making sense of the data generated by the automated measures to answer some high-level questions about the attacks, for example, "What is the current status of an attack?", "How did an attack happen?", and "What might be the next steps of the attackers?". Data analytics conducted by human analysts is crucial because the automated measures are in many cases unable to "comprehend" sophisticated cyber attack strategies even through advanced correlated diagnosis.

To accomplish their tasks, cybersecurity analysts need to analyze the data carefully to identify the true "signals" and "connect the dots" to reason about the storyline of an attack. The data analytics in CSOCs usually involves a series of analysis, including data triage, escalation analysis, correlation analysis, threat analysis, incident response, and forensic analysis [2]. Data triage encompasses examining the details of a variety of data sources (such as IDS alerts and firewall logs), weeding out the false positives, grouping the related indicators so that different attack campaigns (i.e., attack plots) can be separated from each other. Data triage provides a basis for closer inspection in the following analysis to finally generate confidence-bounded attack incident reports. These incident reports will serve as the primary basis for further decision-making regarding how to change current security configuration and act against the attacks.

However, there is a huge gap between the overwhelming data from various security measures (e.g., IDS alerts) and the lack of analytics capabilities, which makes CSOCs still run short of capabilities of detecting and reacting to the intrusions. For instance, data triage is a time-consuming process. Compared to a computer, human brains have orders of magnitudes smaller data processing throughput. In addition, human beings may face some challenges unique to humans such as fatigue, anxiety, and depression. However, neither the network nor the attack campaign is waiting for the human brains. As the data, coming from a variety of data sources, are being continuously generated and their volume is overwhelming.

Therefore, data triage, mostly performed manually by analysts, involves complicated cognitive processes [2, 3]. Since the alert portion of the data contains a large number of false positives, the analysts have to leverage their domain expertise and experience to make fast judgments regarding which parts of the data sources are worthy of further exploration and thus the time pressure is typically huge for them. The analysts have to resort from day shift to night shift transitions to achieve 24*7 coverage. According to a research report by Ponemon Institute [4], only 29% of all alerts received in a CSOC have been inspected and among them, an average of 40% are false positives. FireEye reported that the average annual operational spending of an organization due to false positives is $17.816 million given the default resource capacity informed through common deployments [5].

1.2 Can Cyber Operations Be Made Autonomous?

The challenges faced by real-world CSOCs raise urgent needs for easing the analysts' burden. Although it would be ideal if an autonomous CSOC can be built to perform the data triage tasks as effectively as human analysts, our recent study on data triage processes inside CSOCs indicates that instead of asking whether cyber operations can be made autonomous or not, it seems more appropriate to ask the following questions:

- How to make cyber operations more autonomous?
- What is the right research roadmap for making cyber operations more autonomous?

Due to the following two observations, we think that these two questions are more appropriate. (Observation 1) Human-in-loop and AI (artificial intelligence) are not mutually exclusive. (Observation 2) Human-on-the-loop and AI are not mutually exclusive either. Based on these observations, we believe that the current frontier in building a significantly better CSOC is twofold:

- Frontier A: to identify the specific CSOC "building blocks" which could be made significantly more autonomous. Researches at Frontier A could result in paradigm shifts from human-in-the-loop to human-on-the-loop, and paradigm shifts from human-on-the-loop to human-free.
- Frontier B: optimal co-existence of human-in-the-loop, human-on-the-loop, and autonomous entities inside a CSOC.

1.3 Organization of the Rest of the Paper

In Sect. 2, we provide an overview of data triage processes in CSOCs. In Sect. 3, we review a case study we conducted recently on making data triage operations more autonomous. In Sect. 4, we discuss the lessons we learned from the case study. In Sect. 5, we conclude the paper.

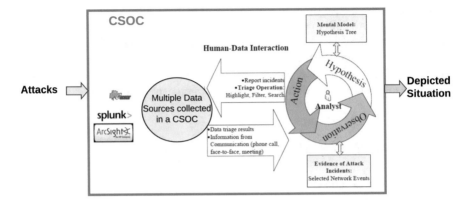

Fig. 1 CSOCs reply on both automated cybersecurity measures and human analysts to achieve cyber situational awareness

2 Cyber Operations in CSOCs

CSOCs employ multiple automated security measures and human analysts to achieve Cyber Situational Awareness (Cyber SA) (shown in Fig. 1). The security measures collect various data (e.g., IDS alerts and firewall logs) from the network. Cybersecurity analysts need to conduct a series of analysis to make sense of the collected data. According to D'Amico et al., in the process of how computer network defense (CND) analysts transform raw data into situational awareness, the raw data are gradually transformed into suspicious activities and incidents [2]. There are different stages of analysis, including triage analysis, escalation analysis, correlation analysis, threat analysis, and incident response analysis. Triage analysis is the first stage that filters the raw input data by weeding out the false alerts or the reports of normal network activities. The triage results will be used in the following escalation and correlation analysis by analysts to gain further awareness of the attack activities and targets. The related data are grouped and transformed into sets of intrusion incidents. Threat and incident response analysis mainly rely on various types of intelligence to conduct prediction and attack forecasting [2].

2.1 Human-in-the-Loop Data Analysis in CSOCs

Considering the essential role of human analysys, the data analysis tasks of various levels in CSOCs are human-in-the-loop processes. Taking the first step of CSOC analysis, data triage, as an example. It usually involves examining the details of alerts and various reports, filtering the data sources of interest for further in-depth analysis, and correlating the relevant data. Figure 2 describes a process of an analyst conducting a series of data triage operations. Each operation is conducted to filter or

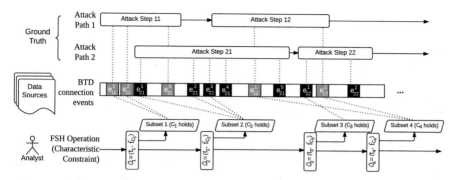

Fig. 2 A scenario of data triage process demonstrates an analyst filtering the network connection events based on characteristic constrains [6]

to correlate the data sources to gain a better understanding of potential attack paths. An **attack path** is a sequence of attack steps and each step is performed based on the previous steps for a malicious goal. **Data sources** refer to the monitoring data collected by various security measures in the CSOC. They are important sources of evidence for analysts to make judgments about the possible attacks. Each item in the sources reports an **network event**. Therefore, the data sources can be represented by a sequence of network events. Only a small portion of the events are suspicious events, which are worthy of further investigation and the suspicious events may belong to different attack paths. To sum up, a data triage analyst's responsibility is to make fast decisions about which events could be related to an attack path and worth further investigation. To accomplish the task, an analyst needs to filter the data sources by tracking a certain characteristic of network events and reason about the possible attack paths based on their previous experience and domain knowledge [7].

2.2 Difficulties in Data Triage Process

2.2.1 Massive and Rapidly Changing Data

The data sources collected in CSOCs are massive and rapidly changing. Bass first pointed out that the data collected from multiple sensors which are used as input into intrusion detection systems are heterogeneous. The data may consist of "numerous distributed packet sniffers, system log-files, SNMP traps and queries, signature-based ID systems, user profile databases, system messages, threat databases and operator commands" [8]. The heterogeneous data vary significantly in types and formats: it can include structured logs and alerts, human intelligence reports, external threat reports, or social media data. In addition, the data change continuously over time together with the attack threats due to the uncertain network activities and unpredictable attacking behaviors.

2.2.2   Weakness and Strength of Human Processing

It is challenging for analysts to transform the massive raw data sources to intrusion sets due to the human cognitive limit. To learn the need of cyber defense analysts, studies have been conducted to investigate how analysts perform data analysis and how the data analysis process can be improved. A security expert has been recognized as an important role in network intrusion detection [9]. Compared with the information processing capability and limited working memory, human brains are much better at interpreting and comprehending the data, generating hypotheses, and making decisions according to the current situation. Senior analysts can perform data triage more efficiently than novice analysts because of the experience learned from the "on-the-job" training [10–12].

The sense-making process of analysts is critical for the data analytics in CSOCs. Cognitive task analysis (CTA) studies have been conducted by researchers to investigate the cognitive processes of analysts. The CTA study of intrusion detection experts conducted by the Air Force identified the cognitive requirements for network intrusion detection [9]. D'Amico et al. studied the roles of analysts in the workflow of data analysis [2]. A further study of network analysts' workflow was conducted through a multi-phase CTA study with a focus on the analysts' needs for visualization and specified analysts' tasks, concerns and goals [13].

2.3   Autonomous Approaches

It is desirable to make cyber operations autonomous, considering the overwhelming information processing tasks and cognitive limits of human analysts. However, it is still too early to fully automate the cyber operations. We start with investigating the limitation of the existing autonomous approaches used in CSOCs. Alert correlation is an important milestone in automated data triage [14]. Alert correlation techniques use heuristic rules (a simple form of automation) to correlate alerts, but can not handle cross-data-source analysis very well. Motivated by the benefits of cross-data-source analysis, SIEM systems (e.g., ArcSight [15]) have been focused on security event correlations across multiple data sources. Rules are usually employed to correlate the event log entries [16].

Although SIEM systems take a big leap forward in generating more powerful data analysis automatons, SIEM systems are extremely expensive for its license cost and the large amount of time and expertise required in constantly system management and customization [17]. Analysts need to develop and test the data triage automatons (e.g. customized filters and complicated correlation rules) that fit the organization's setting [16, 17]. Considering that a large number of complicated data triage automatons need to be generated, the amount of manual effort is enormous. An example of a complicated filtering rule used in a SIEM system is as follows [18]:

```
"Filters -> EventType (In) [Failure], AND,
Context (In) [Context], AND, Destination Port
(In) [DestPort], AND, Protocol (In) [Protocol],
AND, {Source IP (Not In) [ExcludeSrcIP1], OR,
Source IP (Not In) [ExcludeSrcIP2], OR, Source IP
(Not In) [ExcludeSrcIP3] },..."
```

3 Case Study: Leveraging Analysts' Operation Traces for Autonomous Data Triage in CSOCs

3.1 Approach Overview

According to the CTA studies in Cyber SA, data triage is the fundamental step for the further analysis as the first examination of data [2]. Most analysts in CSOCs are conducting data triage and working in shifts to guarantee a 24/7 coverage. Therefore, our conducted a case study which mainly focused on facilitating data triage operations.

Our approach of automating data triage is developed based on three insights. Firstly, it is possible to do non-intrusive tracing of human analysts' concrete data triage operations. Secondly, though challenging, the analysts' traces of data triage operations can be mined in a largely automated way to obtain the good "ingredients" for complicated rules. The above example of SIEM rules can be decomposed into several filtering components [18]. The "EventType (In) Failure" is a basic component containing a data field and a constraint in its value, which is a so-called ingredient. The basic filtering components can be connected by logic connector "AND/OR", and thus form a complicated filtering or correlation rule. Therefore, once the good ingredients are obtained from experts' traces of former data triage operations, analysts can start form them to construct more complicated rules instead of from scratch. The overview of the approach is shown in Fig. 3.

3.2 Formalizing Data Triage Operations

We developed a formal model of data triage process of analysts for enhancing autonomous triage operations. Data triage refer to the analysis performed by analysts, involving examining the details of alerts and various reports, filtering the data sources of interest for further in-depth analysis, and correlating the relevant data. The scenario in Fig. 2 illustrates several key concepts in a data triage process: network connection events, analyst's data triage operations, and the characteristic constraints of events [19].

We consider the attack paths at the abstraction level of network event. A **network event** (written in short as event in this paper) is defined by a tuple with 8 attributes [19],

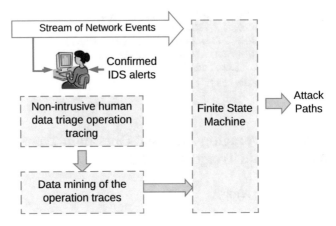

Fig. 3 The overview of our approach

$$e = < time, conn, ip_{src}, port_{src}, ip_{dst}, port_{dst}, protocol, msg >,$$

where $time$ is the time when the connection activity is performed, $conn$ is the type of connection activity (a connection can be "Built", "Teardown", and "Deny"), ip_{src}, $port_{src}$ and ip_{dst}, $port_{dst}$ are the ip address and port of the source and destination respectively, $protocol$ is the connection protocol type, and msg is the message associated with the network connection. A successful TCP communication session usually is created by a "Built" event and ended with a "Teardown" event. A "Deny" event indicates a failed connection. An attack path is represented as a finite sequence of events $(e_1, \ldots, e_n)$.

3.2.1 Analysts' Data Triage Operations

Analysts conduct data triage operations to identify the suspicious network events in the data sources collected from the CSOC's network. According to the study on analysts' operations in data triage [2], these operations can be categorized in three types: filtering the data based on a condition ($FILTER$), searching for a keyword ($SEARCH$) and selecting a subset of events with common characteristics ($SELECT$) as suspicious events. The three types are explained as follows [19].

- FILTER(D_{in}, D_{out}, C): Filter a set of connection events (D_{in}) based on a condition (C) on the attribute values of the connection events and result in a subset (D_{out}).
- SEARCH(D_{in}, D_{out}, C): Search a keyword (C) in a set of connection events (D_{in}). It results in a subset (D_{out}).
- SELECT(D_{in}, D_{out}, C),$D_j \subseteq D_i$: Select a subset of connection events (D_{out}) in a set of connection events (D_{in}), the subset of connection events (D_{out}) has a characteristic (C).

According to the above definition, a data triage operation uses a constraint to identify a subset of events from the larger dataset. The constraint determines the characteristics of the subset events of interest. We define an atomic constraint as follows, which specifies the value range of an attribute of the event,

$$T_i = r_v(attr, val),$$

where r_v is the relationship between values, $r_v = \{=, <>, >, <, <=, >=\}$. Recall the previous example of a SIEM rule in Sect. 2.3. The "EventType (In) Failure" is an atomic constraint represented by $=(attr, \text{'Failure'})$.

A characteristic constraint can be multidimensional because a event has multiple attributes (e.g., SrcIP, DstIP). A constraint can be represented by a predicate in disjunctive normal form, named "**Characteristic Constraint (CC)**",

$$\mathbb{C} = \bigvee (T_1 \wedge \ldots \wedge T_n),$$

where $T_i (1 \leq i \leq n)$ is an atomic predict.

Let $\mathbb{C}$ be a characteristic constraint specified in a data triage operation, and let D be a set of events. A data triage operation is represented by a 2-tuple,

$$O_1 = (t, f_{\mathbb{C}}),$$

where t is the timestamp of the analyst performing this operation, $f_{\mathbb{C}} : P(D) \rightarrow P(D)$, such that $f_{\mathbb{C}}(D) = \{e_k | e_k \in D, C \text{ holds on } e_k\}$, and $P(D)$ is the power set of D.

A **trace** of data triage operations consists of a series of data triage operations performed by an analyst and the underlying temporal and logic relationships between the operations.

3.2.2 Characteristic Constraint Graph

Let $O_1 = (t_1, f_{\mathbb{C}_1}(D))$ and $U_2 = (t_2, f_{\mathbb{C}_2}(D))$ be two different data triage operations performed by an analyst on a set of network events D, we define the following logical relationships between them based on their characteristic constraints: "is-equal-to", "is-subsumed-by" and "is-complementary-with" [19].

$$isEql(O_1, O_2) \iff \mathbb{C}_1 \leftrightarrow \mathbb{C}_2,$$

$$isSub(O_1, O_2) \iff \mathbb{C}_1 \rightarrow \mathbb{C}_2,$$

$$isCom(O_1, O_2) \iff \mathbb{C}_1 \rightarrow \neg\mathbb{C}_2 \text{ and } \mathbb{C}_2 \rightarrow \neg\mathbb{C}_1,$$

where $\rightarrow$ refers to implication, $isEql(\cdot, \cdot)$ and $isCom(\cdot, \cdot)$ are bidirectional relationships but $isSub(\cdot, \cdot)$ is a unidirectional relationship. A special case of "is-complementary-with" is "*is-absolute-complementary-with*": $isCom(O_1, O_2)$ and O_1 and O_2 are absolute complement given a common set of network events, that is, $\mathbb{C}_1 = \neg\mathbb{C}_2$. For example, given a set of network events with a common characteristic "SrcPort <> 80", the data triage operations using the characteristic constraints "SrcPort = 6667" and "SrcPort <> 80 AND SrcPort <> 6667" are absolute complement.

Considering both the logical relationships with the temporal relationships, we use a directed graph to represent an analyst's triage process, and name it "Characteristic Constraint Graph (CC-Graph)", $G(trace) = < V, \{R_l\} >, V = \{O_1, \ldots, O_n\}$, $R_l \subseteq V * V, l \in \{isEql \succ_t, isSub \succ_t, isCom \succ_t\}$. Each node of the graph represents a data triage operations, and a directed edge between two nodes represents a conjunction of a constraint-related logical relationship and a "happen-after" relationship between the operations (i.e. $isEql \succ_t, isSub \succ_t, isCom \succ_t$).

The reason why edges of CC-Graph are defined with both the temporal and logical relationship is that it is worthwhile to consider how an operation is related to the operations that were conducted before it. An analyst may generate several hypotheses about the possible attack paths if he/she found a subset of data noteworthy. To verify these hypotheses, the analyst may perform further data triage operations to narrow down the search space. Therefore, a sequence of operations and their logical and temporal relationships can imply an analyst's data triage strategy [6, 19]. Figure 4 shows an example of a CC-Graph.

3.3 Computer-Aided Tracing of Human Data Triage Operations

To achieve the goal of making data triage more autonomous, a necessary first step is to capture the analysts' **fine-grained** cognitive processes of data triage. A data triage process is a complex human cognitive process. Therefore, we developed a computer-aided method for capturing an analyst's data manipulation actions, observations of suspicious events, and hypotheses generated based on existing observations. The tracing method has two main unique features:

- (C1) The method explicitly records the essential components in a data triage process, including analysts' actions of data filtering, observations of suspicious events, and analysts' hypotheses about possible attack chains.
- (C2) The method is minimum-reactive: it has minimal influence on the analyst's behavior being observed. It is because any distraction may affect analysts' performance when they are working under extremely high pressure.

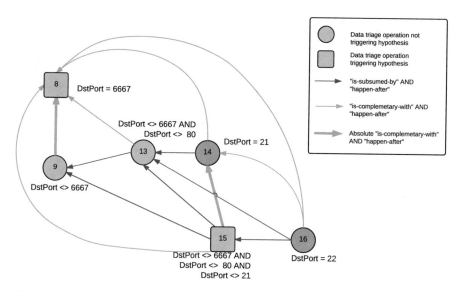

Fig. 4 A partial characteristic constraint graph constructed from an analyst's trace. The nodes are the data triage operations, with the index of their temporal order. A squared node refers to a data triage operation based on which the analyst generated a following hypothesis about the possible attack path. However, circle nodes are the data triage operations that did not result in any hypothesis [6]

The tracing method contains three main components: (1) a representation of analysts' cognitive process in data triage, (2) a computer tool that tracks various analysts' operations while they are performing data triage tasks, and (3) an experiment in which professional analysts were recruited to accomplish a simulated cyber defense situational analysis task with their operations being tracked [20]. The computer tool, named ARSCA, is developed to be used in the experiment to record the traces of analysts' data triage operations in a minimum-reactive way [20].

The user interface of ARSCA is shown in Fig. 5. It contains two main views: (1) a Data View for displaying all the data sources, and (2) an Analysis View for displaying the existing *action, observation* and *hypothesis* instances and their relationships. The functions of ARSCA are detailed as follows [21]: ARSCA supports the data triage operations defined in Sect. 3.2, (*SEARCH, FILTER,* and *SELECT*). In Fig. 5, Region 2 and 3 provide functions of searching by keyword and filtering by condition, thus supporting the operations of *SEARCH* and *FILTER*. Region 4 enables an analyst to make inquiries about a certain port or a specific term appearing in the data sources. Region 5 lets an analyst select the entries in a provided data source as the network events of interest. Once selected, the selected data entries are displayed in another window (Region 6) for the analyst to review and confirm them as the network events of interest, thus supporting the *SELECT* operation. The analyst using this tool can write down his/her hypotheses at a current moment of a certain observation. This function is shown in Region 7

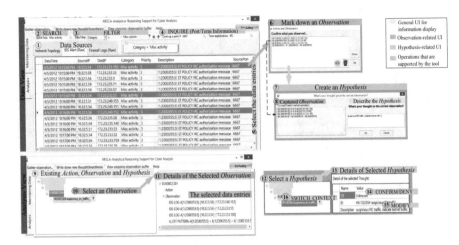

Fig. 5 Main components of the ARSCA user interface (in data view and analysis view) [20]

and 8, which enables the $NEW\ HYPO$ operation. ARSCA visualizes the analyst' existing hypotheses and enables the analyst to modify them. Region 13 enables the analyst to modify the description and truth value of a selected hypothesis, thus enabling the $MODIFY$ and $CONFIRM/DENY$ operation.

Each operation of an analyst is automatically recorded by ARSCA with a timestamp at the back end. For instance, when an analyst conducts a filtering operation, ARSCA will record the time and the filtering condition. After the filtering, the analyst may select the filtered subset as suspicious data, ARSCA will automatically record the subset as an *observation* (Region 5). If a new hypothesis occurs in the analyst's mind based on the observation, he/she can write it down in Region 8, and meanwhile, Region 7 will present the selected suspicious data to the analyst as the current context. At the back end, ARSCA will record the hypothesis and link it to the triggering observation [21].

ARSCA automatically records an analyst's data triage operations while the analyst is performing a data triage task [20]. Once the analyst finishes a task, a piece of trace recording the analyst's data triage operations will be created in the following structural format [6]:

```
<Item Timestamp=[TIMESTAMP]>
[ACTION_TYPE]
([CONTENT])
</item>
```

A sample trace of the data triage operations recorded by ARSCA is demonstrated in Table 1.

Table 1 A sample trace of data triage operations [6]

Operation	Examples in a trace	Description

item_FILTER	`<Item Timestamp= 07/31 13:01:41>`
	
	`FILTER (`
	
	`SELECT * FROM IDS Alerts WHERE`
	`SrcPort = 6667`
	`</Item>`
		Filter the a set of connection events (i.e.IDS Alerts) based on a condition (i.e.SrcPort=6667)

item_SELECT	`<Item Timestamp= 07/31 13:20:29>`
	
	`SELECT (`
	
	`FIREWALL-[4/5/2012 10:15 PM]-`
	`[Built]-[TCP](172.23.233.57/3484,`
	`10.32.5.58/6667),`
	`FIREWALL-[4/5/2012 10:15 PM]-`
	`[Teardown]-[TCP](172.23.233.52`
	`/5694,10.32.5.59/6667),`
	`FIREWALL-[4/5/2012 10:15 PM]-`
	`[Built]-[TCP](172.23.233.57/3484,`
	`10.32.5.58/6667),`
	`FIREWALL-[4/5/2012 10:15 PM]-`
	`[Teardown]-[TCP](172.23.233.58`
	`/3231,10.32.5.51/6667),`
	`</Item>`
		Filter the a set of connection events (i.e. the underlined firewall log entries) with a common characteristics (i.e. DstPort=6667)

item_LINK	`<Item Timestamp= 07/31 13:20:43>`
	
	`LINK (Same DstPort)`
	
	`</Item>`
		Identify the common characteristics (i.e.DstPort) of a selected set of connection events

item_SEARCH	`<Item Timestamp= 08/09 11:08:01>`
	
	`SEARCH (`
	`Firewall Log, 172.23.233.52)`
	`</Item>`
		Search a keyword in a set of connection events specified in the Firewall log.

3.4 The Mining Algorithm

Given the traces of analysts' data triage operations, an approach is further proposed for enhancing autonomous data triage operations. It consists of four steps: (1) identifying the data triage operations from the collected traces along with the characteristics constraints used in these data triage operations; (2) representing the data triage operations in the collected traces and their temporal and logical relationships in a Characteristic Constraint Graph (CC-Graph); (3) mining the traces to constructing useful "patterns" of the noteworthy event chains; and (4) constructing finite state machines based on the "patterns" to automate partial data triage operations for analysts [6].

3.4.1 Step 1: Identifying Data Triage Operations

A trace parser is developed to identify the data triage operations from the traces. The difficulty comes from the mapping from the ARSCA trace items to the data triage operations since it is not a one-to-one matching (an analyst may conduct several successive actions as one data triage operation). Considering all these situations, we mainly refer to the eight types of action sequences in Table 2 to parse an ARSCA trace into a set of data triage operations.

3.4.2 Step 2: Constructing Characteristic Constraint Graph

Given the identified data triage operations, we further identify the relationships among these operations to construct characteristic constraint graphs. An example of characteristic constraint graph is shown in Fig. 4. The nodes in the squares are those triggered at least one hypotheses during an analyst's analysis process, while circles not triggering any hypothesis. There are four different types of edges which corresponds to different logical relationships between data triage operations (i.e., "is-equal-to", "is-subsumed-by", "is-complementary-with" and absolute "is-

Table 2 Identifying data triage operations from ARSCA trace [6]

Item sequence in ARSCA trace	Characteristic constraint in a data triage operation
item_FILTER(cond[a]) → item_OTHER[b]	$\mathbb{C} = \text{cond}$
item_FILTER(cond) → item_SELECT($\{e_i\}$) → item_OTHER	$\mathbb{C} = \text{cond}$
item_FILTER(cond) → item_SELECT($\{e_i\}$) → item_OTHER	$\mathbb{C} = \text{cond}$
item_FILTER(cond) → item_SELECT($\{e_i\}$) → item_LINK(attr[c])	$\mathbb{C} = \text{cond} \cap (\text{attr} = \text{attr}_{e_i})$
item_SEARCH(kwd[d]) → item_OTHER	$\mathbb{C} = (\text{attr}_{infer} = \text{kwd})$
item_SEARCH(kwd) → item_SELECT($\{e_i\}$) → item_OTHER	$\mathbb{C} = (\text{attr}_{e_i} = \text{kwd})$
item_SELECT($\{e_i\}$) → item_OTHER	$\mathbb{C} = \wedge_i \vee_j (\text{attr}_j = \text{val}_{e_i, attr_j})$
item_SELECT($\{e_i\}$) → item_LINK(attr) → item_OTHER	$\mathbb{C} = \wedge_i (\text{attr} = \wedge \text{val}_{e_i, attr})$

[a]Filtering condition
[b]Other ARSCA trace items
[c]The attribute of the events of interest
[d]Search keyword

complementary-with") combined with their temporal relationships (i.e., "*happen-after*". Figure 4 is a partial CC-Graph, with 6 nodes and their relationships. Node 8 is a data triage operation using the constraint "DstPort=6667". It enabled the analyst to gain an observation and triggered a hypothesis. After performing this operation, the analyst screened out the network events with destination port 6667 by conducting another data triage operation (i.e., Node 9). It may indicate that the analyst switched his attention to the unexplored network events with other characteristics after investigating the network events via destination port 6667. The following data triage operations of Node 13 and Node 14 have an "is-subsumed-by" relationship with the data triage operation of Node 9. It implies the analyst gradually narrowed down the searching scope. The data triage operation of Node 14 is the end of this narrowing process and it let the analyst generate another hypothesis. Similarly, the same analysis strategy also exists in the sequence of Node 9, Node 15 and Node 16 [6].

3.4.3   Step 3: Mining Characteristic Constraint Graphs

The next step is to mine useful "patterns" from the CC-Graphs for autonomous data triage. Several steps are taken. Firstly, we identify the critical nodes in the CC-Graphs to be the 'candidates" for constructing state machines. The critical nodes are the data triage operations that lead analysts to key findings. However, the focus of interest of the critical data triage operations may overlap. Therefore, a follow-up step is needed to adjust the critical operations to make sure they contain mutually exclusive characteristic constraints. After that, another step is taken to group the nodes according to which attack chain they may belong to based on heuristics. It is done to make sure each state machine is built up for detecting evidence of one attack chain. The algorithm of each step is described below.

   To identify useful nodes in a CC-Graph, we extract the critical endpoints in "isSub" Subgraphs of the CC-Graph. Given data triage operations O_1 and O_2, $isSub \succ_t (O_2, O_1)$ indicates that O_2 is performed after O_1, and O_2 further narrows the O_1's network event set by using a more strict characteristic constraint. As the case described in Fig. 4, analysts may conduct a series of data triage operations with the "is-subsumed-by" (isSub) relationships to gradually narrow down the network events. The endpoints of such processes can be viewed as the critical characteristic constraints that represent a noteworthy set of network events.

   To enable the constraints of the critical nodes are mutually exclusive, we examine the logic relationships between each two nodes, and add additional characteristic constraints to one of them in the following way [6]. Let V_{ends} be the set of endpoints in an "isSub" subgraph, several steps are taken to make sure every two endpoints in this subgraph have an "isCom" relationship. (1) If two endpoints have an "isEql" relationship, we drop one from V_{ends}. (2) Given V_{ends}, we consider the subgraph induced by V_{ends} from the original CC-Graph, $G_{induced} = < V_{ends}, \{R_{logic}\} >$, where $R_{logic} = \{< v_i, v_j > | isEql(v_i, v_j) \ or \ isSub(v_i, v_j) \ or isCom(v_i, v_j)\}$. Only focusing on the edges of "isCom" relationships in $G_{induced}$, we apply the

Bron–Kerbosch algorithm to find all the maximum cliques in $G_{induced}$. A maximum clique is a subset of the vertexes, represented by $\mathscr{G}_C \in V_{induced}$, such that $\forall v_i, v_j \in \mathscr{G}_C$, $isCom(v_i, v_j)$, and $\nexists v_k \in V_{induced}$, $v_k \notin \mathscr{G}_C$, and $\forall v_i \in \mathscr{G}_C$, $isCom(v_k, v_i)$. The largest maximum clique is denoted as V_{clique}. (3) We add each $v \in V_{ends}$, $v \notin V_{clique}$ into V_{clique} by removing the overlap between v and $v_j \in V_{clique}$. For $v_i \notin V_{clique}$, it overlaps with a $v_j \notin V_{clique}$, iff there exists a network event e satisfies both $\mathbb{C}_i$ and $\mathbb{C}_j$. To remove that overlap, we adjust the characteristic constraint used in v_i (say $\mathbb{C}_i$) to $\mathbb{C}_i \wedge \neq \mathbb{C}_j$. If $\mathbb{C}_i \wedge \neq \mathbb{C}_j$ is not false, we add the adjusted v_i to $V_{clique}(V_{clique} \in \mathscr{G}_C)$.

The adjusted critical nodes are the "candidates" for constructing state machines. The last step is grouping them according to which attack chain they belong. We use heuristics in this step since grouping them requires domain knowledge and experience. One heuristic is to group the operations whose constraints are set on the same IP (e.g., a suspected attack or a potential target), considering the fact that an attack chain usually has one common attacker and target. The second heuristic is that two data triage operations can be grouped if they were arranged in the same path of AOH-Trees [11] by an analyst when he/she was performing a task. According to the design of AOH-Trees, a descendant action node is viewed as a follow-up action for investigating a hypothesis generated based on the previous action. These heuristics are made as readable as SIEM rules so that domain experts could create or modify these heuristics if we apply this approach to the real world.

3.4.4   Step 4: Constructing Finite State Machines

Attack Path Pattern

Attack path patterns are constructed based on the critical nodes and their temporal orders. An attack path pattern is defined by a sequence of characteristic constraints in a temporal order so that a pattern specifies a class of attack path instances. The temporal relationship is a "can-happen-before" relationship between two characteristic constraints, denoted as $\succ_{C_t} (\cdot, \cdot)$. Let $\mathbb{C}_1$ and $\mathbb{C}_2$ be two pre-specified characteristic constraints, $\succ_{C_t} (\mathbb{C}_1, \mathbb{C}_2)$ refers to the analysts' knowledge about the attack: it happened and could happen again if a set of network events satisfied $\mathbb{C}_1$ occurred before the other set of events involving the same hosts that satisfy $\mathbb{C}_2$ in an attack path.

The "can-happen-before" relationships of the nodes in an attack pattern are identified based on the temporal order of the corresponding network events in the task performed by the analyst. Assume that the network events come in sequence over time $E = (e_1, \ldots, e_n)$. We say this sequence of network events satisfies a sequence of characteristic constraints $(\mathbb{C}_1, \ldots, \mathbb{C}_m)$ defined in an attack path pattern $\mathscr{G}_C$, iff we have, $\forall \mathbb{C}_i (1 \leq i \leq m), \exists e_p (1 \leq p \leq n)$ satisfies $\mathbb{C}_i \rightarrow \forall \mathbb{C}_j (1 \leq j < i)$, $\exists e_q (1 \leq q \leq p)$ satisfies $\mathbb{C}_j$. Therefore, given $(\mathbb{C}_1, \ldots, \mathbb{C}_m)$ and E, the attack path instances detected based on $(\mathbb{C}_1, \ldots, \mathbb{C}_m)$ is a sequence of network event sets,

---

Algorithm 1: Identifying "can-happen-before" relationships [6]

Data: D_{task}: a sequence of network event sets;
      C: a set of characteristic constrains
Result: $\mathscr{G}_{\mathscr{C}} =< C, \{\prec_{\mathbb{C}_t}\} >$, an attack path pattern

1   $map < \mathbb{C}, \{e\} > //$ map each characteristic constraint to the
      network events that satisfies it, the network events are
      in temporal order
2   **for** e_i in D_{task} **do**
3   **if** *exists* $\mathbb{C}$ *holds on* e_i **then**
4        $map.put(\mathbb{C}, e_i)$;
5   **end**
6   **end**
7   **for** $\mathbb{C}_1, \mathbb{C}_2$ *in* C **do**
8   Find the first e_1 in $map(\mathbb{C}_1)$, and the first e_1 in $map(\mathbb{C}_1)$ that
      $e_1.\{src, dst\} = e_2.\{src, dst\}$;
9   **if** $e_1.time < e_2.time$ **then**
10   add $\prec_{\mathbb{C}_t} (\mathbb{C}_1, \mathbb{C}_2)$;
11   **end**
12 **end**

$attack_{(\mathbb{C}_1,...,\mathbb{C}_m)}(\mathscr{E}) = \{(\mathscr{E}_1, \ldots, \mathscr{E}_m)\}$, where $\mathscr{E}_{ik}(1 \leq i \leq m) = \{e_{ik} | e_{ik}$ is a network event from $source_{ik1}$ to $destination_{ik2}$ that satisfies $C_i\}$. The algorithm for identifying the "can-happen-before" relationships is shown in Algorithm 1.

State Machine

We construct finite state machines for autonomous data triage and name them "DT-SM". First, we define a state transition as $\delta : S * D \rightarrow S$. Given the current state $S_i \in S$ and a new network event e_i, we have $\delta(S_i, e_i) = S_{(i+1)}$ iff $\exists C_j$, that $\nexists(\mathbb{C}_0, \ldots, \mathbb{C}_n) \in S_i$ and $\mathbb{C}_j \in (\mathbb{C}_0, \ldots, \mathbb{C}_n)$, e_i satisfies C_j and $\exists(\mathbb{C}_0, \ldots, \mathbb{C}_n) \in S_i$, that $\succ_{\mathbb{C}_t} (\mathbb{C}_i, \mathbb{C}_j)$. Therefore, $S_{(i+1)} = S_i - (\mathbb{C}_0, \ldots, \mathbb{C}_i) + (\mathbb{C}_0, \ldots, \mathbb{C}_j)$. Therefore, with a sequence of network events rushing in a CSOC, a DT-SM takes one network event at one time and examine whether it triggers state transition. Once all the network events in a time window have been processed, the DT-SM output the instances of the attack path pattern. Each instance is a sequence of network event sets that satisfy a characteristic constraint sequence specified in the attack path pattern.

3.5 Evaluation

The above autonomous data triage system has been implemented and tested in our experiment. We evaluated (1) the effectiveness of constructing the data triage automatons (DT-SM) based on the traces, (2) the usefulness of the data triage rules mined from the traces and the performance of the constructed DT-SMs, and (3) the impact factors of the DT-SMs' performance.

3.6 Experiment Dataset

3.6.1 ARSCA Traces Collected from a Lab Experiment

Thirty full-time professional cyber analysts were recruited in a previous experiment and asked to accomplish a data triage task. The ARSCA toolkit was used to audit the analysts' operations while they were performing the task [20]. One sample was screened out because the participant didn't accomplish the task due to a technical issue. At last, we collected 29 ARSCA traces in total with 1104 trace items. The average length of the logs is 31.17.

3.6.2 Task Data Sources

To prepare the data triage task, we used the datasets from VAST Challenge 2012, which is a cyber situational awareness task in a setting of a bank's network with approximately 5000 machines. The VAST challenge provides participants with IDS alerts and firewall log from the network. VAST Challenge 2012 asked the participants to identify the noteworthy attack incidents happened in the 40 h covered by the IDS alerts and firewall logs [22]. The entire data sources were composed of 23,595,817 firewall logs and 35,709 IDS alerts. The task scenario underlying the data sources is a multistage attack path that begins with normal network connections, including regional headquarters computers communicating with internal headboards financial server and normal web browsing. The attack starts when an internal workstation was infected with a botnet due to an inserted USB. The botnet replicated itself to other hosts on the network, and meanwhile, the bonnet communicated with several C&C servers. The botnet kept infecting additional computers. It attempted to exfiltrate data using FTP connections but it failed. After that, the botnet successfully exfiltrated data using SSH connections. In the following hours, the majority of the botnet communication and data exfiltration kept happening.

The original data sources provided in the VAST challenge are too large for human analysts to analyze during the limited task time. Therefore, only small portions of data were selected from the original dataset and provided to the participants to enable them to complete the task in the experimental session (60 min). Two time windows were selected and each of them were used to make a cybersecurity analysis task for the subjects in that experiment, which are the time window I and time window II shown in Table 3. In the experiment where ARSCA traces were collected, 10 analysts accomplished the task of time window I, and 19 analysts accomplished the task of time window II.

Table 3 Attack ground truth in 3 selected time windows [6]

Time window	Attack scenario (steps)	Instances	Data sources
Scenario from the beginning (started from 4/5 20:25): An internal workstation got infected with a botnet due to a USB insertion. The botnet spread fast			
I: 4/5 22:15-22:25 (10 min)	(1) The botnet communicated with the external C&C servers using IRC (2) Failed attempted to exfiltrate data using FTP (3) Successful attempted to exfiltrate data using SSH	8 external servers, 105 internal workstation 247 ATTACK PATH PATTERN instances	# IDS Alerts: 239 # Firewall Log: 115,524
Scenario in the middle (about 20 h, 4/5 22:26-4/6 17:56): The IT department noticed the problem and rebooted some infected workstations several times. The data exfiltration drops, but the majority of the botnet traffic still exists			
II: 4/6 18:05-18:15 (10 min)	(1) The botnet spread (inquiring the network hardware) (2) New IRC communications (3) New attempt to exfiltrate data using FTP	11 external servers, 233 internal workstations 233 ATTACK PATH PATTERN instances	# IDS Alerts: 228 # Firewall Log: 48,012
III: 4/6 18:16-19:56 (100 min)	(1) Additional workstations were infected (2) The botnet communication continued (3) FTP exfiltration continued	13 external servers, 517 internal workstations 3055 ATTACK PATH PATTERN instances	# IDS Alerts: 1810 # Firewall Log: 599,489

3.7 Evaluation of DT-SM Construction

3.7.1 Data Triage Operation Identification

We compared the identified data triage operations with the ones identified by two human analysts (served as ground truth). The automatic system identified 348 data triage operations in total. Comparing them with the ground truth, there were 322 data triage operations correctly identified by the system. There were 62 data triage operations in the ground truth but not identified by the system. Therefore, the false positive rate is 0.075 and the false negative rate is 0.161.

3.7.2 Attack Path Pattern Construction

We evaluated these attack path patterns by checking whether its characteristic constraints are critical and mutually exclusive. To decide whether the characteristic

Table 4 Top 10 characteristic constraints in the attack path pattern by analyzing the 29 analysts' data triage operations [6]

1.	DSTPORT = 6667 AND SRCIP = 172.23.*.* AND DSTIP = 10.32.5.* AND PROTOCOL = TCP AND SERVICE = 6667_tcp
2.	SRCPORT = 6667 AND SRCIP = 10.32.5.* AND DSTIP = 172.23.233.* AND PRIORITY = 3 AND DESCRIPTION = [1:2000355:5] ET POLICY IRC authorization message
3.	SRCIP = 172.23.*.* AND DSTIP = 172.23.0.10 AND DSTPORT = 445 AND PRIORITY = 3
4.	SRCIP = 172.23.235.* AND DSTIP = 10.32.5.* AND DSTPORT = 21 AND OPERATION = Deny AND PRIORITY = Warning AND PROTOCOL = TCP AND SERVICE = ftp
5.	SRCIP = 172.23.*.* AND DSTIP = 10.32.5.* AND DSTPORT = 6667 AND OPERATION = Deny
6.	SRCIP = 172.23.*.* AND DSTPORT = 53
7.	SRCIP = 172.23.234.* AND DSTIP = 10.32.5.* AND DSTPORT = 22
8.	SRCIP = 10.32.5.* AND DSTIP = 172.23.1.168 AND DSTPORT = 6667
9.	DSTPORT = 80 AND DSTIP = 10.32.0.100 AND SRCIP > 172.23.0.0
10.	SRCIP = 172.23.0.108 AND DSTPORT = 6667 AND DSTIP = 10.32.5.*

constraints in an attack path schema are critical, we mapped them to the analysts' answer to the task question that asked about the most important observations. In total, we have 32 attack path patterns constructed, containing 81 characteristic constraints. The average number of the nodes in the attack path patterns is 2.781. We found 79 out of the 89 characteristic constraints in the 32 attack path patterns mentioned by the analysts that lead to important observation (88.76%). As for the 10 characteristic constraints not mentioned in analysts' answer, we found 6 of them also lead to hypotheses in analysts' ARSCA trace. All the characteristic constraints in the attack path pattern are mutually exclusive. Table 4 lists the top 10 characteristic constraints included in the attack path pattern.

3.8   Performance of DT-SM

Since the task data sources were selected from a 10-min-time window, we chose a 100-min time window (4/6 18:16-19:56) to collect the testing data sources from the original VAST data sources. It corresponds to the data in time window III in Table 3. Meanwhile, we manually processed the data sources in time window III and tagged each data entry regarding which attack step it is related to define the ground truth for the testing.

A set of DT-SMs was constructed from the traces, each of them can detect a set of event sequences. We combined the results of multiple DT-SMs by selecting the event sequences with high occurrence frequency. Figure 6 demonstrates an example

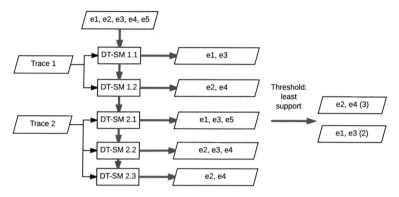

Fig. 6 Identifying suspicious network event sequences based on multiple DT-SMs [6]

of how the DT-SMs results are combined. A threshold can be set up to determine what is the least frequency of occurrence for the event sequences of interest (i.e., "least support"). Given the output of each DT-SM, we calculated the occurrence of frequency of each event sequence and selected those with the occurrence of frequency above the threshold.

The performance of the DT-SM was measured by false positive and false negative rates. We use e^S to denote the network events in the output of the DT-SM S, and e^T to denote the network events included in the ground truth T. We calculated the false positive and false negative rate using the following formula:

$$false\ positive = 1 - \frac{|\cup \{e^T | e^T \in S\}|}{|\cup \{e^S | e^S \in S\}|} \tag{1}$$

$$false\ negative = 1 - \frac{|\cup \{e^T | e^T \in S\}|}{|\cup \{e^T | e^T \in T\}|} \tag{2}$$

The performance of the DT-SMs (i.e., false positive and false negative) built on their traces is shown in Fig. 7. We set the threshold of least support as 1, 2, 5 and 10 respectively. The result shows that, in general, the false positive rates are satisfactory. However, the false negative rates are high. As the threshold increases, the false positive rate decreases while false negative rate increasing. Comparing the results at different thresholds, we found that the best result occurred when the threshold of least support was set as 2. One of the possible reasons for the high false negative rate can be that the participants failed to detect some suspicious network events in the task so that their traces don't involve the effective data triage operations.

Fig. 7 The performance of
DT-SMs with different
thresholds of least support [6]

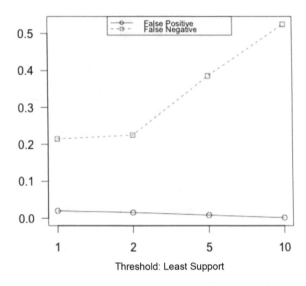

Threshold: Least Support

3.9   Effect of Analysts' Task Performance on the DT-SM's Performance

We know that the performance of a DT-SM is mainly determined by the quality of the attack path patterns mined from the analysts' traces, and analysts' traces are closely related to analysts' task performance. Therefore, we compared the performance of the DT-SMs built on the traces from the analysts with different task performance.

In the experiment in which the traces were captured, analysts were asked about what the attack scenario underlies the provided data sources after accomplishing the task. We evaluated the analysts' task performance by comparing their answers with the ground truth and gave each of them a score in the range of [1, 5]. Among the 29 participants, the first 10 analysts, who participated in the first task working with the data sources of time window I, displayed a diverse range of performance, while the other 19 analysts with the data sources of time window II presented identical results with similar scores. Therefore, we only took the traces of the first 10 analysts into the examination. We used each analyst's trace to construct a DT-SM and then ran the DT-SM on the testing data sources of time window III. We divided the participants into two groups according to their task performance: Group 1 of 5 participants with high task score (i.e., either 4 or 5), and Group 2 of 5 participants with low task score (i.e., either 2 or 3). Table 5 shows the comparison results of the false positive and false negative rates of the DT-SMs built on the traces in these two groups. It shows that the false positive rates in both groups are very small. However, the first group of DT-SMs, which corresponds to higher task performance, have a much smaller false negative rate. It can be explained by the fact that analysts with good performance

Table 5 Performance of the DT-SMs built on the traces from analysts with different task performance

Group	Performance score (1–5)	Performance
High-performance	4–5	False positive: 0.010
		False negative: 0.225
Low-performance	2–3	False positive: 0.015
		False negative: 0.350

The threshold of least support is 2 [6]

in the task were able to detect most of the attack-related network events; their data triage operations may contain more useful characteristic constraints compared with the analysts who performed poorly in the task.

3.9.1 Worst Case Analysis

We noticed a DT-SM built on the trace of an analyst (whose ID is 08239) had the highest false negative rate. We looked into the attack path patterns constructed based on his trace, and found a sequence of 3 characteristic constraints: (1) DSTPORT=6667, (2) DSTIP = 10.32.0.* AND DSTPORT = 80 AND PRIORITY = Info AND PROTOCOL = TCP, and (3) SRCIP = 10.32.5.* AND SRCPORT = 6667 AND DSTIP = 10.32.0.* AND PROTOCOL = TCP. According to the ground truth, the second characteristic constraint is not related to any attack step of the ground truth. It suggests the characteristic constraint is misleading and results in quite a few instances with irrelevant characteristic constraints so that the false negative is much higher. Such a case can be avoided by combining the ARSCA traces of multiple analysts together.

4 Lessons Learned

The main lessons learned from the case study are as follows:

– The analytic processes in CSOCs have been indicated to be intricate and complex cognitive processes in our analysis of the collected traces of analysts' operations. These traces include the details of analysts' data filtering and exploration actions, observations of suspicious events and hypotheses about the possible attack chains. Various strategies of information processing and reasoning have been observed by analyzing the temporal and logic relationships among the analysts' operations. Besides, we observed that the analysts' operations are driven by their mental models (hypotheses) which are dynamically changing with the cyber environment. Therefore, we conclude the CSOC operations are too complicated to be made fully autonomous at this moment.

- Human input is critical for automating CSOC operations, considering that the analytic processes in CSOCs are currently human-in-the-loop. In our case study, the state machines were built based on the traces of the human analysts' data triage operations. Besides, we observed that the performance of the state machines was mainly determined by the analysts' performance in the collected traces. Therefore, it is necessary to have domain experts control the quality of the traces and set up the parameters (e.g., the least support threshold) to achieve a good performance of the automated system. Furthermore, human efforts are necessary when applying the state machines to a different network because the "patterns" mined from the traces need to be modified to fit in a new network setting.
- One limit of the current automated system in our case study lies in the small size of trace collection. We expect the performance of the system to be improved when the size of trace collection increases. However, even if we expand the size of the trace collection, a main challenge for improving the automated system would still remain, that is, how to minimize the false positive and false negative rates. On one hand, having a high false positive rate could prevent CSOCs from adopting such an autonomous system because analysts may need to spend extra efforts filtering out the false positives from the system's output. On the other hand, the system's output might not be very useful with a high false negative rate because it means that the system fails to identify most of the "true signals" from data sources. According to the results of our case study, there is always a trade-off between the false positives and false negatives.
- The results of our case study have shown the feasibility of developing an autonomous system to assist cyber analysis in CSOCs. However, we have to admit that such trace-based learning systems are not capable of handling all kinds of cyber situations, since these traces only capture the past experience of analysts. The autonomous system is built to be a supplementary means rather than a substitute to replace human analysts.
- We believe that human intelligence (of the analysts) will be indispensable in the long run, although CSOCs are evolving to become more autonomous than before. We observed that the analysts use various analytic reasoning strategies to make sense of the data. Despite the human cognitive limits, analysts' insights and reasoning enable them to incorporate new concepts into putative conclusions and to cope with uncertainty associated with incomplete or inaccurate situation information. Such human intelligence and reasoning capacity are often too complex for a computer to fully obtain. Therefore, we believe that the qualitative insights from human analysts will continue to play an essential role in CSOCs.

5   Conclusion

In this paper, we contribute to the debate on whether next-generation cyber-defense solutions should be wholly autonomous in the context of CSOCs, which have been widely established in prominent companies and organizations to achieve cyber situational awareness. Based on the lessons learned from a recent case study on making CSOC data triage operations more autonomous, we conclude that instead of asking whether cyber operations can be made autonomous or not, it seems more appropriate to ask the following questions: (a) How to make cyber operations more autonomous? (b) What is the right research roadmap for making cyber operations more autonomous? We also comment on what should be the current frontier in building a significantly better CSOC.

Acknowledgement This work was supported by ARO W911NF-15-1-0576 and ARO W911NF-13-1-0421 (MURI).

References

1. D. Silver, A. Huang, C. J. Maddison, A. Guez, L. Sifre, G. van den Driessche, J. Schrittwieser, I. Antonoglou, V. Panneershelvam, M. Lanctot, S. Dieleman, D. Grewe, J. Nham, N. Kalchbrenner, I. Sutskever, T. Lillicrap, M. Leach, K. Kavukcuoglu, T. Graepel, and D. Hassabis, "Mastering the game of go with deep neural networks and tree search," *Nature*, vol. 529, pp. 484–489, 2016.
2. A. D'Amico and K. Whitley, "The real work of computer network defense analysts," in *VizSEC 2007*, pp. 19–37, Springer, 2008.
3. J. Yen, R. F. Erbacher, C. Zhong, and P. Liu, "Cognitive process," in *Cyber Defense and Situational Awareness*, pp. 119–144, Springer, 2014.
4. P. Institute, "The state of malware detection and prevention," Cyphort, 2016.
5. FireEye, "The total cost of handling too many alerts versus managing risk," 2016.
6. C. Zhong, J. Yen, P. Liu, and R. F. Erbacher, "Learning from experts' experience: Toward automated cyber security data triage," *IEEE Systems Journal*, 2018.
7. C. Zhong, J. Yen, P. Liu, R. F. Erbacher, C. Garneau, and B. Chen, "Studying analysts' data triage operations in cyber defense situational analysis," in *Theory and Models for Cyber Situation Awareness*, pp. 128–169, Springer, 2017.
8. T. Bass, "Intrusion detection systems and multisensor data fusion," *Communications of the ACM*, vol. 43, no. 4, pp. 99–105, 2000.
9. D. P. Biros and T. Eppich, "Theme: security-human element key to intrusion detection," *Signal-Fairfax*, vol. 55, no. 12, pp. 31–34, 2001.
10. K. A. Ericsson and A. C. Lehmann, "Expert and exceptional performance: Evidence of maximal adaptation to task constraints," *Annual review of psychology*, vol. 47, no. 1, pp. 273–305, 1996.
11. C. Zhong, D. Samuel, J. Yen, P. Liu, R. Erbacher, S. Hutchinson, R. Etoty, H. Cam, and W. Glodek, "Rankaoh: Context-driven similarity-based retrieval of experiences in cyber analysis," in *Cognitive Methods in Situation Awareness and Decision Support (CogSIMA), 2014 IEEE International Inter-Disciplinary Conference on*, pp. 230–236, IEEE, 2014.
12. C. Zhong, T. Lin, P. Liu, J. Yen, and K. Chen, "A cyber security data triage operation retrieval system," *Computers & Security*, vol. 76, pp. 12–31, 2018.
13. R. F. Erbacher, D. A. Frincke, P. C. Wong, S. Moody, and G. Fink, "A multi-phase network situational awareness cognitive task analysis," *Information Visualization*, vol. 9, no. 3, pp. 204–219, 2010.
14. R. Sadoddin and A. Ghorbani, "Alert correlation survey: framework and techniques," in *Proceedings of the 2006 international conference on privacy, security and trust: bridge the gap between PST technologies and business services*, pp. 37–38, ACM, 2006.
15. ArcSight, "Building a successful security operations center," 2010. Research 014-052809-09.

16. D. Nathans, *Designing and Building Security Operations Center*. Syngress, 2014.
17. D. Miller, S. Harris, A. Harper, S. VanDyke, and C. Blask, *Security information and event management (SIEM) implementation*. McGraw Hill Professional, 2010.
18. McAfee, "Siem best practices: Correlation rule and engine debugging," 2014. Report No. PD25633.
19. C. Zhong, J. Yen, P. Liu, and R. F. Erbacher, "Automate cybersecurity data triage by leveraging human analysts' cognitive process," in *Big Data Security on Cloud (BigDataSecurity), IEEE International Conference on High Performance and Smart Computing (HPSC), and IEEE International Conference on Intelligent Data and Security (IDS), 2016 IEEE 2nd International Conference on*, pp. 357–363, IEEE, 2016.
20. C. Zhong, J. Yen, P. Liu, R. Erbacher, R. Etoty, and C. Garneau, "An integrated computer-aided cognitive task analysis method for tracing cyber-attack analysis processes," in *Proceedings of the 2015 Symposium and Bootcamp on the Science of Security*, pp. 8–9, ACM, 2015.
21. C. Zhong, J. Yen, P. Liu, R. Erbacher, R. Etoty, and C. Garneau, "Arsca: a computer tool for tracing the cognitive processes of cyber-attack analysis," in *Cognitive Methods in Situation Awareness and Decision Support (CogSIMA), 2015 IEEE International Inter-Disciplinary Conference on*, pp. 165–171, IEEE, 2015.
22. K. Cook, G. Grinstein, M. Whiting, M. Cooper, P. Havig, K. Liggett, B. Nebesh, and C. L. Paul, "Vast challenge 2012: Visual analytics for big data," in *Visual Analytics Science and Technology (VAST), 2012 IEEE Conference on*, pp. 251–255, IEEE, 2012.

A Framework for Studying Autonomic Computing Models in Cyber Deception

Sridhar Venkatesan, Shridatt Sugrim, Jason A. Youzwak, Cho-Yu J. Chiang, and Ritu Chadha

1 Introduction

Critical cyber systems are under constant attack from adversaries with varying skills and objectives. With an ever-growing laundry list of attack opportunities spanning from software-related issues including known and unknown vulnerabilites to administrative issues such as patch mismanagement, incorrect configuration and noncompliance with best practices, has accelerated the number of attacks in the recent years. Furthermore, these issues have been exacerbated by an increasing reliance on large-scale networking systems to conduct critical missions—thereby, making it very challenging to manage and respond to on-going security incidents in a timely manner.

Cyber attacks are typically preceded by reconnaissance efforts aimed at collecting critical information about the target system. Such information includes network topology, service dependencies, operating systems, and unpatched vulnerabilities. In a multi-step attack, adversaries may conduct additional reconnaissance activities, after the initial compromise, in order to gather additional information that would enable them to further penetrate the network. Unfortunately, when system configurations are static and attackers are given enough time, the attackers will be able to acquire accurate knowledge about the target system through a variety of tools and techniques, and engineer effective exploits.

Current security measures that address these challenges have been reactive, e.g. Intrusion detection systems (IDS). These measures are ineffective at deterring attackers' reconnaissance efforts. Furthermore, due to the possibility of false positives, such measures are implemented with a human-in-the-loop (such as security

S. Venkatesan (✉) · S. Sugrim · J. A. Youzwak · C.-Y. J. Chiang · R. Chadha
Perspecta Labs Inc., Basking Ridge, NJ, USA
e-mail: svenkatesan@perspectalabs.com; ssugrim@perspectalabs.com;
jyouzwak@perspectalabs.com; jchiang@perspectalabs.com; rchadha@perspectalabs.com

© Springer Nature Switzerland AG 2020
S. Jajodia et al. (eds.), *Adaptive Autonomous Secure Cyber Systems*,
https://doi.org/10.1007/978-3-030-33432-1_5

analysts) to verify and validate the alerts before responding to the incident with a security action (e.g., blocking a service, shutting down a system). For large networks, with several IDS sensors deployed at different portions of the network, such solutions require a dedicated team of security analysts to handle these alerts. In a resource-constrained environment, however, such provisioning will be infeasible.

Cyber deception has emerged as a promising approach to increase the amount of effort required to conduct an attack campaign. Cyber deception aims at providing adversaries with an incorrect view of the target system, so that any attack premised on such incorrect information is likely to fail and presents an opportunity for detection. To this end, our earlier research on ACyDS [6] started with the development of an adaptive cyber deception system that leverages the packet header rewriting capability of SDN to provide a unique virtual network view to each host in an enterprise network. A virtual network view can be combined with several deceptive elements such as honeypots and fake broadcast traffic to create a *deceptive network surface* for the host. ACyDS provides the capability to generate deceptive network surfaces that can be tailored for different cyber situations and adversaries.

In a resource-constrained environment, enabling large-scale monitoring, data processing, deception planning and subsequently, deploying a customized deceptive network surface in real-time will be challenging if done manually. We envision that models inspired from the autonomic computing paradigm can efficiently tackle such challenges. To enable the development of such models and provide empirical evidence to validate their efficacy, in this chapter, we will present a framework—called Autonomic models using Adaptive Cyber Deception System A^2CyDS—that can act as a common platform to study different autonomic computing models. It is built on top of the existing ACyDS deception platform. We will describe the current platform and enumerate its capabilities such as sensing the environment and generating deceptive network surfaces. We will also show how different components of a well-known autonomic computing architecture called MAPE-K can be realized through our framework.

2   Overview of ACyDS

ACyDS provides a unique deceptive network view to each host in an enterprise network. That is, a host's view of its network, including subnet topology and IP address assignments of reachable hosts and servers, does not reflect actual network configurations and is different from the view of any other host in the network. For example, each participant of the network will locate network services by contacting the DNS server, but this DNS server will return network address values that are specific to the network view observed by this participant. In a nutshell, ACyDS's deception approach achieves its objective by enabling the following capabilities:

- **View isolation**: Each host is presented with a unique view of the network in terms of IP configurations and network topology. As a result, if multiple hosts are compromised, collusion among them is less likely to be successful.
- **Dynamic view change**: The network view of each host changes on-the-fly to disrupt any knowledge previously acquired by the attacker.
- **Large Search Space**: Each network view can potentially have a large number of subnets and the hosts in a network can be "spread out" over these subnets. As a result, the attacker needs to expand its search space.
- **Active Deception**: ACyDS can actively misinform a host through active deception operations that include injecting fake packets, redirecting requests to honeypots, manipulating OS fingerprints, etc.

ACyDS leverages SDN technologies, including OpenFlow [14] switches and controllers. Our implementation uses Open vSwitch [18] and RYU [20] to seamlessly handle the typical types of IP network traffic and management applications—e.g., ARP, UDP, TCP, ping and traceroute—by dynamically modifying IP header fields at the SDN switch per installed flow rules that implement the network views.

2.1 ACyDS Architecture

ACyDS leverages SDN Controllers, SDN switches, and other components to create individual deceptive network views for hosts. Figure 1 provides a diagrammatic representation of the architecture. The roles played by these components are described below.

The *View Generator* generates network views for hosts and stores generated views in a database. It also changes views for hosts per an administrators directives or based on policies. The View Generator must generate network views that conform to multiple requirements, which are discussed later. The *View Database* stores network views generated by View Generator and provides network view information to other ACyDS components. To implement the *Deception-enabled SDN Controller*, we built a RYU-based controller to manage insertions and deletions of packet rewrite rules and packet forwarding rules in SDN Switch, according to outstanding deception views. To minimize load on the Deception-enabled SDN Controller and allow flexible solution scalability, the *Deception Server* was introduced. The Deception Server handles certain packet body rewrites and generates ARP response that cannot be handled by the SDN Switch. We used Open vSwitch as-is for the SDN Switch, as in our design the SDN switch just needs to enforce its traffic flow rules. Since the TTL field in the IP header is critical for achieving seamless cyber deception, Nicira extensions 0 are used to properly manipulate TTL values.

The *DHCP Server* needs to work seamlessly in an ACyDS-enabled deception network. In our design, we created a deception-aware DHCP Relay to allow use of an unmodified DHCP server while enforcing cyber deception functions. As part of the address assignment procedure, a host is given a unique identifier (which is

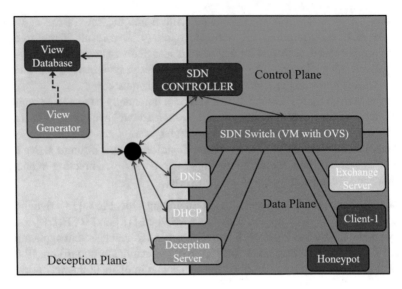

Fig. 1 Existing ACyDS architecture

only visible to the deception system) that identifies the position of this host in
every view. When ACyDS is queried for this host, this unique identifier is used
to provide a view appropriate answer. The initial view for this host is also chosen
during this assignment. Since each host's network view is unique, the *DNS Server*
must be able to return different responses to name queries for a server (e.g., a
common mail server) from different hosts. In our design, we leverage a feature in the
existing BIND implementation, which allows us to achieve this goal by modifying
configuration files rather than modifying code.

2.2 ACyDS Design

Consider the situation in which Client 1 requests its network configuration settings
from the DHCP Server. The DHCP broadcast message reaches the SDN Switch,
which follows an already-installed flow rule to forward DHCP requests from all
hosts to the DHCP Relay. Upon receiving DHCP requests, the DHCP Relay first
notifies the View Generator (VG) to generate a network view for Client 1. The
DHCP Relay sends a request message to the DHCP Server based on the virtual
subnet into which the VG decides to place Client 1, starting the four-way handshake
between Client 1 and the DHCP Server. Client 1 obtains its IP address and DNS
Servers IP address, which it can use to perform name lookups for other servers such
as Exchange server, in its own virtual network view.

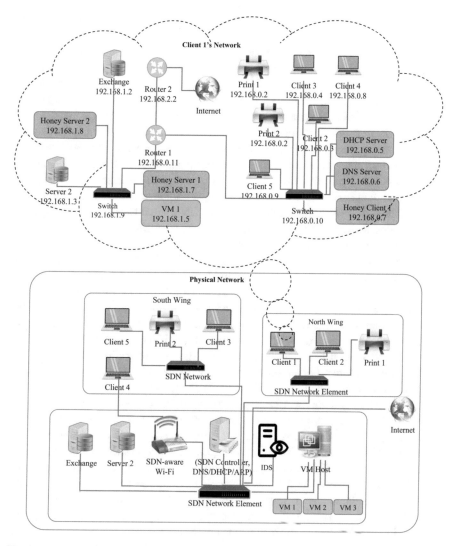

Fig. 2 An example deceptive network surface. In this example, Client 1's network view is different from the underlying physical layout

Suppose Client 1 needs to contact the Exchange Server. If, in the Client 1's view, the IP address of Mail Server happens to be on the same subnet as Client 1, then Client 1 sends an ARP request to get the MAC address of Exchange Server before it can send out IP packets; however, as shown in Fig. 2, if the Mail Server is on a different subnet than Client 1, then Client 1 needs to send an ARP request to get the MAC address of the interface on its default gateway. As each node, including Client 1, is placed in its individual virtual network topology, no such gateways actually exist. To account for proper responses to such ARP requests, the SDN Controller installs a flow rule in the SDN Switch, instructing the switch to always forward ARP requests to the Deception Server. On receiving an ARP request, the Deception Server crafts an appropriate ARP reply and sends it to the requestor, in this case Client 1. This ensures that each requestor will receive replies appropriate to the view that it observes. Client 1 can then start sending IP packets to Exchange Server.

When a packet reaches the SDN Switch, there are always two possible situations: one is that flow rule(s) needed for handling this packet is/are already installed and the other is that no matching rule(s) can be found. For the former, the switch forwards the packet according to the matched flow rule(s); for the latter, the switch buffers the packet and sends a *PacketIn* message to the SDN Controller for instructions. The SDN Controller looks up information in the View Database (VDB) and then generates a *PacketOut* message with instructions on how to handle this packet and possibly install flow rules in SDN Switch for handling this type of packet going forward. In this way, the number of *PacketIn* messages that the SDN Controller needs to process is significantly reduced.

The SDN Controller also needs to install additional rules in the SDN Switch to fulfill the requirements of rendering individual network views to hosts. Consider the first packet sent out by Client 1 to Exchange Server. Both source address and destination address in the packets IP header will follow Client 1's network view, which is different than Exchange Servers network view. However, when the packet reaches Exchange Server, the source address in the IP header must be replaced by Client 1's address in Exchange Servers view and the destination address must be replaced by Exchange Server address in its own view. This is necessary to prevent network view information from leaking between the two network views.

In addition to generating ARP Reply messages, the Deception Server is used by ACyDS for enabling cyber deception. In our design, the Deception Server is used whenever packet processing is considered complicated (e.g., to compute the correct minimum TTL on a route), or to perform packet rewrite functions that cannot be performed by the SDN Switch (e.g., to modify the payload in ICMP messages with embedded IP headers). The DS has to handle payload rewrites because the current OpenFlow standards has no way to perform actions on payloads. The rewrites are required due to the design of certain legacy Internet protocols where source and destination IP addresses are also embedded in the packet payload. We use Deception Server to handle packet header and packet payload rewrite to ensure that deceptive network view information will not be leaked between different views.

Finally, the DNS server must return different responses to name queries of the same domain name from different hosts. This issue appears challenging, but actually can be easily addressed by leveraging a feature that is commonly available in well-known DNS Server implementations such as BIND [4], where DNS query responses can be customized based on IP subnets from where queries originate. Since the host running the DNS server also observes a network view in ACyDS, we assign a virtual view to this host in which each observed view is on a different subnet. The View Generator needs to update the configuration files for DNS Server when a view is added (such as when a new host joins the network) or needs to be changed. Note that it is not possible for a node to spoof DNS queries and receive DNS responses, as such messages will be dropped by the SDN Switch.

2.3 Network View Generation

When a View Generator generates a view, it must satisfy two properties: (1) honor existing access control policy of the underlying host, (2) ensure compatibility with existing view(s). The first property ensures that a host can *reach* only the hosts/services designated by the administrator. Such policies can range from a stringent policy that allows the hosts to communicate only with servers within a network to a more liberal policy that allows all hosts to reach one another. While a stringent policy reduces the attack surface, a liberal policy will be necessary to faciliate proper functioning of network discovery protocol such as NetBIOS. In addition to ensuring compliance with the access control policies, the second property enables transparent switching between views. When changing from one view to another, changing the underlying network configuration (such as IP address) of the host creates an additional overhead and potentially, raises the suspicion of a possible deception to an attacker who has compromised the machine. Therefore, in ACyDS, a host is assigned an IP address by the DHCP server and subsequent renewal requests are responded with the same IP address. Furthermore, in ACyDS, a host is uniquely identified by its IP address and MAC address pair. Hence, to generate a view that is *compatible* with the existing view(s) of a host, the view *must* have the same IP address and MAC address pair.

We have designed a view generation algorithm that satisfies the above two properties. The view generation algorithm takes as input the number of transit nodes, the number of hosts and the number of compatible views per host, and populates the database entries to bootstrap ACyDS. The algorihm first creates a transit subgraph that acts as the backbone network for the view; the nodes of the subgraph correspond to the routers within the view. Next, to each node in the transit subgraph, the algorithm attaches a stub node which represents a subnet to which the host nodes are attached at random. After generating the topology, the algorithm assigns network-relevant information to all the elements. This includes information such as IP blocks for subnets, IP addresses for hosts within view, default gateway, DNS and DHCP server views. To ensure compatibility with between views of a host, the algorithm assigns the same IP address to the host in the generated view(s). An example set of views is provided in Fig. 3.

2.4 Honeypot Support

ACyDS deploys honeypots as yet another host in the network. The honeypot machine is presented with its own network view. and is configured to handle traffic

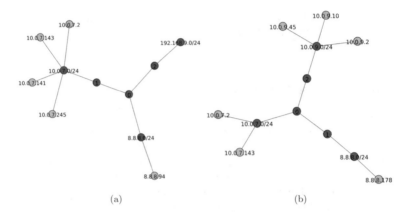

(a)   (b)

Fig. 3 Example views for a host (IP: 10.0.7.143) in two compatible views. The red nodes represent the transit nodes, the blue nodes represent the stub nodes, the green nodes represent the end hosts, the yellow nodes represent the DHCP server and the purple node corresponds to the DNS subnet. (**a**) View 1. (**b**) View 2

that are destined to non-existent IP addresses in the source host's network view. Currently, ACyDS supports a low-interaction honeypot, HoneyD [19], although any honeypot that performs deception above the IP-layer can be supported in a straight-forward manner.

When a host generates traffic to a non-existent destination (in its network view), the SDN controller decides whether to forward traffic to the honeypot or not. If the controller decides to forward (the probability of this occurring is a tunable parameter of the system) to the honeypot, entries are placed into the database to keep track of the decision, so that future attempts to contact this address during this view's lifetime will exhibit the same behavior. The deception server also checks these entries when determining if it needs to form an ARP response. It will generate responses for any honeypot entries that were made.

Honeypots enable the defenders to tailor the network view (presented to the host) based on the history of network activites generated by a host. By tailoring the views, the defenders can solicit additional network activity from a suspicious host to determine whether the host is compromised and also, learn the attacker's intentions. For instance, if the defender observes a port scanning activity originating from a host to a set of hosts within a particular subnet, then the defender can change the network view of the suspicious host to include honeypots within the target subnet. This enables the defender to confirm their suspicion of a malicious scanning activity and potentially, learn about the services that are of interest to the attacker. The optimal honeypot configuration such as number of honeypots and set of open ports in response to suspicious activity is an open problem.

2.5 Fake Broadcast Message

In addition to supporting reactive deception techniques such as honeypots, ACyDS has the capability to engage in proactive deception through fake broadcast message generation. The fake broadcast message generation process is composed of two phase: (1) Traffic profile creation phase, and (2) Traffic generation phase. The traffic profile creation phase is pre-processing phase during which a sample traffic capture is analyzed and is used as a template to build the traffic profiles for different message types (such as NetBIOS, Dropbox) while the traffic generation phase involves generating the broadcast traffic based on the created profiles.

For the first phase, we captured of broadcast traffic on a corporate network and analyzed the frequency of various message types. To synthesize traffic patterns similar to the captured traffic, we extracted the following features for each message type: number of packets per burst, time between packets within a burst, and time between bursts (Fig. 4). Here, a burst is defined as a collection of packets that are within 2 s of one another. We observed that some message types occurred periodically such as announcements by Windows machines and applications such as Spotify and Dropbox. Other types of background traffic appeared less regularly, e.g. DHCP.

After extracting the temporal features for each message type, we computed the mean and standard deviation of the features and modeled them as a normal distribution. Additionally, since every host broadcasts different types of messages, we computed the likelihoods of each message types in a subnet. The likelihood of a message type is computed by calculating the percentage of IP addresses (in the captured traffic) that generated the message type during the capture period. The message type likelihoods and their traffic distribution profiles (the temporal features) for each IP address were stored in a configuration file to bootstrap the next phase.

In the traffic generation phase, first, each host is mapped to a set of message types that it will generate. A message type is chosen based on its likelihood in the captured traffic. Next, for each chosen message type, a distribution profile (composed of the distributions for the three features) is chosen at random and assigned to the host. Finally, after determining the traffic distribution profiles for the host, ACyDS begins the broadcast packet generation process. To generate traffic, it schedules the generation of a burst by randomly choosing a time from the time between bursts distribution and then determines the number of packets within the burst and the time between those packets using the remaining two distribution profiles.

Fig. 4 Features of broadcast traffic

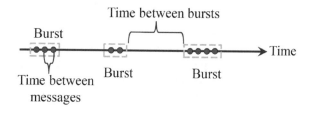

2.6 Dynamic View Change

The generated views can be changed either periodically or on-demand. Such dynamic view changes simulates a Moving Target Defense behavior [15] to invalidate any network-relevant information that an attacker may have acquired during their reconnaissance.While frequent view changes can reduce the time window for reconnaissance and subsequent attack, it can also increase the usability overhead (e.g. lost sessions, interrupted file transfers). In a later section, we provide a cost analysis for such re-configurations.

3 Need for Autonomic Computing Models

Over the past decade, several honey-based technologies have been developed to protect different portions of the network attack surface. These technologies provide protection at different levels including the network-level (e.g., honeypots [7, 19], deceptive networks toplogies [2, 6, 8, 21]), file-system level [3], application-level [17] and user-level [16]. Although individual technologies have proved to be effective at defending a small portion of the attack surface, different techniques need to be combined effectively to protect against adversaries at different stages of an attack campaign. Defense paradigms based on such a combination are referred to as *Deception-in-depth* [1].

Although deploying all known deception techniques would provide maximum protection, there are several constraints that hinder such a deployment. First, in a resource-constrained environment, deploying and managing large number of deception techniques may be infeasible. Monitoring alerts generated by the deception elements is integral to ensure effective deception. In an environment constrained by budget and security analysts, performing large-scale monitoring may be infeasible [10]. Alerts generated by these techniques can range from an early warning of an attack (e.g., port scan, accessing using a honey-password) to a large stream of attacker's action logs from a honeypot after it has been compromised.

Second, deploying multiple deception techniques may reduce utility of the underlying protected system. For instance, when honey-files are deployed, they co-exist with legitimate files within the protected system. If legitimate users erroneously access the honey-files, it increases the number of false positives, and the usability overhead incured by the user. Therefore, planning the configuration and deployment of deception techniques is critical to maximize the utility of the system.

Finally, the number of configurable parameters is large. For instance, Honeyd needs to be configured with a list of IP addresses to respond to and a set of personalities—defined as the OS, port and service scripts–for each IP address. Similarly, honey-file generation requires file properties and file contents. Determining the values of the configurable parameters presents two challenges: (1) Plausibility, and (2) Dynamicity. The main objective of a honey-based technologies is to entice attackers and divert their efforts away from legitimate systems. However, if an attacker is aware of deception, then it is critical to consider the *plausibility* of a legitimate machine/artifact having such a configuration. The plausibility of a configuration is an evaluation from an attacker's viewpoint. For instance, opening all ports on a honeypot may not seem plausible since it is unrealistic for any legitimate machine to host services on all ports. Therefore, if a honeypot is configured with all ports open, then it would not be effective against a deception-aware attacker. Similarly, the contents of honey-files need to be believable for an attacker to take the bait. In fact, in some of the recent attacks on honeywords [11], several honeywords are eliminated due to its implausibility. Therefore, while deploying honey-based technologies, it is critical to configure them such that the resulting deception *seems plausible*.

Additionally, the configuration of the honey-based techniques need to constantly change to evade repeated/persistent attackers. Current deployment of honey-based technologies provide proactive and static protection. However, given enough time, the attacker will be able to learn (either through active or passive operations) the configuration of honey-based technology and avoid it in subsequent attack attempts. Hence, it is critical to dynamically change the configuration of the honey-based technologies. These changes can be either periodic or use a informed-reactive approach, wherein the configuration changes are tailored to the attacker based on the attacker's history of observable actions. For instance, bots may propagate by scanning and compromising machines that have a specific vulnerable service while APT-style attackers may be interested in compromising a particular machine—by exploiting any vulnerable service—and use the machine as stepping stone for the next phase of the attack campaign. For the botnet scenario, it will effective to deploy several honeypots with few ports open (including the port the bot is targeting) to reduce the chances of compromising legitimate machines in subsequent stages. However, for the APT scenario, it would be effective to configure few honeypots with several vulnerable applications to entice the attacker.

Given the environmental constraints and the configurational complexity of deploying multiple deception techniques, we envision that models inspired from the autonomic computing paradigm will efficiently tackle these challenges.

3.1 Autonomic Computing

The goal of autonomic computing paradigm is to develop software systems and applications that can manage themselves based on high-level objectives [12]. Inspired from human autonomic nervous system, an autonomic computing system must be able to protect the system from attacks, recover from faults, reconfigure based on environmental changes and ensure near optimal performance. The paradigm was introduced to manage software intensive systems such as multi-robot system and networked smart homes, while guaranteeing user-specified goals under dynamic conditions.

An autonomic system is composed from autonomic elements that are expected to satisfy several self-management properties. Below, we discuss the central properties of self-management in the context of generating deceptive network surfaces.

- *Self-Configuration*: An autonomic computing system should be able to (re-)configure itself under varying and unpredictable conditions. In the context of deception, the system's configuration space can range from major infrastructure-level (re-)configuration such as deploying additional honeypots to minor policy-level (re-)configuration such as blocking access to a machine's port hosting a legitimate service.
- *Self-Optimization*: An autonomic system should optimize its use of resources. In the context of deception, the autonomic system should be able to manage its resources which includes available honey-based techniques, computational limits to monitor and process alerts, and bandwidth constraints to handle the excess traffic generated due to deception. Furthermore, decisions regarding the usage of these resources must also consider the usability overhead incurred as a result of their deployment.
- *Self-Healing*: An autonomic system should be able to detect and diagnose problems. In deception, the autonomic system must have the capability to monitor the deployed deception techniques. Such a monitoring capability is necessary to understanding the characteristics of the attacker which would be subsequently used for tailoring the deceptive network surface for that attacker.
- *Self-Protection*: An autonomic system protects itself from malicious attacks. In the context of deception, in addition to configuring and deploying the deception techniques as a proactive measures to detect the onset of an attack and an on-going attack, the autonomic system must take actions to minimize the impact of subsequent attacks.

The research challenges to realize systems that satisfy the autonomic computing properties can be divided into two broad categories: (1) Developing models to guide the (re-)configuration of the deceptive network surfaces and (2) System-level realization of the (re-)configuration recommendations by the models. We expand on these challenges in the next two sections.

3.2   Modeling Challenges

Developing a model that recommends a strategy for generating deceptive network surfaces presents four major challenges: (1) Summarizing the network traffic and characterizing the behavior of hosts, (2) Characterizing the overall state of the network, (3) Determining the feasible network surfaces subject to resource-constraints, and (4) Determining the (near-) optimal deceptive network surface for each host in the network that minimizes the impact of an attack.

Characterizing the behavior of a host based on its network traffic is critical to determine the state of the host i.e., whether or not the host is compromised.

Additionally, it is critical to determine the attacker's objectives and their modus operandi to tailor the deception maneuvers for the attacker. While traditional IDS systems inspect traffic for anomalous activities, it is not sufficient to determine the attacker's tactics or intentions. For instance, an IDS system can detect the presence of port scanning activity but cannot provide any information on whether the attacker's scanning style is stealthy or aggressive. Learning the attacker's behavior is critical to tailoring the deceptive network surface for the attacker. In a recent work, we developed hierarchical machine learning models to determine an attacker's risk-averseness and expertise based on their tools usage patterns [22]. Such models can be used to characterize certain behaviors of an attacker. However, a more extensive model is needed to completely characterize the attacker and inform deception maneuvers.

In addition to characterizing the state of a hosts (and the potential adversaries therein), it is critical to determine the overall state of the network to determine the optimal allocation of resources (e.g., honeypots, generation of fake traffic) across the entire network. However, identifying a compact representation of the state of the network is challenging. If the state of the network is coarse-grained (e.g., LOW, MED, HIGH likelihood of an attack), then there may not sufficient information in the state to recommend appropriate actions. On the other hand, if the state of the network is fine-grained (e.g., a vector representing a history of all activities of each host in the network), then it may lead to state space explosion.

The next challenge is determining the cost and expected reward of making modifications to the deceptive network surface for a host. The modification cost can be a combination of several costs such as operational cost (e.g., when introducing additional honey-machines) and usability cost (e.g., when legitimate users accessing honey machines). A nautral approach is to borrow ideas from utility theory to quantify these costs using a common unit of measurement before combining them [9]. Expected reward, on the other hand, is challenging to quantify as we only observe symptoms, if any, of whether or not the recommended action had the intended effect. This is further exasperated by the false positive and false negative rates of the IDS. In a deceptive environment, while modeling the expected reward, we must consider both the expected loss due to the proportion of attack traffic to the legitimate hosts and the expected gain due to proportion of attack traffic to a deceptive element [5].

Finally, the model is expected to make (re-)configuration recommendations that minimizes the impact of an attack. To this end, we envision that several models based on Partially Observable Markov Decision Process (POMDP) and Reinforcement Learning can be leveraged.

3.3 Architectural Challenges

As mentioned above, the model provides recommendations for (re-) configuration that need to be realized by presenting a different deceptive network surface to the hosts. Some of the re-configurations include adding new honeypots, adding background traffic for a particular host etc. To this end, ACyDS can modify the deceptive network surface for hosts within a network. However, one of biggest challenges is developing a framework that enables an *automated* realization of model's recommendations through ACyDS's capability and subsequently, observe the impact of the re-configuration on the adversary's actions, which in-turn, is condensed and forwarded to the model to obtain subsequent recommendations; thereby forming a closed loop. To tackle this challenge, in this chapter, we present a framework—called Autonomic models using Adaptive Cyber Deception System A^2CyDS—that can act as a common platform to study different autonomic computing models. We will first outline a well-known autonomic computing architecture called MAPE-K and then describe how it can be integrated with the ACyDS architecture.

4   Overview of MAPE-K

MAPE-K (monitor-analyze-plan-execute over a knowledge base) has become the de facto reference model to build autonomic systems with feedback loops in software engineering. Developed by IBM, MAPE-K was designed to realize the *autonomic element* architecture for self-adaptive systems shown in Fig. 5. The autonomic element are composed together to build large-scale autonomic systems. The autonomic element, at its core, is composed of a managed element and an autonomic manager with a feedback control loop. The manager consists of two interfaces to the sensors and effectors of the managed element and the MAPE-K engine. The monitor is designed to sense the managed element and its context, process the accumulated data from the sensors and transform them into events in the knowledge base for subsequent analysis. The analyzer references the knowledge base and compares the observed events against known symptom patterns; which subsequently triggers the planning process. The planner interprets the symptoms and

Fig. 5 The autonomic element by IBM [13]

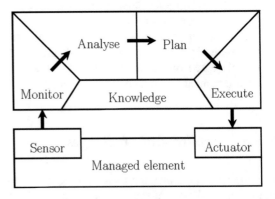

devises a plan that needs to be realized in the managed element using its actuators. The autonomic manager gathers measurement from the managed element and uses information from the history of states while prescribing changes to the managed element. In the next section, we describe how ACyDS can be used to realize some of the components the autonomic element and also, describe how the control theoretic models can be realized in the autonomic element.

5 A^2CyDS: Realizing Autonomic Element in ACyDS

To enable autonomic cyber deception using the autonomic element, we present a framework called A^2CyDS. To develop the framework, we first need to identify its core components; the managed element, the autonomic manager, and its subcomponents. A^2CyDS leverages ACyDS to realize the components associated with the managed element i.e., the sensor and the actuator. We envision that the research on developing autonomic computing models for cyber deception will provide the autonomic manager component of the A^2CyDS framework. Figure 6 provides a diagrammatic representation of the architecture.

In the case of cyber deception, the managed element is the behavior of the adversary in the network. While there are no means to directly observe the adversary's actions, we can infer the adversary's action by observing the traffic generated by the corresponding compromised host. As mentioned earlier, we can leverage existing machine learning models to determine the adversary type [22]. However, additional

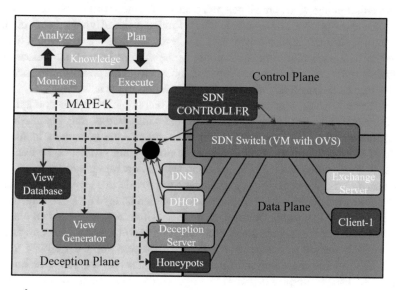

Fig. 6 A^2CyDS: Realizing the autonomic element by integrating MAPE-K with ACyDS

research is required to build an extensive model that characterizes adversaries along multiple dimensions.

In A^2CyDS, the SDN switch acts as the sensor by forwarding the network traffic stream to the monitor component of the autonomic manager. Here, we can configure the SPAN port on the SDN switch to mirror traffic to the monitor component. These ports are typically used to gain nonintrusive access to the traffic between two network devices.

We envision that the autonomic manager's monitor component will digest the input traffic and extract the state of all the hosts that were present in the traffic. The extracted state should be represented in a format compatible with the state of hosts in knowledge base. Since attacks occur infrequently, the analyzer inspects the state of the hosts and the network and determines the subset of hosts whose deceptive network surfaces need to be altered. After determining the candidate hosts, the planner determines the optimal re-configuration for each host. If an optimal action is already known (due to historical observation of the state), then the planner may re-use it to save computation time during the planning and execution stages. Here, the decision regarding how the deceptive network surfaces must be re-configured is governed by control theoretic models. Finally, the re-configuration strategy is passed it to the execution stage for it to take effect.

The execute stage parses the plans from the planner and communicates it to ACyDS. There are two main components to a re-configuration plan: the configuration of the network and the configuration of the deceptive elements. The execute stage interacts with the View Generator and the Deception Server components of ACyDS to implement the re-configuration plan(s). It interacts with the view generator to change the network views of the compromised host. In current implementation, the views are all generated ahead of time to offload the calculations. Using the view generator algorithm, we can make a list of views ahead of time, each with a different level of restriction. The execute stage's action would then be to switch to a particular view appropriate to the current level of suspicion. After switching to the new view, any subsequent requests from the compromised host will receive responses based on the network configuration in the new view.

The execute stage also interacts with the Deception Server to configure the deceptive elements. Two deceptive elements are configured during this interaction: honeypots and the fake broadcast traffic. To configure the honeypots in ACyDS, we have created templates for different operation system profiles to be used with HoneyD. Each profile includes information such as operating system flavor, open and closed ports. We expect the execute stage to provide two pieces of information to configure the honeypots: (1) IP addresses for which honeyd must respond, and (2) the operating system profile for each IP address. Upon receiving the two pieces of information from the execute stage, the deception server updates the configuration file in the honeypot and restarts the HoneyD process for the changes to take effect. The execute stage also informs the Deception server regarding the hosts for which fake background traffic needs to be generated. The Deception Server begins generating the background traffic to the corresponding hosts after a view change.

Finally, the execute stage signals the deception server to change the views of the hosts in the network. The deception server, in turn, updates the database to set the current view of the hosts to their corresponding new view, updates the honeypot configuration and begins generation of the broadcast traffic.

5.1 Overhead Cost Analysis

In this section, we analyze the cost of configuring the network to present different deceptive network surfaces to the hosts. There are two types of overhead cost: (1) instantaneous cost due to re-configuration of the network surface and the (2) maintenance cost to maintain the deceptive network surface. The instantaneous cost is the sum of overhead costs due to the view generation process, configuring the honeypots and usability cost during re-configuration. The maintenance cost is the sum of overhead costs due to packet re-writing process at the switch, generating fake broadcast traffic and usability cost due to broadcast traffic.

The instanenous cost due to the view generation process is composed of two factors: (1) Generating the view and (2) updating the database. The view generation algorithm's overhead is in generating the graph. For a network with V hosts and R transit nodes, then the time taken to generate the transit graph is $O(R \cdot M)$ (where M is a parameter of attachment) and the time taken to attach host nodes is $O(2 \cdot V)$ (one edge per host node). Therefore, the total time is $O(2 \cdot V + R \cdot M)$. After the generating the view, the time taken to update the database was observed to be negligible.

The instanenous cost to configure the honeypots was also observed to be negligible. However, the usability cost during re-configuration, can vary depending on the application type. For instance, HTTP-based applications generate short-lived connections, i.e., a request creates a connection and the response is delivered over that connection. Also, the time between requests is typically greater than the time to reconfigure. Therefore, if each request requires a name resolution to find the location of the server, then the cost of reconfiguration is negligible. However, if the application's state directly depends on the IP address of the server (which was obtained at the start of the session), then re-configuration can prove to be detrimental. Optimal time to switch views remains an open problem.

As mentioned earlier, to ensure network packets appear compatible with the receiving host's view, the switch re-writes the packet headers. We observed that the overhead cost due to this additional re-write operation was negligible. Similarly, we observed that the volume of background traffic generated was insignificant compared to the overall traffic. For instance, during a 1 h traffic capture, we observed that the broadcast traffic contributed to less than 0.1% of the overall traffic. However, introducing fake broadcast traffic can introduce an additional usability cost since fake machines become discoverable to the host. For instance, when fake NetBIOS traffic is introduced, then non-existent Windows machines will show up as NetBIOS-speaking endpoints to the host.

6   Conclusions and Future Work

In this chapter, we presented the challenges of developing an autonomic architecture for cyber deception, broadly categorized as modeling and architectural challenges. To tackle the architectural challenges, we presented a framework called A^2CyDS— that can act as a common platform to study different autonomic computing models. It uses an existing SDN-based architecture, ACyDS, to realize the components associated with the managed element i.e., the sensor and the actuator. ACyDS has the capability to generate views and introduce deceptive elements and present a deceptive network surface to hosts within a network. Current implemention of ACyDS can deploy and configure honeypots, and generate fake broadcast traffic. As part of our future work, we plan to include additional deceptive elements such as honey files and honey users to enrich the deceptive network surface.

Acknowledgements This research was sponsored by the U.S. Army Research Laboratory and was accomplished under Cooperative Agreement Number W911NF-13-2-0045 (ARL Cyber Security CRA). The views and conclusions contained in this document are those of the authors and should not be interpreted as representing the official policies, either expressed or implied, of the Army Research Laboratory or the U.S. Government. The U.S. Government is authorized to reproduce and distribute reprints for Government purposes notwithstanding any copyright notation here on.

References

1. Almeshekah MH, Spafford EH, Atallah MJ (2013) Improving security using deception. Center for Education and Research Information Assurance and Security, Purdue University, Tech. Rep. CERIAS Tech Report 13 (2013).
2. Achleitner S, Porta TL, McDaniel P, Sugrim S, Krishnamurthy SV, Chadha R (2016) Cyber deception: Virtual networks to defend insider reconnaissance. In Proceedings of the 8th ACM CCS international workshop on managing insider security threats, pp. 57–68.
3. Bercovitch M, Renford M, Hasson L, Shabtai A, Rokach L, Elovici Y (2011) HoneyGen: An automated honeytokens generator. In Intelligence and Security Informatics (ISI), 2011 IEEE International Conference on, pp. 131–136. IEEE.
4. BIND. http://www.bind9.ne.
5. Carroll TE, Daniel G (2011) A game theoretic investigation of deception in network security. Security and Communication Networks 4, no. 10: pp. 1162–1172.
6. Chiang CJ, Gottlieb YM, Sugrim S, Chadha R, Serban C, Poylisher A, Marvel LM, Santos J (2016) ACyDS: An adaptive cyber deception system. In Military Communications Conference, MILCOM 2016, pp. 800–805.
7. Dionaea. https://github.com/DinoTools/dionaea. Retrieved on 17 July 2018.
8. Duan Q, Al-Shaer E, Jafarian H (2013) Efficient random route mutation considering flow and network constraints. In IEEE Conference on Communications and Network Security (CNS), pp. 260–268.
9. Fishburn PC (1970) Utility theory for decision making. No. RAC-R-105. Research analysis corp McLean, VA.
10. Ganesan R, Jajodia S, Shah A, Cam H (2016) Dynamic scheduling of cybersecurity analysts for minimizing risk using reinforcement learning. ACM Transactions on Intelligent Systems and Technology (TIST) 8, no. 1: pp. 4.

11. Golla M, Beuscher B, Drmuth M (2016) On the security of cracking-resistant password vaults. In Proceedings of ACM SIGSAC Conference on Computer and Communications Security, pp. 1230–1241. ACM.
12. Huebscher MC, McCann JA (2008) A survey of autonomic computing - degrees, models, and applications. ACM Computing Surveys (CSUR) 40, no. 3: pp. 7.
13. IBM Group (2003) An architectural blueprint for autonomic computing. IBM White paper.
14. OpenFlow. https://www.opennetworking.org/software-defined-standards/specifications/, retrieved on 17 July 2018.
15. Jajodia S, Ghosh AK, Swarup V, Wang C, Wang XS, eds (2011) Moving target defense: creating asymmetric uncertainty for cyber threats.' Vol. 54. Springer Science & Business Media.
16. Juels A, Rivest RL (2013) Honeywords: Making password-cracking detectable. In Proceedings of ACM SIGSAC conference on Computer & communications security, pp. 145–160. ACM.
17. Kippo - SSH Honeypot. https://github.com/desaster/kippo. Retrieved on 3 November 2018.
18. Open vSwitch. https://www.openvswitch.org/. Retrieved on 17 July 2018.
19. Provos N (2003) Honeyd-a virtual honeypot daemon. In 10th DFN-CERT Workshop, Hamburg, Germany, vol. 2, p. 4.
20. RYU. https://osrg.github.io/ryu/. Retrieved on 5 October 2018.
21. Robertson S, Alexander S, Micallef J, Pucci J, Tanis J, Macera A (2015) CINDAM: Customized information networks for deception and attack mitigation. In IEEE International Conference on Self-Adaptive and Self-Organizing Systems Workshops (SASOW), pp. 114–119. IEEE.
22. Venkatesan S, Sugrim S, Izmailov R, Chiang CJ, Chadha R, Doshi B, Hoffman B, Newcomb EA, Buchler N. On Detecting Manifestation of Adversary Characteristics. Accepted in IEEE MILCOM, 2018.

Autonomous Security Mechanisms for High-Performance Computing Systems: Review and Analysis

Tao Hou, Tao Wang, Dakun Shen, Zhuo Lu, and Yao Liu

1 Introduction

High-performance computing (HPC) is a computing paradigm that features an extremely high computational capacity, which is typically measured in floating-point operations per second (FLOPS). Since its first implementation in 1960s by Seymour Cray at the University of Manchester [1], HPC has reached the peta-FLOPS level (e.g., Titan with over 20 peta-FLOPS at Oak Ridge National Laboratory [2]) and played an increasingly important role in various areas, which require significant amounts of computing resources, such as human being's daily life (e.g., weather forecasting [3]), government operations and national security (e.g., government projects [4] and nuclear reaction simulations [5]). Both the industry and governments across the world nowadays are investing abundant resources in the development of HPC, which in turn contributes to the proliferation and real-world impacts of HPC.

Due to important applications of HPC system and its computer and network architectures, there have been increased concerns regarding to security issues in HPC systems [6]. The immediate social impacts, importance and information sensitivity in HPC systems, have also become incentives for hackers or adversaries. As a result, it is necessary to take a careful, rigorous, and comprehensive exam at

T. Hou · Z. Lu (✉) · Y. Liu
University of South Florida, Tampa, FL, USA
e-mail: taohou@mail.usf.edu; zhuolu@usf.edu; yliu@cse.usf.edu

T. Wang
New Mexico State University, Las Cruces, NM, USA
e-mail: taow@nmsu.edu

D. Shen
Central Michigan University, Mount Pleasant, MI, USA
e-mail: dakun.shen@cmich.edu

© Springer Nature Switzerland AG 2020
S. Jajodia et al. (eds.), *Adaptive Autonomous Secure Cyber Systems*,
https://doi.org/10.1007/978-3-030-33432-1_6

109

the autonomous security mechanisms for HPC security and identify all potential vulnerabilities and threats.

Security issues in HPC systems can be inherited from conventional computers and network security issues, such as zero-day attacks that attempt to exploit known or unknown vulnerabilities in software [7]. In the security community, researchers have spent large efforts in improving security in traditional computers and network systems, such as anti-virus, anti-rootkit, intrusion detection, hypervisors, sandboxing and isolation [8]. However, simply retrofitting traditional mechanisms for HPC systems is inappropriate or ineffective for HPC security [9].

HPC systems are essential large-scale computing infrastructures, many of which can be remotely accessed by registered users from different research institutions or companies. This indicates that, on one hand, HPC systems require security protection mechanisms to prevent any suspicious activities or attempts from accessing sensitive information. On the other hand, such security mechanisms must be lightweight in a way that they will not significantly slow down the computing capability of HPC systems. Nor they should incur too much overhead such as memory, communication and storage. Therefore, as being critical infrastructures, HPC systems require a high level of security and efficiency.

In this chapter, we review and investigate potential security attacks and corresponding defense mechanisms for HPC systems, as well as discuss new security issues associated with HPC architectures and characteristics. In particular, we focus on the following perspectives.

- **HPC Design and Architecture Overview:** We provide a broad overview of HPC systems with detailed descriptions of HPC system history, development, state-of-the-art. We also analyze the typical architectures, software and hardware systems, and programming models for HPC systems.
- **Differences between HPC and General Computer:** As aforementioned, simply retrofitting conventional defense mechanisms of general-purpose computers is inappropriate for HPC systems. To better understand the challenges of security issues in HPC systems, we compare the differences between HPC systems and general-purpose computers from multiple aspects (e.g., application domain, system access, management system, programming model).
- **HPC Security Objectives and Threats:** Confidentiality, integrity, and availability are three high-level cyber security objectives. They are all important for HPC systems. We analyze potential security threats and vulnerabilities related to each of the objectives and classify them into four categories: infrastructure vulnerabilities, software bugs, weak access control and insider threats.
- **Security Mechanisms for HPC Systems.** Various security mechanisms have been developed for traditional computer and network systems. We summarize them and discuss in detail their application domains and how they can be used, modified, or tailored for HPC systems in a scalable, lightweight way.

The remainder of this chapter is organized as follows. In Sect. 2, we review the HPC design and architecture, and compare HPC systems with general-purpose computers. In Sect. 3, we describe the security objectives, existing and potential security threats, and case studies for HPC systems. Then, we discuss defense techniques and protection mechanisms for HPC systems in Sect. 4. Finally, we conclude this chapter in Sect. 5.

2 HPC Overview

In this section, we overview the HPC systems from the aspects of hardware, software, and programming model as the preliminary and address the key differences between HPC systems and general-purpose computers.

2.1 HPC Architecture

HPC is designed to deliver a significantly higher computing performance than general-purpose computers. It is widely used in the fields of research, commerce and national security [10]. An HPC system consists of hardware (e.g., CPU/GPU, memory), software (e.g., operating systems and HPC management software) and a high-speed communication network that connects all hardware and software in the system. Figure 1 shows an example of the architecture of HPC systems. In general, an HPC system includes several types of computer/network nodes that can be classified as login nodes, service nodes, compute nodes and storage nodes according to their different functionalities. The supercomputer Titan [11] deployed at Oak Ridge National Laboratory is a representative example of such an architecture shown in Fig. 1.

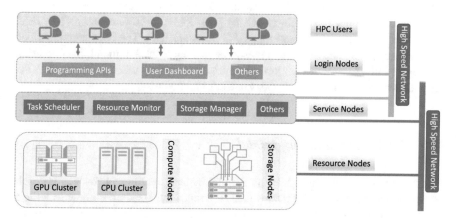

Fig. 1 The general architecture of HPC systems

As Fig. 1 shows, the login nodes work as interfaces between users and HPC core components. Through the login nodes, users can access the HPC system and submit jobs to the service scheduler. The service scheduler usually runs at the service nodes to coordinate the running status of the whole system. A submitted job by a user will be assigned to a (substantial) number of compute nodes in a manner that the loads among all compute nodes are balanced according to a scheduling algorithm. Then, the compute nodes start running the job until the job is finished. The input and output data is stored in the storage nodes. Considering the high computing speed, a high-bandwidth network between nodes is needed for efficient data transportation. A recent network standard, InfiniBand (aiming for a bandwidth of hundreds of GBps), has been developed and deployed widely in HPC today [12].

Since being proposed in 2007 by Nvidia [13], GPUs have been serving as a major computing power in HPC systems to speed up the performance. GPUs' massively parallel architectures (e.g., float point computing) and high power-efficiency are very suitable for scientific computing [14]. Titan is a typical example that benefits from the massive use of GPUs. Titan's computing performance is several times better than its predecessor Jaguar, while only using marginally more electricity and the same occupied space [15].

2.2   HPC Management Platform

How to organize HPC hardware components in a coordinated, balanced manner to yield the highest efficiency is challenging. Torque resource manager [16] and the Simple Linux Utility for Resource Management (SLURM) [17] are two popular applications in HPC systems. Both of them are open-source systems and provide fine-grained resource management as well as easy-to-use user interface. There are also companies developed many commercial solutions to manage HPC systems, such as Cray Linux Environment (CLE) [18], Red Hat HPC solution [19], IBM Spectrum Computing [20], and Sun HPC Software [21]. The core functionalities of these software platforms are (1) resource management that monitors computing resources in HPC systems; (2) job scheduling that decides when to run users' HPC applications in which compute nodes in a coordinated way.

2.3   HPC Programming Model

Message Passing Interface (MPI) is the dominant programming model for developing applications in HPC systems [22]. It defines the standard on how to write a portable and scalable HPC program in an efficient way. C, C++, Fortran and many other languages are able to interface with the libraries that can be used for writing MPI programs that work in the point-to-point mode or the collective communication mode. The newest version of MPI is MPI 3.1 that is proposed in 2016. There are many HPC service vendors that develop improved implementations of MPI. IBM Spectrum MPI [23] and Intel MPI Library [24] are two examples built upon the open-source MPI [25] for better performance and easy-to-use interfaces.

Though MPI is still used widely, a new programming model Map-Reduce [26] has received increasing attention recently. It can work as a complementary to MPI in HPC systems. In general, Map-Reduce can achieve a better performance with a lower requirement of hardware and it is more suitable for data intensive workloads [26]. This model provides a higher abstraction of low level details and is more convenient for users to write parallelized programs. A number of popular systems have been proposed on top of Map-Reduce, such as Hadoop [27], Spark [28], Storm [29], Flink [30], and Samza [31].

2.4 Key Differences Between HPC and General Computer

There are a number of differences between HPC systems and general-purpose computers. To address the HPC security issues in a more comprehensive way, we need to take into account both traditional security issues for general-purpose computers and new problems specifically related to HPC systems. We compare HPC systems and general-purpose computers from the aspects of application domain, system access, users, architecture and hardware, management system, and programming model in Table 1.

3 HPC Security Objectives and Threats

In this section, we first present the security objectives and requirements for HPC systems. Then, we categorize the potential security threats with case studies.

3.1 HPC Security Requirements

Confidentiality, integrity, and availability are three major objectives for security. The security for HPC is no exception. Before introducing the security threats and vulnerabilities, we first introduce the high-level security objectives for HPC from the following three perspectives.

- **Confidentiality**: Ensuring confidentiality implies restrictions on access to or disclosure of sensitive information. For HPC applications which may be related to sensitive business, scientific, or government applications, the data is usually sensitive and it is important for the participants to request a high level of

Table 1 Key differences between HPC systems and general-purpose computers

Aspect	Differing from general-purpose computers	Security challenges and opportunities
Application domain	HPC systems are used for distinct purposes, especially for fields related to scientific research, national security, large business operations and so on. These fields usually are computing resources demanding and also are sensitive to performance overhead	• The security mechanisms implemented in HPC systems must have more fine-grained policies to provide a more stronger protection than on general-purpose computers • The protection mechanisms for HPC systems must take efforts to reduce the performance overhead • The number of HPC applications can be limited, thus the code execution behaviors can be more predictable
System access	HPC systems are usually maintained by professionals in HPC facilities, and the systems can only be accessed remotely by authorized users	• It is difficult to launch traditional attacks that require physical access (e.g., audio monitor and behavior detector) to the computer systems • Due to the privileges for the system administrators and users, HPC systems usually face more serious insider threats which can be launched by internal staff or users • The number of scenarios for user access to the system are limited. Thus, a more restricted and refined access policy can be implemented through hardware or software isolation
Users	Unlike general-purpose computers that only have a limited number of users, HPC systems usually need to serve a large number of users which may come from different research institutions or companies	• HPC system administrators need to carefully examine new user account applications, and grant appropriate levels of authorities to users according to their requirements and HPC applications • User based access control policy can be refined
Architecture and hardware	The architecture of an HPC system consists of distributed compute nodes connected by high-speed networking	• It is more challenging to maintain a steady running status of HPC systems due to the complicated architecture • Due to the distributed architecture of HPC systems, different components usually need to be connected through networks, and thus the communication requirement in HPC systems is also demanding. It is necessary to implement appropriate mechanisms to ensure efficient, reliable data communication

(continued)

Table 1 (Continued)

Aspect	Differing from general-purpose computers	Security challenges and opportunities
Management system	The management systems for HPC usually are Unix/Linux based systems, Only limited system services are allowed to reduce the system performance overhead	• Some traditional security softwares and defense techniques with large overheads may not be applicable for HPC systems, while some traditional attacks may not work either • Unlike the general-purpose computers, the number of system-level defense techniques are limited for HPC management systems due to overhead and architecture constraints. This is also an opportunity for researchers to develop highly customizable HPC security mechanisms
Programming model	Unlike general computers, the key techniques for programming in HPC systems are how to manage the distributed computing resources and how to handle the communications between different components	• HPC programming models usually are developed for specific purposes. The security related tests and evaluations are always inefficient • Some new models (e.g., Hadoop, Spark) are still in their early stages of development. There may also exist vulnerabilities • The communication component and the resource management component may expose some security issues

confidentiality to protect their interests. Therefore, the data in HPC should be carefully protected to ensure confidentiality.

- **Integrity**: Integrity guards against unintended or malicious data or execution flow modification. A loss of integrity means that any data information associated with HPC systems is modified/tampered in an illegal way by potential attackers, hackers, or even insider threats. For HPC, the guarantee of integrity is nontrivial, because even a minimal change of data or execution flow in HPC can lead to a serious impact.
- **Availability**: Ensuring the system resources can be readily accessed by users. Considering that HPC is generally used for important applications (e.g., weather forecast, aerospace research and nuclear simulation), it should have a high level of availability, and make sure users can access the resources in a timely and reliable way.

In what follows, we analyze the potential security threats and vulnerabilities in HPC systems to understand how they may compromise the three major security objectives. Then, we present our case studies of security threats in real-world HPC systems.

3.2   Potential Security Threats and Vulnerabilities

In order to find effective defense mechanisms that can be used for protecting HPC systems from potential security threats and vulnerabilities, we need to carefully look at the objectives of confidentiality, integrity, and availability. An attacker can target one or more security objectives. To this end, attackers may attempt to leverage some vulnerabilities or design flaws. Typical causes of such vulnerabilities, flaws or other exploits that lead to such attacks include infrastructure vulnerabilities, software bugs, weak access control and insider threats.

- **Infrastructure vulnerabilities**: As introduced in Sect. 2, the underlying software and hardware of HPC are specifically designed for specific purposes. HPC developers must pay attention to provide a flexible and scalable system for a high performance. The lack of sufficient security knowledge and skills in the development of the HPC infrastructure may incur vulnerabilities. For example, data exchange among different HPC nodes without encryption will lead to information leaks. Furthermore, as there may exist a limited number of users in an HPC system, insufficient use, testing or evaluation of the system can make users overlook the potential security issues.

  The vulnerabilities in infrastructures will directly influence the availability of HPC systems. The carelessness in design, testing or deployment of infrastructures can result in a high probability of hardware/software accidents, which will lead to dysfunction or even shut the whole system down. The confidentiality and integrity may also be influenced by this type of vulnerability, when the data is damaged by accidents or the vulnerabilities exploited by attackers.

- **Software bugs**: Software bug is the major reason that accounts for various computer vulnerabilities and attacks. It is hard to eliminate software bugs completely. The HPC programming model is more complex than general-purpose computers. Developers need to take into account concurrency, communication, load balancing, job scheduling and some other HPC characteristics. Software bugs may also exist due to the lack of sufficient software testing.

  There are various kinds of software bugs that can be exploited by attackers to target the three major security objectives. A bug may be a flaw, error, failure or fault that affects the running of the system [32], thus leading to a system crash and accordingly the loss of availability. Some serious bugs (e.g., buffer overflow [33]) can be leveraged by malicious users to obtain unauthorized privileges or sensitive information, thereby compromising confidentiality and integrity in HPC systems.

- **Weak access control**: Different users should be granted different levels of privileges to the system resources by access control. Through this mechanism, the administrator can secure the system and prevent the leaking of sensitive information. A strong access control mechanism and careful management of users' accesses are needed for HPC systems. Weak access control in HPC systems can be exploited by existing attack strategies, such as Replay Attacks [34], Non-Control-Data Attacks [35], and Privilege Escalation Attacks [36]. This results in broken confidentiality and integrity of the system.

- **Insider threats**: Insider threats come from the situation that a legitimate user utilizes his/her permission to conduct unauthorized activities that negatively affect the system. These threats may be actively launched by some malicious users or passively activated by carelessness (e.g., running malware in the system or clicking on a phishing link). These threats usually are hard to be noticed and prevented by the protection mechanism and can always lead to a serious effect on the system. Insider threats are increasingly dangerous threats to today's computers, including general-purpose computers and HPC systems. According to CMU-CERT database, there has been more than 1300 insider threat crimes recorded in US since 2001 [37]. It is vital for organizations to detect and deter insider threats.

The incidents involving malicious and inadvertent insiders may lead to a wide range of risks to the system. An inside threat can compromise all the security aspects of an HPC system.

3.3 Case Studies

Next, we use case studies to understand the real-world HPC vulnerabilities, most of which are related to Cray's systems. Cray is a major HPC manufacturer that introduced the world's first supercomputer in 1976 [1]. Cray provides the overall solutions of supercomputers, including both hardware and software. We analyze two exposed vulnerabilities from Common Vulnerabilities and Exposures (CVE) [38] for infrastructure vulnerabilities, software bugs, and weak access control in Cray's HPC systems. We also analyze a recent real-world case [39] to study the insider threats. All the case studies are summarized in Table 2.

4 Defense Techniques and Protection Mechanisms for HPC systems

In the literature, a number of defense techniques and protection mechanisms have been proposed for computer and network security. In this section, we individually review in detail these security strategies and discuss their potential applications to HPC systems.

4.1 Static Analysis and Dynamic Analysis

Software bugs have been a major threat to computer security for decades. The threat of software bugs to HPC systems is more challenging to eliminate due to

Table 2 Case studies on real-world HPC vulnerabilities

Category	The details of the threat or vulnerability
Infrastructure vulnerabilities	**CVE-2014-0748**: APrun and APinit are task schedulers on Cray's supercomputers. APrun accepts the commands from users to run applications, and it forwards an HPC application to APinit which runs on different computing nodes to cooperatively finish the execution of the applications. However, APrun does not validate the user ID in a submitted task, which allows the attacker to execute commands as an arbitrary user and even to escalate his privilege to root
	Spectre (CVE-2017-5753 and CVE-2017-5715) and Meltdown (CVE-2017-5754): These vulnerabilities have very serious impacts on a wide range of devices including Cray's products. These vulnerabilities are caused by the hardware weakness in processors. The operating system and application running on top of the processors are also affected. For these vulnerabilities, malicious users can exploit the system in different ways, however the key technique is side-channel attacks that utilize the speculative execution and branch prediction of processors to disclose unauthorized sensitive information
Software bugs	**CVE-2006-0177**: In Cray UNICOS system, there are multiple buffer overflow vulnerabilities that allow users to locally exploit the system to escalate privileges. The main issue of this vulnerability is that the system lacks the validation of the command strings in various applications with SetUID privileges in UNICOS. The attack can be launched by attaching a long string in the tail of /usr/bin/script, or setting a long file name as the parameter of /etc/nu
	CVE-2001-0891: The Network Queuing System (NQS) is a both batch and device queue system. This vulnerability is a format string vulnerability in NQS daemon service in the Network Queuing Environment (NQE) for CRAY UNICOS system. A local account can use qsub in NQS to submit a task with malicious name that contains formatting characters to escalate his privilege
Weak access control	**CVE-1999-1300**: Command accton usually is used to track a user's behavior and monitor resource consumption. Granting permission is required to use this command. However, Cray UNICOS system has a vulnerability that allows arbitrary users to run accton
	CVE-1999-1468: This vulnerability is caused by the weak access control of program /usr/ucb/rdist. Local users can leverage this vulnerable program to create SetUID programs, and further gain root privileges by compromising the Internal Field Separator parameter
Insider threats	**Report from Russian news service Mash [40]**: It's reported that Russian scientists were arrested by Federal Security Service (FSB) of Russian in Feb, 2018. The reason is that these scientists utilize their access to the supercomputer deployed at Federal Nuclear Centre in Sarov, Russia, to illegally mine Bitcoins. According to the report, this supercomputer is used for nuclear warhead research, and it is one of the most powerful supercomputers in Russia

the wide use of non-type-safe languages (e.g., C and C++) for efficiency and high performance [41]. Discovering and fixing the bugs in HPC softwares are non-trivial and it is challenging for developers to achieve these manually. Many automated techniques have been developed to address this problem in the traditional computer security domain.

Static analysis and dynamic analysis are two important approaches that can be used for the detection of software bugs. Static analysis can discover bugs and logical errors in software without running the code [42]. In contrast, dynamic analysis is used for the run-time testing and evaluation of softwares during the execution [43]. Traditional analysis techniques are time-consuming and not efficient [44, 45]. For HPC systems, many attempts have been made by researchers to reduce the performance overhead. They have proposed many new techniques that can perform static analysis and dynamic analysis in HPC systems.

Clang [46] is widely used for developing HPC applications, it's a C/C++ /Objective-C compiler built on the LLVM architecture [47]. Clang can not only achieve a high performance for compiling, but also provide detailed and useful debug messages. The core part of Clang is Clang Static Analyzer (CSA) [48] that can perform path-sensitive static analysis on target programs to discover bugs. A range of tools was developed on top of Clang to provide a more suitable solution for static analysis. They usually aim at a specific aspect of HPC applications, such as MARMOT [49], MPI-ICFG [50], Spin [51], Umpire [52], and MPI-Checker [53].

DAMPI [54] is a dynamic analyzer that can improve the coverage rate in finding bugs by checking the non-determinism paths of target programs. DAMPI provides scalable run-time analysis of a target program through a decentralized analysis algorithm based on Lamport-clocks [55]. In [56], the authors proposed a lightweight automatic test tool called QuickCheck that can enforce the dynamic analysis in HPC applications. The work in [57] proposed a technique that combines static analysis and dynamic analysis to reduce the overhead and improve the accuracy rate. A tool called Archer is implemented on top of this technique. Archer firstly applies static analysis through a customized version of Clang to identify the safe and unsafe regions of an HPC application. Then, it passes the unsafe regions to the dynamic analysis module which is built based on ThreadSanitizer [58]. By the run-time checking of unsafe regions, it can avoid the false diagnosis and achieve a higher accuracy rate.

Another notable challenge for implementing analysis tools in HPC is that the techniques should be scalable. HPC systems usually are distributed systems with a significant number of nodes. Concurrency and asynchrony are two important features for HPC applications. Wrong configurations of these two features may lead to bugs. When performing analysis in HPC applications, it's vital to take these two features into consideration. In this regard, the traditional bug discovery methods are not effective enough for HPC systems. The authors of [59] proposed a tool called Distributed Execution Minimizer (DEMi) to address this issue. DEMi can discover concurrency and asynchrony related vulnerabilities in a scalable way. DEMi can achieve a low performance overhead as well by minimizing the faulty execution in analysis. ORNL also proposed a tool called Hyperion [60], which can perform static analysis on a binary program to detect vulnerabilities in a scalable way.

4.2   Access Control

HPC systems have usually a number of users that come from different institutions or companies. It is necessary for HPC systems to ensure proper access control policies to protect private data and prevent unauthorized accesses to sensitive resources[61]. Traditionally, there are mainly two families of access control policy: (1) the Discretionary Access Control (DAC) model [62], which delegates the security policy to the users. The owner of an object restricts the access of different subjects to this object by defining an Access Control List. (2) the Mandatory Access Control (MAC) model [63] that is enforced by system administrators with strong security guarantees. MAC defines a set of rules to restrict the ability of a subject to access an object.

Researchers have made substantial efforts to implement access control mechanisms in HPC systems to enhance the security. Linux Security Modules (LSM) [64] is a kernel level security framework that has been adopted in the Linux kernel as a standard component. AppArmor [65], Security-Enhanced Linux (SELinux)[66], Smack [67], TOMOYO Linux [68], and Yama [69] are five widely used security modules included in LSM. These modules enforce DAC or MAC policies to achieve the security goals. They have been integrated in most Linux distributions, including many operating systems developed for HPC. The administrator of an HPC system can select one of these modules to enforce the access control policy according to his/her requirements.

Despite these general enforcement solutions, there are customized, proprietary access control mechanisms. One of the pioneer approaches in implementing access control for HPC is Distributed Security Infrastructure (DSI) [70] by Ericsson. DSI provides APIs for implementing an access control mechanism at the kernel level, and it is highly configurable and easy-to-use in the distributed environment. IBM Security Access Manager (SAM) [71] is a platform that can address the complexity of deployment of access control. In [72], the authors presented a method called RelBAC that can adapt the MAC mechanism to enforce confidentiality and integrity for HPC systems. The authors in [73] proposed an advanced MAC mechanism that can enforce access control for HPC systems in an efficient way.

4.3   Behavior Monitoring

Behavior monitoring can help the administrator to identify malicious activities, so as to stop an attempt to compromise the system or leak of sensitive information. Furthermore, this mechanism can defend against insider threats, in which a person with legitimate access abuses or misuses such access for malicious purposes. In addition, through the analysis of the data from monitoring, we can have an insight of the execution flow of an application, thus may be able to improve the performance and security by optimizing or redesigning a part of the application. However, it is challenging to develop and deploy behavior monitoring mechanisms for HPC systems.

The monitoring system for HPC must be scalable and have less performance overhead on the system. A scalable, high-efficiency monitoring system [74] has been developed at LANL that hosts supercomputers manufactured by various vendors. A monitoring technique has been proposed in [75] to "fingerprint" the code of HPC applications by monitoring and analyzing the communication pattern and computational elements at the application level. This technique can reveal the actual behavior of HPC program execution at a low performance overhead along with a high degree of accuracy. In [76], a monitoring system called DPEM is developed for HPC to detect run-time attacks by identifying the security-relevant behavior.

The main challenge in implementing behavior monitoring is the tradeoff between performance overhead, flexibility, and debugging. Unix kernel functionality Ptrace [77] is used in many implementations (such as [78, 79]) of behavior monitoring. This method is easy-to-implement without modification of the kernel. However, Ptrace is slow and produces a high performance overhead. An alternative approach is modifying the kernel, which reduces the performance overhead but requires more knowledge of the system to modify the kernel and run the monitoring in the privileged mode. In [80], the authors proposed VARAN, an architecture that uses the system calls to monitor the execution. VARAN runs in the user space with a small performance overhead, which is suitable for implementing behavior monitoring for HPC systems.

4.4 Randomization

Randomization is a useful method to defend against memory corruption attacks. Buffer overflow attacks are typically used in memory corruption attacks. The key point of randomization is to make the prediction of the next state of programs's execution more difficult. There are several types of randomization mechanisms that have been developed, such as Address Space Layout Randomization (ASLR) [81], Instruction Randomization (ILR) [82], and Data Space Randomization (DSR) [83]. These mechanisms achieve security by applying location randomization at different levels. ASLR was proposed in Pax Project to prevent the attacks by randomizing memory locations of a process. ILR implements a specific and randomized instruction set for different processes in order to defeat the injection of malicious code. DSR can achieve a wider range of randomization than the previous two methods by randomizing data storage in memory [83].

In HPC systems, randomization is still effective to defend against memory corruption attacks. For example, ASLR can utilize the characteristics of HPC software and hardware to achieve the goal of randomization in a more efficient way. Leveraging software and hardware in HPC differing from general-purpose computers (e.g., heterogeneous chip multiprocessors and heterogeneous-ISA). [84] proposed a mechanism called Heterogeneous-ISA Program State Relocation (HIPStR) to enforce the randomization. The key idea of HIPStR is that the target programs are allowed to run in a random state through the technique of Instruction Set Randomization, which makes it hard to perform code injection attacks.

4.5   Control Flow Integrity

Randomization is mainly used to combat code injection attacks but it lacks the ability to defend against code reuse attacks, such as Return-Oriented Programming (ROP) attacks [85]. Control Flow Integrity (CFI) [86] can be effective in preventing this type of attacks by restricting the execution flow of the program in a validated state. CFI follows a two-phase process: (1) analysis phase, in which a Control-Flow Graph (CFG) is built to indicate the legitimate states for the software execution flow [86], (2) enforcement phase, in which the execution flow must follow the CFG built in the analysis phase. Compared with other memory based defense mechanisms, CFI can assure a higher level of security while making a lower performance overhead [87]. Because of its lightweight overhead, CFI can become a promising protection mechanism for HPC systems.

CFI can be implemented at both compiler level or binary level. Compiler-level CFI is more accurate and efficient due to the availability of source code. Binary-level CFI can be implemented without the source code by reverse-engineering, analyzing and instrumenting the binaries. Binary-level CFI is less accurate than compiler-level CFI; however, it enables CFI to be enforced in a broader and more general way without the requirement of source code.

Existing efforts have been focused on integrating CFI into two widely-used compilers, GCC and LLVM/Clang. In [88], the authors proposed an implementation of a fine-grained, forward-edge CFI enforcement on top of GCC and LLVM. This implementation has been adopted by the Clang community and integrated to the Clang project [89]. The performance overhead of this implementation can be as low as 2% [88]. Binary-level CFI is more difficult to implement, the research community has achieved notable progresses recently. The work in [90] developed a robust CFI enforcement tool called BinCFI for commercial off-the-shelf (COTS) binaries, which includes efficient disassembly, static analysis, and instrumentation for 32-bit binaries.

4.6   Multi-execution

Information leaking [91] may be caused by software bugs or malicious behaviors. For HPC systems, information leaking can raise more concerns because of the sensitivity of HPC data. In [92], the authors introduced an approach called shadow execution that can successfully prevent the leaking of sensitive information. In shadow execution, there are two copies of the original program, they run the same code but with different data. One is the private copy that is isolated from the public network, but its inputs include the user's confidential data. Another copy is the public copy that runs with non-confidential inputs and can access the network. Dominique and Frank in [93] proposed a technique called secure multi-execution. The main idea is to execute a program multiple times with different levels of sensitive data for different security levels, thus stoping the leaking of sensitive information. Their experimental results showed that the execution of secure multi-execution can be even faster than standard execution for certain programs. In [94], the authors implemented multi-execution in a way that does not request different copies for different levels of security. Only a single program is run with multiple variants with different inputs.

Multi-execution achieves a high level of security at the cost of substantial performance overhead. For HPC systems, this challenge can be partly eliminated by parallelism processing and taking advantage of ideal processors. For example, Babak proposed multi-execution environment (MVEE) that engages the idle cores in HPC systems to reduce the performance overhead [79]. This technique uses only a user-space MVEE without any kernel modification.

4.7   Fault Tolerance

HPC systems demand a high degree of availability. Usually, there are multiple users with different jobs running in an HPC system at the same time. The requirement of availability means that HPC systems must be capable of fault tolerance. Several studies have shown that faults occur in a large-scale system and tend to appear more frequently in HPC systems [95–97]. The manufacturing problems, overheating, hardware/software vulnerabilities, or power supply loss all lead to system faults [98]. Furthermore, a fault happening on one node may sequentially affect other nodes in HPC systems. Google recently developed Mega [99] that can work in large-scale distributed systems to address this issue. Microsoft also proposed Byzantine Fault Tolerance (BFT) [100] to tolerate Byzantine faults (e.g., wrong instructions and operator mistakes) by a state machine replication algorithm. Nysiad [101] and Thema [102] are implementation examples of BFT. In contrast to BFT, [103] proposed a scheme named Scalable Error Isolation (SEI). Without the requirement of replication, SEI leads a low space and performance overhead. It ensures fault tolerance with the minimal change of a program and it can be deployed in a scalable manner. SEI can utilize hardware features (i.e., error correction codes) to minimize the overhead.

Table 3 Overview of typical security defense mechanisms in HPC systems

Technique	Detection? Protection?	Addressed threats	Performance overhead
Static analysis	Detection	• Software bugs	No run-time overhead
Dynamic analysis	Detection	• Software bugs	Need to run the code for testing, no run-time overhead
Access control	Protection	• Weak access control	The overhead is low
Behavior monitoring	Detection	• Software bugs • Insider threats	The overhead is high if real-time data collection is needed
Randomization	Protection	• Infrastructure vulnerabilities • Software bugs	The overhead is low
Control flow integrity	Protection	• Infrastructure vulnerabilities • Software bugs	Fine-grained—high Coarse-grained—low
Multi-execution	Protection	• Software bugs	The overhead is high
Fault tolerance	Protection	• Infrastructure vulnerabilities • Software bugs	Traditional methods store replications with a high overhead The new techniques can reduce the overhead

4.8 Summary and Discussion

Overall, we summarize typical defense mechanisms and their potential application domains in HPC systems in Table 3. As shown in Table 3, a defense mechanism is usually developed to address a specific kind of vulnerability. We loosely categorize them in "detection" and "protection" categories. It is vital to develop both detection and protection mechanisms. We can see that the performance overhead is usually low or even no run-time overhead for detection mechanisms. However, protection mechanisms do incur overhead for HPC systems.

In practice, HPC system administrators may choose the proper techniques to achieve the balance between the security and performance to defend against different vulnerabilities be exploited according to their requirements.

5 Conclusions

HPC systems are important in the fields of research, commerce, and national security. It is nontrivial to ensure a fully secure environment for HPC systems. In this chapter, we summarize the efforts that have been made for the purpose of securing HPC systems. We provide an overview of HPC systems, and analyze the potential threats and vulnerabilities in HPC systems. We also carefully review existing defense mechanisms from the aspects of implementation, methodology, application, and performance in HPC systems. This chapter can help HPC administrators and users understand the big picture of HPC security and the potential use of defense strategies in HPC systems.

References

1. Erich Strohmaier, Jack J Dongarra, Hans W Meuer, and Horst D Simon. The marketplace of high-performance computing. *Parallel Computing*, 25(13):1517–1544, 1999.
2. Oak Ridge National Laboratory. Introducing Titan. https://www.olcf.ornl.gov/titan/.
3. J Michalakes, J Dudhia, D Gill, T Henderson, J Klemp, W Skamarock, and W Wang. The weather research and forecast model: software architecture and performance. In *Proc. of ECMWF*, 2005.
4. Lorin Hochstein, Taiga Nakamura, Victor R Basili, Sima Asgari, Marvin V Zelkowitz, Jeffrey K Hollingsworth, Forrest Shull, Jeffrey Carver, Martin Voelp, Nico Zazworka, et al. Experiments to understand HPC time to development. *CTWatch Quarterly*, 2(4A), 2006.
5. Dan Gabriel Cacuci. *Handbook of Nuclear Engineering*, volume 2. Springer Science & Business Media, 2010.
6. Dewayne Adams. Six security risks in high performance computing (HPC). http://patriot-tech.com/six-security-risks-in-high-performance-computing-hpc/.
7. Curtis M Keliiaa and Jason R Hamlet. National cyber defense high performance computing and analysis: Concepts, planning and roadmap. *SANDIA Report*, 2010.
8. Matt Bishop. What is computer security? *IEEE Security & Privacy*, 1(1):67–69, 2003.
9. Alex Malin and Graham Van Heule. Continuous monitoring and cyber security for high performance computing. In *Proc. of ACM CLHS*, 2013.
10. insideHPC. What is high performance computing? http://insidehpc.com/hpc-basic-training/what-is-hpc/.
11. Oak Ridge National Laboratory. Titan user guide. https://www.olcf.ornl.gov/support/system-user-guides/titan-user-guide/.
12. Jiuxing Liu, Jiesheng Wu, and Dhabaleswar K Panda. High performance rdma-based mpi implementation over infiniband. *International J. of Parallel Programming*, 32(3):167–198, 2004.
13. David Luebke. CUDA: Scalable parallel programming for high-performance scientific computing. In *Proc. of IEEE ISBI*, 2008.
14. NVIDIA. What is GPU-accelerated computing? http://www.nvidia.com/object/what-is-gpu-computing,html.
15. Oak Ridge National Laboratory. ORNL debuts Titan supercomputer. https://www.olcf.ornl.gov/wp-content/themes/olcf/titan/Titan_Debuts.pdf.
16. Garrick Staples. Torque resource manager. In *Proc. of ACM/IEEE conference on Supercomputing*, 2006.
17. Amjad Majid Ali, Don Albert, Par Andersson, Ernest Artiaga, Daniel Auble, Susanne Balle, Anton Blanchard, Hongjia Cao, Daniel Christians, Gilles Civario, et al. Simple linux utility for resource management. Technical report, Lawrence Livermore National Laboratory, 2008.
18. Cray. Cray Linux Environment (CLE) software release overview. http://docs.cray.com/books/S-2425-52xx/.
19. Redhat. Redhat HPC solution. http://www.dell.com/downloads/global/solutions/vslc/redhat_hpc_solution.pdf.
20. IBM. IBM Spectrum Computing accelerates high-performance and data-intensive workloads. https://www.ibm.com/spectrum-computing.
21. Stephen Booth and Elson Mourao. Single sided MPI implementations for SUN MPI. In *Proc. of IEEE SC*, 2000.

22. William Gropp, Ewing Lusk, Nathan Doss, and Anthony Skjellum. A high-performance, portable implementation of the MPI message passing interface standard. *Parallel computing*, 22(6):789–828, 1996.
23. IBM. IBM Spectrum MPI. https://www.ibm.com/us-en/marketplace/spectrum-mpi.
24. Intel. Intel MPI Library. https://software.intel.com/en-us/intel-mpi-library.
25. Edgar Gabriel, Graham E Fagg, George Bosilca, Thara Angskun, Jack J Dongarra, Jeffrey M Squyres, Vishal Sahay, Prabhanjan Kambadur, Brian Barrett, Andrew Lumsdaine, et al. Open mpi: Goals, concept, and design of a next generation mpi implementation. In *Proc. of Springer European PVM*. Springer, 2004.
26. Grant Mackey, Saba Sehrish, John Bent, Julio Lopez, Salman Habib, and Jun Wang. Introducing map-reduce to high end computing. In *Proc. of PDSW*, 2008.
27. Andrzej Bialecki, Michael Cafarella, Doug Cutting, and Owen OMalley. Hadoop: a framework for running applications on large clusters built of commodity hardware. *Wiki at http://lucene.apache.org/hadoop*, 11, 2005.
28. Matei Zaharia, Mosharaf Chowdhury, Michael J Franklin, Scott Shenker, and Ion Stoica. Spark: cluster computing with working sets. *HotCloud*, 10:10–10, 2010.
29. Ankit Toshniwal, Siddarth Taneja, Amit Shukla, Karthik Ramasamy, Jignesh M Patel, Sanjeev Kulkarni, Jason Jackson, Krishna Gade, Maosong Fu, Jake Donham, et al. Storm @ twitter. In *Proc. of ACM SIGMOD*, 2014.
30. Paris Carbone, Stephan Ewen, Seif Haridi, Asterios Katsifodimos, Volker Markl, and Kostas Tzoumas. Apache flink: Stream and batch processing in a single engine. *Data Engineering*, page 28, 2015.
31. Rajiv Ranjan. Streaming big data processing in datacenter clouds. *IEEE Cloud Computing*, 1(1):78–83, 2014.
32. T Nakashima, M Oyama, H Hisada, and N Ishii. Analysis of software bug causes and its prevention. *Information and Software technology*, 41(15):1059–1068, 1999.
33. Crispan Cowan, Calton Pu, Dave Maier, Jonathan Walpole, Peat Bakke, Steve Beattie, Aaron Grier, Perry Wagle, Qian Zhang, and Heather Hinton. Stackguard: Automatic adaptive detection and prevention of buffer-overflow attacks. In *Proc. of USENIX Security Symposium*, 1998.
34. Yilin Mo and Bruno Sinopoli. Secure control against replay attacks. In *Proc. of IEEE Communication, Control, and Computing*, 2009.
35. Shuo Chen, Jun Xu, Emre Can Sezer, Prachi Gauriar, and Ravishankar K Iyer. Non-control-data attacks are realistic threats. In *Proc. of USENIX Security Symposium*, 2005.
36. Niels Provos, Markus Friedl, and Peter Honeyman. Preventing privilege escalation. In *Proc. of USENIX Security Symposium*, 2003.
37. Florian Kammüller and Christian W Probst. Modeling and verification of insider threats using logical analysis. 2016.
38. Peter Mell, Karen Scarfone, and Sasha Romanosky. Common vulnerability scoring system. *IEEE Security & Privacy*, 4(6), 2006.
39. Michael Hayden. The insider threat to us government information systems. Technical report, National Security Agency/Central Security Service Fort George G Meade MD, 1999.
40. BBC. Russian nuclear scientists arrested for 'Bitcoin mining plot'. http://www.bbc.com/news/world-europe-43003740.
41. Robert C Seacord. *Secure Coding in C and C++*. Pearson Education, 2005.
42. David Evans and David Larochelle. Improving security using extensible lightweight static analysis. *IEEE software*, 19(1):42–51, 2002.
43. Hossein Safyallah and Kamran Sartipi. Dynamic analysis of software systems using execution pattern mining. In *Proc. of IEEE ICPC*, 2006.
44. Reed Hastings and Bob Joyce. Purify: Fast detection of memory leaks and access errors. In *Proc. of USENIX Security Symposium*, 1991.
45. Nicholas Nethercote and Julian Seward. Valgrind: A program supervision framework. *Electronic notes in theoretical computer science*, 89(2):44–66, 2003.

46. Chris Lattner. Llvm and clang: Next generation compiler technology. In *The BSD Conference*, 2008.

47. Chris Lattner and Vikram Adve. LLVM: A compilation framework for lifelong program analysis & transformation. In *Proc. of IEEE CGO*, 2004.

48. Ted Kremenek. Finding software bugs with the clang static analyzer. *Apple Inc*, 2008.

49. Bettina Krammer, Katrin Bidmon, Matthias S Müller, and Michael M Resch. Marmot: An mpi analysis and checking tool. In *Advances in Parallel Computing*, volume 13, pages 493–500. Elsevier, 2004.

50. Barbara Kreaseck, Michelle Mills Strout, and Paul Hovland. Depth analysis of mpi programs. In *Proc. of AMP*, 2010.

51. Stephen F Siegel. Verifying parallel programs with mpi-spin. In *European Parallel Virtual Machine/Message Passing Interface Users Group Meeting*, 2007.

52. Jeffrey S Vetter and Bronis R De Supinski. Dynamic software testing of mpi applications with umpire. In *Proc. of IEEE SC*, 2000.

53. Alexander Droste, Michael Kuhn, and Thomas Ludwig. Mpi-checker: static analysis for mpi. In *Proc. of ACM LLVM in HPC*, 2015.

54. Anh Vo, Sriram Aananthakrishnan, Ganesh Gopalakrishnan, Bronis R De Supinski, Martin Schulz, and Greg Bronevetsky. A scalable and distributed dynamic formal verifier for mpi programs. In *Proc. of IEEE SC*, 2010.

55. Leslie Lamport. Time, clocks, and the ordering of events in a distributed system. *Communications of the ACM*, 21(7):558–565, 1978.

56. Koen Claessen and John Hughes. Quickcheck: a lightweight tool for random testing of Haskell programs. *Acm sigplan notices*, 46(4):53–64, 2011.

57. Joachim Protze, Simone Atzeni, Dong H Ahn, Martin Schulz, Ganesh Gopalakrishnan, Matthias S Müller, Ignacio Laguna, Zvonimir Rakamarić, and Greg L Lee. Towards providing low-overhead data race detection for large openmp applications. In *Proc. of IEEE LLVM in HPC*, pages 40–47, 2014.

58. Konstantin Serebryany and Timur Iskhodzhanov. Threadsanitizer: data race detection in practice. In *Proc. of ACM WBIA*, pages 62–71, 2009.

59. Colin Scott, Vjekoslav Brajkovic, George Necula, Arvind Krishnamurthy, and Scott Shenker. Minimizing faulty executions of distributed systems. In *Proc. of USENIX NSDI*, 2016.

60. Oak Ridge National Laboratory. ORNL Hyperion Technology. https://www.ornl.gov/partnerships/ornl-hyperion-technology.

61. William Yurcik, Gregory A Koenig, Xin Meng, and Joseph Greenseid. Cluster security as a unique problem with emergent properties: Issues and techniques. In *Proc. of LCI ICLC*, 2004.

62. Butler W Lampson. Protection. *ACM SIGOPS Operating Systems Review*, 8(1):18–24, 1974.

63. D Elliott Bell and Leonard J LaPadula. Secure computer systems: Mathematical foundations. Technical report, DTIC Document, 1973.

64. James Morris, Stephen Smalley, and Greg Kroah-Hartman. Linux security modules: General security support for the linux kernel. In *Proc. of USENIX Security Symposium*, 2002.

65. Z Cliffe Schreuders, Tanya McGill, and Christian Payne. Empowering end users to confine their own applications: the results of a usability study comparing selinux, apparmor, and fbaclsm. *ACM Trans. TISSEC*, 14(2):19, 2011.

66. NSA Peter Loscocco. Integrating flexible support for security policies into the Linux operating system.

67. Andrew Blaich, Douglas Thain, and Aaron Striegel. Reflections on the virtues of modularity: a case study in linux security modules. *Software: Practice and Experience*, 39(15):1235–1251, 2009.

68. Toshiharu Harada, Takashi Horie, and Kazuo Tanaka. Task oriented management obviates your onus on linux. In *Linux Conference*, volume 3, page 23, 2004.

69. Imamjafar Borate and RK Chavan. Sandboxing in linux: From smartphone to cloud. *International J. of Computer Applications*, 148(8), 2016.

70. Makan Pourzandi, Axelle Apvrille, E Gingras, A Medenou, and David Gordon. Distributed access control for carrier class clusters. In *Proc. of PDPTA*, 2003.

71. IBM. IBM Security Access Manager. https://www.ibm.com/us-en/marketplace/access-management.
72. Fausto Giunchiglia, Rui Zhang, and Bruno Crispo. Relbac: Relation based access control. In *Proc. of IEEE SKG*, 2008.
73. Damien Gros, Mathieu Blanc, Jérémy Briffaut, and Christian Toinard. Advanced mac in hpc systems: performance improvement. In *Proc. of IEEE CCGrid*, 2012.
74. Sam Sanchez, Amanda Bonnie, Graham Van Heule, Conor Robinson, Adam DeConinck, Kathleen Kelly, Quellyn Snead, and J Brandt. Design and implementation of a scalable hpc monitoring system. In *Proc. of IEEE PDPSW*, 2016.
75. Sean Peisert. Fingerprinting communication and computation on HPC machines. *Lawrence Berkeley National Laboratory*, 2010.
76. Calvin Ko, Manfred Ruschitzka, and Karl Levitt. Execution monitoring of security-critical programs in distributed systems: A specification-based approach. In *Proc. of IEEE S&P*, 1997.
77. S Sandeep. Process tracing using ptrace. *Linux Gazette*, (81), 2002.
78. Petr Hosek and Cristian Cadar. Safe software updates via multi-version execution. In *Proc. of IEEE ICSE*, 2013.
79. Babak Salamat, Todd Jackson, Andreas Gal, and Michael Franz. Orchestra: intrusion detection using parallel execution and monitoring of program variants in user-space. In *Proc. of ACM European CCS*, 2009.
80. Petr Hosek and Cristian Cadar. Varan the unbelievable: An efficient N-version execution framework. *ACM SIGARCH*, 43(1):339–353, 2015.
81. PaX Team. Pax address space layout randomization (aslr). 2003.
82. Gaurav S Kc, Angelos D Keromytis, and Vassilis Prevelakis. Countering code-injection attacks with instruction-set randomization. In *Proc. of ACM CCS*, 2003.
83. Sandeep Bhatkar and R Sekar. Data space randomization. In *Proc. of Springer DIMVA*, pages 1–22, 2008.
84. Ashish Venkat, Sriskanda Shamasunder, Hovav Shacham, and Dean M Tullsen. HIPStR: Heterogeneous-ISA program state relocation. In *Proc. of ACM ASPLOS*, 2016.
85. Marco Prandini and Marco Ramilli. Return-oriented programming. *IEEE Security & Privacy*, 10(6):84–87, 2012.
86. Martín Abadi, Mihai Budiu, Ulfar Erlingsson, and Jay Ligatti. Control-flow integrity. In *Proc. of ACM CCS*, 2005.
87. Nathan Burow, Scott A Carr, Stefan Brunthaler, Mathias Payer, Joseph Nash, Per Larsen, and Michael Franz. Control-flow integrity: Precision, security, and performance. *arXiv*, 2016.
88. Caroline Tice, Tom Roeder, Peter Collingbourne, Stephen Checkoway, Úlfar Erlingsson, Luis Lozano, and Geoff Pike. Enforcing forward-edge control-flow integrity in gcc & llvm. In *Proc. of USENIX Security Symposium*, 2014.
89. Clang community. Clang 5 documentation: Control Flow Integrity. http://clang.llvm.org/docs/ControlFlowIntegrity.html#publications.
90. Mingwei Zhang and R Sekar. Control flow integrity for cots binaries. In *Proc. of USENIX Security Symposium*, 2013.
91. Aydan R Yumerefendi, Benjamin Mickle, and Landon P Cox. Tightlip: Keeping applications from spilling the beans. In *Proc. of USENIX NSDI*, 2007.
92. Roberto Capizzi, Antonio Longo, VN Venkatakrishnan, and A Prasad Sistla. Preventing information leaks through shadow executions. In *Proc. of IEEE ACSAC*, 2008.
93. Dominique Devriese and Frank Piessens. Noninterference through secure multi-execution. In *Proc. of IEEE S&P*, 2010.
94. Benjamin Cox, David Evans, Adrian Filipi, Jonathan Rowanhill, Wei Hu, Jack Davidson, John Knight, Anh Nguyen-Tuong, and Jason Hiser. N-variant systems: A secretless framework for security through diversity. In *Proc. of USENIX Security Symposium*, 2006.
95. Artem Dinaburg. Bitsquatting: DNS Hijacking without exploitation. *Proceedings of BlackHat Security*, 2011.

96. Andy A Hwang, Ioan A Stefanovici, and Bianca Schroeder. Cosmic rays don't strike twice: understanding the nature of DRAM errors and the implications for system design. In *Proc. of ACM SIGPLAN Notices*, 2012.
97. Edmund B Nightingale, John R Douceur, and Vince Orgovan. Cycles, cells and platters: an empirical analysis of hardware failures on a million consumer PCs. In *Proc. of EuroSys*, 2011.
98. KernelL, Bug Tracker. Data corruption with Opteron CPUs and Nvidia chipsets.
99. Ashish Gupta, Fan Yang, Jason Govig, Adam Kirsch, Kelvin Chan, Kevin Lai, Shuo Wu, Sandeep Govind Dhoot, Abhilash Rajesh Kumar, Ankur Agiwal, et al. Mesa: Geo-replicated, near real-time, scalable data warehousing. *Proc. of the VLDB Endowment*, 7(12):1259–1270, 2014.
100. Miguel Castro and Barbara Liskov. Practical Byzantine fault tolerance and proactive recovery. *ACM Trans. TOCS*, 20(4):398–461, 2002.
101. Chi Ho, Robbert Van Renesse, Mark Bickford, and Danny Dolev. Nysiad: Practical protocol transformation to tolerate byzantine failures. In *Proc. of USENIX NSDI*, 2008.
102. Michael G Merideth, Arun Iyengar, Thomas Mikalsen, Stefan Tai, Isabelle Rouvellou, and Priya Narasimhan. Thema: Byzantine-fault-tolerant middleware for web-service applications. In *Proc. of IEEE SRDS*, 2005.
103. Diogo Behrens, Marco Serafini, Flavio P. Junqueira, Sergei Arnautov, and Christof Fetzer. Scalable error isolation for distributed systems. In *Proc. of USENIX NSDI*, 2015.

Automated Cyber Risk Mitigation: Making Informed Cost-Effective Decisions

Mohammed Noraden Alsaleh and Ehab Al-Shaer

1 Introduction

The proper security configuration of network end-points and their compliance with security policies is a key property to ensure the overall network security because they represent the interface for both benign and malicious users. Traditionally, the compliance of individual hosts with security checklists is evaluated independently and in an isolation from network connectivity. With the increasing role of cyber networks in many human activities, including social, medical, and financial services, a comprehensive cyber risk evaluation requires combining both the compliance states of hosts and network services, and the network infrastructure configuration. For example, in order to evaluate the risk imposed by weaknesses like *"clients with weak passwords are allowed to access the critical financial services remotely."*, we need to: (1) identify the services that do not enforce strong password policies (based on the compliance state) and (2) verify whether they can reach the financial servers (based on the network infrastructure configuration) in which the remote access is enabled. Note that although the strength of the password is not necessarily a software flaw, it indicates a configuration weakness that can have negative consequences on the overall security of the network and it should be considered as part of the risk assessment and mitigation planning process.

The problem of risk assessment and countermeasure selection has attracted considerable attention from academia, government, and industry. Standard vulnerability enumeration and scoring models, such as the Security Content Automation Protocol

M. N. Alsaleh (✉)
Eastern Michigan University, Ypsilanti, MI, USA
e-mail: malsaleh@emich.edu

E. Al-Shaer
University of North Carolina at Charlotte, Charlotte, NC, USA
e-mail: ealshaer@uncc.edu

© Springer Nature Switzerland AG 2020
S. Jajodia et al. (eds.), *Adaptive Autonomous Secure Cyber Systems*,
https://doi.org/10.1007/978-3-030-33432-1_7

(SCAP) [1], have been proposed to communicate security content. Many products and frameworks have demonstrated wide success in automated vulnerability assessment and scanning, such as Nessus [2], Tripwire [3], and OpenVAS [4]. However, vulnerability assessment and scanning in such products are done on the host level. Other solutions based on attack graphs have been proposed to address the same problem [5–7]. This work complements such approaches by incorporating different types of vulnerabilities that can facilitate the attack propagation, and allows for fine-grained mitigation actions.

In this chapter, we present a security analytics framework to assess the global risk of the network and derive cost-effective configuration for risk mitigation. In our previous work [8], we estimated the cyber risk in a network based on the vulnerabilities and configuration weaknesses of network assets, their exposure to threat sources (considering the deployed security countermeasures), and the monetary impact of potential security exploits. In this work, we extend that model by integrating the live activity logs and threat scores of network end-points, collected through host intrusion detection and scoring tools, to reflect the dynamic threat levels of network services. Based on periodic risk assessment, our framework will automatically select a set of risk mitigation actions to bring the risk down given a limited budget. Since the option of patching vulnerabilities, at the host-level, or completely blocking threat sources, at the network-level, may not be feasible due to technical and financial constraints, our framework will consider two types of mitigation actions: host-based (e.g., patching or disabling vulnerable services) and network-based (e.g., blocking threat sources), and select a cost-effective set of actions from both types. Moreover, our solution accounts for (1) the interdependence between vulnerabilities and configuration weaknesses of different network assets when exploiting one vulnerability can increase the potential of exploiting others, (2) the satisfaction of high-level connectivity requirements based on business policies, and (3) the direct and indirect impact of the mitigation actions themselves (e.g., blocking a particular service may seem as a good option when we consider only the direct consumers of that service, but it may not be a feasible option when we consider its dependent services as well).

For a given network configuration, our framework takes three inputs as depicted in Fig. 1: the compliance reports of the different distributed hosts and services in the network, the connectivity between the services, and the live activity and threat scores of network services. The compliance reports are the output of scanning the hosts against given security checklists, which identify the three major types of vulnerabilities: software flaws, configuration weaknesses, and software features that can be misused by malicious users. We utilize the Extensible Configuration Checklist Description Format (XCCDF), a language defined as part of SCAP, for defining security checklists and compliance reports [9]. The service connectivity specifies which services can access others and the threat countermeasures that exist in the network. The live activity and threat scores are reported periodically by the host-based intrusion detection and scoring tools, which run locally on individual hosts, such as OSSEC [10]. Based on these inputs, our framework provides a fine-grained selection of mitigation actions to maximize the ROI considering constraints

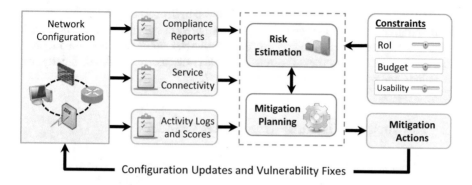

Fig. 1 Risk estimation and mitigation framework

on budget and usability of the network services. The set of mitigation actions is selected from a larger set of actions that are supplied by different sources, including the XCCDF documents themselves, global guidelines and best practices, and local network operators.

The process of cyber risk mitigation is a continuous process especially with the integration of live activity and threat scores. Emerging threats detected by the host-based intrusion detection and scoring tools might require shifting mitigation priorities to focus on the services that exhibit high threat levels over those that do not show any threat activities, even if they are highly vulnerable. Thus, cost-effective mitigation planning must be conducted repeatedly based on live inputs. In each round, our framework will augment the actions recommended from the previous round, reads the live activity and threat scores, and generate a new set of mitigation actions that is most appropriate to the live state of the network.

We formalize the risk mitigation planning as a constraints satisfaction problem and we solve it using the Z3 SMT solver [11]. The Z3 SMT solver provides the theoretical basis to solve linear and non-linear arithmetic constraints, which are required to model our risk metrics and drive the automatic selection of mitigation actions. Since this process will be repeated periodically with minor variations, we do not need to build the entire network and risk models in each round from scratch. Rather, we utilize the *push/pop* mechanism that is available in Z3 to speed up the process. In the first round, we build the entire model using the initial states of hosts security compliance and live activity and threat scores. In the following rounds, we simply *pop* the previous state of security compliance and threat scores and *push* the current state. In this way, only a subset of Z3 assertions that are related to the compliance and threat scores of the network will be changed over the consecutive rounds, while those assertions that are related to the computation of risk and the selection of mitigation actions will stay intact. We evaluated the scalability of our approach on densely connected networks of up to 1500 hosts and the results demonstrate that it is more scalable than the state of the art work in risk mitigation using attack graphs.

The rest of the chapter is organized as follows. In Sect. 2, we present the network configuration and threat models. In Sect. 3, we present our risk assessment model, which is utilized in Sect. 4 to devise cost-effective risk mitigation. Section 5 reports the performance evaluation. The related work is discussed in Sect. 6. Finally, we conclude and present our future plans in Sect. 7.

2   Network Configuration and Threat Model

The network is abstracted as a set of interdependent services, where the traffic flows between the network services are controlled by various types of traffic forwarding and transformation appliances, such as routers, firewalls, intrusion detection systems, VPN gateways, and proxies. A single host in the network can run multiple services, where each service is distinguished by its underlying protocol and port number. The appliances in the network infrastructure operate based on security policies that control the access levels between the interdependent services in the form of *<flow:action>* pairs. Traffic *flows* are represented by the basic IP header fields: the protocol, the source ip address and port number, and the destination ip address and port number. Different appliances support different sets of *actions*. For example, firewalls can either *forward* or *block* traffic, intrusion detection systems can *inspect* the traffic, and IP security gateways and proxies can *protect* the traffic. Organizations may adopt other access control technologies and the set of *actions* will vary accordingly. Our framework does not restrict the set of actions and we leave it to the network operator to add as many actions as available.

Definition 1 We define the network configuration as the three-tuple $(\mathbb{R}, \mathbb{F}, \alpha)$, where $\mathbb{R}$ is the set of services, $\mathbb{F} \subseteq \mathbb{R} \times \mathbb{R}$ is the set of flows, and $\alpha : \mathbb{F} \to \mathbb{A}$ is a function that maps each flow to an action. The set $\mathbb{A} = \{forward, block, inspect, protect, authenticate, \ldots\}$ represents the complete set of traffic control actions supported by the network infrastructure.

For a given network, we can build the initial network configuration model (i.e., the existing configuration before applying risk mitigation actions) automatically using network scanning tools or reachability analysis frameworks. In this work, We utilize a network verification tool called *ConfigChecker* [12], a Binary Decision Diagram (BDD) model checker that models the entire network data-plane configuration and verifies reachability properties. We use ConfigChecker to run reachability queries and determine the connectivity and the traffic control action(s) enforced between all pairs of services in the network.

2.1   Security Compliance State

The compliance state of the network captures the vulnerabilities and configuration weaknesses of all services in the network with respect to pre-defined security checklists. We use the XCCDF documents as the means to communicate security checklists and their scanning results. Multiple security checklists can be evaluated for one service. A security checklist consists of multiple rules that correspond to different types of security weaknesses. NIST Inter-agency Report 7502 [13] categorizes the vulnerabilities into three categories: (1) software flaws (unintended errors in the design or coding of software), (2) security configuration issues (the use of security settings that negatively affects the security), and (3) software feature misuse vulnerabilities (features in the software that provide an avenue to compromise the system). Three standard scoring specifications have been created to measure the severity of these vulnerabilities: the Common Vulnerability Scoring System (CVSS), the Common Configuration Scoring System (CCSS), and the Common Misuse Scoring System (CMSS).

We show in Listing 1 an example of an XCCDF specification that describes a portion (i.e., two XCCDF rules) of the *Red Hat Enterprise Linux 7 Security Guide* [14]. We can see in the example two XML elements: *Benchmark* and *TestResult*. In addition to some metadata, such as the *status, title, platform*, and *version*, the *Benchmark* element in Listing 1 specifies a security checklist that consists of two rules: one to check the encryption of partitions in a system and the other to check the proper configuration of accounts expiration policy. Each rule has a unique *id*, a *severity* score, and a *weight*. Those values are set by the checklist author and they are normally derived from the vulnerability scoring systems: CVSS, CCSS, and the CMSS. The *TestResult* element specifies the results of checking those two rules in one particular host. It specifies the *benchmark* that is being evaluated, its version, the identifier of the *target* machine, and a *rule-result* for each rule in the benchmark.

XCCDF specification defines a set of results that can be assigned to each rule, those are {*Pass, Fail, Error, Unknown, Notapplicable, notchecKed, notSelected, Informational,* or *fiXed*}. In the following discussion, we use the capitalized letters as abbreviations for the results. The complete details of XCCDF structures and the meanings of these results can be found in the XCCDF specification document [9].

Definition 2 We define the security compliance state of the entire network, S_{comp}, as the three-tuple $(\mathbb{R}, \mathbb{V}, \mathbb{M})$, where $\mathbb{R}$ is the set of system services, $\mathbb{V}$ is the set of known vulnerabilities and configuration weaknesses, and $\mathbb{M}$ is a matrix that maps each service to its vulnerabilities. $\mathbb{M}[r, v] \in \{P, F, E, U, N, K, S, I, X\}$ for all $r \in \mathbb{R}$ and $v \in \mathbb{V}$.

The XCCDF rules can reference the common vulnerabilities and configuration weaknesses by their unique IDs that are defined in the public dictionaries, such as the Common Vulnerabilities and Exposures dictionary (CVE) [15] and the Common Configuration Enumeration (CCE) [16]. As shown in the example of Listing 1, the XML tag *ident* is used to map the XCCDF rules to the corresponding CCE identifier. The XCCDF *TestResult* may also include a cumulative compliance score for the whole benchmark on the target machine. There are different scoring models that can be used to calculate this cumulative score utilizing the *weight* attributes of the XCCDF rules. In our risk model, we do not use the cumulative compliance score reported in the XCCDF documents, rather, we use the individual rule results to calculate our own scores as will be shown in the following sections.

Listing 1 An example of a security checklist and its result in XCCDF fromat

```
<Benchmark id="xccdf_org.ssgproject.content_benchmark_RHEL-7">
   <status date="2017-02-06">draft</status>
   <title>
      Guide to the Secure Configuration of Red Hat Enterprise Linux 7
   </title>
   <platform idref="cpe:/o:redhat:enterprise_linux:7"/>
   <platform idref="cpe:/o:redhat:enterprise_linux:7::client"/>
   <platform idref="cpe:/o:redhat:enterprise_linux:7::computenode"/>
   <version>0.1.31</version>
   <Rule id="xccdf_org.ssgproject.content_rule_encrypt_partitions"
      severity="high" weight="10.0">
      <title>Encrypt Partitions</title>
      <description>
         Red Hat Enterprise Linux 7 natively supports partition
         encryption through the Linux Unified Key Setup-on-disk-format
         (LUKS) technology ...
      </description>
      <ident>CCE-27128-8</ident>
   </Rule>
   <Rule id="content_rule_account_disable_post_pw_expiration"
      severity="medium" weight="2.0">
      <title>Set Account Expiration Following Inactivity</title>
      <description xml:lang="en-US">
         To specify the number of days after a password expires
         (which signifies inactivity) until an account is permanently
         disabled ...
      </description>
      <ident>CCE-27355-7</ident>
      <fix system="urn:xccdf:fix:script:sh"
         id="account_disable_post_pw_expiration" complexity="low"
         disruption="medium" reboot="true" strategy="disable">
         [The exact technical procedure to fix the weakness is omitted]
      </fix>
      <fix system="urn:xccdf:fix:script:ansible"
         id="account_disable_post_pw_expiration" complexity="low"
         disruption="low" reboot="false" strategy="enable">
         [The exact technical procedure to fix the weakness is omitted]
      </fix>
   </Rule>
</Benchmark>
<TestResult id="ssgproject-RH-result" end-time="2017-01-26T05:30:48">
   <Benchmark href="xccdf_org.ssgproject.content_benchmark_RHEL-7.xml" />
   <platform idref="cpe:/o:redhat:enterprise_linux:7"/>
   <version>0.1.31<version>
   <organization>org-x<organization>
   <target>host1.org-x.com<target>
   <rule-result idref="xccdf_org.ssgproject.content_rule_encrypt_partitions">
   <result>pass</result>
   <ident>CCE-27128-8</ident>
</rule-result>
<rule-result idref="content_rule_account_disable_post_pw_expiration">
   <result>fail</result>
   <ident>CCE-27355-7</ident>
</rule-result>
<score>85</score>
</TestResult>
```

The exploitability and the impact of the common vulnerabilities and configuration weaknesses can be measured using existing vulnerability scoring systems, which define three groups of metrics: base, temporal, and environmental metrics. These metrics are used to compute an *exploitability* sub-score, an *impact* sub-score, and a final *severity* score for each vulnerability. Six metrics are defined in the base metrics group: three to measure the exploitability (access vector, authentication, and access complexity), and another three to measure the impact (confidentiality-impact, integrity-impact, and availability-impact).

Definition 3 We model the base scores of the common vulnerabilities by the matrix $\$$, with a row for each vulnerability and a column for each of its *exploitability* sub-score (E), *impact* sub-score (I), and *integrity-impact* base score (G). $\$[v, sc] \in [0, 10]$ for all $v \in \mathbb{V}$ and $sc \in \{E, I, G\}$.

The standard vulnerability scoring specifications define the equations to compute the *exploitability* and the *impact* sub-scores, as well as the final *severity* score and report them out of 10.

2.2   Threat Model

The exploits of vulnerabilities and configuration weaknesses are the only sources of threat for the network services in our model. Hence, if a service has no reported vulnerabilities or configuration weaknesses, it is considered secure and it does not impose any risk on the network. The following explains the threat model we use in this work:

- Vulnerability exploits. If a vulnerability exists in a system service, it is likely to be exploited and it imposes certain risk on the entire network.
- Threat sources. A service in the network is considered a threat source if its integrity is likely to be compromised as a result of exploiting its vulnerabilities and configuration weaknesses.
- The threat level of a certain threat source is determined by (1) the number and the *integrity-impact* scores of its vulnerabilities and configuration weaknesses and (2) the malicious activities detected by intrusion detection and monitoring tools.
- Threat propagation. The threat can propagate from a threat source to another victim if the victim is vulnerable and is reachable from the threat source. Thus, the likelihood of threat propagation depends on the number and the *exploitability* of the victim's vulnerabilities and configuration weaknesses in addition to the network configuration (i.e., connectivity).

To capture the threat level of a service, we define the metric *ThreatIndicator*, denoted by ThI, which intuitively measures the ability of the service to establish attacks against others. This metric consists of two components. The first component depends on the live activity and threat scores reported by the host-based intrusion detection tools that monitor and aggregate service activities and assess their threat levels. We call this component the *Malice* score. This score is dynamic and it is likely to change each time the threat levels of network services are evaluated. However, if a service has vulnerabilities that can impact its integrity, it still can be compromised and it can threaten others, even if no malicious activities are detected. Hence, the *Malice* score by itself, which depends solely on the live activity, is not enough. The other component depends on the intrinsic vulnerabilities and configuration weaknesses of the service regardless of whether a malicious activity is detected or not.

The dynamic component, the *Malice* score, of a network service is computed based on intrusion detection, activity logs analysis, and event correlation systems whether they are centralized or distributed, such as security information and event managements systems (SIEM), OSSEC [10], AIDE [17], or Prelude Hybrid-IDS [18]. We assume that each host is always running an agent to collect the activity logs, which will be used to compute a numeric *Malice* score in the range [0, 1], where 1 indicates the highest threat level and 0 indicates no threat. We used OSSEC in our environment and we computed the *Malice* score based on the severity scores reported as part of the alerts raised when malicious activities are detected. The Open Source Security Event Correlator (OSSEC) is a rule-based, free, and cross-platform host-based intrusion detection system that monitors the log files and processes in a system, extracts threat related information, and raise alarms when malicious activities are detected. Rules in OSSEC are configured with severity levels that range between 0 (lowest) and 15 (highest). When a rule is triggered, its severity level is passed as part of the intrusion alert. Based on this model, we calculate the *Malice* score of a particular service during a particular period of time as the highest severity level among the alerts raised within that period, divided by the highest severity. For example, if the highest reported severity level is 8, then the Malice score will be $\frac{8}{15}$.

The static component of the *ThreatIndicator* is computed based on the *integrity-impact* scores of network services. According to NIST Report 7502 [13], integrity refers to the trustworthiness and guaranteed veracity of information. Thus, the integrity-impact measures the ability of an exploited vulnerability to modify the system files and install root-kits, which can be used for spoofing and launching attacks.

The *ThreatIndicator* of the service r, denoted by ThI_r, is formally defined as the addition of two terms as follows:

$$ThI_r = \beta \times \frac{\sum_{u \in V_r} \$[u, E] \times \$[u, G]}{\sum_{v \in \mathbb{V}} \$[v, E] \times \$[v, G]} + (1 - \beta) \times l_r \qquad (1)$$

where $V_r = \{v : v \in \mathbb{V}, \mathbb{M}[h, v] \in \{F, E\}\}$ is the set of active vulnerabilities of the service r. $\$$, $\mathbb{V}$, and $\mathbb{M}$ are defined in Definitions (2) and (3). The first term in this equation, which represents the static component, is expressed as the normalized weighted sum of the *integrity-impact* scores of the vulnerabilities and configuration weaknesses of the service multiplied by the weight β. The *integrity-impact* scores are weighted by the *exploitablity* sub-scores to account for the fact that vulnerabilities that are more likely to be exploited should have larger contributions to the *ThreatIndicator*. The second term, which represents the dynamic component, is expressed as the *Malice* score of the service, denoted by l_r, weighted by $(1 - \beta)$. $\beta \in [0, 1]$ is an arbitrary value that weighs the contribution of the static component to the *ThreatIndicator* score over that of the dynamic component. Setting $\beta = 0$ means that the threat level of services will be totally determined by the *Malice* scores and setting $\beta = 1$ means that the threat level only depends on the vulnerabilities and their *integrity-impact* scores regardless of the detected malicious activity.

3 Risk Assessment

In this section, we define our metric to measure the global risk in a network given its security compliance state, live activity and threat scores, and its data-plane configuration. To be consistent with our network configuration and threat models, the metric (1) captures the interdependence between vulnerabilities (i.e., how exploiting a particular vulnerability increases the likelihood of exploiting others), (2) considers the exposure of network assets to all threat sources inside and outside the network, and (3) recognizes the effectiveness of the deployed countermeasures in the given configuration instance. Before introducing the risk metric itself, we present our model of network threat resistance, which refers to the ability of the security appliances in the network infrastructure to prevent security weaknesses exploits.

3.1 Network Threat Resistance

The network threat resistance is determined by the existence of attack countermeasures in the attack paths from threat sources to vulnerable and weakly configured services. Recall that one of the actions supported by the attack countermeasures is specified for each flow in our network configuration abstract model. As different actions vary in their ability to prevent or deter attacks, we require that an effectiveness value be specified for each possible action in order to quantify the resistance of the network. For example, it is clear that the *forward* action imposes absolutely no threat resistance while the *block* action completely eliminates the threat. However, the effectiveness of other actions, such as *inspect*, is not fixed for all threats because not all vulnerabilities can be mitigated by inspection (e.g., vulnerabilities related to *inadequate encryption strength*), and network-based intrusion detection systems vary in their ability to detect exploits due to limited behavior profiling and detection evasion techniques used by attackers.

In this work, we assume that the effectiveness of all possible actions is given for each vulnerability that exists in the network.

Definition 4 The network threat resistance is defined by the matrix $\mathbb{N}$, with a row for each vulnerability in $\mathbb{V}$ and a column for each action in $\mathbb{A}$. $\mathbb{N}[v, a] \in [0, 1]$ for all $v \in \mathbb{V}$ and $a \in \mathbb{A}$.

The effectiveness of the *forward* action is always 0 and the effectiveness of the *block* action is always 1 for all vulnerabilities, while the effectiveness of other actions lies in the interval $[0, 1]$.

3.2 Threat Exposure

The *Exposure* of a service depends on three factors: (1) the *quantity* of threat sources that can reach the service, (2) the *threat levels* of these threat sources estimated using the *ThreatIndicator* metric, and (3) the network resistance in-between. To calculate the exposure, we build a reachability tree for each service in the network based on the reachability requirements. The reachability requirements determine which services should be connected to each other and they stem from two major sources: business needs (e.g., a library technician workstation can connect to the library's data servers) and functional dependency between different services (e.g., in order to access a web server by its name, we need access to a DNS). The reachability tree captures all the threat sources that can reach the service directly or indirectly. Each node in the reachability tree corresponds to a potential threat source. Recall that threat sources are services with vulnerabilities and configuration weaknesses that jeopardize their integrity.

To define the exposure of a particular service r, let TR_r be the reachability tree of that service and let $(\mathcal{P}_{x,r})$ represent the path in the tree from the node x to the root r. We formally define Exp_r, the *exposure* of the service r, as follows:

$$Exp_r = \sum_{x \in TR_r} ThI_x \times (1 - Res(\mathcal{P}_{x,r})) \qquad (2)$$

where $Res(\mathcal{P}_{x,r})$ is the aggregate resistance of the entire path between x and r, which depends on all the countermeasures deployed in the path and it is calculated according to the following. Let $\mathcal{P}_{x,r} = s_0, s_1, \ldots, s_m$, where $s_0 = x$ and $s_m = r$, and let $a_{i,i+1}$ be the action taken by the attack countermeasures on the flow between s_i and s_{i+1}. This entails that the path $\mathcal{P}_{x,r}$ consists of multiple steps, $\{(s_i, s_{i+1}) \mid 0 \leq i < m\}$, and we compute the aggregate resistance of the entire path considering the actions enforced at all the steps, $\{a_{i,i+1} \mid 0 \leq i < m\}$. However, since the effectiveness of attack countermeasures may vary per vulnerability or configuration weakness as discussed before, the resistance at each step (s_i, s_{i+1}) depends on all the vulnerabilities and weaknesses of the node s_{i+1}, denoted by the set $V_{s_{i+1}}$. The resistance of the entire path is computed as follows:

$$Res(\mathcal{P}_{x,r}) = \max_{0 \le i < m} \{ \min_{v \in V_{s_{i+1}}} \{ \mathbb{N}[v, a_{i,i+1}] \} \} \tag{3}$$

The inner aggregate function, *min*, finds the least effectiveness score of the countermeasure selected for one individual step in the attack path, (s_i, s_{i+1}), with respect to the vulnerabilities of the destination service in that step, $V_{s_{i+1}}$. The intuition behind using the *min* function is that the countermeasure is as effective as it can prevent exploiting all vulnerabilities and configuration weaknesses of the destination. The outer aggregate function, *max*, evaluates the resistance of all the countermeasures in the consecutive steps, not only one step, and takes the maximum resistance among them. That's because preventing exploits at any step in the path is enough to eliminate the threat imposed by that path. In other words, one highly effective countermeasure at one step of the attack path shadows the other less effective countermeasures at the other steps.

3.3 Risk Estimation

We calculate the risk score for each service in the network based on its exposure to threat sources, its asset value, and the impact of exploiting its vulnerabilities and configuration weaknesses. The asset value of each service is given as part of the network configuration and it includes the value of the data stored and managed by the service. The total risk associated with a service, $Risk_r$, is formally defined as:

$$Risk_r = AV_r \times Exp_r \times \frac{\sum_{u \in V_r} (\mathbb{S}[u, E] \times \mathbb{S}[u, I])}{\sum_{v \in \mathbb{V}} (\mathbb{S}[v, E] \times \mathbb{S}[v, I])} \tag{4}$$

where AV_r is the asset value of the service r and Exp_r is the exposure of service r, augmenting the existing network threat resistance. $V_r = \{ v : v \in \mathbb{V}, \mathbb{M}[r, v] \in \{F, E\} \}$ is the set of active vulnerabilities and configuration weaknesses of the service r. $\mathbb{S}$, $\mathbb{V}$, and $\mathbb{M}$ are defined in definitions (2) and (3). The fraction in the right side of the equation is the normalized sum of the *impact* sub-scores of all the vulnerabilities of the service r weighted by their exploitability sub-scores. We use the weighted *impact* sub-scores here to reflect that vulnerabilities or configuration weaknesses that are easy to exploit and have high impacts will have larger contribution to the risk and they should take priority in the risk mitigation plans over those that have low impacts.

The risk is quantified as a portion of the service value. Hence, it is a monetary value that represents the expected loss due to vulnerabilities and configuration weaknesses. The *global risk* of the entire network, denoted by $GR_{\mathbb{S}}$, is calculated as the total sum of the risks associated with all its individual services (i.e., $GR_{\mathbb{S}} = \sum_{r \in \mathbb{S}} Risk_r$).

4 Automated Risk Mitigation

In this section, we show how we model the problem of automated risk mitigation as a constraints satisfaction problem using Z3 SMT solver. We will translate our network configuration, threat, and risk assessment models to linear and non-linear assertions, in such a way that the estimated risk drives the risk mitigation decisions. In Table 1, we she the list of the variables and parameters we used in this formalization.

4.1 Mitigation Objective

A cost-effective risk mitigation plan is the one that returns a benefit greater than the mitigation cost. Traditionally, the cost-effectiveness of a mitigation plan is evaluated by the Return on Investment (ROI) metric, which intuitively measures what an organization profits from the amount spent in risk mitigation. In this work, we use the following popular definition of ROI:

$$ROI = \frac{Benefit - Cost}{Cost} \tag{5}$$

where *Benefit* is the reduction in the risk that results from implementing the selected mitigation actions and the *Cost* is the total cost of implementing them. The *Benefit*

Table 1 Formalization parameters and variables

Parameter	Definition
$\mathbb{R}$	The set of all network services
$\mathbb{A}$	The complete set of network-based mitigation actions
AV_r	The total asset value of the service r
e_j	The *exploitability* sub-score of the vulnerability j
m_j	The *impact* sub-score of the vulnerability j
g_j	The *integrity-impact* base score of the vulnerability j
τ_{roi}, τ_{gr}	thresholds on the ROI and residual risk
B_{high}	Budget threshold
n_p, n_t	Normalization constants
$f\_cost(), f\_use()$	Implementation and usability costs of service-based fixes
$cm\_cost(), cm\_use()$	Implementation and usability costs of network-based actions
$Risk_{init}$	Initial risk before risk mitigation
V_r, T_r	The vulnerabilities and the reachability tree of the service r
$|\mathcal{P}_{k,r}|$	The length of the path from k to r
$\mathcal{P}_{k,r}^i$	The service i in the path from k to r
$\mathbb{N}$	The network threat resistance matrix
β	The weight of service vulnerabilities contribution to its threat level

can be calculated by subtracting the residual risk that remains after implementing the recommended mitigation actions from the initial risk imposed at the network before applying any mitigation actions. Since the risk in our model is quantified as a monetary value, both the *Benefit* and the *Cost* have the same unit.

Based on this definition, we express the objective of risk mitigation as a constraint on the *ROI* value. When $ROI = 0$, there is absolutely no return from the investment. Different organizations may enforce different thresholds on the value of *ROI* (formally, $ROI \geq \tau$). Note that if *ROI* is negative, then the cost is greater than the benefit. Hence, the threshold of *ROI* should be a non-negative value (i.e., $\tau \geq 0$).

4.2 Risk Mitigation Actions

To achieve the mitigation objective, our risk mitigation framework selects a set of actions from a given pool. The decision factors between the different actions include their costs and effectiveness in mitigating the risk. The pool of actions can be populated from different sources, including publicly available security standards, best practices, design principles, security compliance benchmarks, security solutions' vendors and experts, or local network operators. We do not limit our model to particular set of actions. However, costs and effectiveness scores must be supplied for actions in order to plug them into our framework. In Table 2, we show a set of service-based and network-based actions collected from various sources.

Table 2 Examples of mitigation actions

Mitigation actions based on XCCDF	
Configure	Adjust target configuration/settings to match security guidelines.
Disable	Turn off or uninstall a target component
Enable	Turn on or install a target component
Patch	Apply a patch, hotfix, update, etc
Restrict	Adjust permissions, access rights, or other access restrictions
Update	Install upgrade or update to provide new security features
Examples of mitigation actions from CWE	
Authenticate	Authenticate application entities involved in communications.
Redirect	Reroute particular traffic through web application firewall
Migrate	Relocate sensitive assets to a more secure domain/zone.
Validate	Use a proper input validation framework
	Add integrity checks to detect tampering
Other mitigation actions based on network infrastructure capabilities	
Block	Prevent communication based on header or payload content
Inspect-stateful	Apply stateful packet inspection on selected traffic
Inspect-deep	Apply deep packet inspection on the traffic payload
Encrypt-tunnel	Encrypt selected flows using ESP tunnels
Auth-tunnel	Authentication selected flows using AH tunnels

4.2.1 Service-Based Mitigation Actions

Based on our threat model, vulnerabilities are the entry points for attackers and risk can be mitigated by fixing them at the service level. We consider multiple types of vulnerabilities, including software flaws, configuration weaknesses, and feature misuse. Hence, software patching is not the only possible mitigation action. Different types of actions can be taken at the service level to overcome configuration weaknesses and feature misuse vulnerabilities. In the following discussion, we refer to such actions as vulnerability fixes. Software patching is still one example of vulnerability fixes.

Multiple fixes may be applicable to one vulnerability. XCCDF specification provides special constructs to specify one or more fixes for each vulnerability or configuration weakness. Each fix has a set of attributes to specify the cost of the fix, such as whether a reboot is required, an estimate of the potential network performance degradation that the fix might cause, and an estimated complexity or difficulty of applying the fix. In Table 2, we show examples of fixes recommended in XCCDF documents with different strategies. In addition, the XCCDF documents may contain specific fix procedures for particular systems. Those procedures may be specified as a list of target system commands, a list of one or more URLs that contain the resources to apply the fix, a script written in a specific language, or a patch identifier. The specified procedures are supposed to bring the system into compliance with the security checklist. Listing 1 provides examples of vulnerability fixes specified in the XCCDF format using the *fix* element.

For those vulnerabilities and configuration weaknesses that have fixes specified in the XCCDF documents or supplied by the network operator, our framework will decide which vulnerability should be *fixed* and which fix should be taken, in cases where multiple fixes are available, in order to satisfy the mitigation objective.

4.2.2 Network-Based Mitigation Actions

It may be impossible in some cases to achieve the mitigation objective by only considering mitigation actions at the service level because service-based mitigation actions may not be feasible. Instead, the mitigation planner will decide to reconfigure the network infrastructure by introducing appropriate countermeasures and network-based actions to control the communication between services. Those actions will reduce the negative exposure of network assets to threats, which will reduce the risk and satisfy the mitigation objective.

The network resistance model (Sect. 3.1) allows us to incorporate any arbitrary number of mitigation actions at the network level as long as their effectiveness is determined with respect to the network vulnerabilities and configuration weaknesses. The most prominent actions may be traffic blocking, inspection, and encryption. However, organizations may adopt other countermeasures based on the capabilities of the deployed security technologies. The Common Weaknesses Enumeration (CWE), for example, defines a set of recommended mitigation actions for the identified common weaknesses. We enumerated all the mitigation actions available in CWE and they are available as valid mitigation actions in our framework. Table 2 shows some examples of network-based mitigation actions that were extracted from CWE. Some of those actions are general and the exact technical procedures to implement them are to be determined per network if network operators chose to use them. Each of these actions will be assigned an effectiveness score with respect to different vulnerabilities and configuration weaknesses to comply with the network resistance model.

4.2.3 Decision Variables

To model the mitigation actions, which represent the output of our automated risk mitigation process, we define the following two sets of decision variables. The SMT solver will find their values, such that our constraints are satisfied.

$$\mathbb{P} = \{p_{r,j} \in dom(p_{r,j}) \mid j \text{ is a vulnerability of service } r\} \tag{6}$$

$$\mathbb{B} = \{b_{r,j} \mid j \text{ is a threat source that can reach service } r\} \tag{7}$$

The set $\mathbb{P}$ represents the decision variables of the service-based actions, where each variable $p \in \mathbb{P}$ corresponds to a vulnerability or a configuration weakness in the network. For each variable $p \in \mathbb{P}$, the finite set $dom(p) \subseteq \mathbb{Z}^{\geq}$ represents the domain of its possible values, where $\mathbb{Z}^{\geq}$ is the set of non-negative integers. Since the number of available fixes varies per vulnerability, the length of $dom(p)$ varies for each decision variable. If a satisfying solution is found, a value of 0 will be assigned to the variable p if the corresponding vulnerability or configuration weakness is not recommended to be fixed at this time, otherwise the variable p will be assigned a value that represents the index of the service-based action that should be taken to fix the vulnerability.

The set $\mathbb{B}$ captures the recommended network-based mitigation actions. If a satisfying solution is found, a value will be assigned to each of those variables to indicate the appropriate action that should be applied between the corresponding pair of services. Note that a single flow between a particular pair of services may exist in multiple reachability trees of different services. Hence, the network-based action that is selected for that particular flow will have an impact on the risk imposed on the entire network rather than one particular service. While a particular action may be optimal considering a single service, it may not be the case when the entire network is considered. We model the constraint satisfaction problem in such a way that the impact of possible network-based actions is assessed with respect to the entire network as part of the decision making process.

4.3   Mitigation Costs

We assume that a cost can be estimated in advance for each of the mitigation actions, including service-based vulnerability fixes and network-based actions. For accurate estimation of the total mitigation cost, the cost of each mitigation action should account for the following:

- Implementation cost. This is the operational cost that the organization needs to spend in order to apply the mitigation action. This includes the consultation and labor costs, in addition to the price of new hardware or software equipment that may be required.
- Usability cost. Other costs may be incurred due to the service interruptions and customers dissatisfaction. On one hand, applying a vulnerability fix may require disabling a service temporarily or restarting the host machine. On another hand, blocking a service on the network level may have permanent effects on the consumers of that service. These side effects may have significant impacts on the system's mission-critical services. The usability cost may be crucial in some cases to decide between actions that have equivalent implementation costs. For example, inspecting the traffic of a particular service should have less cost on the usability than completely blocking it. If both options can reduce the risk to acceptable levels, our framework will select inspection over blocking. The attributes of vulnerability fixes that are provided in the XCCDF documents quantify the interruption that might be caused by fixes. Those attributes are valuable for estimating the usability cost of mitigation actions.

The following equations formalize the mitigation costs as assertions in the constraints satisfaction problem. The total mitigation cost is captured by the variable $COST$.

$$\underset{r \in \mathbb{R}}{\forall} : \underset{v \in V}{\forall} : \underset{k \in dom(p_{r,v})}{\forall} : (p_{r,v} = k) \implies c_{r,v} = f\_cost(r, v, k) + f\_use(r, v, k)$$
(8)

$$\underset{\substack{r,l \in \mathbb{R} \\ r \neq l}}{\forall} : \underset{k \in \mathbb{A}}{\forall} : (b_{r,l} = k) \implies cm_{r,l} = cm\_cost(r, l, k) + cm\_use(r, l, k) \qquad (9)$$

$$COST = \sum_{r \in \mathbb{R}} \sum_{j \in V_r} c_{r,j} + \sum_{\substack{r,l \in \mathbb{R} \\ r \neq l}} cm_{r,l} \qquad (10)$$

We use the variable $c_{r,v}$ to represent the cumulative cost of applying the appropriate fix to the vulnerability or the configuration weakness v of service r. Since we may have multiple fixes per vulnerability or configuration weakness, the value of this variable is assigned based on the decision variable $p_{r,v}$, which represents the selected fix. The function $f\_cost(i, j, k)$ returns the implementation cost of applying the fix k of the vulnerability or configuration weakness j at service i and $f\_use(i, j, k)$ returns the usability cost of the same fix. Similarly, the variable $cm_{r,l}$ represents the cumulative cost of deploying the appropriate network-based action for the flow from the service r to the service l based on the value of the decision variable $b_{r,l}$. Since it is likely to have multiple possible network-based actions, we use the functions $cm\_cost(r, l, k)$ and $cm\_use(r, l, k)$ to map this variable to the appropriate value for each action k.

4.4   Risk Computation

The risk scores of individual services as well as the entire network are the major decision-making factors in the automated risk mitigation process. We define intermediate variables as part of the constraints satisfaction problem to compute the residual risk in terms of the decision variables. As shown in the following equations, we define the variables ThI_r and Exp_r for each service $r \in \mathbb{R}$ to compute its *ThreatIndicator* and *Exposure*, respectively. The *ThreatIndicator* is computed based on the variables that represent the active vulnerabilities, configuration weaknesses, and the *Malice* scores reported through host-based intrusion detection tools. The set of variables $\mathbb{P}$ has already been defined to represent the vulnerabilities and the configuration weaknesses. We define another set of variables, $\mathbb{L} = \{l_r \mid r \in \mathbb{R}\}$, to represent the *Malice* scores of the services.

$$\forall_{r \in \mathbb{R}} : ThI_r = \beta \times \frac{\left(\sum_{j \in V_r} (p_{r,j} == 0) \times e_j \times g_j\right)}{n_t} + (1 - \beta) \times l_r \qquad (11)$$

$$\underset{r \in \mathbb{R}}{\forall} : Exp_r = \sum_{k \in T_r} \left(ThI_k \times (1 - Res_{k,r})\right), \text{ where} \qquad (12)$$

$$\underset{r \in \mathbb{R}}{\forall} : \underset{k \in T_r}{\forall} : Res_{k,r} = \underset{0 \le i < |\mathcal{P}_{k,r}|}{\max} \left\{ \underset{v \in V_{\mathcal{P}_{k,r}^{i+1}}}{\min} \{\mathbb{N}[v, b_{\mathcal{P}_{k,r}^i, \mathcal{P}_{k,r}^{i+1}}]\} \right\} \qquad (13)$$

As shown in Eq. (11), the vulnerability j contributes to the threat indicator of the service only if it is not selected to be fixed (i.e., when $p_{r,j} == 0$). If the decision variable $p_{r,j}$ has any other value, this condition ($p_{r,j} == 0$) will be false and the vulnerability will have no impact on the threat indicator of the service. Recall that based on our model presented in Sect. 2, the exposure of the service r (represented by the variable Exp_r) depends on the number of threat sources that can reach it (represented by the set T_r), and the threat resistance in the paths that leads to the service (represented by the variables $\{Res_{k,r} \mid k \in T_r\}$). The resistance depends on the mitigation actions taken at the network level. Thus, in Eq. (13), it is expressed in terms of the set of the decision variables in $\mathbb{B}$.

Given that the variables of the *ThreatIndicator* and *Exposure* are defined for each service r, we compute its risk score in terms of these variables as follows:

$$\forall_{r \in \mathbb{R}} : Risk_r = AV_r \times Exp_r \times \left(\sum_{j \in V_r} (p_{r,j} == 0) \times e_j \times m_j \right) / n_p \qquad (14)$$

4.5 Constraints Formalization

We formalize the following three types of constraints to devise a cost-effective set of mitigation actions.

$$ROI \geq \tau_{roi} \qquad (15)$$

$$\sum_{r \in \mathbb{R}} Risk_r \leq \tau_{gr} \qquad (16)$$

$$COST \leq B_{high} \qquad (17)$$

The first constraint, Eq. (15), is the mitigation objective, which sets a threshold, τ_{roi}, on the ROI value. In terms of the variables we defined earlier in our constraints satisfaction problem, the ROI is computed according to the following expression:

$$ROI = \frac{\left(Risk_{init} - \sum_{r \in \mathbb{R}} Risk_r\right) - COST}{COST} \qquad (18)$$

where the variable $COST$ represents the total mitigation cost. Given the initial risk, $Risk_{init}$, we subtract the projected risk after implementing the selected mitigation actions from $Risk_{init}$ to obtain the benefit. Note that $Risk_{init}$ is independent from our decision variables and can be calculated in advance.

The second and third constraints, Eqs. (16) and (17), specify the thresholds, τ_{gr} and B_{high}, for the total residual risk and the total mitigation cost, respectively. The user does not have to provide all the three constraints. Any set of them would be sufficient to devise a mitigation plan, but not necessarily the intended one. The second and third constraints might be needed in some situations to achieve more practical results. For example, assuming the initial risk is 32 and we want to achieve a ROI greater than or equal to 2. This can be achieved by spending a total cost of 8 to reduce the risk from 32 to 8. However, let us assume that a residual risk greater than 4 is not acceptable. In this case, we can add a constraint to find a solution that is restricting the residual risk below 4 instead of 8 and achieve a ROI greater than or equal to 2 at the same time. In this particular example, this is possible if we spend $\frac{28}{3}$ instead of only 8.

4.6 Continuous Risk Mitigation

For continuous risk mitigation, our risk assessment and mitigation actions synthesis must be repeated periodically to mitigate emerging threats based on up to date compliance reports and threat scores. This can be accomplished by building the complete set of assertions that constitute our constraint satisfaction problem from scratch in each round. However, since building these assertions can be time consuming especially for large-scale networks, we utilize the backtracking feature that is available in the Z3 SMT solver using push/pop operations. Utilizing this feature, the continuous risk mitigation is performed according to the process shown in Fig. 2.

The first two steps in this process are performed only once. In the first step, we define all the decision and intermediate variables, including the host-based and network-based actions variables, $\mathbb{P}$ and $\mathbb{B}$, and the *Malice* scores variables, $\mathbb{L}$. In the second step, we build the assertions required to compute the risk and find the set of mitigation actions (Eqs. 8–17), and add them to the constraint satisfaction problem. At this step, these assertions are expressed in terms of the model variables regardless of their exact values.

The remaining three steps will be repeated in every round. In the third step, we push the current values of the variables based on the live compliance reports,

Fig. 2 Continuous risk mitigation using Z3 push/pop operations

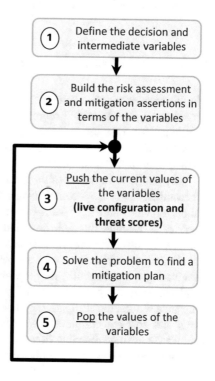

threat scores, and network configuration. We then solve the constraints satisfaction problem to find the appropriate mitigation actions. In the last step, we pop the values of the variables to backtrack to the original model without specific values. This process will reduce the computation in the repeated rounds because the majority of the Z3 assertions will be built only once at the first round, minor changes will be introduced in the later rounds based on the new values of the variables.

5   Implementation and Evaluation

In this section, we present the performance evaluation of our automated risk mitigation planning framework. We implemented our framework using Java to read the network configuration and build the SMT assertions using the Z3 Java API. All the experiments were conducted on a standard PC with 3.4 GHz Intel Core i7 processor and 16 GB of RAM. In our previous work [8], we presented experiments to show that our risk metric returns valid risk estimation compared to the ground-truth collected through attack simulation. The experiments demonstrated that the risk scores calculated using our risk estimation model are valid and consistent with the damage sustained as a result of worm attacks. We show in the following the performance of our automated risk mitigation with respect to different network attributes, including its size and the number of vulnerabilities.

5.1   Real Network Case Study

In this case study, we evaluate the performance of our framework on the Stanford backbone network, which represents a mid-size enterprise network whose entire configuration rule set has been made public for researchers [19]. The network consists of 14 zones connected to two backbone routers via ten layer-2 switches, with a total of 240 hosts.

The public information of the Stanford backbone network includes the topology, forwarding, and access control configuration. However, it does include information about services and their vulnerabilities. In our experiment, we assume that one service is running on each host and we distributed a number of vulnerabilities uniformly on the network services. We used the real forwarding and access control configuration to resolve the connectivity between the services. Since we are evaluating a real network, we generated 25 instances that have the same topology and connectivity, but they defer in the distribution of vulnerabilities. For each instance we ran our mitigation planner multiple times with different values for the ROI and cost constraints and we calculated the average planning time. Figure 3 shows the average planning time for each instance.

The results show that the maximum time was about 15 min for a real mid-size network that has an average of 15 vulnerabilities per service. We believe this is

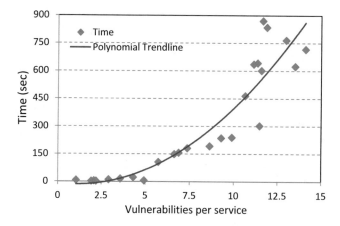

Fig. 3 Real network case study

acceptable since the mitigation planning can be run offline and it does not interfere with the live operation of the network. In addition, we can see that the growth on the planning time is polynomial with respect to the number of vulnerabilities.

5.2 Mitigation Planner Scalability Evaluation

In order to thoroughly study the impact of multiple network parameters on the mitigation planner performance, we generated a large number of synthetic networks. We start by generating a topology using BRITE topology generator [20] according to Waxman model. Then, we distributed a number of services as leaf nodes in the topology. Initially, we add the appropriate forwarding rules to the routers such that all services are reachable from each other. Then, we add access control rules to block the traffic between random pairs of services. Finally, we generate compliance reports for each service by selecting a set of vulnerabilities and assigning a random scanning results (i.e., pass or fail) for each of them.

For all our experimental settings, we ran the mitigation planner multiple times with different ROI and cost thresholds, including some *unsat* cases, where no satisfiable solution is possible. We discuss in the following the impact of the network size, the connectivity degree, and the number of vulnerabilities per host on the time required to solve the satisfaction problem.

The Impact of the Network Size The network size in this experiment refers to the number of end-points (i.e., services). To evaluate the impact of the number of services in the network, we generated a number of networks with varying sizes of up to 1500 services. We fixed the number of vulnerabilities per service to one, and we generated two sets of networks. In one set the connectivity degree was set to 75

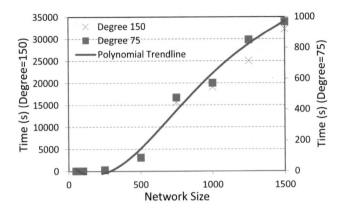

Fig. 4 The impact of network size

(i.e., each service in the network can be directly or indirectly reached by 75 other services), while it was set to 150 in the other set. The average execution time is reported in Fig. 4. The results depict almost the same behavior for both connectivity degree settings. We can see that the processing time may take several hours for networks beyond 500 services due to the non linear operations that are required to calculate the risk. However, the increase in the time requirements is still polynomial and we are working on simplification techniques to reduce the processing time.

The Impact of the Connectivity Degree The connectivity degree refers to the size of the reachability tree of each service, which represents the number of services that can directly or indirectly reach it. Based on our formal model, the number of reconfiguration decision variables (i.e., $|\mathbb{B}|$) is directly proportional to the connectivity degree since we add a decision variable for each node in the reachability tree. In this experiment, we generated multiple networks with average connectivity degrees that varied from 25 to 300. We also generated two sets of networks. In one set, the size (number of services) of the networks was 500 and in the other set, it was set to 250. The results reported in Fig. 5 show that the execution time follows the same behavior in the two sets of networks, that is, the size of the network did not affect the growth order of the processing time. The figure indicates a logarithmic complexity of the execution time with respect to the connectivity degree. We believe this is due to the fact that at large connectivity degrees, it is likely to have redundant paths in the reachability trees of different services. This will help the Z3 solver to simplify the assertions set and consequently reduce the execution time.

The Impact of the Number of Vulnerabilities For this experiment, we generated two sets of networks of fixed sizes, 250 services in one set and 500 services in the other. In both sets, the number of vulnerabilities per service varied between 15 and 80. According to the a report released by NOPSEC [21], the average number of

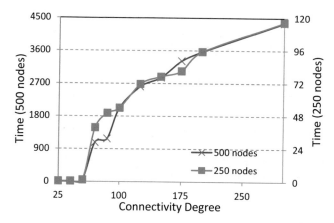

Fig. 5 The impact of the connectivity degree

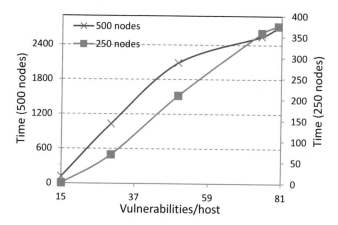

Fig. 6 The impact of vulnerabilities number

vulnerabilities per asset is less than 20. Hence, we believe that 80 is a large number of vulnerabilities to exist in one host and we have not evaluated higher numbers. The results are reported in Fig. 6. We can see that the execution time with respect to the number of vulnerabilities per host is not computationally expensive and it follows a linear trend line.

6 Related Works

In this section, we focus on the recent research conducted in the area of automated risk scoring and mitigation, focusing on those that employ standard specifications and scoring systems, such as XCCDF, OVAL, and CVSS, which have been utilized in many quantitative and qualitative risk assessment models. Houmb et al. [22] derived a frequency and impact metrics based on the CVSS score. They have combined these new metrics to quantitatively estimate the risk level of information systems. Joh and Malaiya [23] employed a stochastic model based on CVSS metrics in a formal quantitative approach for software risk evaluation. None of these works integrates the host vulnerabilities with the network configuration for comprehensive analysis. Homer et al. [5] proposed a security metric model to aggregate vulnerability metrics, in an enterprise network, to measure the likelihood of breaches within a given network configuration through attack graphs. Homer's model and other risk estimation techniques based on attack graphs, such as [24, 25], are driven by specific attack scenarios and they do not provide global quantitative risk scores.

In [26], Barrere et al. present a model for generating vulnerability remediation plans in network systems based on SAT solvers. In [27], the authors use attack graphs that augment feeds from vulnerability scanners in order to prioritize vulnerability patching. These works did not consider network-based reconfiguration actions. Albanese et al. in [28] propose an approximation algorithm to automatically generate network hardening recommendations based on attack graph analysis. Poolsappasit et al. [29] proposed a model that uses the sub-scores reported by CVSS as vulnerability exploitation probabilities that are fed to a Bayesian attack graph for calculating the global risk and they use a genetic algorithm to solve the optimal countermeasure selection problem. Those solutions require complete information about the attack exploits in terms of pre- and post-conditions as attack graphs are inputs for their countermeasure selection algorithms. They are also limited in the types of vulnerabilities that are covered. In [30] and [31], Chung et al. presented a framework called NICE to detect and mitigate vulnerability-exploiting attacks in the cloud virtual networking environment. They used attack graph-based approach to quantify the risk utilizing the base scores of vulnerabilities from CVSS, and recommends the optimal response actions to alerts from a pre-defined list of countermeasures. The selected countermeasure is optimal with respect to a particular node, and not necessarily to the global network, considering the possible attack paths that could have caused the alert. Therefore, it is not clear how this approach can scale with the network size.

In this work, we refine our preliminary risk metrics presented in [8, 32] and we utilize them for fine-grained mitigation planning. We do not directly use the base scores of vulnerabilities as reported in the scoring systems, rather, we utilize their basic sub-scores in our metrics. The exploitability sub-score of potential attack victims and the integrity impact base-metric of the potential threat sources are used to quantify the likelihood of attack propagation, while the impact sub-score is used to quantify the potential loss. We consider all common types of vulnerabilities including configuration weaknesses and feature misuse vulnerability, which can provide more, and normally cheaper, service-level risk mitigation actions. In addition, we integrate live activity and threat scores to tune our risk mitigation decisions based on the dynamic behavior of potential threat sources. Our framework provides the ability to incorporate various technology-specific network-based mitigation options.

We consider the impact of each possible mitigation action on the whole network and the devised risk mitigation plan (that can include multiple mitigation actions) is guaranteed to bring the risk of the global network in compliance with the specified thresholds.

7 Conclusions and Future Work

This paper presents a formal framework for mitigating risk using configuration hardening by analyzing the security compliance reports along with universal vulnerability scores, the live activity and threat scores collected through host-based intrusion detection tools, and the network data-plane configuration. We presented a model for measuring the network global risk and employed it in the automated generation of cost-effective risk mitigation plans. Our framework can formally synthesis the most critical the most critical set of host-based and network-based risk mitigation actions that reduce the residual risk and achieve the desired ROI.

We believe that the contribution of this work is particularly important for automating security hardening based on open standards such as SCAP (specifically, XCCDF documents). Although we managed to run our mitigation planning for networks up to 1500 hosts and high degree of dependency between the hosts, the computation is expected to be more complex in larger networks due to the non-linear arithmetic operations that are needed in order to accurately calculate the global risk. The complete mitigation planning is expected to be conducted offline periodically and it does not affect the normal operation of networks. However, we are planning to investigate simplification techniques to reduce the complexity of our constraints satisfaction problem and reduce the execution time.

References

1. NIST. The Technical Specification for the Security Content Automation Protocol (SCAP). http://csrc.nist.gov/publications/PubsDrafts.html#SP-800-126-Rev-3.
2. Nessus professional. https://www.tenable.com/products/nessus/nessus-professional.
3. Tripwire security vulnerability and risk management. https://www.tenable.com/whitepapers/tenable-network-security-support-portal.
4. Openvas - open vulnerability assessment system. http://www.openvas.org/.
5. John Homer, Su Zhang, Xinming Ou, David Schmidt, Yanhui Du, S Raj Rajagopalan, and Anoop Singhal. Aggregating vulnerability metrics in enterprise networks using attack graphs. *Journal of Computer Security*, 21(4):561–597, 2013.
6. Xinming Ou, Wayne F Boyer, and Miles A McQueen. A scalable approach to attack graph generation. In *Proceedings of the 13th ACM conference on Computer and communications security*, pages 336–345. ACM, 2006.
7. Oleg Sheyner, Joshua Haines, Somesh Jha, Richard Lippmann, and Jeannette M Wing. Automated generation and analysis of attack graphs. In *Security and privacy, 2002. Proceedings. 2002 IEEE Symposium on*, pages 273–284. IEEE, 2002.

8. Mohammed Noraden Alsaleh, Ehab Al-Shaer, and Ghaith Husari. Roi-driven cyber risk mitigation using host compliance and network configuration. *Journal of Network and Systems Management*, 25(4):759–783, 2017.
9. David Waltermire, Charles Schmidt, Karen Scarfone, and Neal Ziring. Specification for the extensible configuration checklist description format (XCCDF) v1.2. http://csrc.nist.gov/publications/nistir/ir7275-rev4/NISTIR-7275r4.pdf, 2012.
10. Rory Bray, Daniel Cid, and Andrew Hay. *OSSEC host-based intrusion detection guide*. Syngress, 2008.
11. Leonardo De Moura and Nikolaj Bjørner. Z3: An efficient smt solver. In *Proceedings of the Theory and Practice of Software, 14th International Conference on Tools and Algorithms for the Construction and Analysis of Systems*, TACAS'08/ETAPS'08, pages 337–340, Berlin, Heidelberg, 2008. Springer-Verlag.
12. Ehab Al-Shaer, Wilfredo Marrero, Adel El-Atawy, and Khalid Elbadawi. Network configuration in a box: Towards end-to-end verification of network reachability and security. In *ICNP*, pages 123–132, 2009.
13. Karen Scarfone and Peter Mell. The common configuration scoring system (CCSS): Metrics for software security configuration vulnerabilities, December 2010.
14. Mirek Jahoda, Ioanna Gkioka, Robert Krátký, Martin Prpič, Tomáš Čapek, Stephen Wadeley, Yoana Ruseva, and Miroslav Svoboda. Red hat enterprise linux 7 security guide. 2017.
15. Common Vulnerabilities and Exposures (CVE). http://cve.mitre.org/, 2017.
16. Common Configuration Enumeration (CCE). http://cce.mitre.org/, 2017.
17. Aide - advanced intrusion detection environment. https://aide.github.io/.
18. Prelude siem - intrusion detection system. https://www.prelude-siem.com/.
19. James Hongyi Zeng and Peyman Kazemian. Mini-Stanford Backbone). https://reproducingnetworkresearch.wordpress.com/2012/07/11/atpg/, 2012.
20. Alberto Medina, Anukool Lakhina, Ibrahim Matta, and John Byers. Brite: An approach to universal topology generation. In *Modeling, Analysis and Simulation of Computer and Telecommunication Systems, 2001. Proceedings. Ninth International Symposium on*, pages 346–353. IEEE, 2001.
21. NOPSEC. State of vulnerability risk management. http://info.nopsec.com/sov, 2015.
22. Siv Hilde Houmb, Virginia N.L. Franqueira, and Erlend A. Engum. Quantifying security risk level from CVSS estimates of frequency and impact. *Journal of Systems and Software*, 83(9):1622–1634, 2010.
23. HyunChul Joh and Yashwant K Malaiya. Defining and assessing quantitative security risk measures using vulnerability lifecycle and cvss metrics. In *The 2011 international conference on security and management (sam)*, 2011.
24. Xinming Ou and Anoop Singhal. Security risk analysis of enterprise networks using attack graphs. In *Quantitative Security Risk Assessment of Enterprise Networks*, pages 13–23. Springer, 2011.
25. Xiaochuan Yin, Yan Fang, and Yibo Liu. Real-time risk assessment of network security based on attack graphs. In *2013 International Conference on Information Science and Computer Applications (ISCA 2013)*. Atlantis Press, 2013.
26. M. Barrere, R. Badonnel, and O. Festor. A sat-based autonomous strategy for security vulnerability management. In *Network Operations and Management Symposium (NOMS), 2014 IEEE*, pages 1–9, May 2014.
27. K. Ingols, R. Lippmann, and K. Piwowarski. Practical attack graph generation for network defense. In *Computer Security Applications Conference, 2006. ACSAC '06. 22nd Annual*, pages 121–130, Dec 2006.
28. M. Albanese, S. Jajodia, and S. Noel. Time-efficient and cost-effective network hardening using attack graphs. In *Dependable Systems and Networks (DSN), 2012 42nd Annual IEEE/IFIP International Conference on*, pages 1–12, June 2012.
29. a N. Poolsappasit, R. Dewri, and I Ray. Dynamic security risk management using bayesian attack graphs. *IEEE Transactions on Dependable and Secure Computing*, 9(1):61–74, Jan 2012.

30. Chun-Jen Chung, Pankaj Khatkar, Tianyi Xing, Jeongkeun Lee, and Dijiang Huang. Nice: Network intrusion detection and countermeasure selection in virtual network systems. *IEEE transactions on dependable and secure computing*, 10(4):198–211, 2013.
31. Chun-Jen Chung, JingSong Cui, Pankaj Khatkar, and Dijiang Huang. Non-intrusive process-based monitoring system to mitigate and prevent vm vulnerability explorations. In *Collaborative Computing: Networking, Applications and Worksharing (Collaboratecom), 2013 9th International Conference on*, pages 21–30. IEEE, 2013.
32. Mohammed Noraden Alsaleh, Ghaith Husari, and Ehab Al-Shaer. Optimizing the roi of cyber risk mitigation. In *Network and Service Management (CNSM), 2016 12th International Conference on*, pages 223–227. IEEE, 2016.

Plan Interdiction Games

Yevgeniy Vorobeychik and Michael Pritchard

1 Introduction

Interdiction seems by its very nature an adversarial act, one perpetrated, if you will, by "bad guys." For example, an attacker may interdict the power flow on an electric power grid, resulting in widespread blackouts [15], or interdict a transportation or a supply network [8, 11]. Consequently, it may be somewhat jarring at first to consider the *defender*—the "good guy"—as the interdictor. We would like to argue that in cybersecurity this is precisely the ultimate goal of the defender: to *interdict* an attack, whether actual or potential. In particular, in this chapter we will illustrate that cyber attacks are naturally viewed as plans, or dynamic decision processes by malicious agents.

At the most basic level, a plan is a sequence of actions which, if successfully executed beginning from an appropriate initial state, accomplishes a planner's goal. Of course, this notion of a plan is quite restricted; for example, if uncertainty is at all salient, an intelligent plan would involve *contingencies*, or a mapping from observed state to action. The perspective we will take in this chapter is that the *attacker is such a planner*. The initial state for the attacker includes the initial vulnerabilities of the target network, as well as any relevant capabilities and information that the attacker possesses. An attack is then a series of actions—perhaps, as a part of a contingent plan of actions—aimed at accomplishing a malicious goal, or perhaps a contingent series of goals, each with a different value to the attacker. The defender, as we had remarked, is the *interdictor*: insofar as the attacker's plan would accomplish goals which are contrary to the defender's desires, the defender would wish to prevent this from happening. A myopic defender would simply attempt to interdict past

Y. Vorobeychik (✉) · M. Pritchard
Department of Electrical Engineering and Computer Science, Vanderbilt University, Nashville, TN, USA
e-mail: michael.j.pritchard@vanderbilt.edu

© Springer Nature Switzerland AG 2020
S. Jajodia et al. (eds.), *Adaptive Autonomous Secure Cyber Systems*,
https://doi.org/10.1007/978-3-030-33432-1_8

attacks; arguably, that is what most cyber-defense is like in practice: preventing attacks which have been identified from succeeding. We argue for a longer, proactive view: the defender can, and should, reason about alternative attack plans that the attacker *could make*, for particular defensive interdiction strategies, and choose an *optimal* interdiction—one that proactively accounts not merely for previously known attacks, but possible future variations which circumvent the defense as well.

Below, we begin with a simple example to illustrate the nature of attack plans and interdictions. Subsequently, we describe several formal modeling approaches for plan interdiction, first when the planning environment is deterministic, and subsequently when it is stochastic. We follow with an in-depth illustration of the approach by using it as a modeling framework for network cyber risk assessment. We then suggest future research directions that consider longer term attack plans, when the defender is able to observe, and react to, some of the attack actions. These directions present interesting questions about optimal adaptive defense, as well as important considerations of adversarial deception.

2   A Simple Example

As a simple illustration, consider the following example of an attack planning problem. The initial state includes the initial attacker capabilities, such as possession of a boot disk and port scanning utilities. Actions include both physical actions (breaking and entering and booting a machine from disk) as well as cyber actions, such as performing a port scan to find vulnerabilities.[1] Figure 1 shows an attack graph (with attack actions as nodes) for this scenario, with the actual attack plan highlighted in red.

Figure 2, on the other hand, shows an example interdiction plan. In this example, we interdict a subset of actions (for example, by patching specific vulnerabilities, or changing the network architecture). A noteworthy observation about the particular interdiction strategy in Fig. 2 is that it still allows the attacker to attack a low-stakes target. This is because, in this specific example, interdicting all possibilities is not cost-effective, relative to the consequence of successful attack.

3   Planning in AI

We begin by formalizing the notion of *planning*, starting with classical planning in deterministic domains, and then considering generalizations that allow us to capture uncertainty.

---

[1]The actions in our example are taken from the CAPEC database (http://capec.mitre.org).

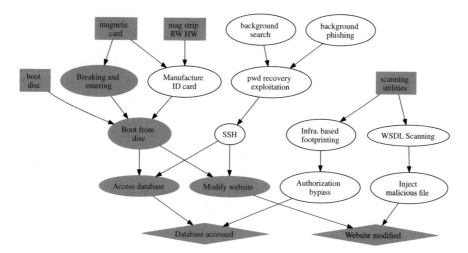

Fig. 1 Example attack graph. Boxes correspond to initial attacker capabilities, ovals are attack actions, and diamonds are attacker goals. An optimal attack plan is highlighted in red

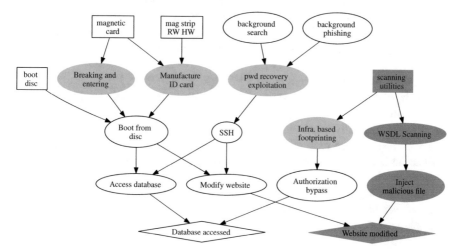

Fig. 2 Example interdiction plan: actions that are blocked are colored in blue, and the final attack plan (circumvention) is highlighted in red

3.1 Classical Planning

Formally, a classical (deterministic) planning problem is a tuple $\{X, A, s_0, G, r, c\}$, where X is the set of literals (binary variables) which represent the state of the world relevant for the planning problem, A is the set of actions, s_0 is the set of literals which are initially true (i.e., the initial state of the world), and G is the set of goals. A plan action $a \in A$ is characterized by a set of *preconditions*, that is, the set of literals that must be true in the current state for the action to be applicable, and a set of *effects*, which either add literals from current state, or delete these, thereby determining transition from one state to another. A reward function r_l assigns a value (utility) to each goal literal $l \in G$ (we assume that the total utility is additive in these). Finally, c_a is the cost of taking an action a. A solution to this planning problem is a plan π, which is a sequence of actions. A number of effective approaches exist for solving such planning problems at scale [5].

3.2 Planning Under Uncertainty

A common formalization of planning under uncertainty makes use of *Markov decision processes (MDPs)*, defined by a tuple $\{S, A, P, r, p_0\}$, where S is the set of states (of the world), A the set of actions, $P(s, a, s') = \Pr\{s'|s, a\}$ a transition function which represents system dynamics as a function of state s and action $a \in A$ taken by the planner, $R(s, a)$ the reward function, and $p_0(s)$ the probability distribution over initial states; below, we assume that there is a fixed starting state s_0 [14]. A solution to the MDP is a policy, π, which determines actions to take as a function of relevant information. If we further assume that the MDP is discrete-time, infinite-horizon, and discounted (future is discounted exponentially, with a discount factor $\gamma \in [0, 1)$), we can restrict attention to policies $\pi(s)$ which map states to actions taken in these states [7, 14].

A major problem with moving from classical planning to MDPs is representational: in MDPs the full state space S is explicitly represented, whereas it is only implicit in classical planning, a result of joint values of state literals. *Factored MDPs (FMDPs)* aim to address this gap. Specifically, instead of specifying the state space S, FMDPs are represented by a collection X of state variables (which we take to be binary henceforth); these are random variables, with $X = x$ denoting a particular instantiation of these to values x. Dynamics are now represented by a Dynamic Bayes Network for each action a; further, we assume that the reward function is additive in state variables, i.e., $r(x, a) = \sum_j r_j(x_j, a)$, where r_j are the variable-specific rewards. Well-known approaches exist for approximately solving FMDPs [9].

4 Plan Interdiction Problem

Our ultimate goal is not merely to compute an optimal plan for the attacker, but rather to compute *an optimal defender interdiction strategy*. To this end, we model the interaction between the defender and attacker as a Stackelberg game in which the defender moves first, choosing to deploy a set of mitigations, and the attacker responds to these by constructing an optimal attack plan given the resulting environment. We can formalize this game as a *plan interdiction problem (PIP)*, defined by $\{\mathcal{M}, c_m, r^D, \phi\}$, where $\mathcal{M}$ is the set of defender mitigation actions,

c_m is the cost of a mitigation $m \in \mathcal{M}$, the defender's reward function $r^D(x) = \sum_j r_j(x_j)$, which is additive over state variables, and the underlying planning problem ϕ for the attacker. The consequence of a mitigation m can be twofold: it can modify current (initial) state s_0, and remove a subset of attacker actions. Thus, if S is a subset of mitigations used by the defender, these modify the attacker's planning problem ϕ; we denote the resulting modified problem by $\phi(S)$, and the associated optimal plan for the attacker by $\pi(S)$. In the PIP, the defender's goal is to choose the optimal set of mitigations S, balancing the defender's utility $V^D(S; \pi(S))$ (total expected discounted reward) and cost of mitigations $c(S) = \sum_{m \in S} c_m$:

$$\max_{S \subseteq \mathcal{M}} V^D(S; \pi(S)) - c(S), \qquad (1)$$

where $\pi(S)$ is the attacker's best response plan, that is, its optimal plan over the restricted planning domain $\phi(S)$.

We first discuss the special case of this problem in the context of deterministic planning, and follow with a more general treatment when uncertainty is involved.

4.1 Interdiction of Deterministic Plans

In the deterministic setting, plan interdiction is focused on goals that can be achieved by the attacker. Recall that G is the set of goal literals, and r_l is the reward to the attacker for achieving a goal literal $l \in G$. We now augment this with a defender's corresponding reward r_l^D (presumably, negative). The plan interdiction problem then becomes

$$\max_{S \subseteq \mathcal{M}} \sum_{l \in G} z_l(\pi(S)) r_l^D - c(S),$$

where z_l is a binary indicator of whether the goal literal l is achieved by the attacker. Letchford and Vorobeychik [10] show that this bi-level optimization problem can be solved using a combination of mixed-integer linear programming and constraint generation, where constraints represent possible attack plans, and are iteratively added by computing approximately optimal plans using state-of-the-art heuristic planning software, such as SGPlan [5].

4.2 Interdicting MDPs

The power of deterministic planning and associated interdiction is that it involves solving highly structured problems, and we can therefore develop a scalable approach for these. The limitation is generality: often, uncertainty in the planning problem faced by the attacker must be appropriately captured.

We model the attacker's planning problem when it faces uncertainty by an MDP, described above. Specifically, we can address the MDP interdiction problem, which can be defined just as its deterministic counterpart above, but using the more general utility function $V^D(S; \pi(S))$. The interdiction problem can then be described very generally by the Eq. (1).

While it is possible to solve MDP interdiction problems using a similar approach for bi-linear optimization as developed by Letchford and Vorobeychik [10], these require that the state space be explicitly represented. Panda and Vorobeychik [13] addressed this technical challenge by integrating state-of-the-art approaches for approximately solving FMDPs by Guestrin et al. [9] with a bi-level framework, and appealing to Fourier representation of a value function over a Boolean space [12].

While the approach by Panda and Vorobeychik [13] enables a considerable advance in solving MDP interdiction problems over factored MDP representations, it is still somewhat limited in scalability. Moreover, a major challenge in plan interdiction approaches to date is that the defender is typically uncertain about the attacker's planning problem, such as the initial vulnerabilities and attacker's access and capabilities, and the resulting Bayesian Stackelberg game is infeasible for current methods for even small problem instances [10].

In recent research, we have taken an alternative approach which integrates reinforcement learning with function approximation. Combined with a restriction that the defender's mitigations only modify initial state (which is without loss of generality, since we can capture action removal by adding associated preconditions to initial state), we can now learn a general value function for the attacker over the state space, and then solve the interdiction problem once, without having to iteratively re-solve the planning problem. Additionally, we can introduce uncertainty about the attacker by capturing it as uncertainty over a subset of initial state variables. In the special case when the value function is linear (or approximated by a linear function), we can transform the Bayesian interdiction problem into a form which can be solved using integer linear programming, a significant advance in scalability compared to prior art.

4.3 Interdicting Partially Observable MDPs

MDPs model an attacker's uncertainty about dynamics. However, they ignore another crucial consideration: attacker's uncertainty about the true state of the system. Insofar as this introduces information asymmetry between the defender and attacker, it introduces a potentially very rich space of interdiction options for the defender. One issue that arises is signaling: if the defender knows aspects of the initial state which are unknown to the attacker, the defender's mitigations can signal to the attacker information about the true initial state. This, in turn, provides an opportunity for deception: the defender may, through particular (costly) mitigations they deploy signal to an attacker that they have vulnerabilities they do not actually have, thereby deceiving the attacker into expending resources into an attack which cannot succeed. In addition, the defender may also control the observations of the attacker about system state, a capability which can provide further leverage.

As we can see, this *partially observable Markov decision process (POMDP) interdiction problem* is exceptionally rich. It is also an open problem from a computational perspective—we would argue, the next important open problem in plan interdiction.

5 Illustration: Threat Risk Assessment Using Plan Interdiction

Having motivated the plan interdiction problem rather abstractly, we now illustrate its value more concretely by using the planning framework for network cyber-risk analysis and mitigation. Specifically, we first define a model for cyber threat assessment using classical planning primitives, augmenting these with stochastic information which represents uncertainty about attacker's access, such as which user accounts the attacker has already compromised. We then describe an implementation of this model, and demonstrate its value through experiments. Finally, we show that by selectively patching a small set of vulnerabilities we can dramatically reduce cyber risk.

5.1 Model

In creating our network threat assessment model, we define six components: a set of hosts H, the system environment T, a dictionary of vulnerabilities V, the target file F, and the attacker A with action set S. Next, we formally describe these components. For illustration, we assume that the attacker aims to exfiltrate a particular file, which may represent sensitive information such as trade secrets.

Each host in our model represents a device within the target environment, with no inherent distinction made among personal computers, servers, mobile devices, etc. Formally, we define a host $h_i \in H$ as possessing three attributes: a set of exploitable vulnerabilities $V_i \subset V$, the set of neighboring hosts $N_i \subset H$, and a flag $F_i \in \{0, 1\}$, which indicates if the target file is present on the host. Vulnerabilities are assigned to a host stochastically, reflecting differences in particular host configurations, non-deterministic exploitation outcomes, and the relative complexity of executing the exploit. The set of neighbors N_i of a host h_i is the set of all hosts which can potentially be accessed from h_i.

The system environment variable T contains the state of each host t_i. The state is represented by a binary vector, and contains information pertaining to the status of the host relative to the attacker. For example, whether the attacker has read or write access to files on the host could be a pair of binary values in the state vector.

Vulnerabilities in the dictionary V are defined by two vectors $R_j, E_j \in \mathcal{R}^E$. The first of these, R_j, is the exploitation requirement vector: the minimum required state of the host (relative to the system environment vector for the host) for successful exploitation. One example of a state requirement would be a vulnerability which requires authentication with user credentials. After successful exploitation of a vulnerability, the state of the host is updated according to the exploitation effects vector, E_j.

The target file F is simply a binary valued variable that is initially set to 0. If the file is accessed by an attacker, it is updated to 1.

The attacker A possesses three attributes. The first of these is a set of hosts $C \subset H$ for which the attacker possesses user credentials (obtained, for example, through a phishing attack). The other two attributes are also sets of hosts, $H_a \subset H$ and $H_c \subset H$, which are those hosts which are accessible to the attacker and have been compromised by the attacker, respectively. In addition to the aforementioned attributes, the attacker has an abstract set of knowledge and tools to assess information about the system environment (e.g. connectivity between hosts). Further, the attacker is assumed to be able to exploit any vulnerability present on an accessible host.

The action set of the attacker, S, contains five categories of deterministic actions encapsulating reconnaissance, exploitation, and data access/exfiltration. These action categories are summarized formally in Table 1. The first two categories of actions, Exploration and Probing, deal with efforts by the attacker to learn information about hosts and the network. Exploration targets a single host h_i (which must in the set of compromised hosts) and results in the union of N_i, the host's neighborhood, with H_a, the set of accessible hosts. Probing examines an accessible host and checks for the presence of particular vulnerabilities.

The next two categories of actions pertain to malicious behavior executed by the attacker. Masquerading, the first of these actions, is the act of accessing a host through normal means (e.g. SSH) with the use of externally acquired user credentials. Naturally, this requires both that the attacker possesses suitable credentials and access to the host. The result of Masquerading is attainment of read and write privileges (denoted r_i and w_i for host h_i) to the target host. Exploitation, the second malicious action available to the attacker, targets a particular accessible host h_i with a vulnerability v_j. Satisfaction of vulnerability requirements R_j are necessary for execution of this action, and the effects of exploitation are according

Table 1 Categories of attacker actions

Preconditions	Action	Effects
$h_i \in H_c$	$Explore(h_i)$	$H_a = H_a \bigcup \{N_i\}$
$h_i \in H_a$	$Probe(h_i, V)$	$\{v_j \in V \mid R_j - (R_j \wedge t_i) = 0\}$
$h_i \in H_a \wedge h_i \in C$	$Masquerade(h_i)$	$r_i, w_i = 1$
$h_i \in H_a \wedge (R_j - (R_j \wedge t_i) = 0)$	$Exploit(h_i, v_j)$	$t_i = t_i \vee E_j$
$h_i \in H_c \wedge r_i = 1$	$Access(h_i)$	$F = 1$

to E_j. The final action available to the attacker is Access. This action targets a particular compromised host h_i and checks for the presence of the target file. If the file is present and the state of the host permits, the attacker accesses the file. Successful execution of this action is the goal for the attacker, and indicates that the system has been compromised successfully.

5.2 Implementing the Model

In this section we describe our implementation of the model given in Sect. 5.1.

5.2.1 Vulnerability Dictionary

To populate our dictionary of vulnerabilities, we turn to the National Vulnerability Database (NVD). Originally created in 2000 by the NIST Computer Security Division, the NVD is an extension of MITRE's Common Vulnerability and Exposures (CVE) dictionary that includes additional vulnerability assessment metrics. One of these metrics, the Common Vulnerability Scoring System (CVSS), is of particular interest to us.

Designed to communicate the characteristics and impact of vulnerabilities, the CVSS provides both quantitative scores and vectors of characteristics. The former indicates the holistic "severity" of the vulnerability, while the latter gives us some indication of the conditions necessary for and the results of successful exploitation. Three sets of metrics comprise the CVSS: base, temporal, and environmental metrics. Of these we only use the base metrics, which cover intrinsic qualities of a vulnerability. Base metrics are divided into exploitability metrics and impact metrics. The former captures information concerning vulnerability accessibility and has three parameters: attack vector (AV), access complexity (AC), and authentication (Au). Impact metrics gauge the potential effects of successful exploitation, divided into confidentiality, integrity, and availability impacts. As detailed in the next section, each of these parameters contributes to our vulnerability model.

5.2.2 Vulnerability Profiles

Having parsed the NVD to generate a vulnerability dictionary, we next construct profiles containing a subset of these vulnerabilities. To this end, we utilize the penetration testing suite Nessus. Specifically, we construct profiles by filtering Nessus vulnerability reports to recover CVE entry IDs, then populate the entries from our dictionary.

Based on CVSS information from the dictionary, we generate the set of exploitation requirements for each vulnerability and derive a value denoting the exploitation probability. Two base metric parameters are retained for later use: attack vector and authentication. The attack vector can take on one of three values, each of which introduces different preconditions for successful exploitation in our model. The most restrictive value, *Local*, requires an attacker to have either direct physical access to the machine or access to a shell account. A corresponding parameter for each host determines whether this level of access is present. *Adjacent Network* access, the second AV value, necessitates some kind of access to either the broadcast or collision domain of the host. In our model, this access is represented by directed edges between an already compromised system and the target system. Finally, *Network* access indicates that the vulnerability is remotely exploitable. Satisfying *Adjacent Access* or the corresponding network access parameter are required for exploitation in this case.

Authentication requirements can also take on one of three values: *None*, *Single*, and *Multiple*. As the latter two values indicate user credentials must be obtained, they introduce an additional precondition for exploitation of the vulnerability.

Exploitation probability is derived from a combination of base metrics and their corresponding weights in the CVSS severity calculation. The initial value of 1.0 is first multiplied by the scoring value associated with access complexity. This attribute captures the relative level of exploitation difficulty due to the presence of specialized access conditions (e.g. non-default software configurations). Low complexity, indicative of no specialized access conditions, has an associated value of 0.71. A value of 0.61 is used for medium complexity—so denoted when "somewhat" specialized access conditions are present. High complexity carries an associated value of 0.35. In the case that multiple authentications are required for exploitation of the vulnerability, the probability is multiplied by an additional factor of 0.8. Finally, we account for the non-deterministic quality of access granted by partial confidentiality impact with a multiplied factor of 0.5. Note that this value is not derived directly from the CVSS formula.

Phishing Attack Probability

Recognizing that attackers are not limited to exploiting software vulnerabilities, we include a phishing attack probability parameter P_P in our framework. Despite the name, the parameter is meant to encapsulate all social engineering vectors which result in the recovery of a user's credentials. In selecting a default value of 0.03, we examined the spear-phishing rate for small businesses (<250 employees) and the overall phishing rate from the 2016 Symantec Internet Security Threat Report.

In precisely defining the utilization of P_P in our model, we say that it is the probability a given host has one or more privileged user accounts whose credentials have been compromised. In so defining the parameter, we avoid the need to generate a set of user credentials and associate them in some manner with the hosts.

Zero-Day Attack Probability

In addition to published vulnerabilities and social engineering vectors, we consider that the attacker may have knowledge of one or more zero-day vulnerabilities which affect hosts. Since the NVD serves as our repository of vulnerabilities, we utilize it to determine our default probability of zero-day attacks. Specifically, we examined all of the CVE entries between 2002 and 2016 and compared the labeled year of the vulnerability (i.e. the year included in the CVE name) with the published date. If the two differed, the vulnerability was considered to have been present and unknown sufficiently long to qualify as a viable zero-day attack. On average across the span of years mentioned, approximately 13% of vulnerabilities meet this criterion.

5.2.3   Host Generation

In general, a host in our model can be any device connected to the network; however, for the initial implementation of the framework we limit ourselves to consideration of servers and personal computers. Hosts are defined fundamentally by a set of three attributes: the vulnerability profile, a list of neighboring hosts, and a set of access levels. A unique host name as well as a boolean value which indicates whether the host serves as a gateway are also included. The gateway indicator is used in our generative network model discussed in section "Organizational Network Generative Model".

Upon initialization of a host object, the set of vulnerabilities in the profile are iterated through, with each vulnerability being retained or discarded stochastically according to the associated probability of exploitation. This results in each host containing a subset of the full profile and reflects differences in host vulnerability due to varying software configurations.

Neighboring hosts in our model are any hosts which satisfy the properties of adjacent access (as defined in the CVSS). Viewing a particular instance of the model as a graph, each neighbor possesses an incoming directed edge.

The access levels list contains information on host properties related to exploit preconditions. In our initial implementation this consists of three values: network, root, and user access. The first indicates that the attacker can execute remote exploits on the host. Root access implies privilege escalation for the attacker on the host has been successfully carried out. Finally, user access indicates that the attacker possesses either user credentials for an account on the host or the means of equivalently authenticating.

5.2.4   Generation of PDDL

The planning domain and problem description for a particular instance are generated sequentially based on instances of the model described in Sect. 5.1. First the domain types and constants are produced. The former consists of three entries: *hosts*, *vulnerabilities*, and *files*. The numbered list of hosts and a single generic file are produced as constants.

Finally, the three actions are constructed. The first of these, the *exploit* action, generalizes the impact of exploiting present vulnerabilities with the intent of gaining read access to the host (to check for the desired file) and, upon failure to locate the file, compromise a neighbor. The base precondition for the action is the presence of a particular vulnerability on the host. Recall that this presence is probabilistic based on the characteristics of the vulnerability and, in the case of heterogeneous host profiles, the vulnerability profile itself. Further, we introduce two additional sets of preconditions that can be added in association with specific vulnerabilities. The first is a requirement of user access, and appears in the event that authentication (single or multiple) is required for exploitation of the vulnerability. The second pertains to the required access vector between the attacker and the host: local, adjacent, or network access. Execution of this action grants read access to the attacker and marks the host as compromised. For each vulnerability that appears on at least one host, an instance of this action is added to the domain.

Figure 3 depicts a sample plan and the effects of each action for a small example network. In the figure, the red arrow indicates that H1 is remotely accessible, and the

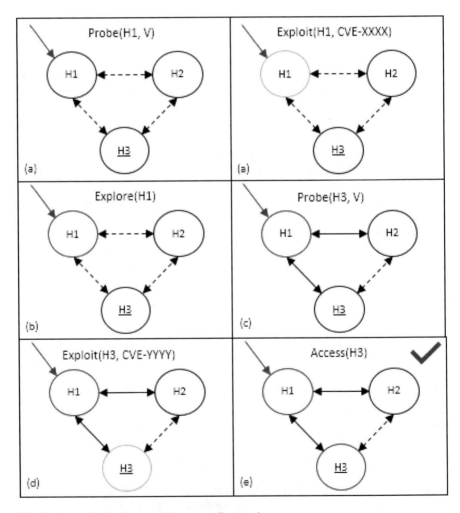

Fig. 3 An attack planning example on a small network

underlined text for H3 indicates that the target file is present on the host. Initially, the attacker can only probe for vulnerabilities on H1. Finding a suitable vulnerability, the attacker next compromises H1 by exploiting the flaw. Having penetrated the network, the attacker can explore to discover the connections between H1 and the other hosts. As before, the attacker then probes for and then exploits a vulnerability, this time on H3. Finally, having gained sufficient privileges on the target host, the attacker accesses the target file, indicating the goal condition has been met.

Once a host has been compromised, the number of types of access vectors available to the attacker must be updated accordingly. To this end, we introduced an artificial action, *update access*, which has two preconditions: a connection between two hosts, and that one of the hosts has been previously compromised. Note that connections between hosts are directed. Once these conditions have been met, the neighboring host is updated to reflect that the attacker now has both network and adjacent access vectors.

The third action fulfills the goal condition of the plan, namely, reading the target file. Execution of the *Access* action requires that the attacker have read access to the host which contains the target file. Taking this action indicates that the file has been read successfully, which satisfies the goal conditions of the plan.

Initial generation of the problem instance follows a straightforward process. First, the target file is randomly assigned to one of the hosts. Next, each host is examined and corresponding predicates are added to the problem definition. An instance of the *connected* predicate is generated for each neighbor (i.e. a host that is accessible from this host) based on the state of neighboring hosts. Instances of *has_vuln* are taken from the specific vulnerability profile of the host. Finally, the presence of initial network, user, or root access are added accordingly. As the final step of problem instance generation, the goal condition of accessing the target file is added.

5.3 Experimental Methods

We illustrate our model of cybersecurity risk assessment using a novel experimental framework which combines a generative model of a network with stochastic generation of hosts based on host images.

5.3.1 Generating Vulnerability Profiles

For our experiments we carefully crafted four vulnerability profiles. Two of these profiles represent generic desktop system configurations, with the remaining two representing server configurations. The operating systems for these profiles were chosen based on compiled OS market share data [1, 2], and software configurations were informed by application use data from WhatPulse [3], a computing habit information aggregator with more than 285,000 active users.

The first desktop configuration was based on a generic Windows desktop setup. As Windows 7 holds the largest share amongst Windows distributions, it was chosen for use with this profile. In addition to the standard software packages installed with Windows 7, the following pieces of third party software were installed:

- Chrome
- Firefox
- Skype
- Java Runtime Environment (JRE)
- Adobe Reader
- Adobe Flash Player

Though Mac OS X holds the second highest market share after Windows for desktops, test images were not readily available for use. This being the case, the second desktop profile was constructed based on Ubuntu Linux version 14.04 (Trusty Tahr).

For server profiles, we again provided both a Windows and Linux variants. The Windows server is a stock image of Windows Server 2012, while the Linux server is again Ubuntu 14.04, but with the addition of software necessary to run an Apache web server.

5.3.2   Generating Network Architecture

We implemented two generative models for constructing random network topologies in the experiments we report on below. The first is the well-known random graph (Erdos–Renyi) model, while the second is a novel generative model aimed at capturing aspects of networks salient in threat modeling.

Erdos–Renyi

The first model implemented was the Erdos–Renyi random graph model [6]. Specifically, we utilize the $G(n, p)$ formulation of the model in which a random graph G is constructed by randomly connecting vertices. For every pair of vertices $v_1, v_2 \in G$, an edge e is added between them with probability p, independently of any other edge.

In addition to specifying arbitrary values of p, we can utilize relationships and established thresholds between n and p to construct graphs with known, potentially interesting characteristics. An example of a known threshold in Erdos–Renyi graphs is $p = \ln(n)/n$. This value represents a sharp connectedness threshold—larger values of p will almost certainly be connected, while smaller values indicate the almost sure certain presence of isolated vertices in the graph. Several of these thresholds are employed in the experimental evaluations detailed in Sect. 5.4.1.

Organizational Network Generative Model

The Erdos–Renyi model offers clean insights, but is known to be overly simplistic to realistic topological characteristics of real networks. Moreover, in modeling security threats on networks one must also make a distinction between types of hosts (such as servers and desktops), as that pertains to the particular OS that is likely to run on such systems (for example, servers will typically not run Microsoft Word, and would not be susceptible to vulnerabilities in this application). To this end, we use a more realistic Block Two-Level Erdos–Renyi (BTER) model proposed in [16], and extend it with host-level characteristics.

Unlike the original Erdos–Renyi model, which treats all vertices identically with regard to edge construction, BTER treats the overall graph structure as a set of interconnected communities, each of which is an Erdos–Renyi random graph. The first phase of BTER graph construction consists of generating a collection of Erdos–Renyi (ER) blocks according to a user-specified degree distribution. These blocks are interconnected in the second phase via nodes in each block that have access degree. The Chung-Lu graph model [4] (which can be framed as a weighted Erdos–Renyi graph) is employed over the excess degrees to form the connections among the blocks.

Our model takes as input a desired node count n, a power law exponent α, a remote access probability P_N, and an optional set of connectivity policies ρ. Construction of a network with our model then follows four primary steps, the explanation of which will be aided by Fig. 4. We first sample n discrete values from a power law sequence with exponent α. In the BTER construction process, these values represent the desired degree of the nodes, and define the size of the communities present within the graph. The sampled values are sorted in ascending order and grouped by value, as seen in panel (a) of Fig. 4. Each entry in the sample list with value 1 represents a device which does not belong to a restricted subnet. As such, we don't consider them when building communities. Starting with the first value greater than 1, groups are formed by selecting and removing the first $d + 1$ entries from the list, where d is the value of the first entry. This procedure continues until the list is empty, at which point all of the groups have been formed. The end result is displayed in panel (b) of Fig. 4: a set of individual nodes and one or more communities of nodes.

Device classification occurs next, with two sets of distinctions made among the devices. First, one node in each community is chosen arbitrarily to serve as the gateway node. Next, each individual node (i.e. those not in communities) is flagged as remotely accessible with probability P_N; those flagged are distinguished as server nodes. In panel (c) of Fig. 4, node 6 is a gateway and node 3 is a server.

Finally, edges are drawn between the nodes as shown in panel (d). By default, all individual nodes are bi-directionally adjacent to each other and the set of gateway nodes. Additionally, each community forms a complete subgraph. As shown later in Sect. 5.4.2, the policies defined in ρ modify the manner in which edges are added.

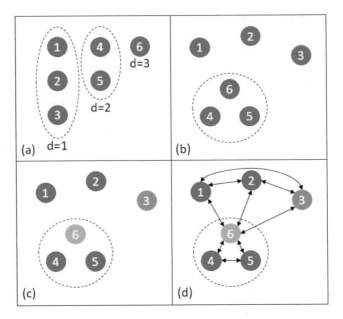

Fig. 4 Generative model network construction

5.4 Experimental Study of Network Cyber Risk

We now present an experimental study of network cyber risk using the experimental setup in Sect. 5.3 which instantiates our planning-based threat analysis framework.

5.4.1 Erdos–Renyi Network Model

As an initial set of experiments, we employ the Erdos–Renyi random graph model with directed edges to generate our network topology. As mentioned in section "Erdos–Renyi", graphs generated using the Erdos–Renyi model possess well-known characteristics based on the relationship between the number of hosts n and the edge probability p. We examine thresholds corresponding to two of these relationships:

1. $np = 1$
2. $p = \frac{ln(n)}{n}$

The first of these, which we will henceforth refer to as $NP1$, produces graphs which almost always contain a maximum component of size $n^{\frac{2}{3}}$. The second relationship, referred to as hereafter as LNN, is the threshold for connectedness in the model [6]. Since the Erdos–Renyi model does not lend itself to differentiation of vertices based on topological characteristics, we generate hosts homogeneously using the Windows desktop vulnerability profile detailed in Sect. 5.3.1.

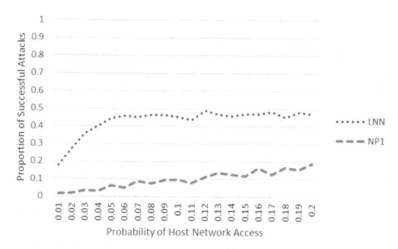

Fig. 5 Cyber risk for Erdos–Renyi Topologies, $n = 100$

Figure 5 shows the effect of varying the host network access probability P_N for a range of values between 0.01 and 0.20. As we might expect, the behavior for the two different values of p differ significantly. For the $NP1$ case, the proportion of successful attacks P_S is much smaller, but increases roughly linearly with P_N (indeed, across the range of values we considered, $P_S \approx P_N$ in this case). We can explain this behavior by examining the structure of the generated networks. Since the attacker does not have the option of physically accessing devices, attack vectors must originate with devices that are remotely accessible. Sparsity of edges, their directed nature, and the inherently disconnected structure of the generated networks limits the ability of the attacker to penetrate further into the network following the compromise of an externally accessible device. Further, since zero-day attacks and utilization of phished user credentials require network access to vulnerable devices, they are of relatively little use for this topology.

With the LNN case, the effect of varying P_N is completely different. Following a sharp increase in P_S across P_N values between 0.01 and 0.05, the proportion of successful attacks reaches a steady state. Given the guarantee of connectedness inherent to the LNN case, any remotely-accessible device will have a path to the target device; however, no guarantees are made that any two remotely-accessible devices will have independent paths to the target. The leveling-off of P_S suggests that independent paths to the target device are saturated beyond $P_N = 0.05$.

5.4.2 Organizational Network Generative Model

As a follow-up to the initial experiments run with the Erdos–Renyi model, similar evaluations with the generative model proposed in section "Organizational Network Generative Model" are executed. Except where otherwise noted, default values for P_P and the zero-day attack probability P_Z are used (0.03 and 0.13, respectively).

For the generative model, we use directed edges and also differentiate vulnerability profiles across the hosts. Gateway and server nodes (remotely accessible nodes not in a community) are assigned either the Linux or Windows server profiles with probabilities 0.664 and 0.336, respectively. All other nodes are assigned either the Windows or Linux desktop profiles with probability 0.7048 and 0.2952. These values represent the proportional ratio of Windows to Linux according to [1]. In addition to varying the network access probability, α value, and host count, we also examine the impact of several network policies and the effect of increased phishing attack probabilities. For the baseline version of the generative model, phishing attacks have an additional effect: if at least one host has compromised credentials, then the attacker is able to utilize a VPN connection, resulting in servers, gateways, and non-community desktop nodes being remotely accessible.

Figure 6 demonstrates the impact of varying network size for the baseline organizational network generative model. For small values of P_N, there are significant differences between P_S across smaller network sizes. These differences become smaller as the largest network sizes are reached. Moreover, risk increases with the number of hosts. The intuition behind these observations is that for smaller networks we expect that phishing attacks are less likely (a lower probability that *some* user account is phished), which limits attack vectors to remotely accessible nodes. Larger networks have more remotely accessible hosts, and a higher likelihood that some credentials are compromised through a phishing attack. Moreover, once even a single credential is phished, the attacker can remotely access a much larger portion of the network, significantly increasing the threat of a successful cyber attack. Consequently, increasing network size increases overall risk in this model.

We next examine the effect of introducing two network connection policies. The first of these is a restriction on outgoing connections from gateway nodes. If enabled, gateways retain outgoing connections only to nodes within their subnet, and all

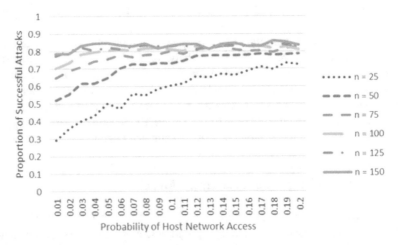

Fig. 6 Cyber risk for the organizational network generative model with varying host counts, no connection restrictions. $\alpha = 2.5$

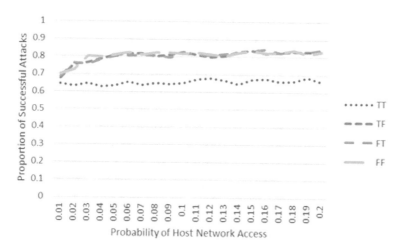

Fig. 7 Cyber risk for the organizational network generative model with varying connection restrictions, $n = 100$. On the legend, the first letter denotes gateway restrictions (True/False), and the second denotes server restrictions

other outgoing connections are removed; incoming connections are not modified. The second policy restricts all outgoing connections from server nodes. In other words, if the second policy is in place, one cannot connect (e.g., SSH) from a server to any other device on the local network. Figure 7 displays each of the combinations of these two policies. On the legend, the first letter denotes gateway restrictions (True/False), and the second denotes server restrictions. We can see that either of these policies by itself does not appreciably improve the security of the network compared to the baseline. Surprisingly, however, combining them results in an average reduction of 0.15 in risk, P_S. Note that because of the attacker's ability to employ VPN connections, there is little sensitivity to changes in P_N.

Next, we study the risk associated with allowing VPN connectivity. As seen in Fig. 8, disabling VPN connections to the network has a significant impact on overall cyber risk. For the unrestricted model across different values of α, we see high initial sensitivity to changes in P_N. As the attacker can no longer bypass attacking remotely accessible servers, the expected number of such servers in the network becomes quite relevant. For a network of 100 nodes, $P_N = 0.08$ marks the beginning of the steady state for P_S. Restricting both gateways and servers results in extremely small values of P_S, and retains only minimal sensitivity to increases in P_N.

In assessing the impact of increased phishing attacks on the system, we varied P_P from 0.01 to 0.20 in increments of 0.01 while keeping P_N at 0.01. The results of this experiment are shown in Fig. 9. As we might expect, both the initial values of P_S and the sensitivity to increases in P_P are markedly higher in larger networks. We've seen that the ability to bypass attack bottlenecks on remotely accessible hosts by utilizing VPN connections has a profound impact on security, and these results reinforce this observation. Even the network of 25 hosts approaches the same level of vulnerability as the 150 host network when P_P becomes large.

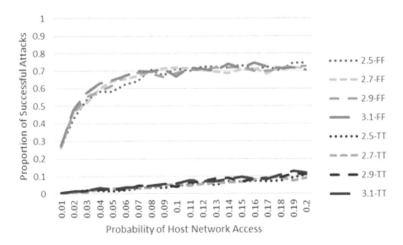

Fig. 8 Cyber risk for the organizational network generative model with no VPN. On the legend, the number denotes the value of α, 'FF' denotes no access restrictions, and 'TT' denotes restricted gateways and servers

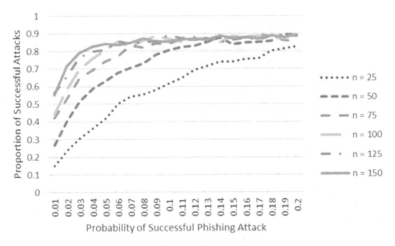

Fig. 9 Cyber risk for the organizational network generative model with varying phishing attack probabilities. $\alpha = 2.5$

5.5 Cyber Risk Mitigation through Plan Interdiction

Our discussion of the risk assessment approach, which leverages AI planning, thus far focused on the attacker modeling. Although experiments demonstrated the value of specific policy changes in mitigating some cyber risk, we only considered a small set of such policies. We now explore systematically a common challenge faced by organizations: of the many vulnerabilities present on the network, which should be prioritized. While in an ideal world, all vulnerabilities are patched, in reality doing so can be both time consuming, and costly in terms of lost productivity. Consequently, in practice a natural question is whether an organization can focus on a small subset of vulnerabilities which are truly critical for this organization, and make these a high priority. Given that our risk analysis framework is based on attack planning, the problem of choosing an optimal subset of vulnerabilities to prioritize is precisely the plan interdiction problem.

To formalize, let V be the set of all vulnerabilities present on a network, and let $S \subseteq V$ be a subset of these which the defender (network administrator) will prioritize. Rather than imposing a cost on patching a given vulnerabilty and minimizing risk, as in our model above, we minimized the number of vulnerabilities that are prioritized, subject to a constraint that risk is below a target threshold θ.

Let $R(S)$ be the risk (probability of a successful attack) faced by the defender when the set S of vulnerabilities is chosen to be prioritized for patching. Implicitly, $R(S)$ depends on the attacker's policy in response to S. However, note that in our framework, the attacker's policy is also a function of additional exogenously specified factors, such as the assignment of (exploitable) vulnerabilities to hosts, and phishing attack success, among others. Let η be a random variable which captures these stochastic factors, and let $\pi(S, \eta)$ be the associated optimal plan for the attacker. If we define $r(S, \pi(S, \eta))$ as a binary variable indicating whether the attack succeeds under exogenous parameters η, risk becomes $R(S) = \mathbb{E}_\eta[r(S, \pi(S, \eta); \eta)]$. The defender's optimization problem is then

$$\min_{S \subseteq V} |S| \quad \text{s.t.} : \quad R(S) \leq \theta. \tag{2}$$

We propose a heuristic solution approach for this problem: greedily add a vulnerability $v \in V$ to S in the order of maximum marginal impact on reducing risk $R(S)$, until we satisfy the condition $R(S) \leq \theta$.

Next, we evaluate the impact that selective patching of vulnerabilities has on cyber risk. For these evaluations, we set $P_N = 0.01$, and used default values for P_P (probability of a successful phishing attack) and P_Z (zero-day probability). Additionally, α was fixed at 2.5. We used the organizational network generative model to generate the network topologies, along with the heterogeneous vulnerability profiles and varied host count to assess the impact of vulnerability patching for different network sizes, as in the earlier experiments. We set the threshold in the optimization problem (2) to $\theta = 0.05$.

Figure 10 shows the results of our heuristic prioritization approach as a function of the number of vulnerabilities being prioritized (until the threshold of $\theta = 0.05$ is reached). As we might expect, the larger networks display higher initial vulnerability; however, the response of each network to the removal of vulnerabilities was very similar in magnitude. Most of the vulnerabilities patched came from the Windows Desktop vulnerability profile, which contributed 81 of the 104 vulnerabilities (after filtering them by year) among all profiles. These initially patched vulnerabilities were consistent in that they possessed a higher than average probability of being exploitable on any given host with the profile. Remarkably, however, we can

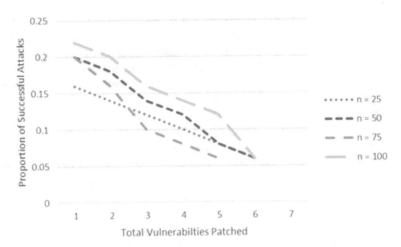

Fig. 10 Threat minimization through vulnerability prioritization. On the legend, the value of n denotes the number of hosts in the network

dramatically reduce cyber attack risk in this model by patching relatively few vulnerabilities ($<$10), as long as we effectively prioritize these.

6   Dynamic Plan Interdiction Games

Thus far, our discussion (and most prior research) had focused on interdiction games in which the defender first makes a fixed decision, and then the attacker devises a dynamic plan, with the possibility of circumventing defender's mitigations. This is most relevant when the defender cannot easily observe adversarial actions as they unfold, and only detects attacks after they have either succeeded or failed. In the remainder of this chapter we briefly discuss ideas for modeling the more general situation in which the defender may detect portions of the attack plan, and can subsequently react to it, for example, deploying additional mitigations in response (including modifications to the observed state).

Let's start with the following scenario: the defender has deployed mitigations, and a detection system. Let's view the detection system as predicting whether or not a particular observed state x involves malicious activity, captured by a binary classifier $f(x)$. Suppose that the detectors are binary, and we can immediately deploy response mitigations that prevent a detected attack from succeeding. The problem of designing such detectors can be viewed as a "basic" plan interdiction problem: we aim to design detectors which minimize loss from undetected attacks, where mitigation (detector design) costs can capture the costs of false positives.

An interesting challenge arises when detectors may detect an attack, but optimal mitigations may be unclear. This arises when the defender is uncertain about the attacker—for example, about the attacker's goals. In this case, the defender may have discovered a subplan (a partial sequence of attack actions), but is uncertain about the full plan. This gives rise to an interesting problem which couples plan interdiction with *plan recognition*: using partial information about the observed plan to infer information about the attacker's planning problem, so that mitigations can be optimally deployed. If the attacker is myopic, this can in principle be addressed through Bayesian updating: the defender may have a prior over the attacker's planning problem aspects (such as the attacker's capabilities and access), and then observations of an actual attack allows them to infer a posterior distribution over these (potentially resolving much of the uncertainty). However, an intelligent attacker may devise plans so as to make such inference difficult, and faces an interesting tradeoff between deceiving the defender, and achieving their goals as efficiently as possible. We view the challenge of addressing such dynamic problems at a sufficiently high resolution to obtain practically meaningful results as a major open problem in plan interdiction games.

7 Conclusion

We introduced the general notion of *plan interdiction games*. In their most basic variation, the defender commits to a collection of mitigations, and the attacker subsequently chooses an optimal attack plan. We illustrate the value of this modeling framework by using it to develop a network cyber threat assessment approach in which network features, as well as vulnerability profiles from standard vulnerability datasets, are used to compute a risk of successful attacks. Our experiments offered several interesting insights into the nature of risk associated with different design choices, such as specific choices about network connectivity and the use of VPN, as well as different exogenous factors, such as susceptibility to phishing attacks. Moreover, we demonstrated an important use case of plan interdiction as a means to prioritize which vulnerabilities are immediately patched, and showed that prioritizing only a few vulnerabilities can have a significant impact on reducing exposure to cyber risk.

While we have made considerable progress modeling the basic plan interdiction problem, as well as advancing technical state of the art to significantly improve scalability and generality of solution approaches, a number of interesting conceptual and technical issues arise when uncertainty is involved either on the part of the attacker about system state, or on the part of the defender about the attacker's planning problem primitives. Dynamics of the problem, in addition to the different aspects of information asymmetry, allow us to consider a very rich space of issues of great relevance in cybersecurity, including adaptive defense and deception both on the part of the defender, and on the part of the attacker. A great deal more research is needed to fully understand the space of plan interdiction problems, develop scalable solutions, and apply these in practical cybersecurity settings.

References

1. Desktop operating system market share. https://www.netmarketshare.com/
2. Developer survey results 2016. https://insights.stackoverflow.com/survey/2016#technology-development-environments
3. Whatpulse: Most used applications. https://whatpulse.org/stats/apps/
4. Aiello, W., Chung, F., Lu, L.: A random graph model for power law graphs. Experimental Mathematics **10**(1), 53–66 (2001). http://eudml.org/doc/227051
5. Chen, Y., Wah, B.W., wei Hsu, C.: Temporal planning using subgoal partitioning and resolution in SGPlan. Journal of Artificial Intelligence Research **26**, 323–369 (2006)
6. Erdos, P., Rényi, A.: On the evolution of random graphs. Publ. Math. Inst. Hung. Acad. Sci **5**(1), 17–60 (1960)
7. Filar, J., Vrieze, K.: Competitive Markov Decision Processes. Springer-Verlag (1997)
8. Ghare, P., Montgomery, D., Turner, W.: Optimal interdiction policy for a flow network. Naval Research Logistics Quarterly **18**(1), 37–45 (1971)
9. Guestrin, C., Koller, D., Parr, R., Venkataraman, S.: Efficient solution algorithms for factored mdps. Journal of Artificial Intelligence Research **19**, 399–468 (2003)
10. Letchford, J., Vorobeychik, Y.: Optimal interdiction of attack plans. In: International Conference on Autonomous Agents and Multiagent Systems, pp. 199–206 (2013)
11. McMasters, A., Mustin, T.: Optimal interdiction of a supply network. Naval Research Logistics Quarterly **17**(3), 261–268 (1970)
12. O'Donnell, R.: Some topics in analysis of boolean functions. In: Proceedings of the fortieth annual ACM symposium on Theory of computing, pp. 569–578. ACM (2008)
13. Panda, S., Vorobeychik, Y.: Near-optimal interdiction of factored mdps. In: Conference on Uncertainty in Artificial Intelligence (2017)
14. Puterman, M.L.: Markov Decision Processes: Discrete Stochastic Dynamic Programming. John Wiley & Sons, Inc. (1994)
15. Salmeron, J., Wood, K., Baldrick, R.: Worst-case interdiction analysis of large-scale electric power grids. IEEE Transactions on Power Systems **24**(1), 96–104 (2009)
16. Seshadhri, C., Kolda, T.G., Pinar, A.: Community structure and scale-free collections of erdős-rényi graphs. Physical Review E **85**(5), 056,109 (2012)

Game Theoretic Cyber Deception to Foil Adversarial Network Reconnaissance

Aaron Schlenker, Omkar Thakoor, Haifeng Xu, Fei Fang, Milind Tambe, and Phebe Vayanos

1 Introduction

Network breaches are a problem of increasing significance given the many major breaches in recent years such as Equifax in 2017 or Yahoo in 2016 [15, 16]. Organizations housing sensitive information are targeted by sophisticated and persistent adversaries who aim to exfiltrate the data or cause damage to important services rendered by the organization. Hackers targeting these organizations first complete a lengthy reconnaissance phase to learn about the vulnerabilities present in the network. The tools used to complete the network reconnaissance include a variety of scanning tools such as Nmap or Nessus [9, 22] that use TCP connections scans, stealth SYN scans, packet sniffing along with others to determine the configurations of systems on a network [18, 23]. These recon tools provide information to an adversary such as the systems on a network, how they are connected, operating systems (OS), the running applications and open ports. Using all of this information in aggregate an adversary then determines the best route for compromising the network.

A. Schlenker (✉) · O. Thakoor · P. Vayanos
University of Southern California, Los Angeles, CA, USA
e-mail: aschlenk@usc.edu; othakoor@usc.edu; phebe.vayanos@usc.edu

H. Xu
University of Virginia, Charlottesville, VA, USA
e-mail: hx4ad@virginia.edu

F. Fang
Carnegie Mellon University, Institute for Software Research, Pittsburgh, PA, USA
e-mail: milind.tambe@harvard.edu

M. Tambe
Harvard University, Cambridge, MA, USA
e-mail: feifang@cmu.edu

© Springer Nature Switzerland AG 2020
S. Jajodia et al. (eds.), *Adaptive Autonomous Secure Cyber Systems*,
https://doi.org/10.1007/978-3-030-33432-1_9

Network administrators use a slew of techniques to protect against these network attacks. These techniques include the use of Intrusion Detection Systems (IDS) [28], the whitelisting of applications, locking down permissions, immediately patching vulnerabilities and others [18]. An interesting recent trend of research has been the use of deceptive techniques to impede cyber adversaries during network attacks. Honeypots are a crucial deceptive tool to learn about the tactics, techniques and procedures of cyber adversaries and identify attacks or reconnaissance activities occurring in the network [20]. Other deceptive tools have focused on thwarting adversarial reconnaissance directly by obfuscating the OS and applications appearing to run on various systems across a network along with altering the viewable network topology [1, 3]. For instance, ACyDS [12] provides the network defender a tool which gives each host on a network a unique view of the present entities (systems) and network topology to significantly improve the difficulty of correctly mapping out a defender's network. Exploits and malware used by an adversary rely on a system having a particular configuration, i.e., an adversary must know the OS and application version to exploit the particular vulnerability he has identified. The approaches mentioned rely on the asymmetric information the defender can utilize to create an interaction where the adversary has substantially higher uncertainty about the *true configuration* underlying a system on the network. However, a major drawback of these previous approaches is the lack of modeling an intelligent, adaptive adversary who aims to take exploit weaknesses in the defender strategies.

Our work concentrates on how the defender can devise a deceptive response scheme to benefit the most from using a mix of true, false and obscure responses to adversarial reconnaissance. To highlight the benefit of the defender using deception, consider a network with 4 systems where 1 is running Nginx and 3 are running Apache Tomcat. Also, assume the adversary has a specific exploit for Nginx, but he does not have exploits for the Apache Tomcat servers. Without deception, the adversary scans all systems to find the one running Nginx and deploys his exploit to compromise that system. However, if the defender lies about the webserver application, the adversary potentially has to test his exploit on all systems to infiltrate the network. Although he would still be successful in this scenario, this example highlights the increased effort and time adversaries must use to compromise the defender's enterprise network. Further, this gives the defender time to mount a better defense and increases the chances the defender catches an attack. The problem for the defender then is to determine how to alter the adversary's perception of the network to minimize her expected loss from an attack.

Our first contribution is the Cyber Deception Game (CDG) model which captures the strategic interaction between the defender and an adversary in network security. In this game, the defender chooses a deceptive response scheme for determining the host (system) responses to network scans while the attacker chooses which system to attack based on the observed responses. For our second contribution, we show that finding the defender's optimal strategy against a powerful attacker who knows the defender's exact deception scheme in CDGs is NP-hard and provide two solution techniques that use Mixed Integer Linear Programming (MILP), an exact reformulation approach and an approximate bisection algorithmic approach, to compute the optimal response scheme. We then propose a greedy algorithm to quickly find good defender strategies in CDGs which is shown to perform well experimentally in a fraction of the time of the reformulated MILP. Third, we show that surprisingly finding the optimal strategy is still NP-hard when faced with naive attackers who act according to prior fixed utilities given budget constraints and propose an algorithm to provide the exact solution. Finally, we present experimental results showing the scalability of our solution techniques and a comparison of the solution quality of proposed techniques for both types of adversaries.

2   Related Work

The use of game theory for security has been studied extensively, which we discuss in Sect. 3. Game theory has also been studied in the context of cybersecurity problems [5, 21, 29, 30]. Kiekintveld et al. [19], Píbil et al. [26], Durkota et al. [14], and Durkota et al. [13] study a honeypot selection game in which a defender chooses the properties of the network and the attacker can use probe actions to test the network where his actions are represented as attack graphs. [11] studies a signaling game where the defender signals to an adversary if a system is either real or a honeypot when the adversary performs a scan. [25] extends the signaling game to account for an adversary who can gain evidence about the true state of a system. In our work, we consider a game scenario in which the defender determines the optimal way to respond to scans sent by a potential adversary given a set of possible responses. Further, we explore different types of adversaries with varying awareness of deception.

Deception has also been widely studied as a means to improve the protection of enterprise networks from potential hackers and intruders [1, 4]. An interesting technical tool that has previously been developed is HoneyD that allows a user to set up and run multiple virtual hosts (potentially honeypots) on a computer network [27]. Albanese et al. [2] uses a graph-theoretic approach to confuse a potential attacker by manipulating his view of systems on the network. However, this work focuses on finding a view which is measurably different from the true state and does not adequately model the response of a strategic adversary. Jajodia et al. [17] is a closely related work where the authors study how to respond to an attacker's scan queries using an annotated probabilistic logic model. We provide a complementary view using game theory to determine how a defender manipulates scan responses to confuse an attacker's view of systems on the network. We also study varying adversary models, which can have a significant impact on the defender's optimal strategy which is not explored in [17].

3   Cyber Deception Game

The *Cyber Deception Game* (CDG) is a zero-sum Stackelberg game between the defender (e.g., network administrator) and an adversary (e.g., hacker). The defender moves first and chooses how the systems should respond to scan queries from an adversary, and the adversary subsequently moves by choosing a system to attack based on the responses. Despite the similarities with game-theoretic models in security domains, such as [7, 8, 31], there are two key differences. First, the defender can only commit to a pure strategy and not an arbitrary mixed strategy. This is because, in these domains, network administrators modify the network very infrequently, and thus, the attackers' view of the network is static. Second, there are no explicit security resources for the defender in CDGs. Consequently, the existing approaches for solving standard Stackelberg games in security domains, cannot be directly applied. The various components of the game and the aforementioned model characteristics are described in detail as follows:

3.1   Systems and True Configurations

The defender aims to protect a set K of systems, from possible exploits and intrusions. Each system has certain attributes, e.g., an operating system, an anti-virus protection mechanism, services hosted, etc. These attributes altogether constitute the *true configuration* (TC) of the system. We denote the set of all possible TCs by F. Each system has an associated utility, which captures how much the adversary would get by attacking it. This utility solely depends on the TC of the system—each $f \in F$ induces a utility denoted by U_f to any system that is assigned f. U_f can be negative if the security level of the system is so high that the attacker's efforts end in vain or the attacker gets fake data from a seemingly successful attack, leading to a loss in the end. It follows that, the *true state of the network* (TSN) can be represented as a vector $N = (N_f)_{f \in F}$, where $N_f \in \mathbb{Z}_{>0}$ denotes the number of systems on the network which have a TC f and $\sum_{f \in F} N_f = |K|$ (We assume $N_f \neq 0$, since such a TC simply need not be considered).

3.2   Observed Configurations

The adversary attempts to gain information about every system on the network, via probes and scans. By scanning a system, the adversary observes certain attributes, which constitute the *observable configuration* (OC) of the system. We denote the set of possible OCs by $\tilde{F}$. We assume that it is possible for the defender to make some of the observable attributes of a system appear different than what they truly are (e.g., altering the TCP/IP stack of a system, spoofing a running service on a port). By means of such alterations at her disposal, the defender controls the OC an attacker sees when probing a system. Note that it may not be possible for an arbitrary TC f to be made to appear as an arbitrary OC $\tilde{f} \in \tilde{F}$—we call such a constraint a *feasibility* constraint, and these are denoted by a (0,1)-matrix π. Iff $\pi_{f,\tilde{f}} = 1$, we say f can be *covered*, or *masked* with $\tilde{f}$. We denote the set of OCs which can mask a TC f, by $\tilde{F}_f = \{\tilde{f} \in \tilde{F} \mid \pi_{f,\tilde{f}} = 1\}$, and similarly, the set of TCs which can be masked by an OC $\tilde{f}$, by $F_{\tilde{f}} = \{f \in F \mid \pi_{f,\tilde{f}} = 1\}$.

From the adversary's perspective, two systems having the same $\tilde{f}$ as their OC are indistinguishable, and hence, his *observed state of the network* (OSN) can be represented as a vector $\tilde{N} = (\tilde{N}_{\tilde{f}})_{\tilde{f} \in \tilde{F}}$ where $\tilde{N}_{\tilde{f}} \in \mathbb{Z}_{\geq 0}$ denotes the number of systems which have an OC $\tilde{f}$. As is the case with the TSN N, we must have $\sum_{\tilde{f} \in \tilde{F}} \tilde{N}_{\tilde{f}} = |K|$.

We assume that masking a TC f with an OC $\tilde{f}$, has a cost of $c(f, \tilde{f})$ incurred by the defender, which typically captures the monetary costs for deploying network modifications necessary for such a deception.

3.3 Defender Strategies

Naturally, F, $\tilde{F}$, π, c and N are known to the defender. Given all this information, the defender must decide her strategy—for each TC f, she must decide how many of the N_f systems having TC f, should be assigned the OC $\tilde{f}$, where $\tilde{f} \in \tilde{F}_f$. Thus, any possible strategy can be represented as a $|F| \times |\tilde{F}|$ matrix ϕ having non-negative integer entries, with $\phi_{f,\tilde{f}}$ representing the number of systems having TC f and OC $\tilde{f}$. Hence, ϕ must satisfy

$$\phi_{f,\tilde{f}} \in \mathbb{Z}_{\geq 0} \qquad \forall f \in F, \forall \tilde{f} \in \tilde{F} \tag{1}$$

Since the TSN N is fixed, ϕ must also satisfy

$$\sum_{\tilde{f} \in \tilde{F}} \phi_{f,\tilde{f}} = N_f \qquad \forall f \in F \tag{2}$$

Since feasibility constraints π are specified, ϕ must also satisfy

$$\phi_{f,\tilde{f}} \leq \pi_{f,\tilde{f}} N_f \qquad \forall f \in F, \forall \tilde{f} \in \tilde{F} \tag{3}$$

Finally, since setting any OC on a system has an associated cost, we assume that the defender's total cost cannot exceed a limit B, which we call the budget constraint. Formally, ϕ must also satisfy

$$\sum_{f \in F} \sum_{\tilde{f} \in \tilde{F}} \phi_{f,\tilde{f}} \, c(f, \tilde{f}) \leq B \tag{4}$$

The set of strategies ϕ which satisfy the constraints (1), (2), (3), and (4), is denoted by Φ.[1] When the defender plays $\phi \in \Phi$, the resulting OSN $\tilde{N}$ is given by $\tilde{N}_{\tilde{f}} = \sum_{f \in F} \phi_{f,\tilde{f}} \; \forall \tilde{f} \in \tilde{F}$.

3.4 Adversary Strategies

Depending on the defender's strategy, the adversary observes $\tilde{N}$ as described above. All systems having the same OC $\tilde{f}$ are indistinguishable to the adversary, and hence, he must be indifferent between all such $\tilde{N}_{\tilde{f}}$ systems when deciding which system to attack. As a result, we assume that he attempts to choose the OC $\tilde{f}$ which gives him the highest expected utility (described momentarily), and attack all the $\tilde{N}_{\tilde{f}}$ systems having this OC with an equal probability. In short, we say "the adversary attacks an OC $\tilde{f}$" to mean he attacks all the systems having OC $\tilde{f}$ with an equal probability. A general mixed strategy for the adversary is to attack the set of OCs with any probability distribution. However, since there always exists a pure best-response strategy in any game, it suffices to consider the adversary's strategies as simply attacking a particular $\tilde{f}$.

3.5 Utilities

When the defender plays a strategy ϕ, the adversary's expected utility on attacking an OC $\tilde{f}$ with $\tilde{N}_{\tilde{f}} > 0$, denoted by $\bar{U}_{\tilde{f}}(\phi)$—or, as $\bar{U}_{\tilde{f}}$ for simplicity, when the underlying ϕ is unambiguously understood—is given by

$$\tilde{U}_{\tilde{f}} = E[U_f | \phi, \tilde{f}] = \sum_{f \in F_{\tilde{f}}} P(f|\phi, \tilde{f})U_f = \sum_{f \in F} \frac{\phi_{f,\tilde{f}}}{\tilde{N}_{\tilde{f}}} U_f \tag{5}$$

Equation (5) follows from computing $P(f|\phi, \tilde{f})$ using the fact that out of $\tilde{N}_{\tilde{f}}$ systems having an OC $\tilde{f}$, $\phi_{f,\tilde{f}}$ have a TC f. Since the game is zero-sum, the defender's expected utility is $-\tilde{U}_{\tilde{f}}$ when $\tilde{f}$ is attacked. Note the attacker cannot attack an OC $\tilde{f}$ with $\tilde{N}_{\tilde{f}} = 0$, or equivalently, his expected utility is $-\infty$ if he does so.

---

[1]The feasibility constraints can simply be captured via the budget constraint by setting the costs of infeasible assignments to be higher than the budget. However, they are essential in the model, since, in some cases, having no budget constraint allows an efficient solution to the problem (e.g. Sect. 5), while still having the very practical feasibility constraints keeps the problem non-trivial.

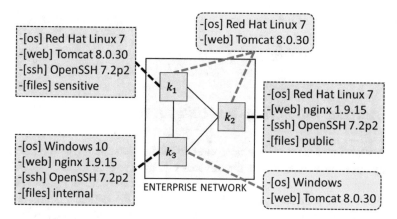

Fig. 1 Simple example of an enterprise network

Next, we illustrate the model using a simple example.

Figure 1 shows a simple example enterprise network which will be used as a running example. We have a set of systems $K = \{k_1, k_2, k_3\}$, set of TCs $F = \{f_1, f_2, f_3\}$ (shown in Fig. 1 as the green boxes) and set of OCs $\tilde{F} = \{\tilde{f}_1, \tilde{f}_2\}$ (shown in Fig. 1 as the yellow boxes). Let the feasibility constraints be given by the sets $F_{\tilde{f}_1} = \{f_1, f_2\}$ and $F_{\tilde{f}_2} = \{f_2, f_3\}$. The TCs are as follows:

$$f_1 = [[os]\ L,\ [web]\ T,\ [ssh]\ O,\ [files]\ S]$$

$$f_2 = [[os]\ L,\ [web]\ N,\ [ssh]\ O,\ [files]\ P]$$

$$f_3 = [[os]\ W,\ [web]\ N,\ [ssh]\ O,\ [files]\ I]$$

For the TCs, the utilities are $U_{f_1} = 10$, $U_{f_2} = 0$, and $U_{f_3} = 6$. The OCs are as follows:

$$\tilde{f}_1 = [[os]\ L,\ [web]\ T] \qquad\qquad \tilde{f}_2 = [[os]\ W,\ [web]\ T]$$

For simplicity, let all the costs $c(f, \tilde{f})$ to be 0, so that there is essentially no budget constraint. Based on the TCs assigned as shown, the state of the network $(N_f)_{f \in F}$ is $(1, 1, 1)$. When the defender assigns OCs as shown in Fig. 1, her strategy ϕ is given by

$$\begin{array}{c} \\ \begin{array}{c} f_1 \\ f_2 \\ f_3 \end{array} \end{array}
\begin{array}{c} \tilde{f}_1\ \tilde{f}_2 \\ \left[\begin{array}{cc} 1 & 0 \\ 1 & 0 \\ 0 & 1 \end{array} \right] \end{array}$$

The expected utility of the adversary (loss of the defender) when he attacks $\tilde{f}_1$ or $\tilde{f}_2$ is respectively given by $\tilde{U}_{\tilde{f}_1} = (10+0)/2 = 5$ and $\tilde{U}_{\tilde{f}_2} = 6/1 = 6$. Thus, attacking $\tilde{f}_2$ leads to the highest expected utility for the attacker.

3.6   Adversary Knowledge and Utility Estimation

The attacker's awareness of the deception and the understanding of the defender's strategy may vary. Note that if the adversary is always able to find the OC with highest expected utility, it is the worst case scenario for the defender given the game is zero-sum. An attacker who is fully aware of how the defender sends the false responses to scan requests (via insider threats, information leakage, etc.) would have such an ability. Formally, we define a *powerful* attacker to be one who knows F, $\tilde{F}$, π, U and ϕ and chooses to attack the OC with the (correct) highest expected utility $\tilde{U}_{\tilde{f}}$ computed through Eq. (5). If the defender chooses a strategy that minimizes the expected utility of a powerful attacker, she gets a robust strategy as the defender can be assured that no matter the extent of the adversary's knowledge, no strategy he plays can lead to a greater loss for the defender, in alignment with the minimax principle.

However, the attacker may not be so powerful. On the other end of the spectrum, if the attacker is unaware of the defender's precise deception scheme or has a very limited understanding of the situation such that he cannot make any meaningful inference, his decision making would be completely dependent on the observed configurations of the systems and some fixed preferences over OCs in terms of the estimated expected utility. Formally, we define a naive attacker to be one who chooses to attack an existing OC $\tilde{f}$ (i.e., one which has at least one system configured to it) with the highest $\tilde{U}_{\tilde{f}}$ where $\tilde{U}_{\tilde{f}}$ is not dependent on the defender's strategy and is known to the defender. This is also equivalent to the case where the attacker just has a fixed preference of the OCs. We analyze CDGs with powerful attackers in Sect. 4, and CDGs with naive attackers in Sect. 5.

4   Optimal Defender Strategy Against Powerful Adversary

In this section, we compute the defender's optimal strategy in a CDG assuming a powerful adversary. The adversary attacks an OC from the set $\text{argmax}_{\tilde{f} \in \tilde{F}} \, \tilde{U}_{\tilde{f}}$ and gets an expected utility of $\max_{\tilde{f} \in \tilde{F}} \tilde{U}_{\tilde{f}}$, denoted in short as $\tilde{U}^*(\phi)$, where the negative value is the defender's expected loss. Hence, the defender aims to minimize her loss by choosing her ϕ from the set $\text{argmin}_{\phi \in \Phi} \, \tilde{U}^*(\phi)$.

4.1 Computational Complexity

We call the problem of finding optimal defender strategy against a powerful adversary in a CDG as $CDG{-}Robust$.

We first investigate a special case. The following proposition provides a tight lower bound on $\min_{\phi \in \Phi} \tilde{U}^*(\phi)$.

Lemma 1 *The expected loss of the defender when playing her optimal strategy, is no lower than the average utility of the systems, i.e.,*

$$\min_{\phi} \tilde{U}^*(\phi) \geq U^{\text{Ave}}(K) = \frac{\sum_{f \in F} N_f U_f}{|K|}$$

***Proof** (Proof Sketch)* Configuring the systems with different OCs effectively partitions the set K into subsets. Since the average utility of all the systems in all these subsets is $U^{\text{Ave}}(K)$, there exist at least one subset whose average utility is no less than $U^{\text{Ave}}(K)$. Therefore the highest expected utility for the attacker, which is the maximum average utility of all these subsets, is no less than $U^{\text{Ave}}(K)$.[2]

Thus, even when the defender plays her optimal strategy, the attacker's expected utility is at least $U^{\text{Ave}}(K)$. Consequently, if the inequality becomes tight for a strategy ϕ, it must be an optimal strategy. It is easy to see that the bound becomes tight if and only if $\tilde{U}^*(\phi) = \tilde{U}_{\tilde{f}}(\phi), \forall \tilde{f}$. Clearly, this is true if and only if $\bar{U}_{\tilde{f}}$ is the same for each $\tilde{f}$ set on any system, and trivially so, if only a single OC is set on all the systems. Thus,

Corollary 1 *If it is feasible for the defender to set the same OC on all the systems making them all indistinguishable to the adversary, doing so is an optimal strategy. Formally, if $\exists \tilde{f}^*$ s.t. $\exists \phi^* \in \Phi$ where $\phi^*_{f,\tilde{f}^*} = N_f, \forall f$, then $\phi^* \in \arg\min_{\phi \in \Phi} \tilde{U}^*(\phi)$.*

It is possible to efficiently check if such an OC exists, by enumeration. However, it may not exist, and we show that $CDG{-}Robust$ is NP-hard in general.

Proposition 1 $CDG{-}Robust$ *is NP-hard.*

Proof We prove the result via a reduction from the Partition problem ($PART$) which is known to be NP-complete. Given a multiset S of n positive integers that sum up to $2r$, $PART$ is the decision problem to determine if S can be partitioned into two subsets S_1 and S_2 such that the sum of integers in S_1 and S_2 are each r. It can be reduced to $CDG{-}Robust$ as follows.

Let the input to $PART$ be a set of integers $S = \{s_1, \ldots, s_n\}$ whose elements sum to $2r$. To construct a CDG, let the set of TCs be $F = \{f_1, \ldots, f_n\} \cup \{f_{n+1}, f_{n+2}\}$, with utilities $U_{f_i} = s_i$ for each $i \in \{1, \ldots, n\}$ and $U_{f_{n+1}} = U_{f_{n+2}} = -r$. Next,

---

[2]A detailed proof can be found in the online appendix: http://teamcore.usc.edu/papers/2018/App_AAMAS_ARS.pdf.

let there be $n + 2$ systems, each having a different TC. Let the set of OCs be $\tilde{F} = \{\tilde{f}_1, \tilde{f}_2\}$, with $\tilde{F}_{f_i} = \tilde{F}$ for each $i \in \{1, \ldots, n\}$, and $\tilde{F}_{f_{n+1}} = \{\tilde{f}_1\}$, $\tilde{F}_{f_{n+2}} = \{\tilde{f}_2\}$. Let all the costs be 0 so that the budget constraint can be ignored. Assuming the adversary to be powerful, these components completely define a $CDG-Robust$ problem.

Note that, by Corollary 1 and the fact that $\sum_f U_f = 0$, we know that the optimal strategy ϕ must have $\tilde{U}^*(\phi) \geq 0$. Now, suppose S can be partitioned into subsets S_1 and S_2 such that the numbers in each sum to r. Then, consider the strategy ϕ which masks the TCs in $\{f_i | s_i \in S_1\}$ and f_{n+1} with $\tilde{f}_1$, and masks the TCs in $\{f_i | s_i \in S_2\}$ and f_{n+2} with $\tilde{f}_2$. It is easy to check that $\tilde{U}_{\tilde{f}_1}(\phi) = \tilde{U}_{\tilde{f}_2}(\phi) = 0 = \tilde{U}^*(\phi)$, making ϕ an optimal strategy. On the other hand, suppose the defender's optimal ϕ yields $\tilde{U}^*(\phi) = 0$. Since $\tilde{f}_1$ must mask f_{n+1}, and $\tilde{f}_2$ must mask f_{n+2}, neither of the OCs are unused. Since $\tilde{U}^*(\phi) = 0$, w.l.o.g., assume $\tilde{U}_{\tilde{f}_1} = 0$. Hence, the sum of utilities of the TCs masked with $\tilde{f}_1$ must be 0. Therefore, the sum of utilities of TCs masked by $\tilde{f}_2$ is also 0. Then, $S_1 = \{s_i | \phi_{f_i, \tilde{f}_1} = 1\}$, and $S_2 = \{s_i | \phi_{f_i, \tilde{f}_2} = 1\}$ form a partition of S, each having sum of the elements r. It follows that, $PART$ should output YES iff $CDG-Robust$ finds an optimal strategy ϕ with $\tilde{U}^*(\phi) = 0$. This reduction, being polynomial-time, proves the claim.

4.2   The Defender's Optimization Problem

The defender's optimal strategy ϕ can be computed by solving the optimization problem given below.

$$\min_{u, \phi} \quad u \tag{6a}$$

$$\text{s.t.} \quad u \sum_{f \in F} \phi_{f, \tilde{f}} \geq \sum_{f \in F} \phi_{f, \tilde{f}} U_f \qquad \forall \tilde{f} \in \tilde{f} \tag{6b}$$

Constraints (1)~(4)

The objective function in Eq. (6a) minimizes the utility u the adversary receives for the game. Equation (6b) enforces that the adversary chooses a best response to the defender's strategy ϕ, where the expected utility for attacking a given $\tilde{f}$ is given by (5). Constraints (1)~(4) represent a feasible defender strategy.

This optimization problem is non-convex due to constraint (6b), which can be linearized, to convert the optimization problem to a MILP as follows. First, we devise an alternate representation of the defender's strategy ϕ, as a $|K| \times |\tilde{F}|$ (0,1)-matrix σ, where $\sigma_{k, \tilde{f}} = 1$ denotes system k is masked with $\tilde{f}$. Further, we represent the TSN N via a vector $\mathbf{x}$, where $x_k \in F$ represents the TC for system k. Then, for each TC f, we have $N_f = |K_f|$ where, $K_f = \{k \in K \mid x_k = F\}$, and $\phi_{f, \tilde{f}} = \sum_{k \in K_f} \sigma_{k, \tilde{f}} \ \forall f, \forall \tilde{f}$. Hence, the alternate representations are indeed equivalent. Then, constraints equivalent to (1)~(4) can be easily formulated for σ and x with an additional constraint $\sum_{\tilde{f}\in\tilde{F}}\sigma_{k,\tilde{f}} = 1 \ \forall k \in K$ to ensure feasibility. More importantly, Eq. (6b) can be reformulated as

$$u\sum_{k\in K}\sigma_{k,\tilde{f}} \geq \sum_{k\in K}\sigma_{k,\tilde{f}}U_{xk} \quad \forall \tilde{f}\in\tilde{F} \tag{7}$$

The left-hand side of (7) can be seen as the sum of a set of terms $u\sigma_{k,\tilde{f}}$, each of which is the product of binary variable $\sigma_{k,\tilde{f}}$ and the continuous variable u. Such an expression can be linearized by introducing variables $z_{k,\tilde{f}}$ for each $k \in K$ and $\tilde{f}\in\tilde{F}$, and enforcing $z_{k,\tilde{f}} = u\sigma_{k,\tilde{f}}$. Consequently, we can rewrite (7) as:

$$\sum_{k\in K}z_{k,\tilde{f}} \geq \sum_{k\in K}\sigma_{k,\tilde{f}}U_{xk} \tag{8}$$

To enforce $z_{k,\tilde{f}} = u\sigma_{k,\tilde{f}}$, we consider $u \in [U^{min}, U^{max}]$ where $U^{min} = \min_{f\in F} U_f$ and $U^{max} = \max_{f\in F} U_f$. With these bounds on u, we then include the constraints for each z variable in the optimization problem as follows:

$$U^{min}\sigma_{k,\tilde{f}} \leq z_{k,\tilde{f}} \leq U^{max}\sigma_{k,\tilde{f}} \tag{9}$$

$$u - (1 - \sigma_{k,\tilde{f}})U^{max} \leq z_{k,\tilde{f}} \leq u - (1 - \sigma_{k,\tilde{f}})U^{min} \tag{10}$$

After this conversion the optimization problem becomes a MILP. The complete formulation can be found in the online appendix.

4.3 MILP Bisection Algorithm

The reformulated MILP presented requires the addition of $|K||\tilde{F}|$ variables and $4|K||\tilde{F}|$ constraints to solve for ϕ. This conversion significantly increases the size of the optimization problem from the original number of $|F||\tilde{F}|$ decision variables in the original optimization problem and can create issues when solving larger CDG instances. The second approach we develop does not require the reformulation and instead solves a sequence of smaller MILPs (same size as (6a)) to find an ϵ-approximate solution for the defender [32]. This is done via a bisection algorithmic framework. The algorithm initially is given an interval that the optimal objective value $\tilde{U}^*$ lies in which for CDGs is $U^* \in [U^{LB}, U^{UB}]$ where $U^{LB} = U^{AVE}(K)$ and $U^{UB} = \max_{f\in F} U_f$. For the algorithm, we introduce two variables $l = U^{LB}$ and $d = U^{UB}$ with the initial width as $\epsilon_0 = d - l$ that contains the optimal value U^* of our optimization problem. The main loop of the algorithm is repeated until the width $d - l \leq \epsilon$. The main loop has the following two steps:

1. Take $\tau = (u + l)/2$ and solve the feasibility problem in Eq. (11a) to find if there exists a solution **n** that satisfies the constraints.
2. **if** *feasible*, take $u := \tau$; **if** *not feasible*, take $l := \tau$.

The algorithm is guaranteed to converge as after each update the interval $[l, u]$ contains the optimal U^* and the width is halved. The number of steps that are needed to find the ϵ-approximate optimal solution is $\lceil \log \frac{\epsilon_0}{\epsilon} \rceil$.

$$\max_{\phi} \quad 1 \tag{11a}$$

$$\text{s.t.} \quad \tau \sum_{f \in F} \phi_{f,\tilde{f}} \geq \sum_{f \in F} \phi_{f,\tilde{f}} U_f \qquad \forall \tilde{f} \in \tilde{f} \tag{11b}$$

Constraints (1)~(4)

While the bisection algorithm may need to solve on the order of a dozen MILPs to arrive at the approximate solution, as we show in the experiments it can significantly outperform the reformulated MILP in computational speed.

4.4 Greedy-Minimax Algorithm

Although we can solve the optimal ϕ via a MILP, it can still be computationally expensive for large instances. Hence, we seek heuristic algorithms which may be suboptimal but run fast and perform well on average. In this section, we describe a simple approach to sequentially assign OCs to the systems, by greedily minimizing attacker's maximum expected utility for the partially built strategy at each stage. Algorithm 1 gives the pseudo-code.

Greedy-Minimax starts by computing for each $f \in F$, the minimum cost of masking f with any feasible OC, and subsequently, the minimum total cost of masking all the systems (Lines 1–2). Next, σ_{best} and $minu^*$ are initialized, which respectively denote the final output strategy of the algorithm and the corresponding utility (Line 3). Subsequently, the algorithm is conducted in a number of iterations. In each iteration, a random shuffle of the set of systems is obtained, referred to as K_{list} above. Subsequently, the strategy σ which is a candidate solution corresponding to this shuffle, the corresponding observed state of the network $(\bar{N}_{\tilde{f}})_{\tilde{f} \in \tilde{F}}$, and the corresponding utilities $(\bar{U}_{\tilde{f}})_{\tilde{f} \in \tilde{F}}$ are all initialized. These are constantly maintained as the algorithm loops through K_{list}, building the solution by assigning an OC to a system one by one (Lines 8–10). The OC to be assigned for a system is determined via the function $GMMAssign()$ which is the essence of this heuristic algorithm. The input to this function is the TC f of the system in question, and the currently built solution in terms of $\sigma, \bar{N}, \bar{U}, remB, reqB$. Given these, the function considers the candidate OCs in $\tilde{F}$ one by one, refutes those which lead to the violation of the budget constraint (i.e., make the resultant minimum required budget to exceed the resultant remaining budget). For every other $\tilde{f}$, it

---

Algorithm 1: Greedy−Minimax

---

1 $minIndCost[] \leftarrow (\min_{\tilde{f}} c(f, \tilde{f}))_{f \in F}$

2 $minTotCost \leftarrow \sum_f N_f * minIndCost[f]$

3 **initialize** $minu^*, \sigma_{best}$

4 **For** $iter = 1 \ldots numIter$

5 $K_{list}[] \leftarrow shuffle(K)$

6   **initialize** $remB \leftarrow B, reqB \leftarrow minTotCost$

7   **initialize** $\sigma[], \bar{N}[], \bar{U}[]$

8   **For** $i = 1 \ldots |K|$

9 $k \leftarrow K_{list}[i], f \leftarrow x[k]$

10 $\sigma[k] \leftarrow GMMAssign(f, \sigma[], \bar{N}, \bar{U}[], remB, reqB)$

11 $\bar{N}[\sigma[k]] \leftarrow \bar{N}[\sigma[k]] + 1$

12 $update(\bar{U}[\sigma[k]])$

13 $remB \leftarrow remB - c(f, \sigma[k])$

14 $reqB \leftarrow reqB - minIndCost[f]$

15   **compute** $u^* = \max_{\tilde{f}} \bar{U}[\tilde{f}]$

16 $update(minu^*, u^*, \sigma_{best}, \sigma)$

17 **return** σ_{best}

18 **Procedure** $GMMAssign(f, \sigma[], \bar{N}, \bar{U}[])$

19   **initialize** $newU^*[]$

20   **For** $\tilde{f} \in \tilde{F}_f$

21   **If** $(reqB - minIndCost[f] + c(f, \tilde{f}) > remB)$ **Then**

22   **Continue**

23 $\sigma[k] \leftarrow \tilde{f}$

24 $newU^*[\tilde{f}] \leftarrow U^*(\sigma)$

25 $\tilde{F}_{best} \leftarrow \operatorname{argmin}_{\tilde{f}} newU^*[\tilde{f}]$

26   **generate** $\tilde{f}_{best} \sim uniRand(\tilde{F}_{best})$

27 **return** $\tilde{f}_{best}$

---

computes resultant $\bar{U}_{\tilde{f}}$ if the system is masked with $\tilde{f}$, and stores it in the array $newU^*$ (Lines 19, 23–24). Finally, based on these, it uniformly randomly chooses an OC from those which minimize the resultant utility $newU^*()$ (Lines 25, 26). Once $GMMAssign()$ returns an OC $\tilde{f}$, it is assigned to the system in question, $\bar{N}_{\tilde{f}}, \bar{U}_{\tilde{f}}$ are updated accordingly, as well as the remaining budget and the minimum required (Lines 11–14). Once the loop through K_{list} is over and the full strategy σ is built, its utility $u*$ is computed, and compared with $minu^*$, to update $minu^*$ and σ_{best} appropriately (Lines 15–16).

It is possible to conceive examples where this heuristic approach does not yield a good solution on an arbitrary shuffle, even for problem instances with small parameters. Such an example with 4 systems, 4 TCs and 2 OCs is discussed in the online appendix. Further, we also show an example (in the online appendix) where the solution value is $\Theta(|K|)$ times as bad as the optimal, on exponentially many shuffles. This motivates getting candidate solutions for a large number of shuffles and choosing the best among them as described above. Since the greedy choice does not guarantee optimality, we also propose *Soft-GMM*, a slight modification of GMM which makes assignment probabilistically, and not deterministically. It works exactly as GMM, except Lines 25, 26—it draws f_{best} from a distribution $P(\tilde{F})$ where, $P(\tilde{f}) \propto \exp(-newU^*[\tilde{f}])$.

4.5   Solving for an Optimal Marginal Assignment n

The prior analysis focuses on finding the optimal pure strategy ϕ for the defender to commit to in the game. This is due to the assumption that adversaries view a fixed (static) version of the network when completing reconnaissance. However, it can also be useful to find the optimal mixed strategy $\mathbf{q}$ for the defender in the game. Formally, we define a mixed strategy as a probability distribution over all possible defender pure strategies $\phi \in \Phi$ where $\sum_{\phi \in \Phi} q_\phi = 1$ and $0 \leq q_\phi \leq 1$. For this game, enumerating the set of pure strategies is infeasible, but it is possible to find the defender's optimal marginal strategy $\mathbf{n} = \sum_{\phi \in \Phi} q_\phi \phi$ due to compactly representing the defender's strategy space. The optimal marginal strategy can be found using the same optimization as (6a) and replacing all instances of $\phi_{f,\tilde{f}}$ with $n_{f,\tilde{f}}$. The optimization problem for finding the defender's optimal marginal strategy can be seen as a generalized fractional linear program.

As in Sect. 4.3, generalized linear fractional programs are solved efficiently using a bisection algorithmic approach which solves a sequence of linear programming feasibility problems to get an ϵ-approximate optimal solution [6]. Similarly to the MILP bisection algorithm, this algorithm is given an interval that U^* lies in which is $U^* \in [U^{LB}, U^{UB}]$. We again introduce the variables $l = U^{LB}$ and $d = U^{UB}$ with the initial width $\epsilon_0 = d - l$ that contains the optimal value U^* of our optimization problem. The main loop is repeated until the width $d - l \leq \epsilon$. The main loop has the following two steps:

1. Take $\tau = (u + l)/2$ and solve the feasibility problem in Eqs. (12)–(17) to find if there exists a solution $\mathbf{n}$ that satisfies the constraints.
2. **if** *feasible*, take $u := \tau$; **if** *not feasible*, take $l := \tau$.

The algorithm is guaranteed to converge as after each update the interval $[l, u]$ contains the optimal U^* and the width is halved. The number of steps that are needed to find the ϵ-approximate optimal solution is $\lceil \log \frac{\epsilon_0}{\epsilon} \rceil$.

$$\max_{u,\sigma} \quad 1 \tag{12}$$

$$s.t. \quad \tau \sum_{f \in F} n_{f,\tilde{f}} \geq \sum_{f \in F} n_{f,\tilde{f}} U(f) \qquad \forall \tilde{f} \in \tilde{f} \tag{13}$$

$$\sum_{\tilde{f} \in \tilde{f}} n_{f,\tilde{f}} = N_f \qquad \forall f \in F \tag{14}$$

$$\sum_{\tilde{f} \in \tilde{F}} \sum_{f \in F} n_{f,\tilde{f}} c(f, \tilde{f}) \leq B \qquad (15)$$

$$n_{f,\tilde{f}} \leq \pi_{f,\tilde{f}} N_f \qquad \qquad \forall f \in F, \forall \tilde{f} \in \tilde{F} \qquad (16)$$

$$n_{f,\tilde{f}} \geq 0 \qquad \qquad \forall f \in F, \forall \tilde{f} \in \tilde{F} \qquad (17)$$

5 Optimal Defender Strategy against Naive Adversary

The robust approach to solving CDGs, i.e., assuming a powerful adversary with knowledge of ϕ, can cause the defender to not fully realize the benefit of her informational advantage when faced with a less powerful attacker. In particular, the adversary may value OCs in a fixed manner that is known to the defender.[3] In this case, the values $\bar{U}_{\tilde{f}}$ are fixed and the defender's strategy does not affect the adversary's expected utility for attacking some $\tilde{f}$. Importantly, if there is no budget constraint we can solve for the defender's optimal strategy ϕ in polynomial time using Algorithm 2. W.l.o.g. we assume the adversary has a strict preference ordering over $\tilde{F}$ as if $\bar{U}_{\tilde{f}}$ is equal for any two OCs, the sets could be merged from the defender's perspective, with the feasibility constraint and cost adjusted accordingly.

Algorithm 2 begins by initializing ϕ, Γ^* (which stores the TCs the adversary attacks) and $\tilde{f}^*$ (the OC the adversary attacks given ϕ). In Line 3 we compute the matrix $minUtil[]$ which stores the lowest utility achievable for each TC which is $\min_{\tilde{f} \in \tilde{F}_f} \bar{U}_{\tilde{f}}$. The **For** loop in Line 4 iterates over all $\tilde{f} \in \tilde{F}$ which is sorted descending by $\bar{U}_{\tilde{f}}$ (Line 2) and determines for each $\tilde{f}$ the best set of TCs to mask if $\tilde{f}$ is attacked by the adversary in Lines 5 through 12. To do this, F is split into 4 separate sets P_1, P_2, P_3 and P_4 and the set of TCs to be masked with $\tilde{f}_i$ is stored in Γ'. Note that for each f we enumerate N_f copies for the algorithm. P_1 contains all TCs which cannot be masked with an $\tilde{f}$ that has $\bar{U}_{\tilde{f}} < \bar{U}_{\tilde{f}_i}$. Intuitively, if this set is non-empty it means the defender is not able to devise a strategy ϕ such that the adversary prefers to attack $\tilde{f}_i$, and hence, all subsequent $\tilde{f}_i$ will never be preferred by the adversary. P_2 (P_4) contain TCs f which must be masked (cannot be masked) with $\tilde{f}_i$. P_3 then contains all TCs f which can be masked with $\tilde{f}_i$ but may also be masked with another OC $\tilde{f}_j \neq \tilde{f}_i$. The function $update(\Gamma', P_3)$ sorts the TCs in ascending order and iterates over the TCs $f \in P_3$ and masks all TC f with $\tilde{f}_i \iff U_f \leq EU(\Gamma')$. In Line 13 $update(\Gamma^*, \Gamma', \tilde{f}^*, \tilde{f}_i)$ sets $\Gamma^* = \Gamma'$ and $\tilde{f}^* = \tilde{f}_i$ if $EU(\Gamma') < EU(\Gamma^*)$. Finally, the function $update(\phi, \Gamma^*, \tilde{f}^*)$ in Line 14 determines the OCs $\tilde{f}'$ for all $f \notin \Gamma^*$ given $\bar{U}_{\tilde{f}'} < \bar{U}_{\tilde{f}^*}$ and the strategy ϕ is returned.

---

[3]As an example, the adversary could estimate his utility according to values derived from the NIST National Vulnerability Database [24].

Algorithm 2: Compute defender's optimal ϕ with fixed $\bar{U}_{\tilde{f}}$

---

1 **initialize** $\phi, \Gamma^*, \tilde{f}^*$
2 sort($\tilde{F}$) //descending by utility $\bar{U}_{\tilde{f}}$
3 minUtil[] $:= (\min_{\tilde{f}} \bar{U}_{\tilde{f}})_f$
4 **For** $i = 1, \ldots, |\tilde{F}|$
5   **initialize** Γ'
6 $P_1 := \{f \mid minUtil[f] > \bar{U}_{\tilde{f}_i}\}$
7   **If** $P_1 \neq \emptyset$
8   **break**
9 $P_2 := \{f \mid minUtil[f] = \bar{U}_{\tilde{f}_i}\}$
10 $P_3 := \{f \mid minUtil[f] < \bar{U}_{\tilde{f}_i} \text{ and } \tilde{f}_i \in \tilde{F}_f\}$
11 $P_4 := \{f \mid minUtil[f] < \bar{U}_{\tilde{f}_i} \text{ and } \tilde{f}_i \notin \tilde{F}_f\}$
12 $\Gamma' := P_2$
13   update(Γ', P_3)
14   update($\Gamma^*, \Gamma', \tilde{f}^*, \tilde{f}_i$)
15 update($\phi, \Gamma^*, \tilde{f}^*$)
16 **return** ϕ

Proposition 2 *Given fixed utilities $\bar{U}_{\tilde{f}}$ and no budget constraint, Algorithm 2 computes the optimal strategy ϕ in $O(|F||\tilde{F}|)$.*

It is possible to efficiently compute the defender's optimal strategy when there is no budget constraint. When the defender has a budget constraint, however, the question arises if her optimal strategy can be found efficiently as well. We call this problem $CDG-Fixed$ and show it is NP-Hard.

Proposition 3 $CDG-Fixed$ *is NP-hard.*

Proof We prove the proposition via a reduction from the 0–1 Knapsack problem (0–1 KP), which is a classical NP-hard problem. Given a budget B and a set of m items each with a weight w_i and value v_i, 0–1 KP is the optimization problem of finding the subset of items Y which maximizes $\sum_{i \in Y} v_i$ subject to the budget constraint $\sum_{i \in Y} w_i \leq B$. We now show that 0–1 KP can be reduced to $CDG-Fixed$. For convenience, we use $[m]$ to denote the set $\{1, 2 \ldots, m\}$ and $S = \sum_{i \in [m]} v_i$ denote the sum of all utilities.

Given a 0–1 KP instance as described above, we construct a CDG instance as follows. Let the set of TCs be $F = \{f_1, \ldots, f_m\} \cup \{f_{m+1}\}$, with utilities $U_{f_i} = v_i, \forall i \in [m]$ and $U_{f_{m+1}} = -W$ for some fixed constant V. Note $N_f = 1 \; \forall f \in F$. Let the set of OCs be $\tilde{F} = \{\tilde{f}_1, \tilde{f}_2\}$, with $\tilde{F}_{f_i} = \tilde{F} \; \forall i \in [m]$ and $\tilde{F}_{f_{m+1}} = \{\tilde{f}_1\}$. Set the costs as $c(f_i, \tilde{f}_1) = 0$, $c(f_i, \tilde{f}_2) = w_i$ for all $i \in [m]$ and $c(f_{m+1}, \tilde{f}_1) = 0$. Set $\bar{U}_{\tilde{f}_1} > \bar{U}_{\tilde{f}_2}$. Assuming a naive adversary, these components completely define a $CDG-Fixed$ problem. Since f_{m+1} is bound to be masked by $\tilde{f}_1$, and $\bar{U}_{\tilde{f}_1} > \bar{U}_{\tilde{f}_2}$, attacking $\tilde{f}_1$ is a dominant strategy for the adversary.

Observe that $\sum_{f \in F} U_f$ is $\sum_{i \in [m]} v_i - V = S - V$. We claim that the optimal objective of the 0–1 KP instance is greater than $S - V$ if and only if the optimal defender utility in the constructed $CDG-Fixed$ problem, i.e., $U^*(\phi)$, is negative. We prove the $\Leftarrow$ direction as the $\Rightarrow$ is a similar proof. Let ϕ^* be the optimal solution to the $CDG-Fixed$ problem. By definition, the set $Y = \{i : \phi^*_{f_i, \tilde{f}_2} = 1\}$ is a feasible solution to the 0–1 KP since the cost of mapping f_i to $\tilde{f}_2$ is w_i. The sum of all utilities of all systems is $S - V$ whereas $U^*(\phi^*) < 0$ means the total utilities of systems mapped to $\tilde{f}_1$ is less than 0, this implies that the total utilities of systems mapped to $\tilde{f}_2$ is at least $S - V$. Note each system mapped to $\tilde{f}_2$ corresponds to an item and hence, the optimal objective of the 0–1 KP is also at least $S - V$.

The above claim shows that for any constant V, we can check whether the optimal objective of the 0–1 KP is greater than $S - V$ by solving a $CDG-Fixed$ instance. Using this procedure as a black-box, we can perform a binary search to find the exact optimal objective of the 0–1 KP with integer values within $O(poly(\log(S)))$ steps (both S and weights are machine numbers with input size $O(\log(S))$). As a result, we have constructed a polynomial time reduction from computing the optimal objective of any given 0–1 KP to solving the $CDG-Fixed$ problem. This implies the NP-hardness of the $CDG-Fixed$ problem.

$CDG-Fixed$ can be solved with Algorithm 2 via a modification to the function $update(\Gamma', P_3)$ in Line 13. Given Γ', we compute the minimum budget B' required to mask all TCs $f \in \Gamma'$ with $\tilde{f}_i$ and mask all TCs $f \in P_3$ and $f \in P_4$ with $\tilde{f}_j$ such that $\bar{U}_{\tilde{f}_j} < \bar{U}_{\tilde{f}_i}$. If $\Gamma' = \emptyset$, then for $f \in P_3$ we mask f with $\tilde{f}_i$ if $c(f, \tilde{f}_i) < B'$. Assuming P_3 is sorted ascending, once the defender assigns $\tilde{f}_i$ to a TC f she is done. If $\Gamma' \neq \emptyset$, the defender must solve multiple MILPs, with $n = n_{\Gamma'}, \ldots, |K|$ to find the best Γ'. Denote $u_{\Gamma'} = EU(\Gamma')$.

$$\min_{\phi} \quad n_{\Gamma'} u_{\Gamma'} + \sum_f \phi_{f,\tilde{f}} U_f \tag{18a}$$

$$\text{s.t.} \quad \sum_f \phi_{f,\tilde{f}_i} \leq n - n_{\Gamma'} \tag{18b}$$

$$\text{Constraints (1) } \sim \text{ (4)}$$

6   Experiments

We evaluate the CDG model and solution techniques using synthetically generated game instances. The game payoffs are set to be zero-sum, and for each TC, the payoffs U_f are uniformly distributed in $[1, 10]$. Each OC $\tilde{f}$ is randomly assigned a set of TCs it can mask, while ensuring each TC can be masked with at least one OC. To generate the TSN, each system is randomly assigned a TC uniformly at random. The costs $c(f, \tilde{f})$ are uniformly distributed in $[1, 100]$ with the budget

B uniformly distributed in-between the minimum cost assignment and maximum cost assignment. All experiments are averaged over 30 randomly generated game instances.

6.1 Powerful Adversary: Scalability and Solution Quality Loss

When solving for the defender's optimal strategy ϕ strategy for enterprise networks, it is important to have solution techniques which can scale to large instances of CDGs. Our first experiment compares the scalability of the reformulated MILP, the bisection algorithm and the Greedy Minimax (GMM) algorithm with 1000 random shuffles along with the solution quality of the approaches. In Fig. 2a we show the runtime results with the runtime in seconds on the y-axis and the number of systems varied on the x-axis. As can be seen, the runtime for solving the reformulated MILP increases dramatically as the number of systems increases while both GMM and the bisection algorithm finish in under 10 seconds in all cases. The results from the bisection algorithm compared to the reformulated MILP are quite surprising given it provides the ϵ optimal solution and highlights the benefit from solving smaller MILP for larger CDG instances.

While GMM is much faster than the reformulated MILP (but comparable to the bisection algorithm), it is not guaranteed to provide the optimal solution or an ϵ-approximate solution. However, our experimental results show that empirically the solution quality loss is very small. In Fig. 2b we compare the solution quality of the MILP to GMM, where the attacker's utility is given on the y-axis and the number of OCs are varied on the x-axis. Importantly, GMM shows a low solution quality loss for the defender compared to the MILP with a minimum loss of 1.68% for 12 systems and a maximum loss of 5.93% for 16 systems. This experiment highlights

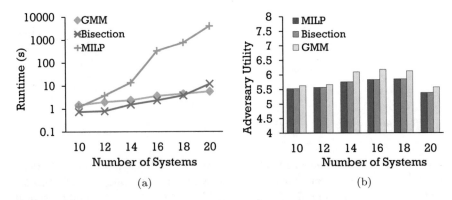

Fig. 2 Runtime comparison and solution quality comparison (20 observables)—reformulated MILP (MILP), the bisection algorithm with $\epsilon = .0001$ (Bisection) and Greedy MaxiMin (GMM) with 1000 random shuffles. (**a**) Runtime. (**b**) Solution quality

the scalability of GMM and shows the loss in solution quality from GMM can give a reasonable trade-off between computational efficiency and solution quality.

An interesting feature of GMM is how often it returns the optimal solution for the defender as the CDG game size changes. Table 1 compares the solution quality of GMM (with 1000 random shuffles) versus the MILP for several game sizes with 10 and 20 systems where the number of OCs are varied from 2 to 10. Interestingly, for CDGs with 10 systems, Hard-GMM is able to find the optimal solution in a vast majority of instances (142 out of 150 instances). However, for CDGs with 20 systems, GMM fails to recover the optimal solution in about a third of the instances (96 out of 150). Nevertheless, the loss of solution quality still remains low (3.18%) even when GMM returns the optimal solution a third of the time.

We also tested the solution quality of a variation of GMM, called Soft-GMM or GMM$-\lambda$. Instead of greedily choosing the OC with minimax expected utility at the stage, we apply a soft-min function [10] with parameter λ controlling the greediness of the next choice. Figure 3 shows the solution quality of GMM (denoted as GMM-H) and GMM$-\lambda$ with varying λ values. GMM$-.01$ is very close to randomly choosing OCs for the systems and performs poorly compared to larger λ values, indicating that GMM is an effective heuristic and performs much better than random assignment. Importantly, the randomness in GMM$-\lambda$ leads to a potential of finding better strategies than GMM since GMM-Hard is restricted to a limited strategy space and GMM$-\lambda$ is not. This can be seen by comparing the results for GMM-Hard and GMM-10 where the latter outperforms the solution quality achieved with GMM-Hard at 8000 and 16000 shuffles. We defer further investigation to future work.

Table 1 Solution quality % loss and number of optimal instances for GMM versus MILP

# OCs	2	4	6	8	10
10 systems	0	0.092%	0.015%	0.028%	0.512%
Optimal instances	30	29	29	29	25
20 systems	0	0.028%	0.615%	1.91%	3.18%
Optimal instances	30	28	17	12	9

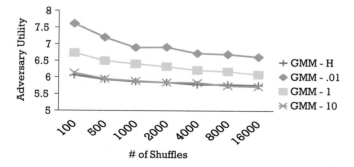

Fig. 3 Solution quality comparison (20 systems and 20 OCs)—comparison of hard-GMM (GMM—H) and soft-GMM (GMM—λ) varying the number of shuffles

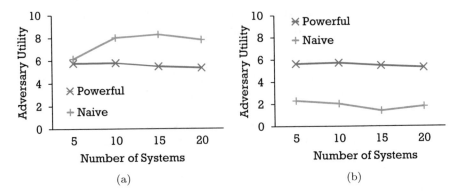

Fig. 4 Solution quality comparison (10 OCs)—in (**a**) we show the solution quality of the two types of defender strategies against a powerful adversary. In (**b**) we show the solution quality of the strategies against a naive adversary. (**a**) Powerful adversary. (**b**) Naive adversary

6.2   Comparing Solutions for Different Types of Adversaries

Our last experiment compares how the optimal strategies for the two adversary models (powerful versus naive) perform in the opposite case. Figure 4a compares the solution quality of the MILP in Sect. 4 to Algorithm 2 when the adversary is assumed to know ϕ with the attacker's utility on the y-axis and the number of systems varied on the x-axis. This figure highlights that for the powerful adversary the MILP performs significantly better than Algorithm 2 (except for 5 systems) and shows the risk of underestimating the adversary's information when devising the defender's strategy ϕ. In Fig. 4b we compare the solution quality of Algorithm 2 to the MILP when the adversary is assumed to have fixed utilities. As the figure shows, the improvement in utility is dramatically higher for Algorithm 2 compared to the MILP. The reason for this difference lies in Algorithm 2 leveraging the adversary's fixed preferences over OCs and minimizes the value of systems masked with the OC the adversary will attack. The MILP, however, minimizes the worst case utility given the adversary may attack any OC and hence, fails to leverage the defender's advantage to a high benefit.

7   Conclusion and Future Work

In this paper, we study the problem of how a network administrator should respond to scan requests from an adversary attempting to infiltrate her network. We show that computing the optimal defender strategy against a powerful adversary is NP-hard and provide two techniques—a reformulation approach and a bisection algorithmic approach—to solve for her optimal strategy. Additionally, we provide a greedy algorithm which quickly finds good defender strategies and performs well empirically. We then show that computing the optimal strategy against a naive attacker is still NP-hard given a budget constraint. Finally, we give extensive experimental analysis demonstrating the effectiveness of our approaches.

Looking to future work, there are several important problems that need to be tackled from CDGs of which we highlight two. First, we assume the adversary only attacks a single system, but in practice, adversaries can attack multiple systems which effects the defender's optimal response scheme. Secondly, our work considers a powerful adversary or one with a fixed set of preferences over OCs. In reality, an adversary's knowledge of the defender's strategy lies in-between these two extremes in the information spectrum. For future work, it will be important to model the adversary's partial information and how it alters the defender's response scheme.

Acknowledgements This work was supported in part by the Army Research Office (W911NF-17-1-0370, W911NF-11-1-0332, W911NF-15-1-0515, W911NF-16-1-0069), National Science Foundation (CNS-1640624, IIS-1649972, and IIS-1526860), and Office of Naval Research (N00014-15-1-2621). Haifeng is partially supported by a Google PhD Fellowship. We also want to thank Solomon Sonya for his invaluable domain knowledge and wonderful discussions.

References

1. Massimiliano Albanese, Ermanno Battista, and Sushil Jajodia. A deception based approach for defeating os and service fingerprinting. In *Communications and Network Security (CNS), 2015 IEEE Conference on*, pages 317–325. IEEE, 2015.
2. Massimiliano Albanese, Ermanno Battista, and Sushil Jajodia. Deceiving attackers by creating a virtual attack surface. In *Cyber Deception*, pages 169–201. Springer, 2016.
3. Massimiliano Albanese, Ermanno Battista, Sushil Jajodia, and Valentina Casola. Manipulating the attacker's view of a system's attack surface. In *Communications and Network Security (CNS), 2014 IEEE Conference on*, pages 472–480. IEEE, 2014.
4. Mohammed H Almeshekah and Eugene H Spafford. Planning and integrating deception into computer security defenses. In *Proceedings of the 2014 Workshop on New Security Paradigms Workshop*, pages 127–138. ACM, 2014.
5. Tansu Alpcan and Tamer Başar. *Network security: A decision and game-theoretic approach.* Cambridge University Press, 2010.
6. Erik B Bajalinov. *Linear-Fractional Programming Theory, Methods, Applications and Software*, volume 84. Springer Science & Business Media, 2013.
7. Nicola Basilico and Nicola Gatti. Automated abstractions for patrolling security games. In *AAAI*, 2011.
8. Nicola Basilico, Nicola Gatti, and Francesco Amigoni. Patrolling security games: Definition and algorithms for solving large instances with single patroller and single intruder. *Artificial Intelligence*, 184:78–123, 2012.
9. Jay Beale, Renaud Deraison, Haroon Meer, Roelof Temmingh, and Charl Van Der Walt. *Nessus network auditing.* Syngress Publishing, 2004.
10. Christopher M Bishop. *Pattern recognition and machine learning.* Springer, 2006.
11. Thomas E Carroll and Daniel Grosu. A game theoretic investigation of deception in network security. *Security and Communication Networks*, 4(10):1162–1172, 2011.
12. Cho-Yu J Chiang, Yitzchak M Gottlieb, Shridatt James Sugrim, Ritu Chadha, Constantin Serban, Alex Poylisher, Lisa M Marvel, and Jonathan Santos. Acyds: An adaptive cyber deception system. In *Military Communications Conference, MILCOM 2016-2016 IEEE*, pages 800–805. IEEE, 2016.

13. Karel Durkota, Viliam Lisỳ, Branislav Bošanskỳ, and Christopher Kiekintveld. Approximate solutions for attack graph games with imperfect information. In *International Conference on Decision and Game Theory for Security*, pages 228–249. Springer, 2015.
14. Karel Durkota, Viliam Lisỳ, Branislav Bosanskỳ, and Christopher Kiekintveld. Optimal network security hardening using attack graph games. In *IJCAI*, pages 526–532, 2015.
15. Vindu Goel and Nicole Perlroth. *Yahoo Says 1 Billion User Accounts Were Hacked*, 2016 (accessed September 10, 2017). https://www.nytimes.com/2016/12/14/technology/yahoo-hack.html.
16. Ines Gutzmer. *Equifax Announces Cybersecurity Incident Involving Consumer Information*, 2017 (accessed October 15, 2017). https://investor.equifax.com/news-and-events/news/2017/09-07-2017-213000628.
17. Sushil Jajodia, Noseong Park, Fabio Pierazzi, Andrea Pugliese, Edoardo Serra, Gerardo I Simari, and VS Subrahmanian. A probabilistic logic of cyber deception. *IEEE Transactions on Information Forensics and Security*, 12(11):2532–2544, 2017.
18. Rob Joyce. Disrupting nation state hackers. San Francisco, CA, 2016. USENIX Association.
19. Christopher Kiekintveld, Viliam Lisỳ, and Radek Píbil. Game-theoretic foundations for the strategic use of honeypots in network security. In *Cyber Warfare*, pages 81–101. Springer, 2015.
20. Christian Kreibich and Jon Crowcroft. Honeycomb: creating intrusion detection signatures using honeypots. *ACM SIGCOMM computer communication review*, 34(1):51–56, 2004.
21. Aron Laszka, Yevgeniy Vorobeychik, and Xenofon D Koutsoukos. Optimal personalized filtering against spear-phishing attacks. In *AAAI*, pages 958–964, 2015.
22. Gordon Fyodor Lyon. *Nmap network scanning: The official Nmap project guide to network discovery and security scanning*. Insecure, 2009.
23. Mandiant. Apt1: Exposing one of China's cyber espionage units, 2013.
24. NIST. *National Vulnerability Database*, 2017. https://nvd.nist.gov/.
25. Jeffrey Pawlick and Quanyan Zhu. Deception by design: evidence-based signaling games for network defense. *arXiv preprint arXiv:1503.05458*, 2015.
26. Radek Píbil, Viliam Lisỳ, Christopher Kiekintveld, Branislav Bošanskỳ, and Michal Pechoucek. Game theoretic model of strategic honeypot selection in computer networks. *Decision and Game Theory for Security*, 7638:201–220, 2012.
27. Niels Provos. Honeyd-a virtual honeypot daemon. In *10th DFN-CERT Workshop, Hamburg, Germany*, volume 2, page 4, 2003.
28. Martin Roesch et al. Snort: Lightweight intrusion detection for networks. In *Lisa*, volume 99, pages 229–238, 1999.
29. Aaron Schlenker, Haifeng Xu, Mina Guirguis, Chris Kiekintveld, Arunesh Sinha, Milind Tambe, Solomon Sonya, Darryl Balderas, and Noah Dunstatter. Don't bury your head in warnings: A game-theoretic approach for intelligent allocation of cyber-security alerts. 2017.
30. Edoardo Serra, Sushil Jajodia, Andrea Pugliese, Antonino Rullo, and VS Subrahmanian. Pareto-optimal adversarial defense of enterprise systems. *ACM Transactions on Information and System Security (TISSEC)*, 17(3):11, 2015.
31. Milind Tambe. *Security and game theory: algorithms, deployed systems, lessons learned*. Cambridge University Press, 2011.
32. Dajun Yue, Gonzalo Guillén-Gosálbez, and Fengqi You. Global optimization of large-scale mixed-integer linear fractional programming problems: A reformulation-linearization method and process scheduling applications. *AIChE Journal*, 59(11):4255–4272, 2013.

Strategic Learning for Active, Adaptive, and Autonomous Cyber Defense

Linan Huang and Quanyan Zhu

1 Introduction

Recent instances of `WannaCry` ransomware, `Petya` cyberattack, and `Stuxnet` malware have demonstrated the trends of modern attacks and the corresponding new security challenges as follows.

- **Advanced**: Attackers leverage sophisticated attack tools to invalidate the off-the-shelf defense schemes such as the firewall and intrusion detection systems.
- **Targeted**: Unlike automated probes, targeted attacks conduct thorough research in advance to expose the system architecture, valuable assets, and defense schemes.
- **Persistent**: Attackers can restrain their malicious behaviors and bide their times to launch critical attacks. They are persistent in achieving the goal.
- **Adaptive**: Attackers can learn the defense strategies and unpatched vulnerabilities during the interaction with the defender and tailor their strategies accordingly.
- **Stealthy and Deceptive**: Attackers conceal their true intentions and disguise their claws to evade detection. The adversarial cyber deception endows attackers an information advantage over the defender.

Thus, defenders are urged to adopt active, adaptive, and autonomous defense paradigms to deal with the above challenges and proactively protect the system prior to the attack damages rather than passively compensate for the loss. In analogy to the classical **Kerckhoffs's principle** in the nineteenth century that attackers know the system, we suggest a new security principle for modern cyber systems as follows:

L. Huang · Q. Zhu (✉)
Department of Electrical and Computer Engineering, New York University, Brooklyn, NY, USA
e-mail: lh2328@nyu.edu; qz494@nyu.edu

© Springer Nature Switzerland AG 2020
S. Jajodia et al. (eds.), *Adaptive Autonomous Secure Cyber Systems*,
https://doi.org/10.1007/978-3-030-33432-1_10

205

Principle of 3A Defense: A cyber defense paradigm is considered to be insufficiently secure if its effectiveness relies on

- Rule-abiding human behaviors.
- A perfect protection against vulnerabilities and a perfect prevention from system penetration.
- A perfect knowledge of attacks.

Firstly, 30% of data breaches are caused by privilege misuse and error by insiders according to Verizon's data breach report in 2019 [1]. Security administration does not work well without the support of technology, and autonomous defense strategies are required to deal with the increasing volume of sophisticated attacks. Secondly, systems always have undiscovered vulnerabilities or unpatched vulnerabilities due to the long supply chain of uncontrollable equipment providers [2] and the increasing complexities in the system structure and functionality. Thus, an effective paradigm should assume a successful infiltration and pursue strategic securities through interacting with intelligent attackers. Finally, due to adversarial deception techniques and external noises, the defender cannot expect a perfect attack model with predicable behaviors. The defense mechanism should be robust under incomplete information and adaptive to the evolution of attacks.

In this chapter, we illustrate three active defense schemes in our previous works, which are designed based on the new cyber security principle. They are defensive deception for detection and counter-deception [3–5] in Sect. 2, feedback-driven Moving Target Defense (MTD) [6] in Sect. 3, and adaptive honeypot engagement [7] in Sect. 4. All three schemes is of incomplete information, and we arrange them based on three progressive levels of information restrictions as shown in the left part of Fig. 1.

The first scheme in Sect. 2 considers the obfuscation of characteristics of known attacks and systems through a random parameter called the player's *type*. The only uncertainty origins from the player's *type*, and the mapping from the type to the utility is known deterministically. The MTD scheme in Sect. 3 considers unknown attacks and systems whose utilities are completely uncertain, while the honeypot engagement scheme in Sect. 4 further investigates environmental uncertainties such as the transition probability, the sojourn distribution, and the investigation reward.

To deal with these uncertainties caused by different information structures, we suggest three associated learning schemes as shown in the right part of Fig. 1, i.e., Bayesian learning for the parameter estimation, distributed learning for the utility acquisition without information sharing, and reinforcement learning for the optimal policy obtainment under the unknown environment. All three learning methods form a feedback loop that strategically incorporates the samples generated during the interaction between attackers and defenders to persistently update the beliefs

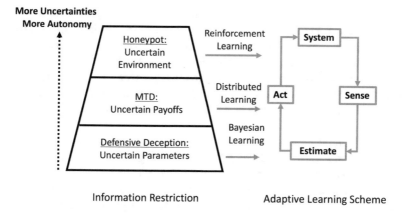

Fig. 1 The left part of the figure describes the degree of information restriction. From bottom to top, the defense scheme becomes more autonomous and relies less on an exact attack model, which also result in more uncertainties. The right part is the associated feedback learning schemes

of known and then take actions according to current optimal decision strategies. The feedback structure makes the learning adaptive to behavioral and environmental changes.

Another common point of these three schemes is the quantification of the tradeoff between security and three different types of cost. In particular, the costs result from the attacker's identification of the defensive deception, the system usability, and the risk of attackers penetrating production systems from the honeynet, respectively.

1.1 Literature

The idea of using deceptions defensively to detect and deter attacks has been studied theoretically as listed in the taxonomic survey [8], implemented to the Adversarial Tactics, Techniques and Common Knowledge (ATT&CK™) adversary model system [9], and tested in the real-time cyber-wargame experiment [10]. Many previous works imply the similar idea of type obfuscation, e.g., creating social network avatars (fake personas) on the major social networks [11], implementing honey files for ransomware actions [12], and disguising a production system as a honeypot to scare attackers away [13].

Moving target defense (MTD) allows dynamic security strategies to limit the exposure of vulnerabilities and the effectiveness of the attacker's reconnaissance by increasing complexities and costs of attacks [14]. To achieve an effective MTD, [15] proposes the instruction set and the address space layout randomization, [16] studies the deceptive routing against jamming in multi-hop relay networks, and [17] uses the Markov chain to model the MTD process and discusses the optimal strategy to balance the defensive benefit and the network service quality.

The previous two methods use the defensive deception to protect the system and assets. To further gather threat information, the defender can implement honeypots to lure attackers to conduct adversarial behaviors and reveal their TTPs in a controlled and monitored environment. Previous works [18, 19] have investigated the adaptive honeypot deployment to effectively engage attackers without their notices. The authors in recent work [20] proposes a continuous-state Markov Decision Process (MDP) model and focuses on the optimal timing of the attacker ejection.

Game-theoretic models are natural frameworks to capture the multistage interaction between attackers and defenders. Recently, game theory has been applied to different sets of security problems, e.g., Stackelberg and signaling games for deception and proactive defenses [6, 16, 21–27], network games for cyber-physical security [28–37], dynamic games for adaptive defense [3, 38–46], and mechanism design theory for security [47–55].

Information asymmetry among the players in network security is a challenge to deal with. The information asymmetry can be either leveraged or created by the attacker or the defender for achieving a successful cyber deception. For example, techniques such as honeynets [22, 56], moving target defense [3, 6, 14], obfuscation [57–60], and mix networks [61] have been introduced to create difficulties for attackers to map out the system information.

To overcome the created or inherent uncertainties of networks, many works have studied the strategic learning in security games, e.g., Bayesian learning for unknown adversarial strategies [62], heterogeneous and hybrid distributed learning [46, 63], multiagent reinforcement learning for intrusion detection [64]. Moreover, these learning schemes are combined to achieve better properties, e.g., distributed Bayesian learning [65], Bayesian reinforcement learning [66], and distributed reinforcement learning [67].

1.2 Notation

Throughout the chapter, we use calligraphic letter $\mathcal{A}$ to define a set and $|\mathcal{A}|$ as the cardinality of the set. Let $\Delta\mathcal{A}$ represent the set of probability distributions over $\mathcal{A}$. If set $\mathcal{A}$ is discrete and finite, $\Delta\mathcal{A} := \{p : \mathcal{A} \mapsto R_+ | \sum_{a \in \mathcal{A}} p(a) = 1\}$, otherwise, $\Delta\mathcal{A} := \{p : \mathcal{A} \mapsto R_+ | \int_{a \in \mathcal{A}} p(a) = 1\}$. Row player P_1 is the defender (pronoun 'she') and P_2 (pronoun 'he') is the user (or the attacker) who controls the column of the game matrix. Both players want to maximize their own utilities. The indicator function $\mathbf{1}_{\{x=y\}}$ equals one if $x = y$, and zero if $x \neq y$.

1.3 Organization of the Chapter

The rest of the paper is organized as follows. In Sect. 2, we elaborate defensive deception as a countermeasure of the adversarial deception under a multistage setting where Bayesian learning is applied for the parameter uncertainty. Section 3 introduces a multistage MTD framework and the uncertainties of payoffs result in distributed learning schemes. Section 4 further considers reinforcement learning for environmental uncertainties under the honeypot engagement scenario. The conclusion and discussion are presented in Sect. 5.

2 Bayesian Learning for Uncertain Parameters

Under the mild restrictive information structure, each player' utility is completely governed by a finite group of parameters which form his/her *type*. Each player's *type* characterizes all the uncertainties about this player during the game interaction, e.g., the physical outcome, the payoff function, and the strategy feasibility, as an equivalent utility uncertainty without loss of generality [68]. Thus, the revelation of the type value directly results in a game of complete information. In the cyber security scenario, a discrete type can distinguish either systems with different kinds of vulnerabilities or attackers with different targets. The type can also be a continuous random variable representing either the threat level or the security awareness level [3, 4]. Since each player P_i takes actions to maximize his/her own type-dependent utility, the other player P_j can form a belief to estimate P_i's type based on the observation of P_i's action history. The utility optimization under the beliefs results in the Perfect Bayesian Nash Equilibrium (PBNE) which generates new action samples and updates the belief via the Bayesian rule. We plot the feedback Bayesian learning process in Fig. 2 and elaborate each element in the following subsections based on our previous work [5].

2.1 Type and Multistage Transition

Through adversarial deception techniques, attackers can disguise their subversive actions as legitimate behaviors so that the defender P_1 cannot judge whether a user P_2's type $\theta_2 \in \Theta_2 := \{\theta_2^g, \theta_2^b\}$ is legitimate θ_2^g or adversarial θ_2^b. As a countermeasure, the defender can introduce the defensive deception so that the attacker cannot distinguish between a primitive system θ_1^L and a sophisticated system θ_1^H, i.e., the defender has a binary type $\theta_1 \in \Theta_1 := \{\theta_1^H, \theta_1^L\}$. A sophisticated system is costly yet deters attacks and causes damages to attackers. Thus, a primitive system can disguise as a sophisticated one to draw the same threat level to attackers yet avoid the implementation cost of sophisticated defense techniques.

Many cyber networks contain hierarchical layers, and up-to-date attackers such as Advanced Persistent Threats (APTs) aim to penetrate these layers and reach specific targets at the final stage as shown in Fig. 3.

At stage $k \in \{0, 1, \cdots, K\}$, P_i takes an action $a_i^k \in \mathcal{A}_i^k$ from a finite and discrete set $\mathcal{A}_i^k$. Both players' actions become fully observable after applied and

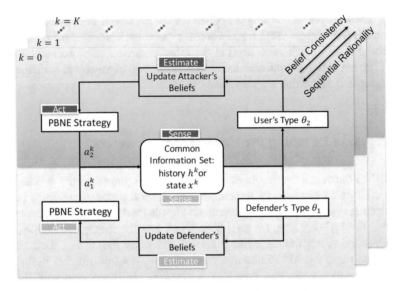

Fig. 2 The feedback loop of the Bayesian learning from the initial stage $k = 1$ to the terminal stage $k = K$. Each player forms a belief of the other player's type and persistently updates the belief based on the actions resulted from the PBNE strategies which are the results of Bayesian learning

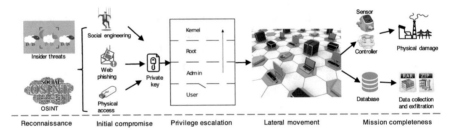

Fig. 3 The multistage structure of APT kill chain is composed of reconnaissance, initial compromise, privilege escalation, lateral movement, and mission execution

each action does not directly reveal the private type. For example, both legitimate and adversarial users can choose to access the sensor, and both primitive and sophisticated defenders can choose to monitor the sensor. Both players' actions up to stage k constitute the *history* $h^k = \{a_1^0, \cdots, a_1^{k-1}, a_2^0, \cdots, a_2^{k-1}\} \in \mathcal{H}^k :=$ $\prod_{i=1}^{2} \prod_{k=0}^{k-1} \mathcal{A}_i^{\bar{k}}$. Given history h^k at the current stage k, players at stage $k + 1$ obtain an updated history $h^{k+1} = h^k \cup \{a_1^k, a_2^k\}$ after the observation a_1^k, a_2^k. A state $x^k \in \mathcal{X}^k$ at each stage k is the smallest set of quantities that summarize information about actions in previous stages so that the initial state $x^0 \in \mathcal{X}^0$ and the history at stage k uniquely determine x^k through a known state transition function f^k, i.e., $x^{k+1} = f^k(x^k, a_1^k, a_2^k), \forall k \in \{0, 1, \cdots, K-1\}$. The state can represent the location of the user in the attack graph, and also other quantities such as users' privilege levels and status of sensor failures.

A behavioral strategy $\sigma_i^k \in \Sigma_i^k : I_i^k \mapsto \Delta(\mathcal{A}_i^k)$ maps P_i's information set I_i^k at stage k to a probability distribution over the action space $\mathcal{A}_i^k$. At the initial stage 0, since the only information available is the player's type realization, the information set $I_i^0 = \Theta_i$. The action is a realization of the behavioral strategy, or equivalently, a sample drawn from the probability distribution $\sigma_i^k(\cdot|I_i^k)$. With a slight abuse of notation, we denote $\sigma_i^k(a_i^k|I_i^k)$ as the probability of P_i taking action $a_i^k \in \mathcal{A}_i^k$ given the available information $I_i^k \in I_i^k$.

2.2 Bayesian Update Under Two Information Structure

Since the other player's type is of private information, P_i forms a belief $b_i^k : I_i^k \mapsto \Delta(\Theta_j), j \neq i$, on P_j's type using the available information I_i^k. Likewise, given information $I_i^k \in I_i^k$ at stage k, P_i believes with a probability $b_i^k(\theta_j|I_i^k)$ that P_j is of type $\theta_j \in \Theta_j$. The initial belief $b_i^0 : \Theta_i \mapsto \Delta\Theta_j, \forall i, j \in \{1, 2\}, j \neq i$, is formed based on an imperfect detection, side-channel information or the statistic estimation resulted from past experiences.

If the system has a *perfect recall* $I_i^k = \mathcal{H}^k \times \Theta_i$, then players can update their beliefs according to the Bayesian rule:

$$b_i^{k+1}(\theta_j|h^k \cup \{a_i^k, a_j^k\}, \theta_i) = \frac{\sigma_i^k(a_i^k|h^k, \theta_i)\sigma_j^k(a_j^k|h^k, \theta_j)b_i^k(\theta_j|h^k, \theta_i)}{\sum_{\bar{\theta}_j \in \Theta_j} \sigma_i^k(a_i^k|h^k, \theta_i)\sigma_j^k(a_j^k|h^k, \bar{\theta}_j)b_i^k(\bar{\theta}_j|h^k, \theta_i)}.$$

(1)

Here, P_i updates the belief b_i^k based on the observation of the action a_i^k, a_j^k. When the denominator is 0, the history h^{k+1} is not reachable from h^k, and a Bayesian update does not apply. In this case, we let $b_i^{k+1}(\theta_j|h^k \cup \{a_i^k, a_j^k\}, \theta_i) := b_i^0(\theta_j|\theta_i)$.

If the information set is taken to be $I_i^k = \mathcal{X}^k \times \Theta_i$ with the Markov property that $\Pr(x^{k+1}|\theta_j, x^k, \cdots, x^1, x^0, \theta_i) = \Pr(x^{k+1}|\theta_j, x^k, \theta_i)$, then the Bayesian update between two consequent states is

$$b_i^{k+1}(\theta_j|x^{k+1}, \theta_i) = \frac{\Pr(x^{k+1}|\theta_j, x^k, \theta_i)b_i^k(\theta_j|x^k, \theta_i)}{\sum_{\bar{\theta}_j \in \Theta_j} \Pr(x^{k+1}|\bar{\theta}_j, x^k, \theta_i)b_i^k(\bar{\theta}_j|x^k, \theta_i)}.$$

(2)

The Markov belief update (2) can be regarded as an approximation of (1) using action aggregations. Unlike the history set $\mathcal{H}^k$, the dimension of the state set $|\mathcal{X}^k|$ does not grow with the number of stages. Hence, the Markov approximation significantly reduces the memory and computational complexity.

2.3 Utility and PBNE

At each stage k, P_i's stage utility $\bar{J}_i^k : \mathcal{X}^k \times \mathcal{A}_1^k \times \mathcal{A}_2^k \times \theta_1 \times \theta_2 \times \mathcal{R} \mapsto \mathcal{R}$ depends on both players' types and actions, the current state $x^k \in \mathcal{X}^k$, and an external noise $w_i^k \in \mathcal{R}$ with a known probability density function ϖ_i^k. The noise term models unknown or uncontrolled factors that can affect the value of the stage utility. Denote the expected stage utility as $J_i^k(x^k, a_1^k, a_2^k, \theta_1, \theta_2) := E_{w_i^k \sim \varpi_i^k} \bar{J}_i^k(x^k, a_1^k, a_2^k, \theta_1, \theta_2, w_i^k), \forall x^k, a_1^k, a_2^k, \theta_1, \theta_2$.

Given the type $\theta_i \in \Theta_i$, the initial state $x^{k_0} \in \mathcal{X}^{k_0}$, and both players' strategies $\sigma_i^{k_0:K} := [\sigma_i^k(a_i^k|x^k, \theta_i)]_{k=k_0,\cdots,K} \in \prod_{k=k_0}^K \Sigma_i^k$ from stage k_0 to K, we can determine the expected cumulative utility $U_i^{k_0:K}$ for P_i, $i \in \{1,2\}$, by taking expectations over the mixed-strategy distributions and the P_i's belief on P_j's type, i.e.,

$$U_i^{k_0:K}(\sigma_i^{k_0:K}, \sigma_j^{k_0:K}, x^{k_0}, \theta_i) := \sum_{k=k_0}^K E_{\theta_j \sim b_i^k, a_i^k \sim \sigma_i^k, a_j^k \sim \sigma_j^k} J_i^k(x^k, a_1^k, a_2^k, \theta_1, \theta_2).$$

(3)

The attacker and the defender use the Bayesian update to reduce their uncertainties on the other player's type. Since their actions affect the belief update, both players at each stage should optimize their expected cumulative utilities concerning the updated beliefs, which leads to the solution concept of PBNE in Definition 1. Note that under PBNE, beliefs are consistent with respect to strategies rather than actions.

Definition 1 Consider the two-person K-stage game with a double-sided incomplete information, a sequence of beliefs $b_i^k, \forall k \in \{0, \cdots, K\}$, an expected cumulative utility $U_i^{0:K}$ in (3), and a given scalar $\varepsilon \geq 0$. A sequence of strategies $\sigma_i^{*,0:K} \in \prod_{k=0}^K \Sigma_i^k$ is called ε-perfect Bayesian Nash equilibrium for player i if the following two conditions are satisfied.

C1: Belief consistency: under the strategy pair $(\sigma_1^{*,0:K}, \sigma_2^{*,0:K})$, each player's belief b_i^k at each stage $k = 0, \cdots, K$ satisfies (2).

C2: Sequential rationality: for all given initial state $x^{k_0} \in \mathcal{X}^{k_0}$ at every initial stage $k_0 \in \{0, \cdots, K\}, \forall \sigma_1^{k_0:K} \in \prod_{k=0}^K \Sigma_1^k, \forall \sigma_2^{k_0:K} \in \prod_{k=0}^K \Sigma_2^k,$

$$U_1^{k_0:K}(\sigma_1^{*,k_0:K}, \sigma_2^{*,k_0:K}, x^{k_0}, \theta_1) + \varepsilon \geq U_1^{k:K}(\sigma_1^{k_0:K}, \sigma_2^{*,k_0:K}, x^{k_0}, \theta_1),$$
$$U_2^{k_0:K}(\sigma_1^{*,k_0:K}, \sigma_2^{*,k_0:K}, x^{k_0}, \theta_2) + \varepsilon \geq U_2^{k:K}(\sigma_1^{*,k_0:K}, \sigma_2^{k_0:K}, x^{k_0}, \theta_2).$$

(4)

When $\varepsilon = 0$, the equilibrium is called Perfect Bayesian Nash Equilibrium (**PBNE**).

□

Solving PBNE is challenging. If the type space is discrete and finite, then given each player's belief at all stages, we can solve the equilibrium strategy satisfying condition C2 via dynamic programming and a bilinear program. Next, we update the belief at each stage based on the computed equilibrium strategy. We iterate the above update on the equilibrium strategy and belief until they satisfy condition C1 as demonstrated in [5]. If the type space is continuous, then the Bayesian update can be simplified into a parametric update under the conjugate prior assumption. Next, the parameter after each belief update can be assimilated into the backward dynamic programming of equilibrium strategy with an expanded state space [4]. Although no iterations are required, the infinite dimension of continuous type space limits the computation to two by two game matrices.

We apply the above framework and analysis to a case study of Tennessee Eastman (TE) process and investigate both players' multistage utilities under the adversarial and the defensive deception in Fig. 4. Some insights are listed as follows.

First, the defender's payoffs under type θ_1^H can increase as much as 56% than those under type θ_1^L. Second, the defender and the attacker receive the highest and the lowest payoff, respectively, under the complete information. When the

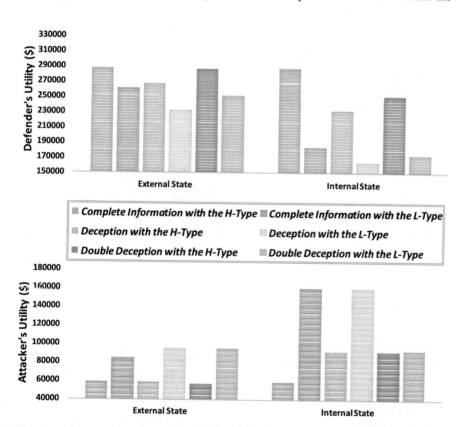

Fig. 4 The cumulative utilities of the attacker and the defender under the complete information, the adversarial deception, and the defensive deception. The complete information refers to the scenario where both players know the other player's type. The deception with the H-type or the L-type means that the attacker knows the defender's type to be θ_1^H or θ_1^L, respectively, yet the defender has no information about the user's type. The double-sided deception indicates that both players do not know the other player's type

attacker introduces deceptions over his type, the attacker's utility increases and the system utility decreases. Third, when the defender adopts defensive deceptions to introduce double-sided incomplete information, we find that the decrease of system utilities is reduced by at most 64%, i.e., the decrease of system utilities changes from \$55, 570 to \$35, 570 under the effectual reconnaissance and type θ_1^H. The double-sided incomplete information also brings lower utilities to the attacker than the one-sided adversarial deception. However, the system utility under the double-sided deception is still less than the complete information case, which concludes that acquiring complete information of the adversarial user is the most effective defense. However, if the complete information cannot be obtained, the defender can mitigate her loss by introducing defensive deceptions.

In conclusion, this work proposes a quantitative defense mechanism to defend against stealthy APTs proactive. The proactive defense does not replace the passive defense which manages to filter out and deter numerous non-target attacks. Proactive defense is useful when the attacker has already evaded the passive defense. Both defense mechanisms should coexist and complement each other to enhance the security of the modern control system.

An analogy is the layered defenses of increasing specificity in the human immune system. The classical passive defense methods such as the firewall and intrusion detection systems are the innate immune system of the modern control system. In particular, the firewall is the first layer of the physical barrier and the intrusion detection system is the second layer of the innate response. The proactive defensive is the adaptive immune system which is designed as the specific response to APTs. The defender learns how to better respond based on the imperfect observation generated during the multi-stage interaction with the user that can be either malicious or legitimate. Since the observation from the detection system is imperfect for the stealthy APT attacks, the proactive defense may also affect the legitimate user negatively, in analogy with the autoimmunity in the immune system. Thus, the proactive defense needs to be quantified and smartly designed to balance the tradeoff between security and usability.

3   Distributed Learning for Uncertain Payoffs

In the previous section, we study known attacks and systems that adopt cyber deception to conceal their types. We assume common knowledge of the prior probability distribution of the unknown type, and also a common observation of either the action history or the state at each stage. Thus, each player can use Bayesian learning to reduce the other player's type uncertainty.

In this section, we consider unknown attacks in the MTD game stated in [6] where each player has no information on the past actions of the other player, and the payoff functions are subject to noises and disturbances with unknown statistical characteristics. Without information sharing between players, the learning is distributed.

3.1 Static Game Model of MTD

We consider a system of N layers yet focus on the static game at layer $l \in \{1, 2, \cdots, N\}$ because the technique can be employed at each layer of the system independently. At layer l, $\mathcal{V}_l := \{v_{l,1}, v_{l,2}, \cdots, v_{l,n_l}\}$ is the set of n_l system vulnerabilities that an attacker can exploit to compromise the system. Instead of a static configuration at layer l, the defender can choose to change her configuration from a finite set of m_l feasible configurations $C_l := \{c_{l,1}, c_{l,2}, \cdots, c_{l,m_l}\}$. Different configurations result in different subsets of vulnerabilities among $\mathcal{V}_l$, which are characterized by the vulnerability map $\pi_l : C_l \to 2^{\mathcal{V}_l}$. We call $\pi_l(c_{l,j})$ the attack surface at stage l under configuration $c_{l,j}$.

Suppose that for each vulnerability $v_{l,j}$, the attacker can take a corresponding attack $a_{l,j} = \gamma_l(v_{l,j})$ from the action set $\mathcal{A}_l := \{a_{l,1}, a_{l,2}, \cdots, a_{l,n_l}\}$. Attack action $a_{l,j}$ is only effective and incurs a bounded cost $D_{ij} \in \mathbb{R}_+$ when the vulnerability $v_{l,j} = \gamma_l^{-1}(a_{l,j})$ exists in the current attack surface $\pi_l(c_{l,k})$. Thus, the damage caused by the attacker at stage l can be represented as

$$r_l(a_{l,j}, c_{l,i}) = \begin{cases} D_{ij}, & \gamma_l^{-1}(a_{l,j}) \in \pi_l(c_{l,k}) \\ 0, & \text{otherwise} \end{cases}. \tag{5}$$

Since vulnerabilities are inevitable in a modern computing system, we can randomize the configuration and make it difficult for the attacker to learn and locate the system vulnerability, which naturally leads to the mixed strategy equilibrium solution concept of the game. At layer l, the defender's strategy $\mathbf{f}_l = \{f_{l,1}, f_{l,2}, \cdots, f_{l,m_l}\} \in \Delta C_l$ assigns probability $f_{l,j} \in [0, 1]$ to configuration $c_{l,j}$ while the attacker's strategy $\mathbf{g}_l := \{g_{l,1}, g_{l,2}, \cdots, g_{l,n_l}\} \in \Delta \mathcal{A}_l$ assigns probability $g_{l,i} \in [0, 1]$ to attack action $a_{l,i}$. The zero-sum game possesses a mixed strategy saddle-point equilibrium (SPE) $(\mathbf{f}_l^* \in \Delta C_l, \mathbf{g}_l^* \in \Delta \mathcal{A}_l)$, and a unique game value $\mathbb{r}(\mathbf{f}_l^*, \mathbf{g}_l^*)$, i.e.,

$$\mathbb{r}_l(\mathbf{f}_l^*, \mathbf{g}_l) \leq \mathbb{r}_l(\mathbf{f}_l^*, \mathbf{g}_l^*) \leq \mathbb{r}_l(\mathbf{f}_l, \mathbf{g}_l^*), \forall \mathbf{f}_l \in \Delta C_l, \mathbf{g}_l \in \Delta \mathcal{A}_l, \tag{6}$$

where the expected cost $\mathbb{r}_l$ is given by

$$\mathbb{r}_l(\mathbf{f}_l, \mathbf{g}_l) := \mathbb{E}_{\mathbf{f}_l, \mathbf{g}_l} r_l = \sum_{k=1}^{n_l} \sum_{h=1}^{m_l} f_{l,h} g_{l,k} r_l(a_{l,k}, c_{l,h}). \tag{7}$$

We illustrate the multistage MTD game in Fig. 5 and focus on the first layer with two available configurations $C_1 := \{c_{1,1}, c_{1,2}\}$ in the blue box. Configuration $c_{1,1}$ in Fig. 5a has an attack surface $\pi_1(c_{1,1}) = \{v_{1,1}, v_{1,2}\}$ while configuration $c_{1,2}$ in Fig. 5b reveals two vulnerabilities $v_{1,2}, v_{1,3} \in \pi_1(c_{1,2})$. Then, if the attacker takes action $a_{1,1}$ and the defender changes the configuration from $c_{1,1}$ to $c_{1,2}$, the attack is deterred at the first layer.

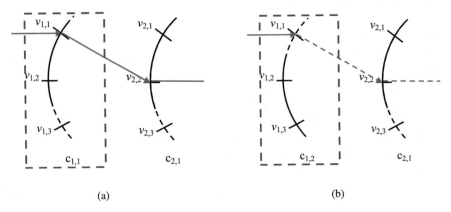

(a)   (b)

Fig. 5 Given a static configuration $c_{1,1}$, an attacker can succeed in reaching the resources at deeper layers by forming an attack path $v_{1,1} \rightarrow v_{2,2} \rightarrow \cdots$. A change of configuration to $c_{1,2}$ can thwart the attacker at the first layer. (**a**) Attack surface $\pi_1(c_{1,1}) = \{v_{1,1}, v_{1,2}\}$. (**b**) Attack surface $\pi_1(c_{1,2}) = \{v_{1,2}, v_{1,3}\}$

3.2 Distributed Learning

In practical cybersecurity domain, the payoff function r_l is subjected to noises of unknown distributions. Then, each player reduces the payoff uncertainty by repeatedly observing the payoff realizations during the interaction with the other player. We use subscript t to denote the strategy or cost at time t.

There is no communication at any time between two agents due to the non-cooperative environment, and the configuration and attack action are kept private, i.e., each player cannot observe the other player's action. Thus, each player independently chooses action $c_{l,t} \in C_l$ or $a_{l,t} \in \mathcal{A}_l$ to estimate the average risk of the system $\hat{r}_{l,t}^S : C_l \rightarrow \mathbb{R}_+$ and $\hat{r}_{l,t}^A : \mathcal{A}_l \rightarrow \mathbb{R}_+$ at layer l. Based on the estimated average risk $\hat{r}_{l,t}^S$ and the previous policy $\mathbf{f}_{l,t}$, the defender can obtain her updated policy $\mathbf{f}_{l,t+1}$. Likewise, the attacker can also update his policy $\mathbf{g}_{l,t+1}$ based on $\hat{r}_{l,t}^A$ and $\mathbf{g}_{l,t}$. The new policy pair $(\mathbf{f}_{l,t+1}, \mathbf{g}_{l,t+1})$ determines the next payoff sample. The entire distributed learning feedback loop is illustrated in Fig. 6 where we distinguish the adversarial and defensive learning in red and green, respectively.

In particular, players update their estimated average risks based on the payoff sample $r_{l,t}$ under the chosen action pair $(c_{l,t}, a_{l,t})$ as follows. Let μ_t^S and μ_t^A be the payoff learning rate for the system and attacker, respectively.

$$
\begin{aligned}
\hat{r}_{l,t+1}^S(c_{l,h}) &= \hat{r}_{l,t}^S(c_{l,h}) + \mu_t^S \mathbf{1}_{\{c_{l,t}=c_{l,h}\}}(r_{l,t} - \hat{r}_{l,t}^S(c_{l,h})), \\
\hat{r}_{l,t+1}^A(a_{l,h}) &= \hat{r}_{l,t}^A(a_{l,h}) + \mu_t^A \mathbf{1}_{\{a_{l,t}=a_{l,h}\}}(r_{l,t} - \hat{r}_{l,t}^A(a_{l,h})).
\end{aligned}
\tag{8}
$$

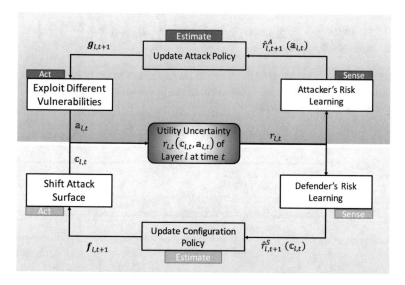

Fig. 6 The distributed learning of the multistage MTD game at layer l. Adversarial learning in red does not share information with defensive learning in green. The distributed learning fashion means that the learning rule does not depend on the other player's action, yet the observed payoff depends on both players' actions

The indicators in (8) mean that both players only update the estimate average risk of the current action.

3.2.1 Security versus Usability

Frequent configuration changes may achieve the complete security yet also decrease the system usability. To quantify the tradeoff between the security and the usability, we introduce the switching cost of policy from $\mathbf{f}_{l,t}$ to $\mathbf{f}_{l,t+1}$ as their entropy:

$$R_{l,t}^S := \sum_{h=1}^{m_l} f_{l,h,t+1} \ln\left(\frac{f_{l,h,t+1}}{f_{l,h,t}}\right). \tag{9}$$

Then, the total cost at time t combines the expected cost with the entropy penalty in a ratio of $\epsilon_{l,t}^S$. When $\epsilon_{l,t}^S$ is high, the policy changes less and is more usable, yet may cause a large loss and be less rational.

$$(\text{SP}): \quad \sup_{\mathbf{f}_{l,t+1} \in \Delta C_l} -\sum_{h=1}^{m_l} f_{l,h,t+1} \hat{r}_{l,t}^S(c_{l,h}) - \epsilon_{l,t}^S R_{l,t}^S. \tag{10}$$

A similar learning cost is introduced for the attacker:

$$(AP): \quad \sup_{\mathbf{g}_{l,t+1} \in \Delta \mathscr{A}_l} \quad -\sum_{h=1}^{n_l} g_{l,h,t+1} \hat{r}_{l,t}^A(a_{l,h}) - \epsilon_{l,t}^A \sum_{h=1}^{n_l} g_{l,h,t+1} \ln \left(\frac{g_{l,h,t+1}}{g_{l,h,t}} \right). \quad (11)$$

At any time $t+1$, we are able to obtain the equilibrium strategy $(f_{l,h,t+1}, g_{l,h,t+1})$ and game value $(W_{l,t}^S, W_{l,t}^A)$ in closed form of the previous strategy and the estimated average risk at time t as follows.

$$f_{l,h,t+1} = \frac{f_{l,h,t} e^{-\frac{\hat{r}_{l,t}(c_{l,h})}{\epsilon_{l,t}^S}}}{\sum_{h'=1}^{m_l} f_{l,h',t} e^{-\frac{\hat{r}_{l,t}(c_{l,h'})}{\epsilon_{l,t}^S}}}, \qquad g_{l,h,t+1} = \frac{g_{l,h,t} e^{-\frac{\hat{r}_{l,t}(a_{l,h})}{\epsilon_{l,t}^A}}}{\sum_{h'=1}^{n_l} g_{l,h',t} e^{-\frac{\hat{r}_{l,t}(a_{l,h'})}{\epsilon_{l,t}^A}}},$$

$$W_{l,t}^S = \epsilon_{l,t}^S \ln \left(\sum_{h=1}^{m_l} f_{l,h,t} e^{-\frac{\hat{r}_{l,t}(c_{l,h})}{\epsilon_{l,t}^S}} \right), \qquad W_{l,t}^A = \epsilon_{l,t}^A \ln \left(\sum_{h=1}^{n_l} g_{l,h,t} e^{-\frac{\hat{r}_{l,t}(a_{l,h})}{\epsilon_{l,t}^A}} \right).$$

$$(12)$$

3.2.2   Learning Dynamics and ODE Counterparts

The closed form of policy leads to the following learning dynamics with learning rates $\lambda_{l,t}^S, \lambda_{l,t}^A \in [0, 1]$.

$$f_{l,h,t+1} = (1 - \lambda_{l,t}^S) f_{l,h,t} + \lambda_{l,t}^S \frac{f_{l,h,t} e^{-\frac{\hat{r}_{l,t}(c_{l,h})}{\epsilon_{l,t}^S}}}{\sum_{h'=1}^{m_l} f_{l,h',t} e^{-\frac{\hat{r}_{l,t}(c_{l,h'})}{\epsilon_{l,t}^S}}},$$

$$(13)$$

$$g_{l,h,t+1} = (1 - \lambda_{l,t}^A) g_{l,h,t} + \lambda_{l,t}^A \frac{g_{l,h,t} e^{-\frac{\hat{r}_{l,t}(a_{l,h})}{\epsilon_{l,t}^A}}}{\sum_{h'=1}^{n_l} g_{l,h',t} e^{-\frac{\hat{r}_{l,t}(a_{l,h'})}{\epsilon_{l,t}^A}}}.$$

If $\lambda_{l,t}^S = 1, \lambda_{l,t}^A = 1$, (13) is the same as (12). According to the stochastic approximation theory, the convergence of the policy and the average risk requires the learning rates $\lambda_{l,t}^A, \lambda_{l,t}^S, \mu_{l,t}^A, \mu_{l,t}^S$ to satisfy the regular condition of convergency in Definition 2.

Definition 2   A number sequence $\{x_t\}, t = 1, 2, \cdots$, is said to satisfy the regular condition of convergency if

$$\sum_{t=1}^{\infty} x_t = +\infty, \quad \sum_{t=1}^{\infty} (x_t)^2 < +\infty. \tag{14}$$

$\square$

The coupled dynamics of the payoff learning (8) and policy learning (13) converge to their Ordinary Differential Equations (ODEs) counterparts in system dynamics (15) and attacker dynamics (16), respectively. Let $e_{c_{l,h}} \in \Delta C_l, e_{a_{l,h}} \in \Delta \mathcal{A}_l$ be vectors of proper dimensions with the h-th entry being 1 and others being 0.

$$\frac{d}{dt} f_{l,h,t} = f_{l,h,t} \left(\frac{e^{-\frac{\hat{r}_{l,t}(c_{l,h})}{\epsilon_{l,t}^S}}}{\sum_{h'=1}^{m_l} f_{l,h',t} e^{-\frac{\hat{r}_{l,t}(c_{l,h'})}{\epsilon_{l,t}^S}}} - 1 \right), h = 1, 2, \cdots, m_l,$$

$$\tag{15}$$

$$\frac{d}{dt} \hat{r}_{l,t}^S(c_{l,h}) = -\mathbb{r}_{l,t}(e_{c_{l,h}}, \mathbf{g}_{l,t}) - \hat{r}_{l,t+1}^S(c_{l,h}), c_{l,h} \in C_l.$$

$$\frac{d}{dt} g_{l,h,t+1} = g_{l,h,t} \left(\frac{e^{-\frac{\hat{r}_{l,t}(a_{l,h})}{\epsilon_{l,t}^A}}}{\sum_{h'=1}^{n_l} g_{l,h',t} e^{-\frac{\hat{r}_{l,t}(a_{l,h'})}{\epsilon_{l,t}^A}}} - 1 \right), h = 1, 2, \cdots, n_l,$$

$$\tag{16}$$

$$\frac{d}{dt} \hat{r}_{l,t+1}^A(a_{l,h}) = \mathbb{r}_{l,t}(\mathbf{f}_{l,t}, e_{a_{l,h}}) - \hat{r}_{l,t+1}^A(a_{l,h}), a_{l,h} \in \mathcal{A}_l.$$

We can show that the SPE of the game is the steady state of the ODE dynamics in (15) and (16), and the interior stationary points of the dynamics are the SPE of the game [6].

3.2.3 Heterogeneous and Hybrid Learning

The entropy regulation terms in (10) and (11) result in a closed form of strategies and learning dynamics in (13). Without the closed form, distributed learners can adopt general learning schemes which combine the payoff and the strategy update as stated in [46]. Specifically, algorithm CRL0 mimics the replicator dynamics and updates the strategy according to the current sample value of the utility. On the other hand, algorithm CRL1 updates the strategy according to a soft-max function of the estimated utilities so that the most rewarding policy get reinforced and will be picked with a higher probability. The first algorithm is robust yet inefficient, and the second one is fragile yet efficient. Moreover, players are not obliged to adopt the same learning scheme at different time. The heterogeneous learning focuses on different players adopting different learning schemes [46], while hybrid learning means that players can choose different learning schemes at different times based on their rationalities and preferences [63]. According to stochastic approximation techniques, these learning schemes with random updates can be studied using their deterministic ODE counterparts.

4 Reinforcement Learning for Uncertain Environments

This section considers uncertainties on the entire environment, i.e., the state transition, the sojourn time, and the investigation payoff, in the active defense scenario of the honeypot engagement [7]. We use the Semi-Markov Decision Process (SMDP) to capture these environmental uncertainties in the continuous time system. Although the attacker's duration time is continuous at each honeypot, the defender's engagement action is applied at a discrete time epoch. Based on the observed samples at each decision epoch, the defender can estimate the environment elements determined by attackers' characteristics, and use reinforcement learning methods to obtain the optimal policy. We plot the entire feedback learning structure in Fig. 7. Since the attacker should not identify the existence of the honeypot and the defender's engagement actions, he will not take actions to jeopardize the learning.

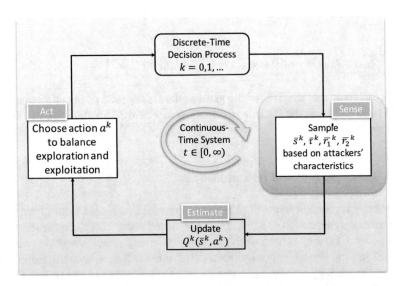

Fig. 7 The feedback structure of reinforcement learning methods on SMDP. The red background means that the attacker's characteristics determine the environmental uncertainties and the samples observed in the honeynet. The attacker is not involved in parts of the green background. The learning scheme in Fig. 7 extends the one in Sect. 3 to consider a continuous time elapse and multistage transitions

4.1 Honeypot Network and SMDP Model

The honeypots form a network to emulate a production system. From an attacker's viewpoint, two network structures are the same as shown in Fig. 8. Based on the network topology, we introduce the continuous-time infinite-horizon discounted SMDPs, which can be summarized by the tuple $\{t \in [0, \infty), \mathcal{S}, \mathcal{A}(s_j), tr(s_l | s_j, a_j),$ $z(\cdot | s_j, a_j, s_l), r^\gamma(s_j, a_j, s_l), \gamma \in [0, \infty)\}$. We illustrate each element of the tuple through a 13-state example in Fig. 9.

Each node in Fig. 9 represents a state $s_i \in \mathcal{S}, i \in \{1, 2, \cdots, 13\}$. At time $t \in [0, \infty)$, the attacker is either at one of the honeypot node denoted by state $s_i \in \mathcal{S}, i \in \{1, 2, \cdots, 11\}$, at the normal zone s_{12}, or at a virtual absorbing state s_{13} once attackers are ejected or terminate on their own. At each state $s_i \in \mathcal{S}$, the defender can choose an action $a_i \in \mathcal{A}(s_i)$. For example, at honeypot nodes, the defender can conduct action a_E to eject the attacker, action a_P to purely record the attacker's activities, low-interactive action a_L, or high-interactive action a_H, i.e., $\mathcal{A}(s_i) := \{a_E, a_P, a_L, a_H\}, i \in \{1, \cdots, N\}$. The high-interactive action is costly to implement yet can both increases the probability of a longer sojourn time at honeypot n_i, and reduces the probability of attackers penetrating the normal system from n_i if connected. If the attacker resides in the normal zone either from the beginning or later through the pivot honeypots, the defender can choose either

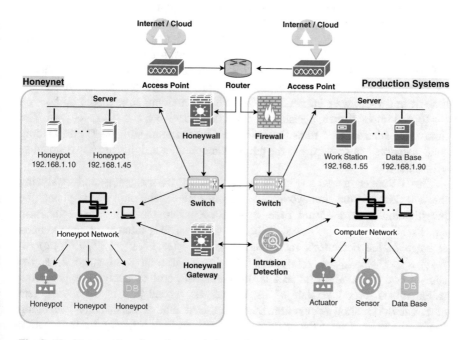

Fig. 8 The honeynet in red emulates and shares the same structure as the targeted production system in green

Fig. 9 Honeypots emulate
different components of the
production system. Actions
a_E, a_P, a_L, a_H are denoted in
red, blue, purple, and green,
respectively. The size of node
n_i represents the state value
$v(s_i), i \in \{1, 2, \cdots, 11\}$

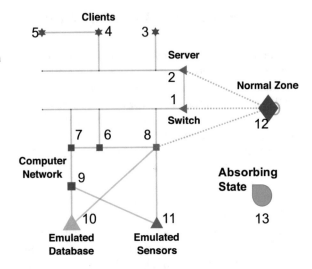

action a_E to eject the attacker immediately, or action a_A to attract the attacker to
the honeynet by generating more deceptive inbound and outbound traffics in the
honeynet, i.e., $\mathcal{A}(s_{12}) := \{a_E, a_A\}$. Based on the current state $s_j \in S$ and the
defender's action $a_j \in \mathcal{A}(s_j)$, the attacker transits to state $s_l \in S$ with probability
$tr(s_l|s_j, a_j)$ and the sojourn time at state s_j is a continuous random variable with
probability density $z(\cdot|s_j, a_j, s_l)$. Once the attacker arrives at a new honeypot n_i,
the defender dynamically applies an interaction action at honeypot n_i from $\mathcal{A}(s_i)$
and keeps interacting with the attacker until she transits to the next honeypot. If the
defender changes the action before the transition, the attacker may be able to detect
the change and become aware of the honeypot. Since the decision is made at the
time of transition, we can transform the above continuous time model on horizon
$t \in [0, \infty)$ into a discrete decision model at decision epoch $k \in \{0, 1, \cdots, \infty\}$. The
time of the attacker's k^{th} transition is denoted by a random variable T^k, the landing
state is denoted as $s^k \in S$, and the adopted action after arriving at s^k is denoted as
$a^k \in \mathcal{A}(s^k)$.

The defender gains an investigation reward by engaging and analyzing
the attacker in the honeypot. To simplify the notation, we segment the
investigation reward during time $t \in [0, \infty)$ into ones at discrete decision
epochs $T^k, k \in \{0, 1, \cdots, \infty\}$. When $\tau \in [T^k, T^{k+1}]$ amount of time elapses
at stage k, the defender's investigation reward $r(s^k, a^k, s^{k+1}, T^k, T^{k+1}, \tau) =$
$r_1(s^k, a^k, s^{k+1})\mathbf{1}_{\{\tau=0\}} + r_2(s^k, a^k, T^k, T^{k+1}, \tau)$, at time τ of stage k, is the
sum of two parts. The first part is the immediate cost of applying engagement
action $a^k \in \mathcal{A}(s^k)$ at state $s^k \in S$ and the second part is the reward rate
of threat information acquisition minus the cost rate of persistently generating
deceptive traffics. Due to the randomness of the attacker's behavior, the information
acquisition can also be random, thus the actual reward rate r_2 is perturbed by an
additive zero-mean noise w_r. As the defender spends longer time interacting with

attackers, investigating their behaviors and acquires better understandings of their targets and TTPs, less new information can be extracted. In addition, the same intelligence becomes less valuable as time elapses due to the timeliness. Thus, we use a discounted factor of $\gamma \in [0, \infty)$ to penalize the decreasing value of the investigation reward as time elapses.

The defender aims at a policy $\pi \in \Pi$ which maps state $s^k \in S$ to action $a^k \in \mathcal{A}(s^k)$ to maximize the long-term expected utility starting from state s^0, i.e.,

$$u(s^0, \pi) = E[\sum_{k=0}^{\infty} \int_{T^k}^{T^{k+1}} e^{-\gamma(\tau+T^k)}(r(S^k, A^k, S^{k+1}, T^k, T^{k+1}, \tau) + w_r)d\tau].$$

(17)

At each decision epoch, the value function $v(s^0) = \sup_{\pi \in \Pi} u(s^0, \pi)$ can be represented by dynamic programming, i.e.,

$$v(s^0) = \sup_{a^0 \in \mathcal{A}(s^0)} E[\int_{T^0}^{T^1} e^{-\gamma(\tau+T^0)}r(s^0, a^0, S^1, T^0, T^1, \tau)d\tau + e^{-\gamma T^1}v(S^1)].$$

(18)

We assume a constant reward rate $r_2(s^k, a^k, T^k, T^{k+1}, \tau) = \bar{r}_2(s^k, a^k)$ for simplicity. Then, (18) can be transformed into an equivalent MDP form, i.e., $\forall s^0 \in S$,

$$v(s^0) = \sup_{a^0 \in \mathcal{A}(s^0)} \sum_{s^1 \in S} tr(s^1|s^0, a^0)(r^\gamma(s^0, a^0, s^1) + z^\gamma(s^0, a^0, s^1)v(s^1)), \quad (19)$$

where $z^\gamma(s^0, a^0, s^1) := \int_0^\infty e^{-\gamma\tau}z(\tau|s^0, a^0, s^1)d\tau \in [0, 1]$ is the Laplace transform of the sojourn probability density $z(\tau|s^0, a^0, s^1)$ and the equivalent reward $r^\gamma(s^0, a^0, s^1) := r_1(s^0, a^0, s^1) + \frac{\bar{r}_2(s^0, a^0)}{\gamma}(1 - z^\gamma(s^0, a^0, s^1)) \in [-m_c, m_c]$ is assumed to be bounded by a constant m_c.

Definition 3 There exists constants $\theta \in (0, 1)$ and $\delta > 0$ such that

$$\sum_{s^1 \in S} tr(s^1|s^0, a^0)z(\delta|s^0, a^0, s^1) \leq 1 - \theta, \forall s^0 \in S, a^0 \in \mathcal{A}(s^0).$$

(20)

□

The right-hand side of (18) is a contraction mapping under the regulation condition in Definition 3. Then, we can find the unique optimal policy $\pi^* = arg \max_{\pi \in \Pi} u(s^0, \pi)$ by value iteration, policy iteration or linear programming. Figure 9 illustrates the optimal policy and the state value by the color and the size of the node, respectively. In the example scenario, the honeypot of database n_{10} and sensors n_{11} are the main and secondary targets of the attacker, respectively. Thus, defenders can obtain a higher investigation reward when they manage to engage the attacker in these two honeypot nodes with a larger probability and for a longer time.

However, instead of naively adopting high interactive actions, a savvy defender also balances the high implantation cost of a_H. Our quantitative results indicate that the high interactive action should only be applied at n_{10} to be cost-effective. On the other hand, although the bridge nodes n_1, n_2, n_8 which connect to the normal zone n_{12} do not contain higher investigation rewards than other nodes, the defender still takes action a_L at these nodes. The goal is to either increase the probability of attracting attackers away from the normal zone or reduce the probability of attackers penetrating the normal zone from these bridge nodes.

4.2   Reinforcement Learning of SMDP

The absent knowledge of the attacker's characteristics results in environmental uncertainty of the investigation reward, the attacker's transition probability, and the sojourn distribution. We use Q-learning algorithm to obtain the optimal engagement policy based on the actual experience of the honeynet interactions, i.e., $\forall \bar{s}^k \in S, \forall a^k \in \mathcal{A}(\bar{s}^k)$,

$$
\begin{aligned}
Q^{k+1}(\bar{s}^k, a^k) = & (1 - \alpha^k(\bar{s}^k, a^k)) Q^k(\bar{s}^k, a^k) + \alpha^k(\bar{s}^k, a^k) [\bar{r}_1(\bar{s}^k, a^k, \bar{s}^{k+1}) \\
& + \bar{r}_2(\bar{s}^k, a^k) \frac{(1 - e^{-\gamma \bar{\tau}^k})}{\gamma} - e^{-\gamma \bar{\tau}^k} \max_{a' \in \mathcal{A}(\bar{s}^{k+1})} Q^k(\bar{s}^{k+1}, a')],
\end{aligned}
\tag{21}
$$

where $\alpha^k(\bar{s}^k, a^k) \in (0, 1)$ is the learning rate, $\bar{s}^k, \bar{s}^{k+1}$ are the observed states at stage k and $k + 1$, $\bar{r}_1, \bar{r}_2$ is the observed investigation rewards, and $\bar{\tau}^k$ is the observed sojourn time at state s^k. When the learning rate satisfies the condition of convergency in Definition 2, i.e., $\sum_{k=0}^{\infty} \alpha^k(s^k, a^k) = \infty, \sum_{k=0}^{\infty} (\alpha^k(s^k, a^k))^2 < \infty, \forall s^k \in S, \forall a^k \in \mathcal{A}(s^k)$, and all state-action pairs are explored infinitely, $\max_{a' \in \mathcal{A}(s^k)} Q^{\infty}(s^{\infty}, a')$, in (21) converges to value $v(s^k)$ with probability 1.

At each decision epoch $k \in \{0, 1, \cdots\}$, the action a^k is chosen according to the ϵ-greedy policy, i.e., the defender chooses the optimal action $arg \max_{a' \in \mathcal{A}(s^k)} Q^k(s^k, a')$ with a probability $1 - \epsilon$, and a random action with a probability ϵ. Note that the exploration rate $\epsilon \in (0, 1]$ should not be too small to guarantee sufficient samples of all state-action pairs. The Q-learning algorithm under a pure exploration policy $\epsilon = 1$ still converges yet at a slower rate.

In our scenario, the defender knows the reward of ejection action a_A and $v(s_{13}) = 0$, thus does not need to explore action a_A to learn it. We plot one learning trajectory of the state transition and sojourn time under the ϵ-greedy exploration policy in Fig. 10, where the chosen actions a_E, a_P, a_L, a_H are denoted in red, blue, purple, and green, respectively. If the ejection reward is unknown, the defender should be restrictive in exploring a_A which terminates the learning process. Otherwise, the defender may need to engage with a group of attackers who share similar behaviors to obtain sufficient samples to learn the optimal engagement policy.

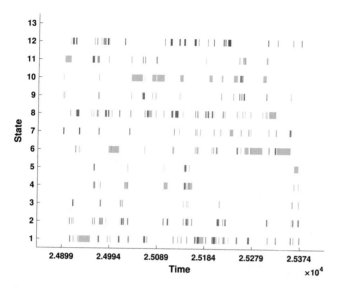

Fig. 10 One instance of Q-learning on SMDP where the x-axis shows the sojourn time and the y-axis represents the state transition. The chosen actions a_E, a_P, a_L, a_H are denoted in red, blue, purple, and green, respectively

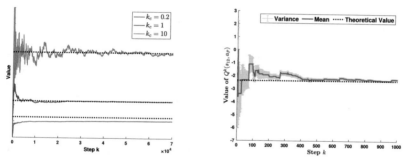

(a) The convergence rate under different values of k_c.

(b) The evolution of the mean and the variance of $Q^k(s_{12}, a_P)$.

Fig. 11 Convergence results of Q-learning over SMDP. (**a**) The convergence rate under different values of k_c. (**b**) The evolution of the mean and the variance of $Q^k(s_{12}, a_P)$

In particular, we choose $\alpha^k(s^k, a^k) = \frac{k_c}{k_{\{s^k, a^k\}} - 1 + k_c}, \forall s^k \in \mathcal{S}, \forall a^k \in \mathcal{A}(s^k)$, to guarantee the asymptotic convergence, where $k_c \in (0, \infty)$ is a constant parameter and $k_{\{s^k, a^k\}} \in \{0, 1, \cdots\}$ is the number of visits to state-action pair $\{s^k, a^k\}$ up to stage k. We need to choose a proper value of k_c to guarantee a good numerical performance of convergence in finite steps as shown in Fig. 11a. We shift the green and blue lines vertically to avoid the overlap with the red line and represent the corresponding theoretical values in dotted black lines. If k_c is too small as shown in the red line, the learning rate decreases so fast that new observed samples hardly update the Q-value and the defender may need a long time to learn the right value. However, if k_c is too large as shown in the green line, the learning rate decreases so slow that new samples contribute significantly to the current Q-value. It causes a large variation and a slower convergence rate of $\max_{a' \in \mathcal{A}(s_{12})} Q^k(s_{12}, a')$.

We show the convergence of the policy and value under $k_c = 1, \epsilon = 0.2$, in the video demo (See https://bit.ly/2QUz3Ok). In the video, the color of each node n^k distinguishes the defender's action a^k at state s^k and the size of the node is proportional to $\max_{a' \in \mathcal{A}(s^k)} Q^k(s^k, a')$ at stage k. To show the convergence, we decrease the value of ϵ gradually to 0 after 5000 steps. Since the convergence trajectory is stochastic, we run the simulation for 100 times and plot the mean and the variance of $Q^k(s_{12}, a_P)$ of state s_{12} under the optimal policy $\pi(s_{12}) = a_P$ in Fig. 11. The mean in red converges to the theoretical value in about 400 steps and the variance in blue reduces dramatically as step k increases.

5   Conclusion and Discussion

This chapter has introduced three defense schemes, i.e., defensive deception to detect and counter adversarial deception, feedback-driven Moving Target Defense (MTD) to increase the attacker's probing and reconnaissance costs, and adaptive honeypot engagement to gather fundamental threat information. These schemes satisfy the Principle of 3A Defense as they actively protect the system prior to the attack damages, provide strategic defenses autonomously, and apply learning to adapt to uncertainty and changes. These schemes possess three progressive levels of information restrictions, which lead to different strategic learning schemes to estimate the parameter, the payoff, and the environment. All these learning schemes, however, have a feedback loop to sense samples, estimate the unknowns, and take actions according to the estimate. Our work lays a solid foundation for strategic learning in active, adaptive, autonomous defenses under incomplete information and leads to the following challenges and future directions.

First, multi-agent learning in non-cooperative environments is challenging due to the coupling and interaction between these heterogeneous agents. The learning results depend on all involving agents yet other players' behaviors, levels of rationality, and learning schemes are not controllable and may change abruptly. Moreover, as attackers become aware of the active defense techniques and the learning scheme under incomplete information, the savvy attacker can attempt to interrupt the learning process. For example, attackers may sacrifice their immediate rewards and take incomprehensible actions instead so that the defender learns incorrect attack characteristics. The above challenges motivate robust learning methods under non-cooperative and even adversarial environments.

Second, since the learning process is based on samples from real interactions, the defender needs to concern the system safety and security during the learning period, while in the same time, attempts to achieve more accurate learning results of the attack's characteristics. Moreover, since the learning under non-cooperative and adversarial environments may terminate unpredictably at any time, the asymptotic convergence would not be critical for security. The defender needs to care more about the time efficiency of the learning, i.e., how to achieve a sufficiently good estimate in a finite number of steps.

Third, instead of learning from scratch, the defender can attempt to reuse the past experience with attackers of similar behaviors to expedite the learning process, which motivates the investigation of transfer learning in reinforcement learning [69]. Some side-channel information may also contribute to the learning to allow agents to learn faster.

Acknowledgements This research is partially supported by awards ECCS-1847056, CNS-1720230, CNS-1544782, and SES-1541164 from National Science of Foundation (NSF), award 2015-ST-061-CIRC01 from U. S. Department of Homeland Security, and grant W911NF-19-1-0041 from Army Research Office (ARO).

References

1. Verizon, "Data breach investigation report," (2019), Retrieved from https://enterprise.verizon.com/resources/reports/dbir/
2. D. Shackleford, "Combatting cyber risks in the supply chain," *SANS. org*, 2015.
3. L. Huang and Q. Zhu, "Adaptive strategic cyber defense for advanced persistent threats in critical infrastructure networks," *ACM SIGMETRICS Performance Evaluation Review*, vol. 46, no. 2, pp. 52–56, 2019.
4. ——, "Analysis and computation of adaptive defense strategies against advanced persistent threats for cyber-physical systems," in *International Conference on Decision and Game Theory for Security*. Springer, 2018, pp. 205–226.
5. L. Huang, Q. Zhu, "A dynamic games approach to proactive defense strategies against Advanced Persistent Threats in cyber-physical systems," *Computers & Security*, vol. 89, 101660, 2020. https://doi.org/10.1016/j.cose.2019.101660
6. Q. Zhu and T. Başar, "Game-theoretic approach to feedback-driven multi-stage moving target defense," in *International Conference on Decision and Game Theory for Security*. Springer, 2013, pp. 246–263.
7. L. Huang and Q. Zhu, "Adaptive Honeypot Engagement through Reinforcement Learning of Semi-Markov Decision Processes," *arXiv e-prints*, p. arXiv:1906.12182, Jun 2019.
8. J. Pawlick, E. Colbert, and Q. Zhu, "A game-theoretic taxonomy and survey of defensive deception for cybersecurity and privacy," *arXiv preprint arXiv:1712.05441*, 2017.
9. F. J. Stech, K. E. Heckman, and B. E. Strom, "Integrating cyber-d&d into adversary modeling for active cyber defense," in *Cyber deception*. Springer, 2016, pp. 1–22.
10. K. E. Heckman, M. J. Walsh, F. J. Stech, T. A. O'boyle, S. R. DiCato, and A. F. Herber, "Active cyber defense with denial and deception: A cyber-wargame experiment," *computers & security*, vol. 37, pp. 72–77, 2013.
11. J. Gómez-Hernández, L. Álvarez-González, and P. García-Teodoro, "R-locker: Thwarting ransomware action through a honeyfile-based approach," *Computers & Security*, vol. 73, pp. 389–398, 2018.
12. N. Virvilis, B. Vanautgaerden, and O. S. Serrano, "Changing the game: The art of deceiving sophisticated attackers," in *2014 6th International Conference On Cyber Conflict (CyCon 2014)*. IEEE, 2014, pp. 87–97.
13. J. Pawlick, E. Colbert, and Q. Zhu, "Modeling and analysis of leaky deception using signaling games with evidence," *IEEE Transactions on Information Forensics and Security*, 2018.

14. S. Jajodia, A. K. Ghosh, V. Swarup, C. Wang, and X. S. Wang, *Moving target defense: creating asymmetric uncertainty for cyber threats.* Springer Science & Business Media, 2011, vol. 54.

15. G. S. Kc, A. D. Keromytis, and V. Prevelakis, "Countering code-injection attacks with instruction-set randomization," in *Proceedings of the 10th ACM conference on Computer and communications security.* ACM, 2003, pp. 272–280.

16. A. Clark, Q. Zhu, R. Poovendran, and T. Başar, "Deceptive routing in relay networks," in *International Conference on Decision and Game Theory for Security.* Springer, 2012, pp. 171–185.

17. H. Maleki, S. Valizadeh, W. Koch, A. Bestavros, and M. van Dijk, "Markov modeling of moving target defense games," in *Proceedings of the 2016 ACM Workshop on Moving Target Defense.* ACM, 2016, pp. 81–92.

18. C. R. Hecker, "A methodology for intelligent honeypot deployment and active engagement of attackers," Ph.D. dissertation, 2012.

19. Q. D. La, T. Q. Quek, J. Lee, S. Jin, and H. Zhu, "Deceptive attack and defense game in honeypot-enabled networks for the internet of things," *IEEE Internet of Things Journal*, vol. 3, no. 6, pp. 1025–1035, 2016.

20. J. Pawlick, T. T. H. Nguyen, and Q. Zhu, "Optimal timing in dynamic and robust attacker engagement during advanced persistent threats," *CoRR*, vol. abs/1707.08031, 2017. [Online]. Available: http://arxiv.org/abs/1707.08031

21. J. Pawlick and Q. Zhu, "A Stackelberg game perspective on the conflict between machine learning and data obfuscation," in *Information Forensics and Security (WIFS), 2016 IEEE International Workshop on.* IEEE, 2016, pp. 1–6. [Online]. Available: http://ieeexplore.ieee.org/abstract/document/7823893/

22. Q. Zhu, A. Clark, R. Poovendran, and T. Basar, "Deployment and exploitation of deceptive honeybots in social networks," in *Decision and Control (CDC), 2013 IEEE 52nd Annual Conference on.* IEEE, 2013, pp. 212–219.

23. Q. Zhu, H. Tembine, and T. Basar, "Hybrid learning in stochastic games and its applications in network security," *Reinforcement Learning and Approximate Dynamic Programming for Feedback Control*, pp. 305–329, 2013.

24. Q. Zhu, Z. Yuan, J. B. Song, Z. Han, and T. Başar, "Interference aware routing game for cognitive radio multi-hop networks," *Selected Areas in Communications, IEEE Journal on*, vol. 30, no. 10, pp. 2006–2015, 2012.

25. Q. Zhu, L. Bushnell, and T. Basar, "Game-theoretic analysis of node capture and cloning attack with multiple attackers in wireless sensor networks," in *Decision and Control (CDC), 2012 IEEE 51st Annual Conference on.* IEEE, 2012, pp. 3404–3411.

26. Q. Zhu, A. Clark, R. Poovendran, and T. Başar, "Deceptive routing games," in *Decision and Control (CDC), 2012 IEEE 51st Annual Conference on.* IEEE, 2012, pp. 2704–2711.

27. Q. Zhu, H. Li, Z. Han, and T. Basar, "A stochastic game model for jamming in multi-channel cognitive radio systems," in *ICC*, 2010, pp. 1–6.

28. Z. Xu and Q. Zhu, "Secure and practical output feedback control for cloud-enabled cyber-physical systems," in *Communications and Network Security (CNS), 2017 IEEE Conference on.* IEEE, 2017, pp. 416–420.

29. ———, "A Game-Theoretic Approach to Secure Control of Communication-Based Train Control Systems Under Jamming Attacks," in *Proceedings of the 1st International Workshop on Safe Control of Connected and Autonomous Vehicles.* ACM, 2017, pp. 27–34. [Online]. Available: http://dl.acm.org/citation.cfm?id=3055381

30. ———, "Cross-layer secure cyber-physical control system design for networked 3d printers," in *American Control Conference (ACC), 2016.* IEEE, 2016, pp. 1191–1196. [Online]. Available: http://ieeexplore.ieee.org/abstract/document/7525079/

31. M. J. Farooq and Q. Zhu, "Modeling, analysis, and mitigation of dynamic botnet formation in wireless iot networks," *IEEE Transactions on Information Forensics and Security*, 2019.

32. Z. Xu and Q. Zhu, "A cyber-physical game framework for secure and resilient multi-agent autonomous systems," in *Decision and Control (CDC), 2015 IEEE 54th Annual Conference on.* IEEE, 2015, pp. 5156–5161.

33. L. Huang, J. Chen, and Q. Zhu, "A large-scale markov game approach to dynamic protection of interdependent infrastructure networks," in *International Conference on Decision and Game Theory for Security*. Springer, 2017, pp. 357–376.

34. J. Chen, C. Touati, and Q. Zhu, "A dynamic game analysis and design of infrastructure network protection and recovery," *ACM SIGMETRICS Performance Evaluation Review*, vol. 45, no. 2, p. 128, 2017.

35. F. Miao, Q. Zhu, M. Pajic, and G. J. Pappas, "A hybrid stochastic game for secure control of cyber-physical systems," *Automatica*, vol. 93, pp. 55–63, 2018.

36. Y. Yuan, Q. Zhu, F. Sun, Q. Wang, and T. Basar, "Resilient control of cyber-physical systems against denial-of-service attacks," in *Resilient Control Systems (ISRCS), 2013 6th International Symposium on*. IEEE, 2013, pp. 54–59.

37. S. Rass and Q. Zhu, "GADAPT: A Sequential Game-Theoretic Framework for Designing Defense-in-Depth Strategies Against Advanced Persistent Threats," in *Decision and Game Theory for Security*, ser. Lecture Notes in Computer Science, Q. Zhu, T. Alpcan, E. Panaousis, M. Tambe, and W. Casey, Eds. Cham: Springer International Publishing, 2016, vol. 9996, pp. 314–326.

38. Q. Zhu, Z. Yuan, J. B. Song, Z. Han, and T. Basar, "Dynamic interference minimization routing game for on-demand cognitive pilot channel," in *Global Telecommunications Conference (GLOBECOM 2010), 2010 IEEE*. IEEE, 2010, pp. 1–6.

39. T. Zhang and Q. Zhu, "Strategic defense against deceptive civilian gps spoofing of unmanned aerial vehicles," in *International Conference on Decision and Game Theory for Security*. Springer, 2017, pp. 213–233.

40. L. Huang and Q. Zhu, "Analysis and computation of adaptive defense strategies against advanced persistent threats for cyber-physical systems," in *International Conference on Decision and Game Theory for Security*, 2018.

41. ——, "Adaptive strategic cyber defense for advanced persistent threats in critical infrastructure networks," in *ACM SIGMETRICS Performance Evaluation Review*, 2018.

42. J. Pawlick, S. Farhang, and Q. Zhu, "Flip the cloud: Cyber-physical signaling games in the presence of advanced persistent threats," in *Decision and Game Theory for Security*. Springer, 2015, pp. 289–308.

43. S. Farhang, M. H. Manshaei, M. N. Esfahani, and Q. Zhu, "A dynamic bayesian security game framework for strategic defense mechanism design," in *Decision and Game Theory for Security*. Springer, 2014, pp. 319–328.

44. Q. Zhu and T. Başar, "Dynamic policy-based ids configuration," in *Decision and Control, 2009 held jointly with the 2009 28th Chinese Control Conference. CDC/CCC 2009. Proceedings of the 48th IEEE Conference on*. IEEE, 2009, pp. 8600–8605.

45. Q. Zhu, H. Tembine, and T. Basar, "Network security configurations: A nonzero-sum stochastic game approach," in *American Control Conference (ACC), 2010*. IEEE, 2010, pp. 1059–1064.

46. Q. Zhu, H. Tembine, and T. Başar, "Heterogeneous learning in zero-sum stochastic games with incomplete information," in *49th IEEE conference on decision and control (CDC)*. IEEE, 2010, pp. 219–224.

47. J. Chen and Q. Zhu, "Security as a Service for Cloud-Enabled Internet of Controlled Things under Advanced Persistent Threats: A Contract Design Approach," *IEEE Transactions on Information Forensics and Security*, 2017. [Online]. Available: http://ieeexplore.ieee.org/abstract/document/7954676/

48. R. Zhang, Q. Zhu, and Y. Hayel, "A Bi-Level Game Approach to Attack-Aware Cyber Insurance of Computer Networks," *IEEE Journal on Selected Areas in Communications*, vol. 35, no. 3, pp. 779–794, 2017. [Online]. Available: http://ieeexplore.ieee.org/abstract/document/7859343/

49. R. Zhang and Q. Zhu, "Attack-aware cyber insurance of interdependent computer networks," 2016.

50. W. A. Casey, Q. Zhu, J. A. Morales, and B. Mishra, "Compliance control: Managed vulnerability surface in social-technological systems via signaling games," in *Proceedings of the 7th ACM CCS International Workshop on Managing Insider Security Threats*. ACM, 2015, pp. 53–62.
51. Y. Hayel and Q. Zhu, "Attack-aware cyber insurance for risk sharing in computer networks," in *Decision and Game Theory for Security*. Springer, 2015, pp. 22–34.
52. ——, "Epidemic protection over heterogeneous networks using evolutionary poisson games," *IEEE Transactions on Information Forensics and Security*, vol. 12, no. 8, pp. 1786–1800, 2017.
53. Q. Zhu, C. Fung, R. Boutaba, and T. Başar, "Guidex: A game-theoretic incentive-based mechanism for intrusion detection networks," *Selected Areas in Communications, IEEE Journal on*, vol. 30, no. 11, pp. 2220–2230, 2012.
54. Q. Zhu, C. A. Gunter, and T. Basar, "Tragedy of anticommons in digital right management of medical records." in *HealthSec*, 2012.
55. Q. Zhu, C. Fung, R. Boutaba, and T. Başar, "A game-theoretical approach to incentive design in collaborative intrusion detection networks," in *Game Theory for Networks, 2009. GameNets' 09. International Conference on*. IEEE, 2009, pp. 384–392.
56. T. E. Carroll and D. Grosu, "A game theoretic investigation of deception in network security," *Security and Commun. Nets.*, vol. 4, no. 10, pp. 1162–1172, 2011.
57. J. Pawlick and Q. Zhu, "A Stackelberg game perspective on the conflict between machine learning and data obfuscation," *IEEE Intl. Workshop on Inform. Forensics and Security*, 2016.
58. T. Zhang and Q. Zhu, "Dynamic differential privacy for ADMM-based distributed classification learning," *IEEE Transactions on Information Forensics and Security*, vol. 12, no. 1, pp. 172–187, 2017. [Online]. Available: http://ieeexplore.ieee.org/abstract/document/7563366/
59. S. Farhang, Y. Hayel, and Q. Zhu, "Phy-layer location privacy-preserving access point selection mechanism in next-generation wireless networks," in *Communications and Network Security (CNS), 2015 IEEE Conference on*. IEEE, 2015, pp. 263–271.
60. T. Zhang and Q. Zhu, "Distributed privacy-preserving collaborative intrusion detection systems for vanets," *IEEE Transactions on Signal and Information Processing over Networks*, vol. 4, no. 1, pp. 148–161, 2018.
61. N. Zhang, W. Yu, X. Fu, and S. K. Das, "gPath: A game-theoretic path selection algorithm to protect tor's anonymity," in *Decision and Game Theory for Security*. Springer, 2010, pp. 58–71.
62. A. Garnaev, M. Baykal-Gursoy, and H. V. Poor, "Security games with unknown adversarial strategies," *IEEE transactions on cybernetics*, vol. 46, no. 10, pp. 2291–2299, 2015.
63. Q. Zhu, H. Tembine, and T. Başar, "Distributed strategic learning with application to network security," in *Proceedings of the 2011 American Control Conference*. IEEE, 2011, pp. 4057–4062.
64. A. Servin and D. Kudenko, "Multi-agent reinforcement learning for intrusion detection: A case study and evaluation," in *German Conference on Multiagent System Technologies*. Springer, 2008, pp. 159–170.
65. P. M. Djurić and Y. Wang, "Distributed bayesian learning in multiagent systems: Improving our understanding of its capabilities and limitations," *IEEE Signal Processing Magazine*, vol. 29, no. 2, pp. 65–76, 2012.
66. G. Chalkiadakis and C. Boutilier, "Coordination in multiagent reinforcement learning: a bayesian approach," in *Proceedings of the second international joint conference on Autonomous agents and multiagent systems*. ACM, 2003, pp. 709–716.
67. Z. Chen and D. Marculescu, "Distributed reinforcement learning for power limited many-core system performance optimization," in *Proceedings of the 2015 Design, Automation & Test in Europe Conference & Exhibition*. EDA Consortium, 2015, pp. 1521–1526.
68. J. C. Harsanyi, "Games with incomplete information played by "bayesian" players, i–iii part i. the basic model," *Management science*, vol. 14, no. 3, pp. 159–182, 1967.
69. M. E. Taylor and P. Stone, "Transfer learning for reinforcement learning domains: A survey," *Journal of Machine Learning Research*, vol. 10, no. Jul, pp. 1633–1685, 2009.

Online Learning Methods for Controlling Dynamic Cyber Deception Strategies

Marcus Gutierrez and Christopher Kiekintveld

1   Introduction

As we become a more interconnected society and place increasing amounts of trust in our cyber infrastructure, cyber threats have also become more pervasive and more sophisticated. Cyber deception has become an increasingly important and unique defensive tool for combating these threats. Cyber deception techniques are diverse, and so are the goals they accomplish for defense. Deception techniques can be used to learn about attackers, including detecting their presence or actions, learning about specific tactics and goals, and capturing examples of malware and other tools. Deception can also be focused on mitigating the effectiveness of attacks by confusing attackers, potentially leading to less effective attacks, delayed or conservative decisions, and wasted time and other resources.

Honeypots are one of the best known forms of cyber deception. These fake hosts and services are deployed in a network, often to waste the resources of an attacker and log attack activity to inform the network administrator [36]. Over time, honeypots have been used for many different purposes, and have evolved to be much more sophisticated with greater abilities to mimic real hosts and to capture useful information about attackers [6, 21, 24]. The sophistication of honeypots can vary dramatically, from limited low-interaction honeypots to sophisticated high interaction honeypots [13, 21, 27]. A significant amount of research has been devoted to designing convincing honeypots that are hard to tell apart from real systems, as well as to designing different types of honeypots.

M. Gutierrez · C. Kiekintveld (✉)
The University of Texas at El Paso, El Paso, TX, USA
e-mail: mgutierrez22@miners.utep.edu; cdkiekintveld@utep.edu

© Springer Nature Switzerland AG 2020
S. Jajodia et al. (eds.), *Adaptive Autonomous Secure Cyber Systems*,
https://doi.org/10.1007/978-3-030-33432-1_11

Another important set of research challenges for the use of cyber deception methods is at the strategic level: given that we have effective deception capabilities, how can these be used most effectively to improve cyber defense? The use of deception techniques is costly; there are costs to design and maintain the deceptive objects, and there is the potential to confuse legitimate users, administrators, or to inadvertently present new attack surfaces. This means that deception should be used strategically, to accomplish particular goals while considering the costs. In addition, the defensive strategy may need to be adapted over time due to changes in the underlying network being protected, or due to changes in the nature of the current threat environment. Due to the rapid pace of these events in a cybersecurity context, decisions about how to deploy and dynamically adapt the deception strategy should be automated as much as possible using artificial intelligence methods.

Currently, many deception strategies such as honeypots are deployed statically, on a mostly ad-hoc basis. For example, a network administrator may decide to set up a certain set of honeypots on the network, configuring either open source or commercial products by hand and then leaving them in place on the network. A more sophisticated approach is to adopt the principles of Moving Target Defense (MTD) and randomly change the configurations of honeypots deployed over time, for example by randomly switching between a set of pre-configured profiles at periodic intervals [38]. A number of recent game-theoretic approaches take this basic MTD idea further and optimize a randomization strategy based on a game-theoretic model (these will be surveyed in more detail in the following section). While very useful in some cases, the game theory approaches require a detailed model of the adversary, and generally do not have the ability to learn and adapt to opponents over time based on repeated interactions.

Here, we discuss using methods from machine learning to design adaptive strategies for cyber deception, focusing on examples using honeypots. We compare these with game theoretic approaches and show that in some settings the adaptive approaches have significant advantages. In particular, if the defender has the ability to make observations and adjust the strategy based on repeated interactions with attackers, these models can adapt and fine-tune a defensive policy based on the actual threat environment, without relying on a correct and detailed model up front. In addition, they can account for novel events (e.g., zero-day vulnerabilities) using exploration and rapidly adapt to new environments.[1] Finally, they provide many of the same advantages of randomized strategies in that they are quite difficult for attackers to predict and learn to play well against, as we show using data from a study with human participants in a simple cyber deception game.[2]

---

[1] This work was first presented in the Artifical Intelligence for Cyber Security workshop in San Francisco, CA in 2017 [15].

[2] Complete description of this work found in the proceedings in 41st CogSci conference [14]

1.1 Game Theory for Cyber Deception

Game theory is one of the primary tools for strategic decision making in adversarial environments, so it is a natural candidate approach for analyzing strategic decisions in cyber deception. If the designer of a solution fully understands the action space and state space of an interaction and the size of the proposed game is tractable, then game theory provides precise solutions with guarantees of optimality without the need for training sets or learning from direct interaction with an adversary.

Several recent works have investigated the game-theoretic approach to cyber deception. Notably, Píbil et al. introduced the Honeypot Selection Game (HSG) [16, 26]. The HSG models a network administrator selecting from honeypot configurations to capture an intelligent and rational attacker, which closely matches the problems described in Sects. 2 and 3.

Several other game-theoretic models have been developed to address other cyber defense problems [1, 19, 31, 32], including some specifically for deception [30, 43], however these consider attribute obfuscation as the means of deception rather than use of decoy objects.

Wang et al. investigated the use of honeypots in the smart grid to mitigate denial of service attacks through the lens of Bayesian games [42]. La et al. also model honeypots mitigating denial of service attacks in similar fashion, but in the Internet-of-Things domain [18]. Du et al. tackle a similar "honeypots for denial of service attack" problem with Bayesian game modeling in the social networking domain [10]. These works demonstrate the vast amounts of domains honeypots can aid in.

A couple of works also consider the notion of two-sided deception, where the defender not only deploys real-looking honeypots, but also fake-looking real hosts. Rowe et al. demonstrated mathematically that deploying two-sided deception offers an improved defense by scaring off attackers [28]. Caroll and Grosu introduce the signaling deception game where deployed honeypot deception is bolstered through the use of signals [9]. Shi et al. introduce the mimicry honeypot framework which combines real nodes, honeypots, and fake-looking honeypots to derive equilibria strategies to bolster defenses [35]. They validated their work in a simulated network.

1.2 Online Learning for Cyber Deception

Online learning fundamentally contrasts game theory in that it is retrospective, focusing on adapting based previously experience. In particular, reinforcement learning concerns itself with optimizing the overall reward over repeated interactions [37]. This paradigm often requires less computational power and makes fewer assumptions about the environment as the primary problem it needs to solve is to effectively balance exploration and exploitation while gradually improving the solution.

These attributes of reinforcement learning have many benefits when addressing cyber deception. One of the major issues that arises in the cybersecurity domain is the vast and complex environments. We do not yet fully understand the complex relationships between software, users, and vulnerabilities. However, reinforcement learning can explore different defenses to find the best one and then play optimally. Adaptive online learning solutions can even maintain a balance of exploration and exploitation when the environment changes over time (e.g., vulnerabilities are patched or discovered).

Online learning is not new to cyber deception, and several works have investigated this combination of concepts. Interestingly, online learning can be used to further aid in successfully committing cyber deception [20, 25, 40, 41] or in detection of deceptive cyber threats [29, 33, 34, 39, 44]. One limitation of online learning is a relative lack of guarantee in solution quality as opposed to game-theoretic solutions.

Another issue that arises when attempting to transfer to real world applications is *observability*. Reinforcement learning, in particular, requires constant feedback when actions are performed. If the deployed defense did not detect any malicious attacks for long periods of time, the defense algorithms may incorrectly penalize the chosen solutions when there were no attacks at all (and in essence, there was nothing to detect). Lastly, online learning does require time before it matches (or even surpasses) the defensive quality of its game-theoretic counterpart. A newly deployed system built from game-theoretic solutions will likely outperform a newly deployed system with reinforcement learning for an initial period.

2   Online Learning for Deception in a Dynamic Threat Environment

One of the dominant characteristics of cybersecurity is the constant and quickly changing nature of the threat landscape, as new offensive and defensive techniques are developed and improved daily. When new vulnerabilities are discovered, cybersecurity experts try to detect them as quickly as possible and develop countermeasures. However, this takes significant time and it is not always possible to completely fix all vulnerabilities, or to disseminate patches to all affected systems. A zero-day exploit is an undisclosed application vulnerability that can be exploited to negatively affect hardware, applications, data or the network [5]. The time before zero-day attacks have been fixed, and patches have been applied is critical since there is often time for substantial damage. Most Intrusion Detection Systems (IDS) have difficulties detecting these zero-day attacks because they rely on previously observed signatures or hard-coded rules, or imperfect methods for detecting other types of malicious behavior. Honeypots and other deception techniques provide hope for improving the detection and tracking of this evolving space of vulnerabilities and exploits since they can provide high quality alerts even for previously unknown types of attacks. However, optimizing the ability of honeypots to detect the changing threat landscape will also require methods to adapt the honeypot deployment strategy to track the current threat environment. We propose an approach for doing this using methods from online learning to adapt a deception strategy over tiem.

We model the problem of a network administrator selecting from a set of pre-configured, high-interaction honeypot profiles to detect ongoing attacks. Here, we consider an attack to be the full set of actions needed to exploit a specific system. This includes probing the network, the intrusion into the network, and the delivery of a malicious payload. Attacks utilize exploits to inflict harm to the integrity of a system, but exploits are not a static threat. New exploits are developed all the time and older exploits wane in utility as their vulnerabilities are patched. This aspect of exploits forms an evolutionary life cycle [22]. These dynamically changing exploits make the attacker's arsenal of attacks inherently dynamic. Defender solutions should be resilient and adapt to the constantly shifting capability of the adversaries. We model these dynamically shifting exploits based on the vulnerability life cycles studied by Frei [11].

In this work, we model a repeated interaction wherein each round, a defender must select from a set of specific honeypot configurations that can detect some attacks by an adversary. Each honeypot configuration exposes a different attack surface to the attacker. There are a vast number of honeypot configurations (e.g., different combinations of protocols, server operating systems, application types, application versions, services offered, etc.). The defender's ultimate goal is to detect and learn from attacks that would harm the current network the defender is tasked with protecting. Each set of honeypot configurations (i.e., honeynet) exposes a unique attack surface and provides different value in the detection capability depending on the current life cycles of the adversary's attacks and their potential to harm the given network. Exposing all attack surfaces would be infeasible, significantly harm the overall performance of the network, and would be impossible to maintain. So, the defender needs to reason strategically to make the best of use limited honeynet resources to track the current threat environment by exposing targeted attack surfaces.

Our primary contributions are twofold. First, we present a realistic cybersecurity configuration that captures adaptive opponents learning from one another using honeypots and exploits in a constantly evolving threat environment. We then propose a solution method for the defender based on method from the Multi-Armed Bandit (MAB) reinforcement learning framework. We demonstrate that using standard MAB solutions, the defender is capable of adapting to the attacker regardless of the dynamically changing environment.

2.1 Model

We now introduce a formal model that captures two important features of the exploit detection problem. First, the defender has limited resources and must selectively

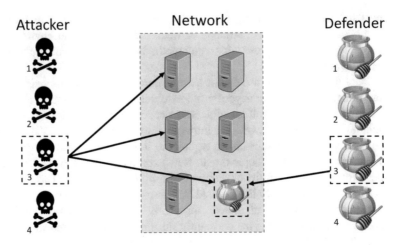

Fig. 1 High-level visualization of model. Defender inserts honeypots into the network and the adversary selects an attack that targets the servers on the network (which may be honeypots)

choose which types of honeypots to deploy. Second, the set of exploits that can be used (and detected) changes dynamically over time, both by introducing new exploits and changing the value of existing exploits. Here, we consider a repeated interaction between a defender and an attacker. The defender faces a choice in each round of which set of available honeypot configurations to deploy in that round. The attacker's decision in each round is which exploit to deploy to try to execute a successful attack. A high-level visualization of the interaction is show in Fig. 1.

A key aspect of our model is that systems in a network (real or fake) have specific configurations, and each exploit can affect only systems that have these specific configurations. For example, an exploit may take advantage of a vulnerability in a specific version of an operating system. We model the configuration of a system as a vector of binary variables, which represent whether a particular configuration feature is true or not for a specific system.[3] We will refer to the set of all possible configurations as D, the number of configurations using k^d, and individual configurations as $D_i \in \{0, 1\}^f$ where f is the total number of features and i is an index variable such that $1 \leq i \leq k^d$. We note that the number of legal configurations is generally less than 2^f since some may not represent feasible configurations, but may still be extremely large. Each configuration represents a possible system, or a possible honeypot.

We assume that the defender has a static network N of real systems to protect (in general, this could also change over time, but we adopt this for simplicity). These are represented using the same configuration vectors as the honeypots, but we use the variable $N_s \in \{0, 1\}^f$ to refer to a real system, and $k^n \geq 1$ to refer to the number

---

[3]This could easily be generalized to include non-binary features, but it is not necessary for our purposes.

of real systems in the network. In addition, each real system has a value V_s that describes how important it is to either the defender or attacker. In each round, the defender will select a set of honeypots to add to the network from the set D, which will be added to the systems in N to form the modified network for that round.

The attacker's actions represent possible exploits that can be used to attack systems on the network. We represent exploits using a binary vector similar to that used for system configurations. However, these vectors represent the *required* system configuration features that must be present for a system to be vulnerable to the exploit. The set of all currently known exploits is given by A, and individual exploits by $A_m \in \{0, 1\}^f$. A system (real or fake) is vulnerable to exploit A_m if and only if it has a 1 for all features where A_m has a 1.

Another key aspect of our model is that the set of available exploits changes over time, as does the effectiveness of the exploits. In our model, we add a new (previously unknown) exploit to the set A at the end of each round with probability $p(t)$. Therefore, the total number of exploits k_t^a varies over time, and the attacker can select any exploit that is available in A at time t.

We also model the severity/effectiveness of different exploits. The National Institute of Standards and Technology uses the Common Vulnerability Scoring System (CVSS) to assess the severity, difficulty of implementation, and impact of exploits [23]. We capture the severity of different exploits, but also model how this severity evolves over the typical lifecycle of an exploit [11]. Initially, an exploit may be known only to the initial discoverer, and there are no known patches or mitigations. These are the most dangerous exploits, and are known as *zero-day attacks*. At some point the exploit becomes broadly known. During this time it may be widely used to conduct attacks by many different groups, while mitigations are still being developed. Eventually, patches and other mitigations are developed to reduce or eliminate the exploit. However, they may take time to be fully adopted and distributed, so the effectiveness of the exploit is gradually reduced over time.

We use a function $AttackVal_m(Z_{m,t})$ for each specific exploit to model how the effectiveness changes over time. These functions are (weakly) monotonically decreasing with respect to the number of times the exploit m has been detected by the defender by round t, denoted by $Z_{m,t}$. We allow for many different functional forms, since the pattern may be different for different types of exploits/attacks. Figure 2 in the experiments section shows examples of the types of functions we use in our simulations.

The defender and the attacker receive scores in each round depending on whether or not the attack was detected, the values of the (real) systems affected by the attack, and the severity of the exploit used in the attack. In round t the defender adds a set of honeypots to the network $D_i \in D$, and the attacker selects one exploit $A_m \in A$. If at least one of the honeypots added by the defender is vulnerable to A_m, then the defender *detects* the attack; otherwise the attack is not detected. If the defender does not detect the attack, he loses a value proportional to the total value of the systems that are vulnerable to the attack multiplied by the severity score for the attack given by $AttackVal_m(Z_{m,t})$, and the attacker gains this value. If the attack is detected, the payoffs are reversed. More formally, we define the defender's reward $R_{i,m,t}$ in round t as:

$$R_{i,m,t} = \begin{cases} AttackVal_m(Z_{m,t}) \cdot \frac{\phi_m}{2T} & \text{if } D_i \text{ detects } A_m, \\ -AttackVal_m(Z_{m,t}) \cdot \frac{\phi_m}{2T} & \text{if } D_i \neg\text{detects } A_m. \end{cases} \tag{1}$$

The values for each function range between $[0,1]$. T denotes the summation of the values of every host s in the network where $1 \leq s \leq k^n$, such that $T = \sum_{s=1}^{k^n} V_s \phi_m$ represents the sum of the values of all hosts on the network vulnerable to exploit m. We note that the reward values lie in the range $[-1,1]$, where a value of -1 signifies that the defender failed to detect an exploit with the highest possible severity that successfully exploits every host on the network. Similarly, a reward value of 1 signifies the detection of this extreme exploit. We assume a zero-sum scenario, so the attacker's payoffs are defined in the same way, but with the opposite sign.

2.2 Attacker Model

Our focus in this paper is on developing effective defender strategies using online learning methods. However, we also need to consider a realistic model of an adaptive adversary to evaluate our defender strategies. Real-world attackers are not likely to adopt optimal learning policies (especially when viewed as a large, diverse group), but are likely to adapt over time to choose more beneficial strategies more often. We use a simple adaptive attacker strategy to model this, based on fictitious play (a similar adversarial attacker is also used in Klíma et al. [17]).

The attacker estimates the historical value of playing each exploit m by keeping a running average of the utility values received each time m is played. The agent discounts the older values to weight newer information more heavily to allow for a gradual learning rate. Specifically, the Adversarial Attacker assesses each exploit m's Utility U_u in time t using the formula:

$$U_m(t) = CurrVal_m(t) + \lambda * AttackTotal_m(t - 1)$$

where λ is a discount parameter and $AttackTotal(m, t)$ is the total rewards received from exploit m up to the current time step. $CurrVal_m(t)$ represents the attacker reward for the current timestep. For our experiments, we used a discount value $\lambda = 1.0$, such that the value of the current attack and its past successes are weighted roughly the same. This attacker differs from the Adversarial Attacker described by Klíma in that it is not deterministic. Instead, this agent uses a distribution that updates according its beliefs and randomly selects from this distribution each round to play an exploit. The learning rate λ affects how quickly the attacker shifts towards the best response exploit.

2.3 Defender Strategies

The basic problem the defender faces in our model is to learn the best honeypot configurations to select in each round. If the environment and attacker behavior were static, this would map directly to a classic multi-armed bandit problem, where the key challenge is to balance the exploitation of current information with exploration to learn new information. However, our model is highly dynamic, since the value of using any given honeypot configuration will change over time as the exploits and their values change, and the attacker learns better attack policies. There are variations of the multi-armed bandit setting that account for different forms of non-stationary environments, but none that map exactly to our setting. Nevertheless, we believe that these methods are a very promising starting point for designing learning strategies for the exploit detection problem, so we evaluate versions of several algorithms to evaluate their effectiveness in this domain.

2.4 Baseline Defense Strategies

A naïve strategy that is commonly used in practice for deploying honeypots can be characterized as the "set and forget" strategy. The defender chooses a honeypot configuration to play at the beginning of the game and deterministically plays this configuration for the remainder of the game. This limits the defender's possible attack surface coverage drastically and we show that adaptive methods can provide much stronger strategies and better coverage to detect attacks. For the remainder of the paper, we refer to this defense strategy as a Pure strategy.

Random defense strategies should improve over the Pure strategy. A Uniform Random defense agent plays each possible honeypot configuration with equal probability in each round. This strategy is hard to predict and maximizes exploration, but it does not attempt to exploit information from past experience. The Fixed Random agent plays according to a randomized policy for selecting honeypot configurations. However, it does not adapt this policy over time, so this agent offers a random, but exploitable defense.

2.5 Multi-Armed Bandits

Multi-Armed Bandits (MAB) capture a central tradeoff in machine learning: balancing exploration vs exploitation. In a standard MAB, an agent must repeatedly select from a set of arms. It receives a reward drawn from an initially unknown distribution of values, with a different distribution for each arm. The goal is to learn which arm has the highest expected value as quickly as possible, therefore minimizing the cumulative regret. One standard setting is the "stochastic" model, where the distribution of rewards is stochastic, but does not change over time. A setting at the opposite extreme is the "adversarial" model, where the rewards can be changed arbitrarily by an adversary.

The defender in our model faces a problem that maps naturally to the high-level bandit problem. The defender chooses from a set of options in each round, and receives feedback about the success of this choice. The value of selecting each honeypot configuration is initially unknown, but can be learned over time. Unfortunately, our model does not map exactly to either the stochastic or adversarial bandit model in the assumptions about how the rewards may change over time. In our model the distribution of rewards for choosing a specific honeypot change over time as the adversary learns, and as the exploits and their values evolve. However, these changes are not as extreme as in the standard adversarial model; the rewards change in an adversarial direction, but not arbitrarily.

Since our setting lies somewhere between the stochastic and adversarial models, we consider algorithms designed for both types of models so see which one yields better performance in our setting. We evaluate the performance of these solutions based on regret, which is the difference between the expected value of the best honeypot configuration θ and the expected value of a defender in a given round. We define the expected value of θ as,

$$E[\theta] = \max_{\theta} \sum_{\theta \in D} \sum_{m \in A} X_t(\theta) * Y_t(m) * R_{\theta,m,t}$$

where $R_{\theta,m,t}$ is the defender's reward in round t when playing the optimal honeypot configuration θ and the attacker plays exploit m. We then define regret as,

$$Regret_t = E[\theta] - \sum_{i \in D} \sum_{u \in A} X_t(i) * Y_t(m) * R_{D_i,A_m,t}$$

where $X_t(i)$ is the defender's probability for playing honeypot configuration i in round t and $Y_t(m)$ is the attacker's probability for playing exploit m in round t. Ideally, the defender wishes to minimize regret, which corresponds to playing the optimal honeypot configuration in each round.

In the stochastic setting, there are k^d arms to choose from, each with their own independent reward distributions on $[0, 1]$. We use the most common solution for this class of MAB, the Upper Confidence Bound (UCB) method first described by Auer et. al. [2]. Though our defender plays against an adversary, the adversary is constrained by the available exploits. The typical adversarial MAB setting assumes that an opponent determines the expected rewards of each arm, potentially with some external randomization [7]. We utilize the Exponentially weighted algorithm for Exploration and Exploitation (EXP3), which is the most well-known adversarial bandit algorithm [3]. EXP3 differs from UCB in that it is not deterministic. At the end of each round, it has a probability for selecting each arm. This prevents an intelligent attack from using pattern recognition or simply knowing the algorithm, which may be beneficial in a security context.

2.6 Experiments

We conducted several experiments to evaluate different online learning methods for the exploit detection problem in comparison with several baseline methods described previously. We consider four types of functions for how the severity of an exploit evolves over time, as shown in Fig. 2. The steep exploit has high initial value, but decreases rapidly and approaches zero. The constant exploit provides a low, but consistent value. The steady exploit provides a linearly decreasing value function that stops near zero. The traditional exploit, modeled by Frei, acts similar to a non-increasing step function, representing the life cycle stages of a vulnerability [11]. In all cases, exploits provide the highest value when they have not been detected previously.

In every experiment, the defender and attacker repeatedly interact for 20,000 rounds. We use a set of 50 possible system configurations for our experiments, where each configuration has between 8 and 12 positive features. This is enough to provide a diverse set of attack surfaces, but also in a reasonable range for the type of systems that could be present in a modest network, and that could be crafted as honeypot configurations. The attacker starts with $k^a = 10$ exploits, but each round the attacker has a 10% chance to discover a new exploit.

In Fig. 3, we show that the two bandit algorithms outperform the three naïve baselines, providing a strong case for MAB algorithms as a foundation for solving this problem. One argument against using UCB is the fact that is deterministic. Our attacker agent does not perform any sophisticated learning, but if an attacker had knowledge that the defender is employing UCB, they could exploit the defender and avoid detection 100% of the time. On the other hand, EXP3 assumes that the opponent is actively trying to minimize the agent's expected rewards. To combat this, EXP3 randomly selects an arm in each round according to a calculated distribution.

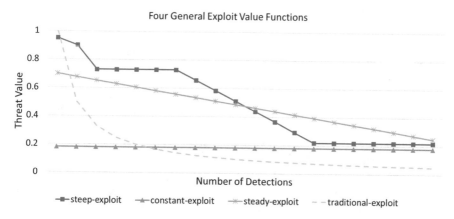

Fig. 2 Example value functions for four exploit types: steep, traditional, constant, and steady

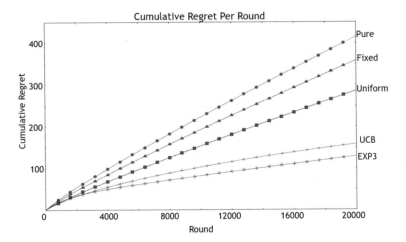

Fig. 3 Cumulative regret over time

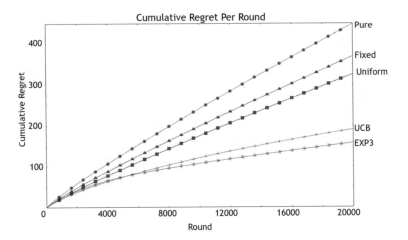

Fig. 4 Second experiment, increasing the number of configurations and features

In our second experiment, we keep the same parameters, but increase the number of honeypot configurations to $k^d = 100$ and the number of possible configuration features to $f = 100$. This increases the complexity and number of strategies for the defender. As seen in Fig. 4, the naïve strategies perform similarly, continuously being exploited by the Adversarial Attacker. UCB and EXP3 perform only slightly worse than in the first experiment. In the first 4000 rounds, EXP3 appears to perform worse than UCB, unlike in the first experiment. This is most likely caused by the increased number of honeypot configurations and therefore, an increased amount of exploration.

3   Online Learning Algorithms for Deception Against Humans

Another important aspect of the success of cyber deception strategies is whether they can be learned and exploited by an intelligent adversary. Of particular interest are human adversaries, who may be able to easily detect and exploit patterns in how deceptive objects are used, and avoid them to attack only real systems. Game theoretic models consider this problem by using randomized strategies to make it difficult for adversaries to exploit specific patterns in defensive strategies. However, adaptive strategies that learn to respond to opponents may also be hard to predict, and have many of the same advantages of the game theoretic randomized strategies. Here, we consider both game theoretic and adaptive strategies against human opponents in a basic cyber deception game using honeypots.

3.1   Model

For this study we designed a model that focuses on the learning aspects of an adversarial cybersecurity interaction, motivated by honeypot deception. In this scenario, an attacker and defender compete over multiple resources (nodes) in the network belonging to the defender with the following parameters: v_i is the value of node i, c_i^a is the cost to attack node i, and c_i^d is the cost to defend node i. At the beginning of the interaction, each node is initialized with the non-negative parameters. At the beginning of each round, the defender spends some budget D to turn some subset of the nodes into honeypots, such that the total cost of defended nodes is $\leq D$.[4]

Once the defender deploys honeypots, the attacker selects a node to attack or passes. If the attacker's chosen node i is undefended, the attacker receives the reward $v_i - c_i^a$, and the defender receives a reward of 0. On the other hand, if the attacker's chosen node i was a honeypot, the attacker receives the negative reward $-c_i^a$, and the defender receives the positive reward v_i.[5] At the end of the round, the interaction resets, and the process repeats each round.

The only feedback the attacker receives is the reward for her action. Therefore, the attacker can only partially and indirectly observe the defender's behavior. The defender observes the individual honeypot placements. So, if the defender captures the attacker with a honeypot, the defender knows which honeypot node was responsible for the capture. If the defender does not capture the attacker and there are more than 1 undefended nodes, the defender can never be certain about which

---

[4]Sections 2 and 3 are updated excerpts from separate works. Please consider these mathematical symbols found in these sections in isolation in the case of conflicting definitions.

[5]We assume $v_i > c_i^a$ and $\sum_{i \in N} c_i^d > D$.

node the attacker chose. This style of feedback is known as semi-bandit feedback in the MAB literature. Given our focus on the study of high-level decision-making, only general cognitive skills are needed from those humans playing the role of the attacker. Cybersecuriy knowledge does not play a role in making decisions regarding "honeypot" configuration or realism [4].

We designed a repeated adversarial interaction with 6 arms (which we will refer to as nodes) to be played over 50 rounds as seen in Fig. 5. We recruited 304 human participants on Amazon's Mechanical Turk [8]. Of the 304 participants, 130 reported female and 172 reported male with 2 participants reporting as other.

All participants were above the age of 18 and had a median age of 32. The experiment averaged roughly 10 min from start to finish and the participants were paid US $1.00 for completing the experiment. The participants were given a bonus payment proportional to their performance in the 50 round game, ranging from US $0 to an extra US $3.25. This bonus payment was intended to incentivize participants to play as best they could.

In a realistic cybersecurity environment, the domain knowledge of the attacker plays an important role as to which vulnerabilities to exploit and how to gain access to a system. When recruiting the participants in our study, we held no requirements or assumptions about the cybersecurity knowledge of the participants. To address this, we take the pessimistic assumption that if the participant (as the attacker) tries to attack a non-honeypot node, they perform a guaranteed successful attack. All that remains for the attacker is deliberate which node to target for an attack, which boils down to basic human cognition. Real world expert hackers will share the same level of cognition with our participants, allowing the recruited participants to accurately represent real cyberattackers at the described level of abstraction [4].

3.2 Scenario

The defender has a budget $D = 40$ that limits the number of honeypot configurations (i.e., combinations of defended nodes). In each round, the participant attacks a node and receives either a positive reward $v_i - c_i^a$ or a negative reward $-c_i^a$ depending on the defender's action.

The setup in Fig. 5 was the same for every participant. For ease of the participant, we simplified the visible rewards on the nodes, where the reward $v_i - c_i^a$ for attacking a non-honeypot appears as the positive top number in the node. Meanwhile, the loss for attacking a honeypot $-c_i^a$ appears as the lower, negative number inside the node. Table 1 shows the actual parameters for each node.

We designed the nodes such to fit a variety of risk-reward archetypes (e.g., low-risk/low-reward, high-risk/high-reward, low-risk/high-reward). The intuition is to allow for differences in strategies and learning. These differences in known parameters provide a noticeable difference from the traditional MAB. For instance, in the first round, the attacker is making an informed decision based on the attack costs and rewards.

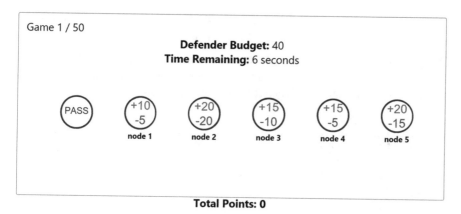

Fig. 5 User interface for the honeypot intrusion game

Table 1 Node parameters for online human experiment		Pass	Node 1	Node 2	Node 3	Node 4	Node 5
	v_i	0	15	40	25	20	35
	c_i^a	0	5	20	10	5	15
	c_i^d	0	10	20	15	15	20

3.3 Defenders

We deployed 3 different defenders to analyze the impact an online learning defense has on human learning as opposed to randomized and static defenses. We use the *Static Pure Defender*, the *Static Equilibrium Defender*, and the *Adaptive LLR Defender* that learns from its own action observations. Each defender creates a different level of learning complexity for the human participants. Here we are not investigating the best defense strategy versus humans. Instead, we are interested in analyzing the impact that varying levels of defense complexity have on human learning and decision making as a whole.

Static Pure Defender This defender employs a "set and forget," purely static defense that attempts to maximize its total value by assuming it must commit to a single, pure, non-stochastic strategy for a single round. This defender tries to spend its budget to protect the highest valued nodes. For the scenario seen in Fig. 5, the defender always defends nodes 2 and 5, leading to nodes 3 and 4 as optimal nodes for attacking. This defender acts as a baseline for human learning. With this defender, we investigate the upper bound on how quickly humans can learn a defense.

Static Equilibrium Defender This defender plays over a fixed distribution of defenses (combinations of nodes to be honeypots). The defense is a Mixed Strategy Nash Equilibrium. It optimizes the defender's expected utility assuming only a

single, non-repeated interaction against a fully rational attacker. An optimal strategy
of the attacker in this equilibrium is to attack node 4.

Adaptive Learning with Linear Rewards Defender The last defender, Learning
with Linear Rewards (LLR) [12], provides a deterministic, yet adaptive defense as
it tries to maximize its reward by balancing exploration and exploitation.

Algorithm 1 Learning with linear rewards (LLR)

1: //INITIALIZATION
2: If $max|\mathcal{A}_a|$ is known, let $L = max|\mathcal{A}_a|$; else, $L = N$
3: **for** $t = 1$ to N **do**
4:     Play any action a such that $t \in \mathcal{A}_a$
5:     Update $(\hat{\theta}_i)_{1 \times N}$, $(m_i)_{1 \times N}$ accordingly
6: **end for**
7: //MAIN LOOP
8: **for** $t = N + 1$ to ∞ **do**
9:     Play an action a which solves the maximization problem

$$a = \underset{a \in \mathcal{F}}{\operatorname{argmax}} \sum_{i \in \mathcal{A}_a} a_i \left(\hat{\theta}_i + \sqrt{\frac{(L+1)\ln n}{m_i}} \right), \tag{2}$$

10:     Update $(\hat{\theta}_i)_{1 \times N}$, $(m_i)_{1 \times N}$ accordingly
11: **end for**

Algorithm 1 describes the LLR algorithm where $\mathcal{A}_a$ defines the set of all
individual basic actions (nodes to defend). In the scenario from Fig. 5, $\mathcal{A}_a$ is the set
containing all 5 nodes. LLR uses a learning constant L, which we set to $L = 3$ for
our scenario since this is the maximum number of nodes we can play in a defense.
LLR has an initialization phase for the first $N = 5$ rounds where it guarantees
playing each node at least once. $(\hat{\theta}_i)_{1 \times N}$ is that vector containing the mean observed
reward $\hat{\theta}_i$ for all nodes i. $(m_i)_{1 \times N}$ is the vector containing m_i, or number of times
arm i has been played. After each round these vectors are updated accordingly.

After the initialization phase, LLR solves the maximization problem in Eq. (2)
and deterministically selects the subset of nodes that maximizes the equation each
round until the end of the game. This deterministic nature of LLR indirectly adapts
to the attacker's moves. It has no concept of an opponent, but instead is trying to
balance between nodes with high observed means (i.e., have captured the attacker
often in the past) and less frequently played nodes (which the attacker may move
to in order to avoid capture). We say that LLR indirectly adapts to the attacker's
actions.

In this scenario, the attacker can never fully exploit the deterministic strategy
of the defender because of the partial observability aspect of the interaction. This
defense leads to the optimal node(s) changing in each round as adaptive LLR learns.

3.4 Behavioral Results

Analysis of human data shows clear performance patterns among the 3 defenders. The pure defender predictably performed the worst, yielding an average score of 611.93 points to the human attackers, just over 100 points short of the maximum possible points achievable against the pure defender. Next, the equilibrium defender performed significantly better, yielding only an average of 247.81 points to the human attackers, a full 200 points short of the maximum expected points achievable by a human attacker. Finally, the LLR was the most resilient defender versus the human attackers with an average of 172.6 points yielded to the participants. Table 2 shows the aggregate data of the human attacker performance.

Figure 6 shows the cumulative utility frequencies among the participants. Visually, we can see the pure defender yielded many points to many participants with only a couple of outliers. The participant who received −375 points vs the static pure defender likely tried to speed through the game without trying to optimize total reward.

LLR is designed to solve a combinatorial MAB problem that tries to optimize over a static, stochastic environment. Here, LLR does not take into account the attacker's adaptive nature. We do not make any claims that LLR is as a perfect way to respond to human decision-making. However, we note that LLR clearly outperforms the randomized and static defenders.

When analyzing the proportion of the human population that played optimally per round, we can see the differences in learning curves among the various

Table 2 Aggregate data of participants' end-game attacker rewards

	Average	Std. dev.	Median	Min	Max
Pure	611.93	168.88	675	−375	750
Equ.	247.81	149.60	290	−185	570
LLR	172.6	123.02	160	−85	640

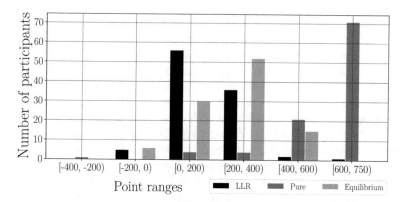

Fig. 6 Frequencies of total cumulative utility ranges

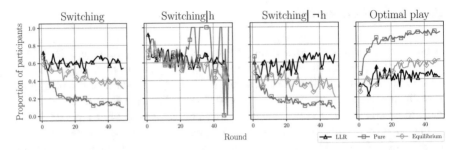

Fig. 7 The proportions of participants switching nodes to attack or playing optimally over time. The high switching after triggering a honeypot seen in round 26 from participants facing the static pure defender is a small portion of the population as less than 10% of the population were triggering honeypots past round 25

defenders. The rightmost graph in Fig. 7 shows the frequency of optimal decisions over the course of the 50 rounds.

Figure 7 details other measures that help describe the differences in human attacker performances. We can see that each defender case leads to drastic differences in switching (i.e., attacking different knows in consecutive rounds) and conditional switching (i.e., switching after triggering a honeypot or not). High switching suggests a more exploratory state, while low switching indicates a more exploitative state. We can see the noticeably higher switching in the LLR case as opposed to the other defenses. Combine this with the results seen in proportion of optimal play and it is clear that the human participants are struggling to adapt to the adaptive LLR defense.

4 Conclusion

Cyber deception methods including honeypots and other related technologies present a useful set of tools for detecting attackers and mitigating some types of attacks. Since attackers consistently use deception and misinformation to gain advantage, utilizing this set of tools is necessary to level the playing field for defenders. However, these methods must be used strategically to maximize the value they provide to defense, relative to the considerable costs of developing and maintaining effective deceptions. Research on moving target defense and related game theoretic approaches has provided useful paradigms for reasoning about some aspects of these decisions, but most of this work does not consider the aspect of dynamically adapting to a changing and evolving adversary and threat landscape.

We present here a framework and some initial results using online learning and adaptation paradigms that can adapt to a specific but evolving threat environment over time. This has both strengths and weaknesses relative to methods in MTD and game theory. It has the ability to learn to respond effectively to a specific threat environment based on experience, while retaining the flexibility to adapt to new threats over time. MTD approaches mostly focus on modifying the defenses without a specific adversary model, so they cannot adapt to specific threats. Game theory approaches rely on an accurate (and typically static) model of the adversary to optimize decisions. Our adaptive learning approach has advantages over both of these in many cases, but it can also be blended with both MTD and game theory models to achieve even better results.

We also consider how well these adaptive strategies perform against humans. In particular, we are interested in whether these adaptive strategies have similar advantages as the randomized game theoretic strategies in playing against humans in a strategic setting. We see that human attackers are capable of learning incredibly quickly against static defenses. The randomized defender strategies based on game theory performed much better, but humans struggled even more to learn an effective strategy against the adaptive defender. This shows that the adaptive strategies have many of the same advantages of being difficult to predict as the equilibrium policies, but with the added advantage of adapting well to exploit specific opponents.

Acknowledgements The work found in Sect. 2 first appeared in the *Artificial Intelligence for Cyber Security* workshop held at the 31st AAAI Conference on Artificial Intelligence in San Francisco, CA in 2017 [15].

The work found in Sect. 3 is currently in press for the 41st Annual Meeting of the Cognitive Science Society (2019) to be held in Montreal, Canada at the time this was written [14]. The authors would like to thank Jakub Černý, Palvi Aggarwal, Noam Ben-Asher, Efrat Aharonov, Branislav Bošanský, Orsolya Kovacs, and Cleotilde Gonzalez for their contributions to this work.

References

1. Alpcan, T., Başar, T.: Network security: A decision and game-theoretic approach. Cambridge University Press (2010)
2. Auer, P., Cesa-Bianchi, N., Fischer, P.: Finite-time analysis of the multiarmed bandit problem. Machine learning **47**(2–3), 235–256 (2002)
3. Auer, P., Cesa-Bianchi, N., Freund, Y., Schapire, R.E.: Gambling in a rigged casino: The adversarial multi-armed bandit problem. In: Foundations of Computer Science, 1995. Proceedings., 36th Annual Symposium on, pp. 322–331. IEEE (1995)
4. Ben-Asher, N., Gonzalez, C.: Effects of cyber security knowledge on attack detection. Computers in Human Behavior **48**, 51–61 (2015)
5. Bilge, L., Dumitras, T.: Before we knew it: an empirical study of zero-day attacks in the real world. In: Proceedings of the 2012 ACM conference on Computer and communications security, pp. 833–844. ACM (2012)
6. Bringer, M.L., Chelmecki, C.A., Fujinoki, H.: A survey: Recent advances and future trends in honeypot research. International Journal of Computer Network and Information Security **4**(10), 63 (2012)
7. Bubeck, S., Cesa-Bianchi, N.: Regret analysis of stochastic and nonstochastic multi-armed bandit problems. arXiv preprint arXiv:1204.5721 (2012)
8. Buhrmester, M., Kwang, T., Gosling, S.D.: Amazon's mechanical turk: A new source of inexpensive, yet high-quality, data? Perspectives on psychological science **6**(1), 3–5 (2011)
9. Carroll, T.E., Grosu, D.: A game theoretic investigation of deception in network security. Security and Communication Networks **4**(10), 1162–1172 (2011)

10. Du, M., Li, Y., Lu, Q., Wang, K.: Bayesian game based pseudo honeypot model in social networks. In: International Conference on Cloud Computing and Security, pp. 62–71. Springer (2017)
11. Frei, S., May, M., Fiedler, U., Plattner, B.: Large-scale vulnerability analysis. In: Proceedings of the 2006 SIGCOMM workshop on Large-scale attack defense, pp. 131–138. ACM (2006)
12. Gai, Y., Krishnamachari, B., Jain, R.: Combinatorial network optimization with unknown variables: Multi-armed bandits with linear rewards and individual observations. IEEE/ACM Transactions on Networking (TON) **20**(5), 1466–1478 (2012)
13. Garg, N., Grosu, D.: Deception in honeynets: A game-theoretic analysis. In: 2007 IEEE SMC Information Assurance and Security Workshop, pp. 107–113. IEEE (2007)
14. Gutierrez, M., Černý, J., Ben-Asher, N., Aharonov, E., Bošanský, B., Kiekintveld, C., Gonzalez, C.: Evaluating models of human adversarial behavior against defense algorithms in a contextual multi-armed bandit task. In: 41st Annual Meeting of the Cognitive Science Society (CogSci 2019), Montreal, QC (2019 in press)
15. Gutierrez, M.P., Kiekintveld, C.: Adapting honeypot configurations to detect evolving exploits. In: Workshops at the Thirty-First AAAI Conference on Artificial Intelligence (2017)
16. Kiekintveld, C., Lisỳ, V., Píbil, R.: Game-theoretic foundations for the strategic use of honeypots in network security. In: Cyber Warfare, pp. 81–101. Springer (2015)
17. Klíma, R., Lisỳ, V., Kiekintveld, C.: Combining online learning and equilibrium computation in security games. In: International Conference on Decision and Game Theory for Security, pp. 130–149. Springer (2015)
18. La, Q.D., Quek, T.Q., Lee, J., Jin, S., Zhu, H.: Deceptive attack and defense game in honeypot-enabled networks for the internet of things. IEEE Internet of Things Journal **3**(6), 1025–1035 (2016)
19. Laszka, A., Vorobeychik, Y., Koutsoukos, X.D.: Optimal personalized filtering against spear-phishing attacks. In: AAAI (2015)
20. Luo, T., Xu, Z., Jin, X., Jia, Y., Ouyang, X.: Iotcandyjar: Towards an intelligent-interaction honeypot for iot devices. Black Hat (2017)
21. Mairh, A., Barik, D., Verma, K., Jena, D.: Honeypot in network security: a survey. In: Proceedings of the 2011 international conference on communication, computing & security, pp. 600–605. ACM (2011)
22. McQueen, M.A., McQueen, T.A., Boyer, W.F., Chaffin, M.R.: Empirical estimates and observations of 0day vulnerabilities. In: System Sciences, 2009. HICSS'09. 42nd Hawaii International Conference on, pp. 1–12. IEEE (2009)
23. Mell, P., Kent, K.A., Romanosky, S.: The common vulnerability scoring system (CVSS) and its applicability to federal agency systems. Citeseer (2007)
24. Nawrocki, M., Wählisch, M., Schmidt, T.C., Keil, C., Schönfelder, J.: A survey on honeypot software and data analysis. arXiv preprint arXiv:1608.06249 (2016)
25. Pauna, A., Iacob, A.C., Bica, I.: Qrassh-a self-adaptive ssh honeypot driven by q-learning. In: 2018 international conference on communications (COMM), pp. 441–446. IEEE (2018)
26. Píbil, R., Lisỳ, V., Kiekintveld, C., Bošanský, B., Pěchouček, M.: Game theoretic model of strategic honeypot selection in computer networks. In: International Conference on Decision and Game Theory for Security, pp. 201–220. Springer (2012)
27. Provos, N.: Honeyd-a virtual honeypot daemon. In: 10th DFN-CERT Workshop, Hamburg, Germany, vol. 2, p. 4 (2003)
28. Rowe, N.C., Custy, E.J., Duong, B.T.: Defending cyberspace with fake honeypots. JOURNAL OF COMPUTERS **2**(2), 25 (2007)
29. Sagha, H., Shouraki, S.B., Khasteh, H., Dehghani, M.: Real-time ids using reinforcement learning. In: 2008 Second International Symposium on Intelligent Information Technology Application, vol. 2, pp. 593–597. IEEE (2008)
30. Schlenker, A., Thakoor, O., Xu, H., Fang, F., Tambe, M., Tran-Thanh, L., Vayanos, P., Vorobeychik, Y.: Deceiving cyber adversaries: A game theoretic approach. In: AAMAS (2018). http://dl.acm.org/citation.cfm?id=3237383.3237833

31. Schlenker, A., Xu, H., Guirguis, M., Kiekintveld, C., Sinha, A., Tambe, M., Sonya, S.Y., Balderas, D., Dunstatter, N.: Don't bury your head in warnings: A game-theoretic approach for intelligent allocation of cyber-security alerts. In: IJCAI, pp. 381–387 (2017)

32. Serra, E., Jajodia, S., Pugliese, A., Rullo, A., Subrahmanian, V.: Pareto-optimal adversarial defense of enterprise systems. ACM Transactions on Information and System Security (TISSEC) **17**(3), 11 (2015)

33. Servin, A., Kudenko, D.: Multi-agent reinforcement learning for intrusion detection. In: Adaptive Agents and Multi-Agent Systems III. Adaptation and Multi-Agent Learning, pp. 211–223. Springer (2005)

34. Servin, A., Kudenko, D.: Multi-agent reinforcement learning for intrusion detection: A case study and evaluation. In: German Conference on Multiagent System Technologies, pp. 159–170. Springer (2008)

35. Shi, L., Zhao, J., Jiang, L., Xing, W., Gong, J., Liu, X.: Game theoretic simulation on the mimicry honeypot. Wuhan University Journal of Natural Sciences **21**(1), 69–74 (2016)

36. Spitzner, L.: Honeypots: tracking hackers, vol. 1. Addison-Wesley Reading (2003)

37. Sutton, R.S., Barto, A.G.: Reinforcement learning: An introduction. MIT press (2018)

38. Tsikerdekis, M., Zeadally, S., Schlesener, A., Sklavos, N.: Approaches for preventing honeypot detection and compromise. In: 2018 Global Information Infrastructure and Networking Symposium (GIIS), pp. 1–6. IEEE (2018)

39. Venkatesan, S., Albanese, M., Shah, A., Ganesan, R., Jajodia, S.: Detecting stealthy botnets in a resource-constrained environment using reinforcement learning. In: MTD@ CCS, pp. 75–85 (2017)

40. Wagener, G., Dulaunoy, A., Engel, T., et al.: Self adaptive high interaction honeypots driven by game theory. In: Symposium on Self-Stabilizing Systems, pp. 741–755. Springer (2009)

41. Wagener, G., State, R., Engel, T., Dulaunoy, A.: Adaptive and self-configurable honeypots. In: 12th IFIP/IEEE International Symposium on Integrated Network Management (IM 2011) and Workshops, pp. 345–352. IEEE (2011)

42. Wang, K., Du, M., Maharjan, S., Sun, Y.: Strategic honeypot game model for distributed denial of service attacks in the smart grid. IEEE Transactions on Smart Grid **8**(5), 2474–2482 (2017)

43. Wang, W., Zeng, B.: A two-stage deception game for network defense. In: Decision and Game Theory for Security (2018)

44. Xu, X., Xie, T.: A reinforcement learning approach for host-based intrusion detection using sequences of system calls. In: International Conference on Intelligent Computing, pp. 995–1003. Springer (2005)

Phishing URL Detection with Lexical Features and Blacklisted Domains

Jiwon Hong, Taeri Kim, Jing Liu, Noseong Park, and Sang-Wook Kim

1 Introduction

Cyberattacks incur huge damage to our society. According to a reputable source [10], cyberattacks cost US economy between \$57B and \$109B in 2016 alone. However, the surrounding environments are getting worse as attackers are becoming more sophisticated than ever and the scale of cyberattacks is sharply increasing. Because of that, many enterprises invest a lot in deploying intrusion detection systems and firewalls as well as hiring skilled security experts. But attackers try to circumvent the defensive methods by phishing. It is common for many cyberattacks that in their initial phase, attackers disseminate phishing emails with camouflaged contents. Careless employees may visit the malicious web pages and their machines are then infected by malware. After the initial compromise, the attacker can intrude the enterprise network through the infected machines, totally evading other intrusion detection systems and firewalls. At the same time, those infected machines provide shelters for the attacker.

It was reported by IBM Security that Dyre malware, one Trojan, caused more than one million USD loss for many enterprise organizations. Dyre was first spread through phishing emails to victims in 2014 and compromises the victims' computer

Jiwon Hong, Taeri Kim, and Jing Liu are listed in alphabetical order and equally contributed. Noseong Park and Sang-Wook Kim are the co-corresponding authors.

J. Hong · T. Kim · S.-W. Kim
Hanyang University, Seoul, South Korea
e-mail: nowiz@hanyang.ac.kr; taerik@hanyang.ac.kr; wook@hanyang.ac.kr

J. Liu · N. Park (✉)
George Mason University, Fairfax, VA, USA
e-mail: jliu30@gmu.edu; npark9@gmu.edu

© Springer Nature Switzerland AG 2020
S. Jajodia et al. (eds.), *Adaptive Autonomous Secure Cyber Systems*,
https://doi.org/10.1007/978-3-030-33432-1_12

if installed. Once infected victims try to log in any bank websites that are monitored by Dyre, they are redirected to a fake bank website, where they are asked to enter all login credentials. As a result, attackers can illegally transfer money with the stolen credentials. Sometimes, Dyre releases a new binary code version very quickly (e.g., in 3 days). It is hard for antivirus software, which uses known malware signatures for detection, to identify such fast-evolving malware. In this case, techniques in rapidly detecting phishing URLs are desired to eliminate potential threats. If we successfully detect phishing URLs contained by phishing emails and prevent them from being accessed by employees, the majority of cyberattacks can be thwarted in their initial phase.

To this end, various methods to detect phishing URLs have been proposed. One of the simplest methods among them relies on blacklisted IP addresses and domains. This method is computationally lightweight. However, it is not easy to keep the blacklist up to date. One more weak-point is that sometimes attackers implant their phishing web pages in a benign server after compromising it, in which case the blacklist-based method cannot detect.

Other popular methods are machine learning-based methods. Many machine learning models have been proposed to detect phishing URLs. They can be broadly categorized into (1) content-based and (2) string-based models. The former reads a web page and decide if it is phishing or not. The latter uses only URL string patterns and makes decisions. For various practical reasons, the latter is more preferred than the former in many real-world environments (see Sect. 2 for detailed descriptions).

In this work, we conduct an in-depth study about the string-based methods assisted by a blacklist, which is one of the most powerful configurations to detect phishing URLs. We survey literature to collect widely-used string features and build a state-of-the-art machine learning model. This overall workflow is shown in Fig. 1. First, we crawl a crowdsourced repository of phishing URLs to test the

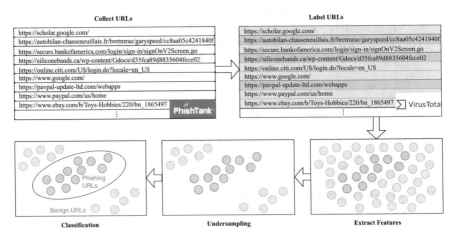

Fig. 1 Overall workflow of our study

method against recent phishing URL patterns. Although there exist several other open dataset for phishing URL detection, most of them are outdated due to the fact that attacker patterns evolve quickly. We need to collect recent phishing URLs on our own. Second, we acquire the blacklist from VirusTotal.com to label collected URLs.

From the literate survey, we identified 18 string features describing URLs, such as string entropy, the length of URL, and so forth. The blacklist adds one more binary feature to denote if a URL's domain is blacklisted. Therefore, each URL is represented by an 19-dimensional vector in our experiments.

One common pitfall in phishing URL detection is the notorious class imbalance problem where the benign URL class outnumbers the other phishy URL class. In many existing works, researchers manually sorted out them to balance them, which is practically ill-chosen direction. We apply state-of-the-art under/oversampling methods which work on the 19-dimensional vector space to create artificial training samples (vectors). After oversampling the minority class or undersampling the majority class, we can balance them.

After that, we apply many existing classifiers such as RandomForest, AdaBoost, etc. These classifiers try to find the best hyper-plane to bisect the two classes of the vectors. We also consider deep learning models which read the raw string URLs rather than their vector representations and predict if an input URL is benign or phishy.

Among all methods we tested, RandomForest shows the best recall, precision, and F-1 while another deep learning-based method shows the best accuracy. We also conducted feature importance analysis and found that string entropy and the KL divergence from English are effective in detecting phishing URLs.

2 Related Work

Phishing URL detection has been widely studied for decades and various detection solutions have been proposed. Most of them can be categorized into two groups: content-based detection methods and string-based detection methods. Each of them has pros and cons. For content-based detection methods, more information about a specific web-page can be obtained for improving the detection performance. However, one drawback of content-based methods is that actual executions of one URL are needed, which might cause safety issues. In order to mitigate potential safety issues, disposable virtual machines are required to implement those detection techniques in a controlled experimental environment, which is resource intensive and thus impractical for some vendors. While string-based detection is easier in data collection and safer in implementing, as it only looks at the URL strings and extracts useful features. But sometimes extracted information is not sufficient enough to identify phishing URLs. In this section, researches on content-based detection methods and string-based detection methods are reviewed.

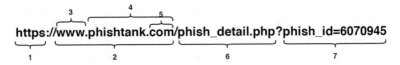

Fig. 2 Components in one URL

2.1 URL Structure

Before reviewing related work, the structure of one URL is briefly introduced in
this subsection. A URL is typically composed by several components. One example
URL with seven components is presented in Fig. 2. To be specific, component "1"
is the protocol used by the URL. In this example, HTTPS is used, while there are
also other available protocols such as HTTP and FTP. Component "2" is host or
hostname, which is the device name connected to computer network. It contains
subdomain (i.e., component "3": *WWW*), and domain name (i.e., component "4"),
which needs to be registered in the Domain Name System (DNS). Component
"5" represents *Top-Level-Domain, TLD*, a web-address suffix. Component "6" is
path, which refers to a location (e.g., file or directory) on the webserver. The last
component "7" includes parameter and value. In this case, parameter is *phish_id*,
value is 6,070,945 which is the *phish_id* we intend to look for. In one URL,
parameters are started following "?".

2.2 Content-Based Phishing URL Detection

After crawling web-pages, many features can be extracted by analyzing contents
contained in one web-page. One type of features is statistics on classical characteristics identified through domain knowledge. For instance, some common features
based on HTML document contents such as the maliciousness of URLs in one
web page, the number of *forms* (for taking victims' sensitivity information), and
the number of external links are used in [17, 20, 42, 44]. More features are also
identified in [17], such as the number of distinct word, document length, word
length, the number of NULL characters, and number of word in one line. Usually,
legitimate web-pages contain more information, thus having more distinct words
and of longer length; while malicious web-pages are more focus on words serving
for attack purposes and of shorter length. Similarly, 19 features extracted from
HTML contents, such as the count of *iframe* tags (one iframe embeds another
document into the current HTML document), the count of unknown tags, and the
count of elements coming from external domains are used by *Prophiler* [7].

Similar statistics can be drawn from JavaScript contents as well. Besides the
usage of HTML, [7] incorporates JavaScript based heuristic features including
the average length of script lines, number of long variables, number of strings

containing malicious tags, number of strings containing *iframe*, and etc. It is also found that attackers use certain native JavaScript functions very often, such as *eval()*, *escape()*, *unescape()*, *exec()*, *setTimeout()*, *setInterval()*, *and ubound()*, which are critical elements in detecting malicious URLs.

Additionally, some advanced calculations are performed on top of web-page contents to extract more features. N-gram models are adopted for modeling dynamical HTML content [17] and characters used in JavaScript [9]. In [9], string entropy is also calculated upon N-gram (specifically, 1-gram is used). It is found that malicious web-pages are with lower entropy as only certain characters are used. Some studies also tried to use visual similarity to identify similar phishing web-pages for legitimate ones. In [40], authors decompose one web-page into different segments and measure similarities in three perspectives: block, layout, and overall style. One web-page is considered as phishing if its similarity with one legitimate web-page is larger than a preset threshold. Similarly, authors in [27] evaluate visual similarity from three aspects: visual text, visual image, and overall look-and-feel. One difference from [40] is they identify legitimate candidates by their own algorithms. Instead of measuring similarity from different perspectives, some research attempts to treat one web-page as a whole and measure the similarity. For instance, [14] first converts one web-page into an image and then measures its similarity with known phishing web-pages. They use Earth Mover's Distance (EMD) to measure the similarity of each color and its coordinates in images. Following Gestalt theory, [8] adopts the concept of supersignals to model a web-page as an indivisible unit, and then further converts supersignals to numerical values for measuring visual similarity between two web-pages.

Content-based detection requires the access to malicious URLs in order to crawl web-page contents. Attacks can happen at the same time. Therefore, multiple researchers explored the possibility of detecting phishing URLs only by analyzing URL strings and their related external information.

2.3   String-Based Phishing URL Detection

As found in previous studies [15, 21], it is possible to detect phishing URLs only with features directly extracted from URL strings (i.e., lexical features) or indirectly related to information extracted from URL strings (i.e., host related features).

One type of classical string-based phishing URL detection methods is blacklist, where a list of known malicious URLs are maintained. If one URL appears in the blacklist, security warnings will pop-up when users try to access it. As it only requires string comparison for detecting phishing URLs, it is easy to implement yet effective, thus widely used in most anti-virus systems. Traditionally, those malicious URLs in the blacklist are collected through user reporting and honeypots [3, 30].

However, it is impossible to keep a comprehensive and up-to-date list of all malicious URLs, thus leading to high false negative rates. In [35], authors analyzed four main blacklists and found them having 35–98% false negative rates. Especially numerous new phishing URLs can be generated, deployed, and then disappear in a rapid speed [21]. An empirical study was conducted in [34] on blacklist and concluded that blacklist can only detect 20% zero-hour attack. Although most blacklists can include 47–83% new phishing URLs after 12 h, it is not effective because 63% phishing campaigns only last for less than 2 h as depicted in their dataset.

Instead of relying on blacklists only, multiple studies attempt to extract information from blacklists in order to automatically extend existing blacklists or include it as additional features for building machine learning models in detecting phishing URLs. In [13], authors first extracted malicious domains and further new unknown malicious domains by analyzing name server and registration information related to those domains. The authors observed that the name servers of around 90% malicious domains are younger than 1 year and usually share the same name with domains. WHOIS information is incorporated for further narrowing down the new inferred malicious domains. More methods are proposed in [32, 37] for automatically extending existing blacklists. [21] used the occurrence of one URL in six blacklists and one white-list (i.e., binary variable) as an additional feature set and other 16 feature sets to classify if one URL is phishing or not. As the result shown, adding the blacklist features improves the error rate by 8% for one dataset.

It is found that statistical characteristics are different for phishing URLs and benign ones [26, 38]. Lexical features such as URL length, domain length, and the number of special characters (e.g., "%", "$") are widely used to identify malicious URLs [2, 5]. To pretend legitimate, some phishing URLs are generated by simply manipulating benign ones. [15] studied the phishing URLs' structure and identified four common types of obfuscation used by hackers: replacing host with IP address, mimicking redirect-URLs by adding valid domain names in the path, manipulating well-known hostnames (e.g., adding strings before or after good hostnames), and mistyping domain names. In order to be robust to obfuscation, they use four feature categories and build a logistic regression model to classify benign URLs and phishing URLs. Specifically, they included PageRank [31] (phishing URLs tend to have lower PageRank), page quality score maintained by Google, the presence of the domain in White Domain Table, and bag-of-word features of one URL string. Instead of extracting words from one entire URL, [21, 23] maintain separate tokens by components in one URL (e.g., Host, domain, path).

Another type of common features is host-based features. Host information is first extracted from the URL string and more external information related to the host can be included as extral features. [21, 23] has shown that information such as host location, registration date, and time-to-live provides non-trivial contributions in detecting phishing URLs.

2.4 Phishing URL Classification Algorithms

After converting URLs into feature space, the phishing URL detection problem can be modeled as binary classification and then solved by a plenty of classification algorithms. Logistic regression is one classical method used for binary classification and frequently adopted in multiple previous work [7, 15, 21, 43]. Besides, several ensemble learning methods are employed by many recent work on malicious URL detection. [33] adopted AdaBoost to build a URL classifier with features extracted from website contents by LDA (Latent Dirichlet Allocation). In [11] and [12], seven independent classifiers are built, namely J48, Random Tree, Random Forest (RF), Naive Bayes, Bayes Net, Support Vector Machines (SVM), and Logistic Regression. The authors developed different algorithms to ensemble predictions from the seven classifiers. In [25], the authors compared the above mentioned seven classifiers on their dataset. They showed Random Forest achieved the best performance with 95.22% accuracy, while SVM has the worst performance with 86.31% accuracy.

In addition, several studies attempt to use deep learning methods to classify URLs. For instance, [5] uses long short-term memory (LSTM) cells to build a sequence (i.e., URL) classification model. As the results show, the LSTM-based approach without any manual-created features (e.g., lexical features) can achieve 5% better accuracy than a RF classifier with lexical features and statistical features of URLs. [18, 19] also share the same idea in modeling a URL as a sequence for classification, but with different deep learning architectures. [19] uses one-dimensional convolution (1DConv) neural network, while [18] combines LSTM and 1DConv.

3 Data Collection

There exist a couple of open dataset for phishing URL detection. However, they were developed several years back. Considering quickly evolving attack patterns, we decided to collect recent phishing URLs rather than relying on the old datasets. Phishytank.com is one of the most famous crowdsourced repository of potentially malicious URLs where people can freely upload their detected URLs. However, they do not provide ground-truth labels of benign/phishy for their reported URLs and many of reported URLs are not phishy.

We carefully selected three target vendors and collected their URLs after reading Phishing Activity Trends Report [4] by Anti-Phishing Working Group, one of the most well-reputed reports about phishing attack patterns. The report released the list of hundreds of vendors most frequently targeted by attackers that includes Bank of America, eBay, and PayPal. Many URLs were reported for the three vendors when we were monitoring the web site and collecting URLs.

Many phishing URLs reported in the web site do not last long. Attackers usually maintain the phishing web page for a short time and clean their traits from the Internet. Therefore, we could not access the contents of the reported URLs in a stable manner.

4 Lexical Features

In this subsection, we describe lexical features used for our study.

1. *Length of one URL*
   Attackers usually use long URLs to lower the detection probability. So phishing URLs is longer than legitimate URLs. In this work, we use the following rule in [28] to identify phishing URLs.

$$\text{AURLis} \begin{cases} \text{benign, if its length} \leq 53 \\ \text{neutral, if } 54 \leq \text{its length} \leq 75 \\ \text{phishing, if its length} \geq 76 \end{cases}$$

2. *Usage of IP instead of domain name*
   It is found that phishing URLs tend to use IP instead of domain names. For one URL, if IP is used, this feature is turned on.
3. *Number of subdomain*
   It is reported that if a URL has more than one subdomain, then it is phishing. For this feature, we count the number of dots in the domain parts. If there are more than three dots (i.e., more than one subdomain), the URL is phishing.
4. *Number of TLD in one URL's path*
   Phishing URLs try to include TLD from legitimate URLs in the path for making them appear to be authentic. We count the number of TLDs in the path as one feature.
5. *Occurrence of phishing keywords*
   There are multiple keywords that phishing URLs usually have. For instance, many phishing URLs have "suspend", "account", "login", "admin", "confirm". We keep a list of phishing keywords and use their occurrence as one feature to determine the maliciousness of a URL.
6. *Occurrence of "@"*
   By taking advantage of the fact that web browsers ignore everything appearing before "@", attackers usually put a phishing URL following a benign URL separated by "@" to deceive victims. For instance, a URL like "http://www.google.com@phishing.com" actually direct victims to "phishing.com" rather than anything related to Google.

7. *Occurrence of "-" in domain*

Phishing URLs tend to impersonate legitimate ones through adding prefix or suffix to their domain. It leads to the occurrence of "-" in domain. We check whether there is "-" in domain for this feature.

8. *Number of special symbols*

We count the number of punctuation symbols (i.e., .!&,#$%;) as one feature. [39] found that legitimate URLs have less punctuation symbols than phishing URLs.

9. *Entropy of one URL*

Entropy is to measure the amount of information carried by data. A smaller value indicates more information. A legitimate URL is more meaningful than a phishing URL, which usually is composed by random strings. We can identify phishing URLs through entropy values. It was already demonstrated by [5].

10. *Kullback–Leibler (KL) divergence of one URL from English*

KL divergence is used to measure the distance between two distributions. For this feature, we calculate the KL divergence between character frequency of one URL and that of English. We observed the KL divergence value for legitimate URLs is different from that of phishing URLs.

11. *Ratio of vowel to consonant in the hostname*

For this feature, we calculate the ratio between vowel and consonant in the hostname. Phishing URLs have a different ratio range from legitimate URLs

12. *Occurrence of digits in domain names*

In general, domain names of legitimate URLs are meaningful and do not contain any digits. A URL containing digits in the domain name is malicious.

13. *Ratio of digits to letters*

Legitimate URLs keep a balanced ratio between digits and letters. The ratios for legitimate URLs and phishing URLs are different.

14. *Variant of well-known domain names*

To easy fool victims, phishing URLs tend to use altered famous domain names. One typical strategy is simply adding prefix or suffix, such as "g-google.com" and "ebay-y.com". From Alexa, we identify top 1000 most visited websites and use them as well-known domain names. For this feature, we identify variants of those 1000 domain names.

15. *Number of "-" in the path*

As phishing URLs tends to add prefix or suffix to legitmate URLs, the number of dash in the path is higher for phishing URLs than legitmate URLs.

16. *Length of the hostname*

Phishing URLs usually have either too long hostname or too short hostname, while legitimate URLs maintain a reasonable length of hostname. We use two features in representing the maliciousness of one URL considering the length of hostname. If hostname of one URL is longer than 22 characters (i.e., one feature) or shorter than 5 characters (i.e., the other feature), it is malicious.

17. *Number of ":" in the hostname*

one common attempt using by phishing URL is manipulating port number, thus leading to the frequent occurring of colon ":".

5 Blacklist of Domains

There are several bodies releasing a list of blacklisted domains. Among them, virustotal.com releases the largest and up-to-date list. We contacted them and they allowed us to access their blacklist for research purposes. They collected many malicious domain by analyzing malware codes with hard-coded domains and evaluating reported malicious domains.

We do not use whitelist because attackers sometimes compromise a whitelisted domain and implant their phishing web pages. According to Phishing Activity Trends Report [4], it becomes more popular that attackers try to evade detection methods in this way. Therefore, we do not use any of whitelisted domain information.

6 Experiments

In this section, we describe our experimental environments and results. We test with about 50K URLs collected from other works and phishtank.com. We also compare state-of-the-art phishing URL detection models.

6.1 Experimental Environments

We introduce the dataset we collected and classification methods. We also describe how we choose the best hyper-parameters for each method.

6.1.1 Datasets

We crawled three sets of URLs related to Bank of America, eBay, and PayPal reported in phishtank.com for a couple of months in 2017. However, ground-truth labels are not given for each URL—phishtank.com only provides user-voted ratings for URLs and because of its open nature that allows even the attackers themselves to vote, the ratings are unreliable.

For this reason, we labeled the collected URLs using an outside source. virustotal.com provides the predicted labels from over 60 anti-virus products for a given URL. We took a majority vote for each URL's label from seven most popular and reliable anti-virus products including Avast, Kaspersky, McAfee, Norton, and Trend Micro.

In addition to our three crawled datasets, we examined existing open phishing URL detection datasets. We found two open datasets with raw URL strings [1, 36]. The other open datasets we found [22, 29, 41] do not include raw URLs for generating features we need.

Table 1 The number of phishy/benign URLs for each dataset

Dataset	VirusTotal threshold	Phishy URLs	Benign URLs
eBay	$\frac{4}{7}$	8529	18,800
PayPal	$\frac{4}{7}$	9690	17,572
Bank of America	$\frac{4}{7}$	4610	9408
Sorio et al. [36]	N/A	40,439	3637
Ahmad et al. [1]	N/A	62,231	344,800
Total	N/A	119,012	381,734

Note that the datasets from [36] and [1] already have ground-truth labels and we did not use virustotal.com to label them. There are some URLs in common among datasets so the total number of URLs is slightly smaller than their sum

We compiled these five distinct datasets into one very large dataset. The statistics of the combined dataset are shown in Table 1. For the experiments, we adopt fivefold cross validation so that the data is divided into 80:20 ratio for training and testing.

6.1.2 Phishing URL Detection Methods

In our experiments, we consider the following popular feature-based classification methods: Adaboost, Random Forest, and SVM. We also consider three string-based deep learning classifiers: 1DConv, LSTM, and 1DConv+LSTM. For feature-based classifiers, we used all the features we gathered from literature (listed in Sect. 4).

We adopt under/oversampling to deal with the class imbalance problem of our dataset as the number of benign URLs are much larger than the number of phishy URLs. We adopt total of 16 under/over-sampling methods including synthetic minority oversampling [6], adaptive synthetic sampling [16], and more.

There are a huge number of possible combinations of classifiers, under/over-sampling methods, and their parameters. We perform grid search for each classification method to find its best performing combination.

6.2 Experimental Results

The results are summarized in Table 2. Random Forest shows the best recall, precision, and F-1 score among all classification methods. However, 1DConv+LSTM shows better accuracy than Random Forest. Due to its low recall, 1DConv+LSTM fails to detect many phishing URLs.

Table 2 Prediction results of the classification methods

Method	ecall (phishy)	Precision (phishy)	F-1	Accuracy
AdaBoost	0.830	0.830	0.830	0.831
SVM	0.762	0.720	0.734	0.720
RandomForest	**0.840**	**0.850**	**0.840**	0.847
1DConv	0.677	0.735	0.689	0.864
LSTM	0.697	0.710	0.688	0.857
1DConv+LSTM	0.788	0.806	0.784	**0.902**

The best results are indicated by bold font

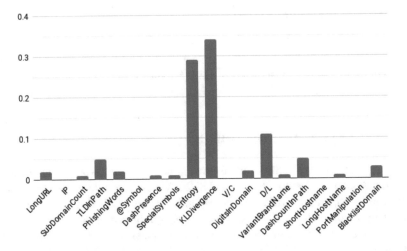

Fig. 3 Importance value for 19 features

6.3 Feature Importance

We analyzed the importance of each feature. The results are shown in Fig. 3. the KL divergence between one URL and English and entropy of one URL are top two most important features in detecting phishing URLs. The ratio between digital and letters also plays an important role. The presence of TLD in path and the number of dash in path are two critical features in identifying malicious URLs as well.

7 Conclusion and Future Work

We presented a phishing URL detection method with state-of-the-art lexical features and blacklist. We crawled our own data from a crowdsourced repositories and collected 18 popular lexical feature after extensive literature survey. We applied state-of-the-art machine learning techniques that consists of under/oversampling and classifiers. Surprisingly, this feature engineering-based method outperforms other deep learning models. In addition, we analyzed the importance of features in detection phishing URLs.

However, there exist several underexplored topics for phishing URL detection. First, evasion and poisoning are two popular adversarial techniques to neutralize machine learning. Evasion in our contexts is a technique to create counter-evident phishing URLs so that machine learning techniques cannot correctly detect them. For instance, phishing URLs running on whitelisted domains are popular evasion techniques—in response, we do not use any of whitelists. To our knowledge, there is only one work to design a robust detection method against evasion [24]. However, this work is based on content features rather than lexical features and in practice it is not easy to apply to real-world environments for the reason we mentioned in our related work section. In that perspective, there is almost no research for robust phishing URL detection. Poisoning means injecting noisy training samples, which requires an access to training samples. In many cases, however, training samples are confidential and only a small number of personnel are authorized to access. It is unknown how phishing URL detection models react when training samples are poisoned. We conjecture that poisoned training samples can be cleaned during its pre-processing step and before training the model.

Second, advanced machine learning techniques cannot be adopted in many cases where users have machines with limited capacity. These days many anti-virus products have their own phishing URL detection engine internally. However, their users are so diverse in terms of computing power, which creates a non-trivial challenge in designing their engines. Thus, the engine should be lightweight and at the same time, powerful, which contradict to each other.

References

1. Ahmad F (2017) https://github.com/faizann24/using-machine-learning-to-detect-malicious-urls
2. Anand A, Gorde K, Moniz JRA, Park N, Chakraborty T, Chu BT (2018) Phishing url detection with oversampling based on text generative adversarial networks. In: 2018 IEEE International Conference on Big Data (Big Data), IEEE, pp 1168–1177
3. Anderson DS, Fleizach C, Savage S, Voelker GM (2007) Spamscatter: Characterizing internet scam hosting infrastructure. In: USENIX Security Symposium
4. Anti-Phishing Working Group (2018) APWG Phishing Attack Trends Reports. https://www.antiphishing.org/resources/apwg-reports
5. Bahnsen AC, Bohorquez EC, Villegas S, Vargas J, González FA (2017) Classifying phishing urls using recurrent neural networks. In: 2017 APWG Symposium on Electronic Crime Research (eCrime), IEEE, pp 1–8
6. Bowyer KW, Chawla NV, Hall LO, Kegelmeyer WP (2011) SMOTE: synthetic minority over-sampling technique. CoRR abs/1106.1813, http://arxiv.org/abs/1106.1813
7. Canali D, Cova M, Vigna G, Kruegel C (2011) Prophiler: a fast filter for the large-scale detection of malicious web pages. In: Proceedings of the 20th international conference on World wide web, ACM, pp 197–206

8. Chen TC, Dick S, Miller J (2010) Detecting visually similar web pages: Application to phishing detection. ACM Transactions on Internet Technology (TOIT) 10(2):5
9. Choi Y, Kim T, Choi S, Lee C (2009) Automatic detection for javascript obfuscation attacks in web pages through string pattern analysis. In: Proceedings of the 1st International Conference on Future Generation Information Technology, Springer-Verlag, Berlin, Heidelberg, FGIT '09, pp 160–172
10. of Economic Advisers TC (2018) https://www.whitehouse.gov/wp-content/uploads/2018/03/the-cost-of-malicious-cyber-activity-to-the-u.s.-economy.pdf
11. Eshete B, Villafiorita A, Weldemariam K (2012) Binspect: Holistic analysis and detection of malicious web pages. In: International Conference on Security and Privacy in Communication Systems, Springer, pp 149–166
12. Eshete B, Villafiorita A, Weldemariam K, Zulkernine M (2013) Einspect: Evolution-guided analysis and detection of malicious web pages. In: 2013 IEEE 37th Annual Computer Software and Applications Conference, IEEE, pp 375–380
13. Felegyhazi M, Kreibich C, Paxson V (2010) On the potential of proactive domain blacklisting. In: Proceedings of the 3rd USENIX Conference on Large-scale Exploits and Emergent Threats: Botnets, Spyware, Worms, and More, USENIX Association, Berkeley, CA, USA, LEET'10, pp 6–6, http://dl.acm.org/citation.cfm?id=1855686.1855692
14. Fu AY, Wenyin L, Deng X (2006) Detecting phishing web pages with visual similarity assessment based on earth mover's distance (emd). IEEE transactions on dependable and secure computing 3(4):301–311
15. Garera S, Provos N, Chew M, Rubin AD (2007) A framework for detection and measurement of phishing attacks. In: Proceedings of the 2007 ACM workshop on Recurring malcode, ACM, pp 1–8
16. He H, Bai Y, Garcia EA, Li S (2008) Adasyn: Adaptive synthetic sampling approach for imbalanced learning. In: IEEE International Joint Conference on Neural Networks, pp 1322–1328
17. Hou YT, Chang Y, Chen T, Laih CS, Chen CM (2010) Malicious web content detection by machine learning. Expert Systems with Applications 37(1):55–60
18. Kilby M (2017) https://github.com/incertum/cyber-matrix-ai/tree/master/malicious-url-detection-deep-learning
19. Le H, Pham Q, Sahoo D, Hoi SC (2018) Urlnet: Learning a url representation with deep learning for malicious url detection. arXiv preprint arXiv:180203162
20. Ludl C, Mcallister S, Kirda E, Kruegel C (2007) On the effectiveness of techniques to detect phishing sites. In: Proceedings of the 4th International Conference on Detection of Intrusions and Malware, and Vulnerability Assessment, Springer-Verlag, Berlin, Heidelberg, DIMVA '07, pp 20–39
21. Ma J, Saul LK, Savage S, Voelker GM (2009) Beyond blacklists: learning to detect malicious web sites from suspicious urls. In: Proceedings of the 15th ACM SIGKDD international conference on Knowledge discovery and data mining, ACM, pp 1245–1254
22. Ma J, Saul LK, Savage S, Voelker GM (2009) Beyond blacklists: Learning to detect malicious web sites from suspicious urls. In: KDD, pp 1245–1254
23. Ma J, Saul LK, Savage S, Voelker GM (2009) Identifying suspicious urls: an application of large-scale online learning. In: Proceedings of the 26th annual international conference on machine learning, ACM, pp 681–688
24. Mao J, Tian W, Li P, Wei T, Liang Z (2017) Phishing-alarm: Robust and efficient phishing detection via page component similarity. IEEE Access 5:17020–17030, DOI 10.1109/AC-CESS.2017.2743528
25. Marchal S, François J, State R, Engel T (2014) Phishscore: Hacking phishers' minds. In: 10th International Conference on Network and Service Management (CNSM) and Workshop, IEEE, pp 46–54
26. McGrath DK, Gupta M (2008) Behind phishing: An examination of phisher modi operandi. LEET 8:4

27. Medvet E, Kirda E, Kruegel C (2008) Visual-similarity-based phishing detection. In: Proceedings of the 4th international conference on Security and privacy in communication netowrks, ACM, p 22
28. Mohammad RM, Thabtah FA, McCluskey L (2012) An assessment of features related to phishing websites using an automated technique. In: 7th International Conference for Internet Technology and Secured Transactions, pp 492–497
29. Mohammad RM, Thabtah F, McCluskey L (2014) Predicting phishing websites based on self-structuring neural network. Neural Computing and Applications 25(2), DOI 10.1007/s00521-013-1490-z, https://doi.org/10.1007/s00521-013-1490-z
30. OpenDNS (2019) Phishtank - out of the net, into the tank, https://www.phishtank.com/
31. Page L, Brin S, Motwani R, Winograd T (1999) The pagerank citation ranking: Bringing order to the web. Tech. rep., Stanford InfoLab
32. Prakash P, Kumar M, Kompella RR, Gupta M (2010) Phishnet: Predictive blacklisting to detect phishing attacks. In: Proceedings of the 29th Conference on Information Communications, IEEE Press, Piscataway, NJ, USA, INFOCOM'10, pp 346–350, http://dl.acm.org/citation.cfm?id=1833515.1833585
33. Ramanathan V, Wechsler H (2012) Phishing website detection using latent dirichlet allocation and adaboost. In: 2012 IEEE International Conference on Intelligence and Security Informatics, IEEE, pp 102–107
34. Sheng S, Wardman B, Warner G, Cranor L, Hong J, Zhang C (2009) An empirical analysis of phishing blacklists
35. Sinha S, Bailey M, Jahanian F (2008) Shades of grey: On the effectiveness of reputation-based "blacklists". In: 2008 3rd International Conference on Malicious and Unwanted Software (MALWARE), IEEE, pp 57–64
36. Sorio E, Bartoli A, Medvet E (2013) Detection of hidden fraudulent urls within trusted sites using lexical features. 2013 International Conference on Availability, Reliability and Security pp 242–247
37. Sun B, Akiyama M, Yagi T, Hatada M, Mori T (2016) Automating url blacklist generation with similarity search approach. IEICE TRANSACTIONS on Information and Systems 99(4):873–882
38. Teraguchi NCRLY, Mitchell JC (2004) Client-side defense against web-based identity theft. Computer Science Department, Stanford University Available: http://cryptostanfordedu/SpoofGuard/webspoofpdf
39. Verma R, Dyer K (2015) On the character of phishing urls: Accurate and robust statistical learning classifiers. In: Proceedings of the 5th ACM Conference on Data and Application Security and Privacy, DOI 10.1145/2699026.2699115, http://doi.acm.org/10.1145/2699026.2699115
40. Wenyin L, Huang G, Xiaoyue L, Min Z, Deng X (2005) Detection of phishing webpages based on visual similarity. In: Special interest tracks and posters of the 14th international conference on World Wide Web, ACM, pp 1060–1061
41. Whittaker C, Ryner B, Nazif M (2010) Large-scale automatic classification of phishing pages. In: NDSS '10, http://www.isoc.org/isoc/conferences/ndss/10/pdf/08.pdf
42. Xiang G, Hong J, Rose CP, Cranor L (2011) Cantina+: A feature-rich machine learning framework for detecting phishing web sites. ACM Transactions on Information and System Security (TISSEC) 14(2):21
43. Xu L, Zhan Z, Xu S, Ye K (2013) Cross-layer detection of malicious websites. In: Proceedings of the third ACM conference on Data and application security and privacy, ACM, pp 141–152
44. Zhang Y, Hong JI, Cranor LF (2007) Cantina: a content-based approach to detecting phishing web sites. In: Proceedings of the 16th international conference on World Wide Web, ACM, pp 639–648

An Empirical Study of Secret Security Patch in Open Source Software

Xinda Wang, Kun Sun, Archer Batcheller, and Sushil Jajodia

1 Introduction

Recent years have witnessed an accelerating use of open source software (OSS), particularly in cloud environments. As one of the biggest hosting service providers, GitHub announced that there had been 31 million developers working across 96 million repositories in 2018 [4]. As the popularity of open source software impressively grows, so does the number of its vulnerabilities. A report from Snyk shows the number of published open source vulnerabilities almost doubles in the last two years (2017 and 2018) [27].

Different from propriety software whose source code is closed, the source code of OSS can be carefully scrutinized by attackers to discover the unknown vulnerabilities. Particularly, the security patches of OSS vulnerabilities explicitly point out the vulnerable code, which enlightens attackers on how to generate exploits for attacking the unpatched versions. For instance, just one day after the remote code execution vulnerability in Apache Struts 2 (CVE-2017-5638) was publicly disclosed and fixed, exploit scripts were spread in the wild. Several months later, without patching its system, Equifax got attacked and millions of sensitive personal data including social security number were exposed [18].

Timely patching the vulnerability is an effective defense against those "N-day" attacks. However, such good practice is hard to enforce in real world. A system may bundle multiple open source libraries and each library may release multiple patches once in a while. In this case, developers have to handle a large number

X. Wang · K. Sun (✉) · S. Jajodia
George Mason University, Fairfax, VA, USA
e-mail: xwang44@gmu.edu; ksun3@gmu.edu; jajodia@gmu.edu

A. Batcheller
Northrop Grumman Corporation, Falls Church, VA, USA
e-mail: archer.batcheller@ngc.com

© Springer Nature Switzerland AG 2020
S. Jajodia et al. (eds.), *Adaptive Autonomous Secure Cyber Systems*,
https://doi.org/10.1007/978-3-030-33432-1_13

of patches or new versions that are composed of security fixes, bug fixes, and new features. Applying such patches or updating to the newest version increases the service system downtime and introduces extra workload for admins. Since it is difficult to make all software up to date, developers tend to refer to security advisories like Common Vulnerabilities and Exposures (CVE) [3] or change log to prioritize security related patches [14].

Software vendors may secretly patch their vulnerabilities without creating CVE entries or even explicitly describing the security issue in its change log. One reason is the concern that too many CVE records or vulnerability fixes in the change log may hurt the quality reputation of their software. In addition, they may intend to block the publication of related CVE entries until they believe it is safe to publicly release them. However, since the related patch or new version has already been publicly available, attackers can still carefully analyze the code changes from the patch or the difference between two versions and then generate the corresponding exploits to attack the unpatched versions. Moreover, due to the similar design/implementation logic or code clone [12], software packages providing similar functionalities may contain the same vulnerability. Therefore, when attackers discover a security patch in one software package, they may apply these exploits to other software packages that have not fixed the vulnerability. In such case, a system is still exposed to attackers even if the admin updates the system to the newest version timely. We consider it as one type of "0-day" vulnerability.

To defend this, developers and users need an approach to identify the existence of secret security patches in not only bundled software but also other similar software so that they can patch their system in time. Moreover, software vendors should pay attention to security update of similar software. Therefore, it is critical to figure out the existence of secret security patches and thus provide insights to solve this problem. In this work, we aim to solve two problems: (1) How to identify security patches from non-security patches? and (2) To what extent does the secret security patch exist? To answer these questions, we develop a machine learning based system and toolset to help automatically identify security patches, and then we perform a case study on three popular open source SSL libraries.

We solve three challenges when developing the system. The first challenge is that there is no available large-scale security patch dataset to study. Seulbae et al. [11] collected data from eight Git repositories. Zhen et al. [16] built a Vulnerability Patch Database from 19 products. Such databases may introduce biases that threaten the practical use. Though Li et al. [15] proposed a methodology to build a large-scale database based on all the Git related records in NVD, they do no release an open-sourced version. In this work, we collect a more complete CVE-security patch mapping dataset. Besides Git repositories, our dataset also includes security patches from projects hosted on other websites.

The second challenge is how to extract effective patterns/features to distinguish between security patches and non-security patches. To address this problem, we manually analyze our collected security and non-security patches. Then we identify a number of specific characteristics where security and non-security patches may have different distributions. Previous work [15, 33] focuses on basic characteristics that come from documentation text or metadata generated by *diff* command. Since software vendors may manipulate documents to cover their secret patches, features from text documentation may not be reliable. Instead, our work considers more high-level features that can be extracted from source code.

The third challenge is to choose the most effective machine learning techniques. With the identified features, we try multiple popular machine learning techniques and compare their performance. Finally, we choose to use Random Forest [1] with random under-sampling to deal with the imbalanced dataset. The experimental results show that our model achieves good performance with 80.0% true positive rate and 31.1% false positive rate.

We conduct a case study on three popular SSL libraries, including OpenSSL [22], LibreSSL [21], and BoringSSL [6]. We identify 12 secret security patches. We conclude our observation and propose our suggestions to software vendors. We believe joint efforts are needed to remove this type of "0-day" vulnerability and improve the security of open source ecosystem.

We summarize our contribution as follows:

- We build the first open-sourced large-scale security patch dataset by querying each CVE entries [3] from year 1999–2018. We collect 3738 security patches on C/C++.
- We propose a set of features to profile the differences between security patches and non-security patches. Based on manual analysis of security patches and non-security patches, we identify 63 features that can be divided into three categories, namely, basic feature, syntactic feature, and semantic feature.
- We develop a machine learning based system to distinguish security patches from non-security patches, which can be used to automatically identify the existence of security patches by software developers and end users.
- We perform a case study on three open source SSL libraries and discover 12 secret security patches. We summarize our observations and give a series of suggestions to reduce the number of this type of "0-day" vulnerability.

The remaining of the chapter is organized as follows. Section 2 gives an overview of our machine learning based system. Section 3 describes how we collect the datasets for both security patches and non-security patches. Section 4 shows the list of useful features on identifying security patches. Section 5 details the quantitative evaluation and analysis of our model. Section 6 describes the case study on three popular SSL libraries. Section 7 discusses the limitations and potential extension of our system. We describe related works in Sect. 8. Finally, we conclude the paper in Sect. 9.

2 System Overview

Figure 1 shows an overview of our system. The first step is to construct a security and non-security patch dataset for (1) extracting features that can distinguish security patches from non-security patches, (2) training a machine learning based

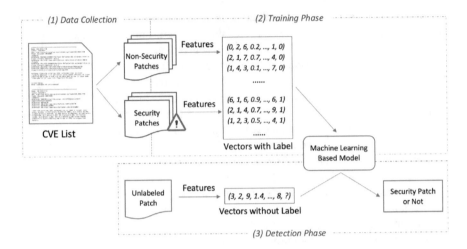

Fig. 1 System overview

model to help automatically identify the security patch in the training phase, and (3) evaluating the effectiveness of our model in the detection phase. To the end, we query all the CVE entries in 1999–2018 from at least 898 open source projects. Among them, we focus on projects written in C/C++, the languages with the highest number of vulnerabilities [30].

Based on previous work [15, 29] and our observation, we propose a set of features consisting of basic features, syntactic features, and semantic features to distinguish between security patches and non-security patches. Each patch can be transformed into a vector with the corresponding label mapping to the identified features. In the training phase, we randomly choose 80% of our dataset for training purpose. We adopt the Random Forest algorithm [1] with random under-sampling technique, which can achieve the best performance in our scenario.

In the testing phase that evaluates our system performance, we use the remaining 20% as the testing dataset. Once the user receives a new patch, our system transforms it into a vector using our proposed features and then our machine learning model generates a prediction result, i.e., if it is a security patch or not.

3   Patch Database Collection

Since there is no open-sourced large-scale patch dataset, we construct one[1] using the CVE list [28] in order to study the patterns of the security and non-security patches. The CVE list is composed of multiple CVE entries, that are used to build the U.S.

---

[1]The dataset is available at https://github.com/SecretPatch/Dataset.

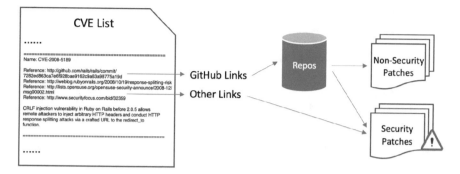

Fig. 2 Overview of data collection

National Vulnerability Database (NVD). Each CVE entry is for a publicly disclosed vulnerability, which contains the description and related references (e.g., the URLs of the corresponding patches). Figure 2 illustrates how we collect the patch datasets.

We make the assumption that all the information provided in CVE is correct. Then, we collect a CVE-security patch mapping dataset by crawling all the related URLs in the CVE list. For the non-security patch dataset, we use the remaining commits in the open source repositories that appear in the CVE list. We describe the methodology in the following.

3.1 Security Patch Dataset

From 1999 to 2018, the CVE list consists of 126,491 CVE entries. Each CVE entry is identified by a CVE ID and includes pertinent reference links of reports, advisories, and patches (if any). One option is to simply crawl all these links to check if it contains a patch. However, considering the huge number of reference links, we propose a more efficient method to collect security patches from the CVE list. Based on our observation, the reference URLs can be divided into two categories according to the repository's adopted hosting service: GitHub URLs and other URLs. We download the security patches from projects hosted on GitHub and outside GitHub, respectively.

Projects Hosted on GitHub For projects hosted on GitHub, we find that the reference URLs that contain security patches are in the following form:

https://github.com/{owner_name}/{repo_name}/commit/{commit_hash}.

The owner name and repository name are corresponding to the project itself. The commit hash is a hash value that can uniquely identify a commit, i.e., the patch of the CVE entry. In this case, after using regular expression, the corresponding security patch can be downloaded from the URL with an appendix *.patch*, i.e.,

https://github.com/{owner_name}/{repo_name}/commit/{commit_hash}.patch.

Therefore, for vulnerable GitHub repositories, instead of crawling all the reference listed, we only need to access a few URLs per CVE entry. In this way, we collect over 4,000 security patches.

Project Hosted Outside GitHub For the project hosted on other sites, there is no uniform pattern of the reference link that can tell if it contains security patches. To further extend our dataset, we crawl all the reference links of the CVE entries where no GitHub commit URLs exist. After using specific notations, i.e., *diff*, @@, +++, and − − −, as the indicators of existence of the patch, we remove the HTML/CSS labels and other unrelated contents. The remaining part is downloaded as a security patch. Since many reference links before 2010 are no longer available, we collect 692 security patches.

3.2 Non-security Patch Dataset

To study the difference between security and non-security patches and train our classifier, we also need a non-security patch dataset. Theoretically, a patch is corresponding to a vulnerability fix, bug fix, or feature update. However, due to different version control philosophies, some software vendors may release a big patch that mingles multiple patches. Also, for projects that are not hosted in control version system like GitHub, we may only generate a unified *.diff* file between an original and a modified source tree as a big patch that contains multiple patches. We leave how to divide a big patch into multiple single patches as our future work. Here, we download the commits from 898 vulnerable GitHub repositories in CVE lists and assume that each GitHub commit is for a vulnerability fix, bug fix, or feature upgrade. For each repository, the Git command `git log` is used to get all the history commits. Further, we remove all the commits with the same hash value as commits in the security dataset so that our collected security patches would not appear in the non-security dataset.

3.3 Collected Database

Since patches written in different programming languages may have different syntactic and semantic patterns, it is hard to cover the syntax of all kinds of languages. Our work focuses on patches of projects mainly written in C/C++ that are the languages with the highest number of vulnerabilities [30]. After filtering out all the commits of projects in languages other than C/C++, we find that even the patches of C/C++ projects may contain modifications on files other than *.c/.cpp/.h/.hpp*. About half of these security patches are only composed of C/C++ files. Others contains files such as *.changelog, .kconfig, .sh, .phpt*, and etc. Although our identifying approach only considers C/C++ parts of security patches, we need to figure out the role of non-C/C++ files in the security patches instead of simply removing them. By manually checking, we find most of these non-C/C++ files are documentation modification or changes corresponding to modifications of C/C++ files. Only 27 out of 3,765 (less than 1%) security patches make key modifications on non-C/C++ files, e.g., .S files to solve the dependency problem. After excluding them from the security patches, we get 3,738 security patches.

For the non-security patch dataset, since manually filtering out patches that do not aim to fix the C/C++ files is time-consuming, we simply take all the patches that only involve C/C++ files into consideration and thus the size of our non-security patch dataset is 455,014.

4   Security Patch Identification

It is important to identify useful features for improving the effectiveness of classification algorithms. Previous work [29] has concluded several features to identify the security fixes and bug fixes from feature upgrade patches. By studying 3,738 security patches in our dataset, we propose a set of features that could further distinguish security patches from non-security patches. These features can be classified into three categories: basic features, syntactic features, and semantic features, which are used in supervised machine learning techniques to automatically detect security patches.

4.1   Feature Extraction

A patch [5] contains differences between old and new version files and some context information. Figure 3 shows an example of the patch for CVE-2014-3158. Each patch may modify several files. Each modification that is corresponding to a file, i.e., difference, starts with a *diff a/{folder_name}/{file_name} b/{folder_name}/{file_name}* (e.g., line 1), and each difference may contain multiple change hunks that are lines before and after modification. In other words, one change hunk includes consecutive lines marked with − and +. For instance, lines 9 and 10 is a change hunk, and there are four hunks in this patch.

After studying our security and non-security patch dataset, we make the following observation:

```
1  diff --git a/pppd/options.c b/pppd/options.c
2  index 45fa742..e9042d1 100644
3  --- a/pppd/options.c
4  +++ b/pppd/options.c
5  @@ -1289,9 +1289,10 @@ getword(f, word, newlinep, filename)
6                  /*
7                   * Store the resulting character for the escape sequence.
8                   */
9  -                if (len < MAXWORDLEN-1)
10 +                if (len < MAXWORDLEN) {
11                      word[len] = value;
12 -                ++len;
13 +                    ++len;
14 +                }
15
16                  if (!got)
17                      c = getc(f);
18 @@ -1329,9 +1330,10 @@ getword(f, word, newlinep, filename)
19                  /*
20                   * An ordinary character: store it in the word and get another.
21                   */
22 -                if (len < MAXWORDLEN-1)
23 +                if (len < MAXWORDLEN) {
24                      word[len] = c;
25 -                ++len;
26 +                    ++len;
27 +                }
28
29                  c = getc(f);
30          }
```

Fig. 3 An patch example (CVE-2014-3158)

- Security patches are more likely to modify less code than non-security patches since the non-security patches often introduce something new to implement new functionalities or modify relatively larger code base to improve current efficiency or fix the design or implementation bugs.
- Security patches often make small modifications to some operators and operands. For example, some overflow vulnerabilities are often caused by an improper boundary value, which can be easily fixed by changing > to >= or n to n-1.
- The lines before and after modifications in security patches are similar since minor changes are made.
- Security patches have a better chance to make the same or similar modifications multiple times, for instance, Fig. 3 contains two same modifications (hunks) when not considering the indentation.
- Security patches are always involved with modification on conditional statements, i.e., adding new conditionals or modifying existed conditions
- Security patches are always involved with memory related operations.
- Security patches contain more data type conversion since wrongly using data type causes vulnerabilities like integer overflow.

Table 1 List of features

No.	Description	Type
1	# of changed files	Basic
2	# of hunks	
3–6	# of removed/added/total/net lines	
7–10	# of removed/added/total/net characters	
11–14	# of removed/added/total/net conditional statements	Syntactic
15–18	# of removed/added/total/net loops	
19–22	# of removed/added/total/net function calls	
23–24	# of total/net modified functions	
25–28	# of removed/added/total/net arithmetic operators	
29–32	# of removed/added/total/net relation operators	
33–36	# of removed/added/total/net logical operators	
37–40	# of removed/added/total/net bitwise operators	
41–44	# of removed/added/total/net memory operators	
45–48	# of removed/added/total/net variables	
49–51	AVE/MIN/MAX Levenshtein distance within hunks (before abstraction)	
52–54	AVE/MIN/MAX Levenshtein distance within hunks (after abstraction)	
55	# of same hunk (before abstraction)	
56	# of same hunk (after abstraction)	
57	# of data type conversion	
58	Removed and added hunks are the same (True or False)	
59–60	# and % of affected files	Semantic
61–62	# and % of affected functions	
63	Any data dependency changes (True or False)	

- Security patches may simply move several lines to another place almost without modifications, for instance, to solve the use after free vulnerabilities. Another example is that moving a conditional statement to the outer layer is common to fix a resource management vulnerability.

Based on the above observation, we propose a set of features that fall into three categories: basic, syntactic, and semantic features. Table 1 lists these features. The *removed* and *added* mean the corresponding characteristics existed on previous vulnerable lines that are marked with - and modified lines that are marked with +, respectively. The *total* refers to the sum of *removed* and *added* number of the corresponding characteristics. The *net* refers to the *added* number minus *removed* number. Basic features (1–10) are basic characteristics of patches that consider the number of changed files, hunks, lines and characters. Syntactic features 11–18 consider the number of conditional statements and loops. These features (1–18) are borrowed from Tian et al.'s work [29], which are proved to be effective in distinguishing vulnerability and bug fixing patches from new feature patches. To further differentiate security patches from bug fixes, we conclude 40 more syntactic features:

- **# of total/net modified functions.** Different from previous function calls which are represented by the function name or pointer in change hunks, the number of modified functions represents how many functions are involved by the change hunks. This number helps assess the directly affected range of a patch. For instance, for a patch which contains three change hunks within a function, this number is counted as three in total and one in net.
- **# of total/net/removed/added basic operators.** We count the total and net number of basic operators including arithmetic, relation, logical, and bitwise operators which occur in each patch. Also, we count these numbers in the removed part and added part, respectively.
- **# of total/net/removed/added memory operators.** We consider the corresponding number of C/C++ memory related operators which occur in each patch, e.g., `malloc`, `calloc`, `realloc`, `free`, and `sizeof`.
- **AVE/MIN/MAX Levenshtein distance within hunks (before abstraction).** Levenshtein distance is a measure of the similarity [24]. In our work, Levenshtein distance within a change hunk is the number of deletions, insertions, and substitutions required to transform the previous lines into modified lines within a hunk. Since there are always many hunks within one patch, the average, minimum, and maximum Levenshtein distance values are used to describe such a patch.
- **AVE/MIN/MAX Levenshtein distance within hunks (after abstraction).** To further measure the similarity of each pair of previous and modified hunks, we abstract the code. After removing the space and comment, we replace all the identifiers with a uniform character (e.g., $). Then, we calculate the corresponding Levenshtein distance on this abstracted code.
- **# of same hunks (before abstraction).** We consider every two exact same change hunks as a pair of the same hunks.
- **# of same hunks (after abstraction).** To count the pair of similar hunks, we exclude the exact same hunk. After abstracting the code, we regard every two same abstracted change hunks as a pair of similar hunks.
- **# data type conversion.** We only consider hunks where the modification is on the data type. Then, we count the number of data type conversion in these hunks.
- **If removed and added hunks are the same.** Here, we consider the hunks that only contain removed lines or added lines. If both the hunk with removed lines and the hunk with added lines exist and are the same (i.e., the patch just moves some lines to another location), this value is True. Otherwise, it is False.

Moreover, we propose five semantic features:

- **# and % of affected files.** The number of affected files is computed by counting the number of files that call the modified functions in the given patch. The percentage is calculated by dividing the number of affected files with the total file number.

- **# and % of affected functions.** We consider the functions that call the functions involved in a patch as the affected functions. If the patch contains modification on the conditional expression, the functions that are called within the corresponding body are also regarded as affected functions. The percentage is calculated by dividing the number of affected functions with the total function number.
- **Any changes of data dependency.** If previous variables are changed or new variables are introduced after modification, we regard this as an indicator of data dependency change and the value is True. Otherwise, it is False.

4.2 System Modeling

Since the distribution of security patch and non-security patch dataset is imbalanced, we first try SVM algorithm [2] that is insensitive to the imbalanced dataset. However, the results do not reach our expectation. Instead, we perform the random under-sampling to avoid the model being in favor of the majority class and then apply Random Forest provided by Weka [8]. In addition, previous work has discovered that some vulnerabilities of security patches were not reported to CVE [15, 31]. In other words, there may exist some secret security patches in our security patch dataset, which may threaten the accuracy of our model. Therefore, we manually remove them from non-security patch dataset. After that, our dataset consists of 3,738 security patches and 3,575 non-security patches.

We randomly choose 80% security and non-security patch dataset and transform each of them to a vector of values on above 63 features with its label "1" (i.e., security patch) or "0" (i.e., non-security patch) as the input training data. In the testing phase, we transform the remaining 20% patches in our datasets to vectors and then apply our model. If a vector is assigned "1", the corresponding patch is detected as a security patch. Otherwise, the corresponding patch is detected as a non-security patch.

5 Evaluation

To evaluate the effectiveness of our model, we split our dataset into training and testing datasets. We randomly choose 80% of our dataset as the training dataset and the remaining 20% as the testing dataset. Using the training dataset, we adopt a tenfold cross-validation to choose the best parameter configuration. Our experiments are conducted on a machine with 3.1 GHz Intel Core i7 CPU and 16GB RAM. The training phase (including 5,850 patches) takes 87s and the testing phase (including 1,463 patches) takes 21s. Figure 4 illustrates the ROC curve of our model. We adopt the configuration with 80.0% true positive rate and 31.1% false positive rate for our case study.

Fig. 4 ROC curve

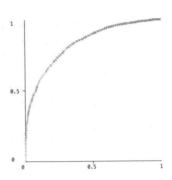

6   Case Study

To understand the current status of secret security patches, we perform a case study on three popular SSL libraries, i.e., OpenSSL, LibreSSL, and BoringSSL. First, we apply our model on commits of these projects to identify the security patches. Once a security patch is identified, we use code similarity/clone detection techniques [7, 9] along with our expertise to see if other libraries contain the same or similar vulnerable or patched code.

Table 2 summarizes 12 secret security patches and the corresponding fix information in OpenSSL, LibreSSL, and BoringSSL. The first column shows the CVE ID of each security patch and the affected software mentioned in NVD (here we omit CVE- prefix due to space limitation). The *Fix Date* column of each project is obtained from the commit date in the patch (commit) of each vulnerability that represents the actual fix date. The grey background cell denotes the earliest fix date of each vulnerability. The dash (–) means such vulnerability does not apply to this project. Each project's *Delay* is the date difference between the first fixed date among all three projects and its own fixed date, during which other similar type of software is exposed to attackers. *Not yet* means the project contains such vulnerability and it has not been fixed until our study date (06/20/2019). The *Public Disclosure* is the earliest date between patched version's official release date (if found) and NVD publishing date. Note that all the dates shown in this table are in the form of MM/DD/YY. We get the second to the last column by manually checking the advisory in CVE entry or its official hosted website. The *Secret Day* can be computed as date difference between the CVE ID belonging project's first fix date and the public disclosure date, which can be utilized by attackers to attack unpatched versions.

6.1   Identified Secret Security Patches

In the following, we go through all these 12 secret security patches that we discover to give a profile of the existence of the same vulnerabilities in similar software.

Table 2 Secret security patches among three SSL libraries

CVE ID (CVE-*)	OpenSSL		LibreSSL		BoringSSL		Public disclosure	Secret day
	Fix date	Delay	Fix date	Delay	Fix date	Delay		
2018-5407 (OpenSSL)	04/19/18	–	Not yet†	427+	–	–	11/15/18	210
2018-0734 (OpenSSL)	10/23/18	–	Not yet†	240+	Not yet†	240+	10/30/18	7
2018-0732 (OpenSSL)	06/11/18	974	06/13/18	976	10/11/15	–	06/12/18	975
2018-0739 (OpenSSL)	03/22/18	–	08/06/18	137	03/27/18	5	03/27/18	5
2017-3731 (OpenSSL)	01/18/17	–	02/01/17	14	–	–	01/26/17	8
2016-7053 (OpenSSL)	10/16/16	849	07/11/14	21	06/20/14	–	11/10/16	874
2016-7052 (OpenSSL)	08/22/16	–	–	–	09/26/16	35	09/26/16	35
2016-6305 (OpenSSL)	09/10/16	–	Not yet†	1013+	–	–	09/22/16	12
2016-6304 (OpenSSL)	09/09/16	–	09/27/16	18	–	–	09/22/16	13
2016-6308 (OpenSSL)	09/10/16	–	Not yet†	1013+	–	–	09/22/16	12
2018-8970 (LibreSSL)	01/22/15	–	03/22/18	1135	–	–	03/24/18	2
2018-12434 (LibreSSL)	06/19/18	982	06/13/18	976	10/11/15	–	06/14/18	977

† Until 06/20/2019

CVE-2018-5407 OpenSSL computes an Elliptic curve scalar multiplication in constant time that can enable local users to implement a side-channel timing attack. This vulnerability involves three functions in *crypto/bn/bn_lib.c* and *crypto/ec/ec_mult.c* and has been fixed on April 19, 2018. However, the same vulnerable code still exists in LibreSSL's newest version 2.9.2, which means there has been already 427 days after OpenSSL patched the same vulnerability. Moreover, there is more than half a year between the patch committed date and NVD publishing date.

CVE-2018-0734 This vulnerability can be exploited to recover the private key from manipulated variations in the signing algorithm. OpenSSL fixed this timing side-channel vulnerability in *crypto/dsa/dsa_ossl.c* in November 2018 while other two libraries have not patched it after more than 450 days. Also, the NVD entry only mentions OpenSSL as the affected software.

CVE-2018-0732 During OpenSSL key agreement in a TLS handshake, a very large prime value can be sent to the client, which causes an unreasonably long period to generate a key for this prime. This could be exploited as a denial-of-service attack. This vulnerability exists in *generate_key* of */crypto/dh/dh_key.c* on OpenSSL and LibreSSL until June 2018 while BoringSSL patched this vulnerability in its first version as early as November 2015. Also, the NVD only mentions outdated OpenSSL would be affected.

CVE-2018-0739 A denial-of-service attack can be launched by a malicious input in functions of *crypto/asn1/asn1_err.c* that could lead to an excessive recursion. OpenSSL patched this by limiting the stack depth in March 2018. BoringSSL patched this quickly after OpenSSL while LibreSSL released the patched version 4 months later. The NVD does not list LibreSSL and BoringSSL as affected software, either.

CVE-2017-3731 This vulnerability can be triggered by a truncated packet that results in an out-of-bounds read of accessible memory. OpenSSL fixed it by limiting the length in *crypto/evp/e_aes.c* and *crypto/evp/e_chacha20_poly1305.c*. LibreSSL rapidly patched the same vulnerability in its next version, though only OpenSSL is mentioned in NVD.

CVE-2016-7053 This is caused by mishandling ASN.1 CHOICE type that can result in a NULL pointer dereference in *crypto/asn1/tasn_dec.c*. OpenSSL fixed this in November 2016. However, both the first version of LibreSSL and BoringSSL exempted this vulnerability as early as 2014, which leaves over 2 years when OpenSSL was exposed to attackers.

CVE-2016-7052 This vulnerability may cause a denial-of-service by triggering a CRL operation in *crypto/x509/x509_vfy.c*. OpenSSL fixed this first in August 2016. BoringSSL promptly patched this vulnerability after it was publicly disclosed, while only OpenSSL is listed by NVD.

CVE-2016-6305 This vulnerability may be used to cause a denial of service (infinite loop) by triggering a zero-length record in *ssl3_read_bytes* function of *ssl/record/rec_layer_s3.c*, which was fixed by OpenSSL in September 2016. Similar vulnerability of LibreSSL in *ssl/s3_pkt.c* has not been patched.

CVE-2016-6304 Remote attackers can trigger a denial of service (memory consumption) via large OCSP Status Request extensions in *ssl/t1_lib.c*. OpenSSL fixed this first in September 2016 and LibreSSL patched this in its next version. Also, only OpenSSL was mentioned in NVD.

CVE-2016-6308 By crafting DTLS message with an excessive length, a denial of service (memory consumption) can be triggered in OpenSSL. NVD publicly released this several months later. Currently, the similar vulnerable code still exists in LibreSSL after almost three years.

CVE-2018-8970 Using the zero length of host name would bypass the verification and thus lunch a man-in-the-middle attack to spoof servers. LibreSSL fixed this in 2018 which is 3 years later than OpenSSL. Also, a CVE entry that mentions LibreSSL is created.

CVE-2018-12434 LibreSSL patched a memory-cache side-channel vulnerability by rejecting excessively large primes during DH key generation (*crypto/dh/dh_key.c*). Other software fixed similar vulnerabilities within 1 week. Only LibreSSL is identified as affected software by NVD.

6.2 Observation and Insight

Below are several worth-considering phenomena we observe. They also provide us with insights to improve the security of open source software ecosystem.

Incomplete Affected Software Versions in NVD For each vulnerability listed in the Table 2, though two or more projects are involved, only one project is mentioned in the description part and/or known affected software configurations in NVD. We categorize them into two cases:

1. A project first fixes a vulnerability and requests (or is requested by other users) a CVE entry for this issue. After that, other projects just silently patch without requesting a new CVE or merging their information into the existing CVE.
2. A project first fixes a vulnerability but not reports this issue to CVE. Some time later, other projects are found similar vulnerabilities and there would be a CVE entry for these projects other than the first fixing project.

Among these three SSL libraries, most of the first projects that fix the vulnerability have the corresponding CVE entries. There are about half of these cases where other project vendors silently patched after the NVD publicly disclosed. Some first-fixing projects did not request a CVE entry for their vulnerabilities. In this situation, other projects' fix dates are much later than the first fix date. Without a CVE advisory, it is hard for other vendors to realize their similar vulnerability. Therefore, the first project should always create a CVE entry to list its affected versions and try to notify other similar software vendors. On the other hand, since the CVE advisory plays an important role when users decide whether to patch or update, we suggest latter-fixing software vendors to merge their vulnerability information into an existing CVE entry instead of silent patching.

Poor Channel of Peer Information Sharing In our study, three quarters of vulnerabilities have an over 1 year fix delay, e.g., more than 3 years for LibreSSL to realize CVE-2018-8970. One reason is that the first project to figure out the vulnerability did not explicitly and timely publish essential information, e.g., BoringSSL's fixes for CVE-2018-0732, CVE-2016-7053, and CVE-2018-12434. Also, similar projects did not pay close attention to the new modification made by other projects. This indicates that similar software vendors do not have a good channel to share such kind of information. Lack of joint efforts from both the first-fixing vendors and followers lead to years of exposure, which are likely to be used for attacking other similar software. Under such circumstances, normal users are powerless to resist this "0-day" attack even if they have tried their best to timely update to the newest version every time. To improve the open source ecosystem, similar software vendors should strengthen their cooperation in the aspect of vulnerability detection.

Better Chance to Secret Patch for Big Vendors When a normal user like us wants to request a CVE for newly found vulnerability, we should first figure out if the vulnerability's corresponding software vendor is a participating CVE Numbering Authority (CNA) [25]. If so, we need to contact these vendors directly. Otherwise, we could contact the CVE Program Root CNA. In practice, when we find OpenSSL contains the same LibreSSL's vulnerability (CVE-2018-12434), we contact its corresponding participating CNA, i.e., OpenSSL Software Foundation. However, they replied to us that this vulnerability could only cause a local-host side channel attack, so no CVE is needed. In contrast, there is no participating CNAs for LibreSSL and thus it was assigned with a CVE ID. We can see that the CNA mechanism may provide big software vendors an opportunity to secretly patch their vulnerability without creating a CVE ID. In this case, when comparing OpenSSL with LibreSSL, users may draw a biased conclusion that OpenSSL is more reliable than LibreSSL since the number of its recent CVE records is smaller than that of LibreSSL.

Nonstandard and Inconsistent Software Maintenance It is understandable that different vendors have different software maintenance philosophy. However, it would be better to follow a uniform rule in the aspect of vulnerability tracking and fixing. At least, the vulnerability disclosed in the most influential public vulnerability database (i.e., NVD) should be evaluated using the same metrics. Take OpenSSL and LibreSSL in the previous subsection for instance, it is inappropriate that the same vulnerability in two similar software is given different evaluation results: qualified and unqualified for CVE assignment. There should be some standardized metrics to help evaluate if a vulnerability should be included in the NVD. Moreover, for the same software, vendors should maintain it consistently. Although CVE-2018-8970 (missing verification of a zero length name that may cause a man-in-the-middle attack) was assigned to LibreSSL, LibreSSL described this as a bug fix in its change log without mentioning any security related issues. However, after we check the history change log, we find LibreSSL usually explicitly classifies all the patches into security fix, bug fix, and new feature. In this case, when a user only focuses on its change log, high chances are that he regards this as a fix of small bugs that can be tolerated in their system at that time. To avoid this, LibreSSL should keep classifying patches into categories as before. For all the software vendors, a good practice is to keep their maintenance behavior consistently.

Improper Sequence between Patch Release and Advisory Publishing In our study, we notice that some software vendors may release vulnerability patch several weeks ahead NVD official discloses, which may incur some problems. There may exist some necessary processes in NVD that delays the actual advisory public disclose date. However, our suggestion is not to publish security patches before advisories are publicly disclosed. Using the CVE description information to generate exploits is relatively hard, but on the contrary, analyzing the vulnerability patches that point out vulnerable code to generate exploits is much easier, especially when modifications are minor between two neighboring software versions. In such case, several weeks before CVE advisory publishing may be enough for attackers to attack unpatched versions. Also, in our opinion, CVE advisory has a better chance to encourage users to patch their old versions than the new version release note. It would be better for software vendors to release their patch after the advisory is publicly disclosed.

7 Discussion and Limitations

Vulnerability Database Bias The CVE list we adopted as dataset source may be biased to some specific kinds of vulnerabilities. Previous work has proved that not all the vulnerabilities reported in CVE have known approaches to trigger them and there are also a number of vulnerabilities without CVE IDs that can be triggered [20]. Therefore, not all the vulnerabilities are included in the CVE list. In such case, since we collect security patches from the CVE list, our dataset may be biased to severe or high-exploitable vulnerabilities. For instance, we have mentioned that OpenSSL refused to assign a CVE ID for a local-host side channel vulnerability due to its low exploitability in their opinion. The ideal solution is to manually identify more vulnerability outside the CVE list and then add them to the current dataset. However, this requires huge efforts and domain experts. We argue that since CVE list covers numerous cyber security products and services all over the world, we assume our model which is trained by security patches from CVE list could be applicable to most open source patches. Also, even though our current model is in favor of severe or high-exploitable vulnerabilities, it is reasonable since such vulnerabilities should be taken precedence over other vulnerabilities in practice.

Race Between Attackers and Defenders There are some concerns about possibilities that our approach may also be leveraged by attackers. Actually, we wonder attackers might have already misused secret security patches to some extent. In this work, we are not only to provide a toolset for identifying the security patches. Our final goal is to improve the global open source ecosystem. On one hand, users can make use of this toolset to prioritize the security patch deployment and thus reduce the attack surface. On the other hand, if software vendors know there is such a tool that can discover their secret or mislabeled patches, they will be more likely to avoid to do so in the future for their quality reputation. In addition, our case study has revealed the importance of keeping an eye on similar software's update. Therefore, our work could help promote software vendors to maintain their products more normatively, increase the collaboration between each other on information sharing, and finally eliminate this secret patch caused "0-day" attacks from the source.

Extension to Projects Hosted Outside GitHub Our current work focus on projects hosted on GitHub. In practice, although GitHub is the most popular open source software hosting service provider and most vulnerable open source software that appears in CVE list is hosted on GitHub, there are some projects hosted on its own website or both on GitHub and its own sites with unsynchronized maintenance, e.g., LibreSSL. Applying our tool to these projects requires extra efforts. On GitHub, we can simply regard a commit as a patch since one commit is corresponding to one issue (vulnerability fix, bug fix or new functionality) in most cases (only 0.1% exception in security dataset by manually checking). For open source software hosted on other websites, vendors may release a big patch that mingles security and non-security patches together or we could only acquire a patch by generating a *diff* file from the source code of neighboring versions. In this case, the *diff* file may consist of a number of change hunks that belong to multiple patches. If the modifications are few, we can separate them through some simple approaches like keyword matching. However, when changes are complicated, for instance, main version releases that introduce a large number of modifications, it is hard to separate it into individual patches as the input of our current tool. We leave this as an open problem.

Adaption to Languages Other Than C/C++ Since our syntactic and semantic features are dependent on the programming languages, our current system only supports to identify security patch of open source projects written in C/C++. Currently, we focus on C/C++ since they are languages with the highest vulnerabilities. Actually, our system can be adapted to other programming languages by modifying features according to the targeted programming languages, e.g., syntax parsing related features 11–58 and 61–63. We leave extension to other types of programming languages and even multiple programming languages as future work.

8 Related Work

Vulnerability Detection Open Source Software vulnerability detection has become an active research area. There are two main research directions: vulnerable code similarity comparison and vulnerability pattern recognition. For vulnerable code similarity detection, the traditional token-based techniques remove all the white space as well as comments and then replace variable and function names with a specific character to detect Type-1 and Type-2 code clone [26] that only makes few modifications of identifiers, comments, and whitespace. The tree-based techniques [10, 32] mainly transform the program into Abstract Syntax Tree (AST) and then compare the longest common sequence (LST). Graph-based techniques [13, 19] use control and data dependence graph to detect code clones as isomorphic subgraphs. For vulnerability pattern recognition, machine learning or deep learning approaches are proposed by extracting the patterns from the vulnerable code and then searching the code with the same pattern. VulPecker [16] uses different sets of features to detect different types of software vulnerabilities. VulDeepecker [17] trained a neural network to detect buffer overflow and resource management errors caused by library/API call. Certain secret security patches have been reported ad hoc during these studies. Zhen et al. [17] found Xen silently patched the vulnerability after the disclosure of CVE-2016-9104 in Qemu. Their results also revealed the secret security patches between Seamonkey and Firefox (CVE-2015-4517) as well as between Libav and FFmeng (CVE-2014-2263). This work motivates us to perform an empirical study on the secret security patches.

Patch Dataset Collection Since the patch contains both the vulnerable code and modification at the same time, most of current vulnerability detection work gets the vulnerability dataset by collecting security patches. Seulbae et al. [11] collected data from eight well-known Git repositories, and Zhen et al. [16] built a Vulnerability Patch Database (VPD) from 19 products. However, the size of these datasets is not sufficient for performing a machine learning based study. Considering thousands of CVE records on open source projects, Li et al. [15] built a large-scale security patch database based on the Git repositories. However, they do not provide an open-sourced version for further research.

Patch Analysis Actually, some researchers have paid attention to patch analysis. Zame et al. [33] made a case study on the difference between security and performance patches in Mozilla Firefox. Perl et al. [23] showed many statistic difference between vulnerability contributing commits and other commits. However, they do not distinguish between vulnerability fixes and non-security bug fixes. Li et al. [15] conducted the first large-scale empirical study between security patches and non-security bug fixes, and it provides analysis on the basic characteristics and life cycles of security patches. Xu et al. [31] presented a scalable approach to identify security patches through the semantic analysis of execution traces. However, it cannot handle cross-function security patches and some specific kinds of non-security patches that are similar to security patches on the binary level.

9   Conclusion

In this paper, we develop a machine learning based security patch identification system, which can be used by users and developers to automatically identify secret security patches and decide if it is the time to update to the new version or apply the patches. We point out that once a security patch is identified, its corresponding vulnerability may be detected in other similar types of software and if detected, this patch could be utilized to patch similar vulnerabilities. To evaluate the effectiveness of our model, we build a database that is composed of the security patches in the CVE list. We make it open-sourced to promote public research on improving the security of the global open source software environment. We propose a set of syntactic and semantic code features to profile security patches. With these features, our system can achieve good detection performance. To figure out the existence of secret security patches, we apply our system to three open source SSL library projects, discover 12 secret security patches, and find some interesting phenomena. With these observations, we suggest software vendors could maintain their products more normatively, increase the collaboration with each other, and finally eliminate this kind of "0-day" vulnerability.

Acknowledgements We would like to thank Shu Wang and Fuxun Yu for their valuable suggestions on this work. This work is partially supported by the NSF grant CNS-1822094, IIP-1266147 and ONR grants N00014-16-1-3214, N00014-16-1-3216, and N00014-18-2893.

References

1. Breiman L (2001) Random forests. Machine learning 45(1):5–32
2. Chang CC, Lin CJ (2011) LIBSVM: A library for support vector machines. ACM transactions on intelligent systems and technology (TIST) 2(3):27
3. Common Vulnerabilities and Exposures (CVE) (2019) https://cve.mitre.org/cve/identifiers/index.html
4. GitHub (2019) The state of the octoverse 2018. https://octoverse.github.com
5. GNU Diffutils (2016) https://www.gnu.org/software/diffutils/
6. Google Inc (2019) BoringSSL. URL https://boringssl.googlesource.com/boringssl/
7. Grune D (2017) The software and text similarity tester SIM. https://dickgrune.com/Programs/similarity_tester/
8. Hall M, Frank E, Holmes G, Pfahringer B, Reutemann P, Witten IH (2009) The WEKA data mining software: an update. SIGKDD Explorations 11(1):10–18
9. Harris S (2015) Simian. https://www.harukizaemon.com/simian/
10. Jiang L, Misherghi G, Su Z, Glondu S (2007) Deckard: Scalable and accurate tree-based detection of code clones. In: Proceedings of the 29th international conference on Software Engineering, IEEE Computer Society, pp 96–105
11. Kim S, Woo S, Lee H, Oh H (2017) Vuddy: A scalable approach for vulnerable code clone discovery. In: Security and Privacy (SP), 2017 IEEE Symposium on, IEEE, pp 595–614
12. Knight JC, Leveson NG (1986) An experimental evaluation of the assumption of independence in multiversion programming. IEEE Transactions on software engineering (1):96–109
13. Krinke J (2001) Identifying similar code with program dependence graphs. In: Reverse Engineering, 2001. Proceedings. Eighth Working Conference on, IEEE, pp 301–309
14. Kula RG, German DM, Ouni A, Ishio T, Inoue K (2018) Do developers update their library dependencies? Empirical Software Engineering 23(1):384–417
15. Li F, Paxson V (2017) A large-scale empirical study of security patches. In: Proceedings of the 2017 ACM SIGSAC Conference on Computer and Communications Security, ACM, pp 2201–2215
16. Li Z, Zou D, Xu S, Jin H, Qi H, Hu J (2016) Vulpecker: an automated vulnerability detection system based on code similarity analysis. In: Proceedings of the 32nd Annual Conference on Computer Security Applications, ACM, pp 201–213
17. Li Z, Zou D, Xu S, Ou X, Jin H, Wang S, Deng Z, Zhong Y (2018) Vuldeepecker: A deep learning-based system for vulnerability detection. arXiv preprint arXiv:180101681
18. Lily Hay Newman (2017) Equifax offically has no excuse. https://www.wired.com/story/equifax-breach-no-excuse/
19. Liu C, Chen C, Han J, Yu PS (2006) Gplag: detection of software plagiarism by program dependence graph analysis. In: Proceedings of the 12th ACM SIGKDD international conference on Knowledge discovery and data mining, ACM, pp 872–881

20. Mu D, Cuevas A, Yang L, Hu H, Xing X, Mao B, Wang G (2018) Understanding the reproducibility of crowd-reported security vulnerabilities. In: 27th USENIX Security Symposium (USENIX Security 18), USENIX, pp 919–936
21. OpenBSD Foundation (2019) LibreSSL. URL https://www.libressl.org
22. OpenSSL Software Foundation (2019) OpenSSL. URL https://www.openssl.org
23. Perl H, Dechand S, Smith M, Arp D, Yamaguchi F, Rieck K, Fahl S, Acar Y (2015) Vccfinder: Finding potential vulnerabilities in open-source projects to assist code audits. In: Proceedings of the 22nd ACM SIGSAC Conference on Computer and Communications Security, ACM, pp 426–437
24. Pieterse V, Black PE (1999) Algorithms and Theory of Computation Handbook. CRC Press LLC
25. Request CVE IDs (2019) https://cve.mitre.org/cve/request_id.html
26. Roy CK, Cordy JR (2007) A survey on software clone detection research. Queen's School of Computing TR 541(115):64–68
27. Snyk (2019) The state of open source security 2019. https://snyk.io/stateofossecurity/
28. The MITRE Corporation (2019) CVE list. https://cve.mitre.org/cve/
29. Tian Y, Lawall J, Lo D (2012) Identifying linux bug fixing patches. In: Proceedings of the 34th International Conference on Software Engineering, IEEE Press, pp 386–396
30. White Source Software (2019) The state of open source vulnerabilities management. https://www.whitesourcesoftware.com/open-source-vulnerability-management-report/
31. Xu Z, Chen B, Chandramohan M, Liu Y, Song F (2017) SPAIN: security patch analysis for binaries towards understanding the pain and pills. In: Proceedings of the 39th International Conference on Software Engineering, IEEE Press, pp 462–472
32. Yang W (1991) Identifying syntactic differences between two programs. Software: Practice and Experience 21(7):739–755
33. Zaman S, Adams B, Hassan AE (2011) Security versus performance bugs: a case study on firefox. In: Proceedings of the 8th working conference on mining software repositories, ACM, pp 93–102

Printed in the United States
By Bookmasters